The
Oldsmobile
Nº 1
THE
LINCOLN HIGHWAY ASSOCIATION
CONTRIBUTOR'S TICKET
ISSUED TO
ASSOCIATED
ETHYL
GASOLINE
DRIVE-IN
CHRYSLER
MOTORS
DATSUN
SAVES

OLDSMOBILE

GTO

JIM HEIMANN · PHIL PATTON

100 YEARS OF AUTOMOTIVE ADS

100 JAHRE AUTOWERBUNG 100 ANS DE PUBLICITÉ AUTOMOBILE

TASCHEN

THE DEVELOPMENT OF AUTOMOBILE TECHNOLOGY AND THE AUTOMOBILE BUSINESS PARALLELED THE DEVELOPMENT OF MODERN ADVERTISING – AND MODERN MEDIA…WHOSE COMBINED REACH EXTENDED INTO ALMOST EVERY AMERICAN HOME.

DIE ENTWICKLUNG VON AUTOTECHNIK UND -INDUSTRIE ZEIGT PARALLELEN ZUR ENTWICKLUNG DER MODERNEN WERBUNG UND DER MODERNEN MEDIEN – DIE ZUSAMMENGENOMMEN FAST JEDEN US-HAUSHALT ERREICHTEN.

PARALLÈLEMENT AUX PROGRÈS DE LA TECHNOLOGIE AUTOMOBILE ET À L'ESSOR DE CE SECTEUR INDUSTRIEL, LA PUBLICITÉ ET LES MÉDIAS MODERNES SE DÉVELOPPENT. OUTRE LA RADIO PUIS LA TÉLÉVISION, LES REVUES SE MULTIPLIENT, ET TOUCHENT LA QUASI-TOTALITÉ DES FOYERS AMÉRICAINS.

INTROD

AMERICA IN THE AUTOMOBILE AGE
AMERIKA IN DER ÄRA DES AUTOMOBILS
L'AMÉRIQUE À L'ÂGE DE L'AUTOMOBILE

UCTION

LOZIER

"The Choice of Men Who Know"

ON touring highways, at the seashore, on the boulevard, in the mountains, at the country club,—wherever you meet people of wealth and refinement, there, in increasing numbers, you find the Lozier.

Big Six. Touring Cars $5,000, Limousines and Landaulets $6,500.

"LIGHT SIX" $3,250 to $4,450.

LOZIER MOTOR COMPANY

2403 Mack Avenue Detroit, Michigan

Factory Branches in New York, Chicago, Boston Philadelphia and San Francisco

Plymouth Belvedere, 1955
Frontispiece Pontiac GTO, 1965
Page 474 Pontiac Firebird, 1978

All images are from the Jim Heimann collection unless otherwise noted. Any omissions for copy or credit are unintentional and appropriate credit will be given in future editions if such copyright holders contact the publisher.

Timeline image credits: Burton Holmes Historical Archive, www.burtonholmes.org: Chicago World's Fair (1933). Jim Cherry Collection: Lincoln Futura (1955), Firebird III (1959). Library of Michigan, an agency of the Department of History; Arts and Libraries: My Merry Oldsmobile (1905). Missouri Department of Transportation: Federal-Aid Highway Act (1956). Sam DeVincent Collection of Illustrated American Sheet Music, Archives Center, National Museum of American History, Smithsonian Institution: Henry's Made a Lady Out of Lizzie (1927). Smithsonian Institution, NMAH/Transportation: Alexander Winton in the "Bullet No. 1" (1901), President Woodrow Wilson's Lincoln Highway Association membership card (1913), homemade turn signal (1921), Dual brand parking meter (1935).

The publisher would like to thank Leslie Kendall and Tony Thacker for their fact-checking expertise; and Cara Walsh, Thomas Chung, Tyler Flatt, Maurene Goo, and Christopher Kosek for their invaluable assistance in getting this book produced.

Hohenzollernring 53, D-50672 Köln
www.taschen.com

Art direction: Josh Baker, Los Angeles
English-language editor & project management: Nina Wiener, Los Angeles
Design: Marco Zivny, Los Angeles
Cover lettering: Michael Doret
Editorial coordination: Jutta Hendricks and Viola Krauß, Cologne
Production: Nadia Najm, Cologne
German translation: Helmut Roß, Krenglbach
French translation: Françoise Fauchet, Coulobres

Printed in China
ISBN 978-3-8365-1463-7

> "I WILL BUILD A MOTOR CAR FOR THE GREAT MULTITUDE… CONSTRUCTED OF THE BEST MATERIALS, BY THE BEST MEN HIRED… SO LOW IN PRICE THAT NO MAN MAKING A GOOD SALARY WILL BE UNABLE TO OWN ONE…"
>
> — HENRY FORD, FORD MOTOR COMPANY, 1908

"THE POETRY OF MOTION! THE REAL WAY TO TRAVEL! THE ONLY WAY TO TRAVEL!" intoned Mr. Toad in Kenneth Grahame's classic children's book *The Wind in the Willows* (1908). It was probably the first literary testimonial to the fascination of the car, the emerging automotive obsession. Those first cars were toys for the rich. Motoring was a hobby for the wealthy, like yachting or mountain climbing. Used less for trips to the office or shop than for leisurely weekend excursions out into nature, cars required special equipment and, in most cases, specialized employees in the form of drivers and mechanics.

Early automobiles were custom-made, ordered almost like fine suits or dresses from a tailor. Typically, the chassis and engine were sold as a unit, while bodies were purchased from an entirely different manufacturer — often carriage-makers or coach-builders who might still be supplying the horse-and-buggy market.

The first motorists (or "automobilists," as they were called) were men like W. K. "Willy" Vanderbilt, heir to the railroad and shipping fortune. A classic early adopter of technological innovation, his enthusiasm resembled that of Mr. Toad. He spent freely on early automobiles, buying a Stanley Steamer, a Mercedes he called the "Red Devil," and a Daimler he called the "White Ghost." In 1904, Vanderbilt set a speed record of 92 mph on the sand at Ormond Beach, Florida — at a time when 30 mph was a zippy pace for most cars.

The first U.S. automobile ad ran in 1896, for the Duryea Motor Wagon Company's first U.S. car. In the decades that followed, most ads were for high-end makes like Pierce-Arrow and Packard, as well as for automotive accessories. More often than not, these ads were aimed at people who took care of cars rather than at car owners. In those days, oil and water had to be changed every few miles. Flat tires were frequent. Cars were open, requiring a special wardrobe of goggles, scarf, and wraparound coat, or "duster."

The development of automobile technology and the automobile business paralleled the development of modern advertising — and modern media. These media included not just radio and, later, television, but also magazines, from *Collier's* and *The Saturday Evening Post* to *Life*, *Fortune*, and *Time*, whose combined reach extended into almost every American home.

Indeed, several of the most prominent ad campaigns, slogans, and individual pieces of advertising of the 20th century were for cars. One of these was the famed "Penalty of Leadership" ad run by Cadillac in 1915. The company prided itself, then as now, on excellence and technical innovation, but one of its models had shown flaws, and rival Packard had criticized it. Cadillac responded with an all-type ad written by adman Theodore F. MacManus. "When a man's work becomes a standard for the whole world, it also becomes a target for the shafts of the envious few," he rebutted, not mentioning any specific model or product but burnishing the brand. Cadillac had not only defended its honor, it established its brand for the next half century.

IN 1908, HENRY FORD INTRODUCED THE MODEL T AND BROUGHT CARS TO THE MASSES. Ford envisioned fathers taking their families from unhealthy cities to the country on weekends. But the impact was far larger. The T established the idea and reality of universal automobility.

Ford promised that when he finished lowering the price of a car, "No man earning a decent salary will be able to be without one." He was pretty much right: By 1920, cars had moved from mere novelty to something close to necessity.

Henry Ford was so convinced that the Model T, which he termed the "universal car," would sell itself, that he declined to do much to advertise it. "Ford advertising never attempts to be clever," the company boasted in 1912. In fact, its customers and fans sold the Model T. As with such products of today as the iPod, the Model T developed a fan base, a popular culture, and an accessory industry. There were even Model T jokes, somewhat akin to "blonde jokes" in a later era.

But when the Model T was finally upgraded, in 1928, to the Model A, Ford hired the N. W. Ayer agency, which created

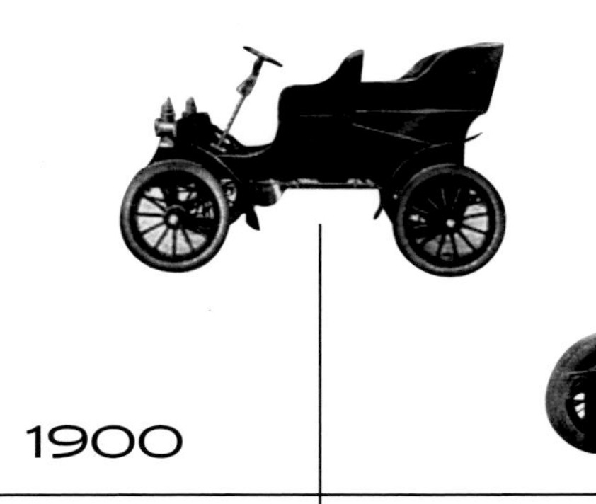

1900

1900 Steering wheel begins to replace tiller

Lenkhebel zunehmend durch Lenkrad abgelöst

Le volant remplace peu à peu la poignée

1901 Alexander Winton sets world speed record at 57.8 mph with his Bullet No. 1

Alexander Winton erzielt Geschwindigkeitsweltrekord mit 92 km/h in seinem Bullet No. 1

Alexander Winton établit un record de vitesse à 93 km/h au volant de sa Bullet n°1

1905 Oldsmobile sponsors first transcontinental race (New York – Portland, Oregon)

Oldsmobile sponsert erstes Transkontinentalrennen (New York – Portland, Oregon)

Oldsmobile sponsorise la première course transcontinentale (New York – Portland, Oregon)

1905 First car reported stolen

Erstes Auto als gestohlen gemeldet

Première déclaration de vol de voiture

one of the most memorable ad campaigns of the era, framing the cars in reassuring family vignettes, in a happy, white-picket-fence *Our Town*. No longer would Fords sell simply on low price. More and more people were buying not just their first but their second or third cars.

Another promotional approach to the car came from General Motors, also founded in 1908. This combine of brands—including Cadillac, Oldsmobile, and Buick—would become known for offering variety. "A car for every purse and purpose" was the phrase of GM's boss, Alfred Sloan: cars varying in style and sophistication. GM changed models each year, a move Sloan said was aimed at "manufacturing discontent." It also became an American ritual, like a holiday, fed by advertising. As surely as they returned to school each September, American kids peeked into car dealerships, eager to spot the new models.

The Model T was famously available in "any color you want as long as it's black." General Motors made that simply "any color you want" by offering new, fast-drying Duco lacquers, created by DuPont chemists in the early 1920s, starting with True Blue, the offering available exclusively on the 1924 Oakland model. The new paints made possible mass production in color. Color stood for General Motors' willingness to offer more and more choices to the consumer.

To bring more excitement into new cars, Sloan looked to Hollywood. There, movie stars and directors drove elaborately customized cars, were often photographed in front of them for publicity purposes, and were sometimes featured in advertisements as early celebrity endorsers. Many of the custom cars were the work of one man, Harley Earl. His clients included producer Cecil B. DeMille—his next-door neighbor—and actors Mary Pickford, Tom Mix, and Fatty Arbuckle. Impressed with the way Earl conceived each car as a whole by working with clay models, Sloan hired him to design a new car, the 1927 LaSalle, and to create the General Motors Art and Color Section, which would design new cars for each new year—like fashion.

WHILE WOMEN WERE AT FIRST SECONDARY TARGETS OF AUTO ADVERTISING, THEY SOON BECOME THE MAIN FOCUS FOR MANY MODELS. Cars were being used in areas where women shopped and, increasingly, worked. From new colors to automatic transmissions, many innovations were created with women buyers in mind, and manufacturers were placing ads in *Vogue*, *Good Housekeeping*, *Ladies' Home Journal*, and other magazines, specifically to reach women.

By 1930, the designs of the cars themselves had become an important part of selling them, and advertising had to be brought into harmony with the look of new models. Painters helped present the new steel bodies; they made the roofs look taller and made sure the highlights struck the right point on the cars' beltlines.

Thanks largely to loans and the used-car market, the United States quickly became the world leader in cars per capita. By the end of the 1930s, the United States had a 22.7% rate of car ownership, while the UK had only 5.4%; Germany's rate was half that of the UK, and Italy's rate was even lower, with only about 10 cars per thousand people. In Russia, the rate was even lower: fewer than five cars per thousand. So common were cars in the U.S. and so comparatively rare in the rest of the world that when the film of John Steinbeck's *The Grapes of Wrath* was screened in Europe, audiences were baffled. They saw how the Joad family made its way to California in a broken-down old jalopy. But how can this family be poor? the Europeans wondered. Didn't they own a car?

The Depression killed or mortally wounded many of the great luxury marques, like Pierce-Arrow and Duesenberg. Packard, previously the top of the social ladder, was supplanted in status by Cadillac, which, as part of the General Motors family, had other brands to lean on. Packard would linger on into the mid-'50s, with bloated cars that were mere echoes of their earlier elegance.

Introduced commercially in 1938, color photography had nearly replaced illustration in most print advertising by the '50s; but in automobile advertising, painting hung on.

1907

1907 Demountable rims allow drivers to fix their own flat tires

Abnehmbare Felgen gestatten es dem Fahrer, Reifenpannen selbst zu beheben

Les jantes démontables permettent aux automobilistes de réparer eux-mêmes leurs pneus crevés

1908 Michelin Tire builds first plant outside of France in Turin, Italy

Michelin-Reifen errichtet im italienischen Turin erstes Werk außerhalb Frankreichs

Michelin installe sa première usine à l'étranger : à Turin, en Italie

1908 Ford releases Model T; 15 million will be built

Ford lanciert sein Model T: 15 Millionen Exemplare werden einen Käufer finden

Ford lance le modèle T ; il sera construit à 15 millions d'exemplaires

1909 Baker offers 17 models of electric vehicles; 38% of cars on road electric by 1900

Baker offeriert 17 verschiedene Elektroautos; um 1900 besitzen noch 38 Prozent aller Autos einen Elektroantrieb

Baker propose 17 modèles de véhicules électriques ; en 1900, 38 % des voitures sur la route sont électriques

Lozier, 1912 ◄◄

Ford Model T, 1908

► Erskine Six, 1927

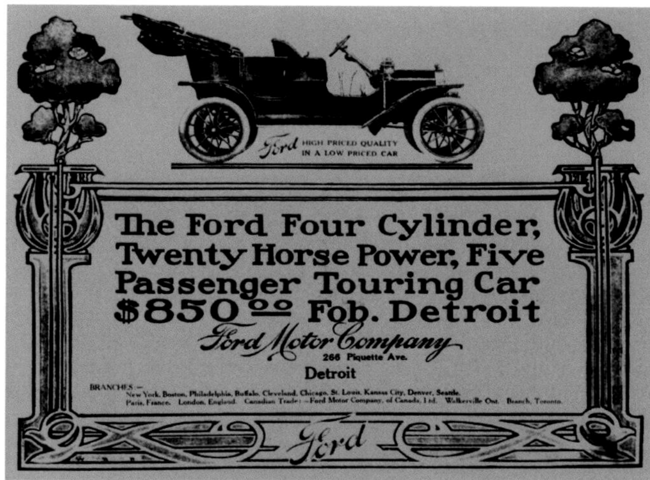

Painters could render effects that photographers in that pre-digital age could not. They made cars seem futuristic; they elongated and widened them, romanticized them by emphasizing highlights and shadows and bringing out their sculptural qualities. Illustrators of car ads received secret, advance photos of the next year's new cars to use as models. Some of the leading ad painters worked in pairs, including Art Fitzgerald and Van Kaufman, who often put their initials on license plates in the paintings. They were renowned for images promoting Pontiac's "Wide Track" feature — Pontiacs were sold as being low and wide, supposedly for added stability on the road. Illustration also allowed advertising men to flatter the proportions of cars, to make them seem longer or taller. Sometimes photos were cut apart and used as models for "stretch" paintings, with roofs suddenly tall enough to enclose a man wearing a hat.

By the middle of the century, the car was inextricably tied to the wider culture. Jack Kerouac took to the road in an old Hudson to write *On the Road*, typing it out on what he called "the scroll" — a 120-foot roll of standard-size tracing paper, taped together sheet by sheet, which, according to legend, Kerouac unrolled like the road itself across his first editor's desk. The first rock 'n' roll song, written by Ike Turner, appeared in 1951, and it was named after and inspired by a car: "Rocket 88" took its title from Oldsmobile's new high-compression V8 engine. It marked the beginning of a tradition linking cars and pop music that continued through the Beach Boys and Smokey Robinson to Prince and Snoop Dogg. If industrial designer Raymond Loewy castigated American cars as "rolling jukeboxes," what was wrong with that, given that Elvis, Chubby Checker, and Buddy Holly were on the real jukeboxes?

During the Eisenhower years, superhighways and television changed life and changed the car. Tail-finned cars were like sharks to poet Robert Lowell; they swam across the world of Sloan Wilson's *The Man in the Gray Flannel Suit*. *Time* magazine called Ford's design chief, George Walker, the "Cellini of Chrome." And Virgil Exner created Chrysler's extreme "Forward" look: "Suddenly, it's 1960!" But Ford's 1957 launch of its Edsel brand into the teeth of an economic recession signaled that the wave had crested.

IN 1959, THE NEW YORK ADVERTISING AGENCY DOYLE DANE BERNBACH LANDED THE NATIONAL VOLKSWAGEN ACCOUNT AND LAUNCHED THE "THINK SMALL" CAMPAIGN, generally regarded by advertising professionals and historians as one of the best ad campaigns of all time. Using simple black-and-white photos of the Beetle and Bus, along with wry copy, the ads played to understatement and modesty. Created by copywriter Julian Koenig and art director Helmut Krone, the ads gently mocked the annual model change and all the chrome, glint, and feature-creep of American models. "'Think small' was thinking quite big, actually," wrote advertising historian Bob Garfield. "Beetle ownership allowed you to show off that you didn't need to show off."

1911 Inaugural Indianapolis 500 race

Erstes Indianapolis 500 Rennen

Inauguration de la course des 500 miles d'Indianapolis

1912 Cadillac offers first electric starter, making motoring more accessible to women

Cadillac präsentiert den ersten elektrischen Anlasser, was besonders den Frauen entgegenkommt

Cadillac propose le premier démarreur électrique, facilitant l'accès des femmes à la conduite automobile

1912 Ford begins Five Dollar Day: $5 pay for eight-hour shift at Illinois plant

Ford startet den Five Dollar Day: 5 US-Dollar Lohn für eine Acht-Stunden-Schicht im Werk Illinois

Ford lance la journée à cinq dollars : paye de 5$ pour huit heures de travail à l'usine installée dans l'Illinois

1915 Packard president Henry Joy drives Lincoln Highway (Detroit – San Francisco) in 21 days

Packard-Präsident Henry Joy fährt den Lincoln Highway (Detroit – San Francisco) in 21 Tagen

Henry Joy, président de Packard, parcourt la Lincoln Highway (Detroit – San Francisco) en 21 jours

"WHAT IS GOOD FOR THE COUNTRY IS GOOD FOR GENERAL MOTORS, AND WHAT'S GOOD FOR GENERAL MOTORS IS GOOD FOR THE COUNTRY."

–CHARLES WILSON, GENERAL MOTORS, 1955

Showing off was still what most domestic cars were about. While America was at the height of its power, in 1960, car models and ads reflected that power. But questions began to appear. Suddenly, Americans thought about the safety of the huge, powerful cars they drove. Industry critic Ralph Nader's book *Unsafe at Any Speed* became a bestseller, and Nader's testimony before congressional committees led to legislation requiring seat belts and other improvements.

Americans also wanted more personalized cars. Introduced at the New York World's Fair in 1964, the Ford Mustang was presented as the first personal — or at least "personalizable" — car. Its short rear deck and long hood became a reflection of the miniskirt era. Ford executive Lee Iacocca billed it as "the car you design yourself," thanks to a long list of optional equipment. The Mustang became symbolic of the newly liberated, young, single woman, embodied in the hit song, "Mustang Sally," by Mack Rice. Wilson Pickett's cover of the song sold more than 400,000 copies in its first year.

While Detroit coped with the "youth quake" and pervasive counterculture of the '60s by using such slogans as "Dodge Fever," American Motors offered "blue-jean editions" of cars, to appeal to kids. For women, there were highly customizable pony cars, such as the Chevy Camaro, and, for men, highly customizable muscle cars like the Pontiac GTO.

With the '70s came energy crises and the arrival, in force, of Japanese imports in the United States. In October 1973, an alliance of oil-producing Middle Eastern countries declared an embargo against countries supporting Israel in the Yom Kippur War, and oil prices soared to $12 a barrel. Gasoline prices in the U.S. quadrupled within weeks, and rationing began; Congress adopted a 55 mph national speed limit. Small-car sales zoomed, but Detroit built few small models. Ford, General Motors, and Chrysler hastily imported models from their European branches or sister companies in Asia and re-badged them. But the Japanese makers were the ones who benefited. In 1958, Japanese makers together sold fewer than 1,500 cars in the United States. A decade later, that number was 150,000, and by 1975 their sales made up 10% of the U.S. market.

Toyota's Corona and Honda's Civic quickly gained a word-of-mouth reputation no advertising could match. The Datsun Z-cars — beginning with the 240Z, in 1969 — gained fans among young people as an economical sports car. The Z-car also won awards from auto magazines, ratifying the reputation of Japanese cars. By the mid-'70s, Japanese imports overshadowed European ones, and, despite clever ads like Renault's "Le Car" campaign, French and Italian imports declined. After it replaced the Beetle, in 1974, Volkswagen languished too.

It took a good decade, but Detroit's Big Three aimed to adopt their competitors' methods. In 1989, General Motors unveiled Saturn, which was advertised under the slogan "A different kind of company. A different kind of car." New types of vehicles showed up in new types of ads. The minivan, developed by Chrysler in 1983 to succeed the familiar wood-sided station wagon as the quintessential American family car, was most often depicted in advertisements via an interior view. And the sport-utility vehicle arrived — an offspring of the military jeep and the pickup truck — to keep alive the dream of the open road.

If the rock-solid Toyota Corollas and Honda Civics in millions of driveways updated Henry Ford's promise of inexpensive, dependable, practical automobility, the SUVs of the 1990s represented a return to the rugged early days of cars. They promised that one could drive anywhere, road or not; they provided symbolic security in a dangerous world.

The history of the automobile is the story of the industrial economy. Tied as it is to fashion, art, film, and music, the automobile is not only a cultural force, but an economic one as well. Just as we've come to call earlier eras the Stone Age and the Bronze Age, the car has played such a large role in our lives that today's era might easily be called the age of the automobile.

The PENALTY OF LEADERSHIP

1915

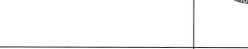

1915 Cadillac runs famed Penalty of Leadership ad in response to criticism

Cadillac reagiert auf Kritik mit der berühmt gewordenen Anzeige „Penalty of Leadership"

En réponse aux critiques, Cadillac publie sa célèbre annonce « La sanction du plus fort »

1917 America enters World War I

Die USA treten in den Ersten Weltkrieg ein.

Les États-Unis entrent en guerre

1923 Jordan Playboy becomes first car advertised on emotional appeal alone

Der Jordan Playboy ist das erste Auto mit rein emotional orientierter Werbung

La Jordan Playboy est la première voiture dont la publicité repose uniquement sur la psychologie

1925 First motel—or motorist's hotel—erected in San Luis Obispo, California

Erstes Motel (Motorist's Hotel) im kalifornischen San Luis Obispo errichtet

Premier motel – ou hôtel pour automobilistes – inauguré à San Luis Obispo, en Californie

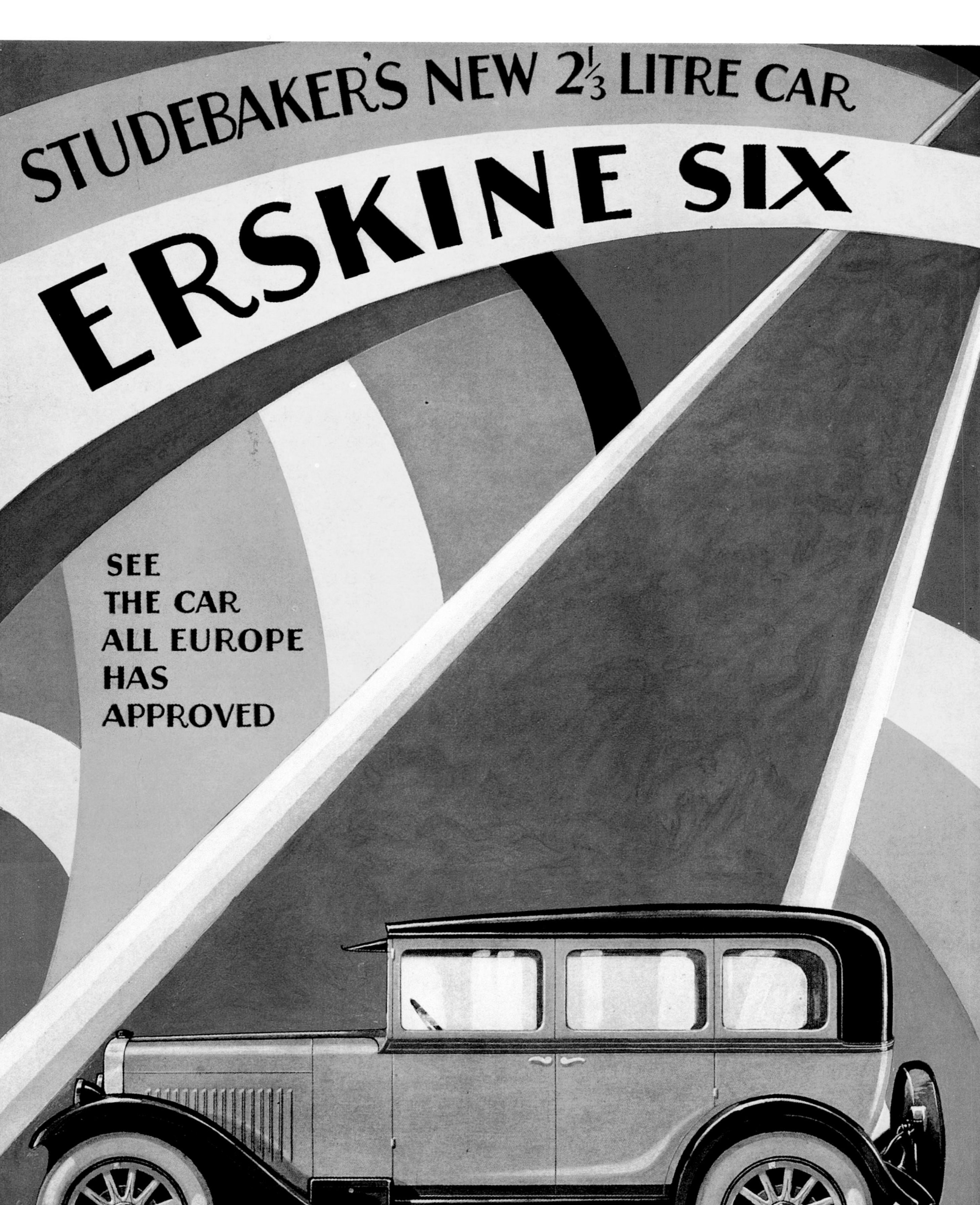
STUDEBAKER'S NEW 2⅓ LITRE CAR
ERSKINE SIX
SEE
THE CAR
ALL EUROPE
HAS
APPROVED
ERSKINE SIX CUSTOM SEDAN—$985 f.o.b. factory

BUICK

1939

„DIE POESIE DER BEWEGUNG! DIE WAHRE ART ZU REISEN! DIE EINZIGE ART ZU REISEN!", schwärmte Herr Kröterich in dem Kinderbuch-Klassiker *Der Wind in den Weiden* von Kenneth Grahame aus dem Jahr 1908. Vermutlich war dies das erste literarische Zeugnis von der Faszination, ja der beginnenden Obsession Auto. Bei den ersten Autos handelte es sich noch um ein Spielzeug der Reichen. Autofahren war ein Hobby der Wohlhabenden, ähnlich dem Segeln oder Bergsteigen. Das Auto diente weniger dazu, ins Büro oder zum Einkaufen zu fahren. Lieber unternahm man an den Wochenenden gemütliche Spritztouren aufs Land. Hierzu bedurfte es allerdings einer speziellen Ausrüstung und meist auch fachkundigen Personals in Gestalt von Chauffeuren und Mechanikern.

Die frühen Automobile waren Sonderanfertigungen, vergleichbar mit einem Maßanzug, den man beim Schneider bestellte. Fahrgestell und Motor wurden in der Regel als Einheit verkauft, während die Karosserie von einem ganz anderen Hersteller stammte, nicht selten von einem Stellmacher oder Karosseriebauer, der womöglich auch weiterhin Pferdewagen fertigte.

Die ersten „Automobilisten" waren Männer wie W. K. „Willy" Vanderbilt, Erbe des Schiffs- und Eisenbahnkönigs Cornelius Vanderbilt. Die Begeisterung dieses frühen Anhängers der neuen Technik war der des Herrn Kröterich durchaus nicht unähnlich. Vanderbilt gab beträchtliche Summen für Autos aus. So etwa erwarb er einen Stanley Steamer, einen Daimler, den er „White Ghost" taufte und einen Mercedes namens „Red Devil". Auf dem Sand von Ormond Beach, Florida erzielte Vanderbilt 1904 mit 148 km/h einen neuen Geschwindigkeitsrekord – wobei damals 50 km/h bei den meisten Autos bereits als ziemlich flottes Tempo galten.

DIE ERSTE AUTOWERBUNG IN DEN USA ERSCHIEN 1896 UND GALT DEM ERSTEN US-AUTOMOBIL, GEFERTIGT VON DER DURYEA MOTOR WAGON COMPANY. Die meisten Anzeigen der folgenden Jahrzehnte warben für Nobelmarken wie Pierce-Arrow und Packard oder für Zubehör. Die Zielgruppe bestand indes eher aus jenen, die sich um die Autos kümmerten als aus den eigentlichen Besitzern. Damals nämlich mussten noch alle paar Kilometer Öl und Wasser nachgefüllt werden, Reifenpannen waren an der Tagesordnung und die offenen Autos erforderten eine spezielle Kluft aus Brille, Schal und weitem Staubmantel.

Die Entwicklung von Autotechnik und -industrie zeigt Parallelen zur Entwicklung der modernen Werbung und der modernen Medien – neben dem Radio (und später dem Fernsehen) auch Zeitschriften von *Collier's* und *The Saturday Evening Post* bis zu *Life*, *Fortune* und *Time*, die zusammengenommen fast jeden US-Haushalt erreichten.

In der Tat galten einige der herausragenden Werbekampagnen, Slogans und Anzeigen des 20. Jahrhunderts dem Auto. Berühmt wurde Cadillacs Anzeige „Penalty of Leadership" von 1915. Cadillac war damals wie heute stolz auf seine Top-Qualität und technischen Neuerungen. Bei einem Modell waren indes Mängel aufgetreten, was vom Mitbewerber Packard kritisiert wurde. Cadillac reagierte mit einer allgemein gehaltenen Anzeige aus der Feder von Theodore F. MacManus. „Wenn das Tun eines Mannes zum Standard für die ganze Welt wird, dann wird es auch zum Ziel für die Spitzen der paar Neider", erwiderte er, um das Markenimage aufzupolieren, ohne dabei ein spezielles Modell oder Produkt zu erwähnen. Damit hatte Cadillac nicht nur seine Ehre gerettet, sondern sich für die nächsten fünfzig Jahre zugleich auch als Marke etabliert.

ALS HENRY FORD 1908 SEIN MODEL T VORSTELLTE, BRACHTE ER DAS AUTO ZU DEN MASSEN. Ford hatte die Vorstellung, dass die Väter ihre Familien nun an den Wochenenden von den ungesunden Städten hinaus aufs Land bringen würden. Die Auswirkungen waren indes noch viel weitreichender, denn das Model T sollte die Idee und Realität der „universalen Automobilität" etablieren.

1926

1926 Route 66—aka "Main Street of America"—runs from Chicago to Los Angeles

Die Route 66 alias „Hauptstraße Amerikas" verbindet Chicago und Los Angeles

La mythique Route 66 relie Chicago à Los Angeles

1927 Cadillac releases first "styled" car, the LaSalle, designed by Harley Earl

Cadillac präsentiert mit dem von Harley Earl entworfenen LaSalle den ersten „durchgestylten" Wagen

Cadillac lance son premier modèle « design » : la LaSalle, dessinée par Harley Earl

1933 Cadillac unveils Aero-Dynamic coupe at Chicago World's Fair

Cadillac stellt das Aero-Dynamic Coupé auf der Weltausstellung in Chicago vor

Cadillac dévoile son coupé aérodynamique à la foire internationale de Chicago

1934 Bank robbers Bonnie Parker and Clyde Barrow use Ford V8s as getaway cars

Die Bankräuber Bonnie Parker und Clyde Barrow benutzen Fluchtautos mit Ford V8-Motor

Les braqueurs Bonnie Parker et Clyde Barrow apprécient les Ford V8

Buick Eight, 1939 ◂◂

▸ DeSoto, 1956

Wenn er den Preis eines Autos immer weiter senken würde, so versprach Ford, „wird kein Mann, der ein anständiges Gehalt verdient, ohne eines sein können". Damit lag er ziemlich richtig, denn schon 1920 war das Auto keine bloße Neuheit mehr, sondern bereits fast eine Notwendigkeit.

Das Model T, sein „universales Auto", würde sich von selbst verkaufen. Davon war Henry Ford überzeugt und deshalb kümmerte er sich kaum um Werbung. „Ford-Werbung will niemals clever sein", rühmte man sich 1912. In der Tat fand das Model T auch so zahlreiche Kunden und Anhänger. Vergleichbar mit heutigen Produkten wie dem iPod ließ das Model T eine entsprechende Fangemeinde, Populärkultur und Zubehörindustrie entstehen. Es gab sogar Model-T-Witze, den späteren Blondinenwitzen nicht unähnlich.

Als 1928 dem Model T schließlich das hochwertigere Model A folgte, wandte sich Ford an die Werbeagentur N.W. Ayer. So entstand eine der nachhaltigsten Werbekampagnen jener Zeit, die das Auto als Teil der intakten Familie in heimeligen Szenen hinter weißem Lattenzaun propagierte. Ford konnte nicht mehr allein mit dem niedrigen Preis punkten, denn zunehmend mehr Menschen kauften nun nicht ihr erstes, sondern bereits ihr zweites oder gar drittes Auto.

Eine andere Werbestrategie verfolgte das ebenfalls 1908 gegründete Unternehmen General Motors. Diese Union von Marken wie Cadillac, Oldsmobile und Buick sollte für die gebotene Vielfalt bekannt werden. „Ein Auto für jeden Zweck und Geldbeutel" lautete der Slogan von GM-Direktor Alfred Sloan. GM brachte jedes Jahr neue Modelle mit unterschiedlichem Stil und Raffinement. Der alljährliche Modellwechsel sollte, so Sloan, „Unzufriedenheit erzeugen". So entstand zugleich ein durch Werbung gespeistes amerikanisches Ritual, ähnlich den Ferienterminen. So gewiss wie die Kinder jeden September in die Schule zurückkehrten, hielten sie bei den Autohändlern aufgeregt Ausschau nach den neuesten Modellen.

Das Model T gab es „in jeder Farbe, sofern es Schwarz ist". General Motors machte daraus „jede Farbe, die Sie wünschen" – dank der Anfang der 1920er-Jahre von DuPont entwickelten, schnell trocknenden Duco-Lacke. Neue Farben wie das „True Blue", das es für den 1924er Oakland gab, machten die Massenproduktion „in Farbe" möglich – wobei „Farbe" für GMs Bereitschaft stand, dem Kunden eine zunehmend größere Auswahl zu bieten.

Um den neuen Modellen mehr Faszination zu verleihen, orientierte sich Sloan an Hollywood. Hier fuhren die Filmstars und Regisseure aufwendige Sonderanfertigungen. Oft wurden sie vor ihren Karossen stehend abgelichtet und traten mitunter in Anzeigen als frühe Werbeträger in Erscheinung. Zahlreiche dieser Anfertigungen waren das Werk eines Mannes: Harley Earl. Zu seinen Kunden gehörten der Filmproduzent Cecil B. DeMille (sein unmittelbarer Nachbar) und die Schauspieler Mary Pickford, Tom Mix und Fatty Arbuckle. Sloan beeindruckte, wie Earl anhand von Tonmodellen jedes Auto komplett konzipierte und beauftrage Earl, einen neuen Wagen zu entwerfen (den 1927er LaSalle) und die General Motors „Art and Color Section" auf die Beine zu stellen, die jedes Jahr mit neuen Modellen aufwarten würde – wie in der Welt der Mode.

WÄHREND FRAUEN IN DER AUTOWERBUNG ZUNÄCHST NUR EINE ZWEITRANGIGE ZIELGRUPPE DARSTELLTEN, sollte sich dies bei zahlreichen Modellen schon bald ändern. Autos kamen dort zum Einsatz, wo Frauen einkauften und zunehmend auch arbeiteten. Viele Neuerungen, von neuen Farben bis zu Automatikgetrieben, entstanden mit Blick auf weibliche Käufer. Um Frauen gezielt anzusprechen, inserierte man in Zeitschriften wie *Vogue*, *Good Housekeeping* oder *Ladies' Home Journal*.

Um 1930 war das Design selbst zu einem bedeutenden Verkaufsaspekt geworden und es galt, die Werbung auf den Look der neuen Modelle abzustimmen. Die Zeichner halfen

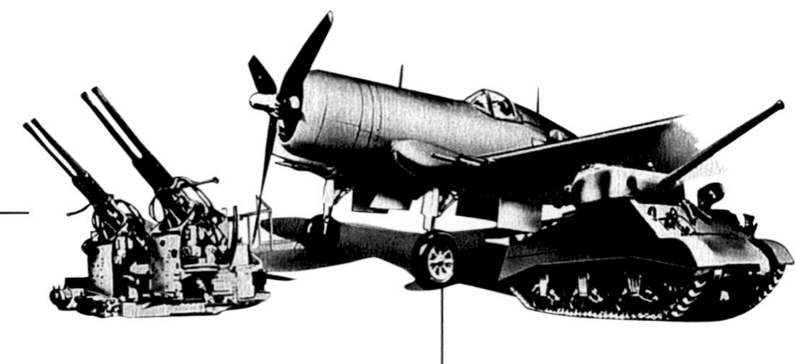

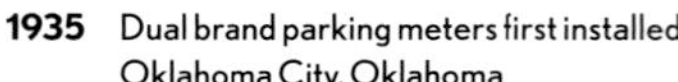

1935

1935 Dual brand parking meters first installed, Oklahoma City, Oklahoma

Erste Parkuhren in Oklahoma City (Oklahoma) aufgestellt

Premiers parcmètres de la marque Dual installés à Oklahoma City, en Oklahoma

1942 World War II causes civilian car production shut down in U.S.

Zweiter Weltkrieg bringt die zivile Autoproduktion in den USA zum Erliegen

La Seconde Guerre mondiale entraîne une chute de la production automobile civile aux États-Unis

1945 U.S. gas rationing ends with end of WWII

Benzinrationierung in den USA nach dem Zweiten Weltkrieg aufgehoben

Le rationnement de l'essence aux États-Unis cesse avec la fin de la Seconde Guerre mondiale

1945 Postwar passenger-car production resumes

Die ersten Nachkriegs-Pkw laufen vom Band

La production de voitures particulières reprend après la guerre

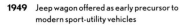

1949 Jeep wagon offered as early precursor to modern sport-utility vehicles

Jeep Wagon als früher Vorläufer der modernen SUVs angeboten

La Jeep est présentée comme le précurseur des 4x4 actuels

1949 Virgil Exner joins Chrysler as director of styling; will introduce Forward Look

Virgil Exner tritt bei Chrysler als Design-Direktor ein und wird den „Forward Look" erfinden

Virgil Exner devient directeur de création chez Chrysler ; il lancera le look Forward

1951 Oldsmobile's high-compression engine inspires first rock 'n' roll song, "Rocket 88"

Oldsmobiles hoch komprimierter Motor steht Pate beim ersten Rock 'n' Roll-Song „Rocket 88"

Le moteur à haute compression d'Oldsmobile inspire la première chanson de rock'n'roll : Rocket 88

1951 GM design chief Harley Earl dreams up Le Sabre concept car

GM-Chefdesigner Harley Earl kreiert das Concept-Car Le Sabre

Harley Earl, designer en chef chez GM, imagine le concept-car Le Sabre

Ford Mustang, 1967

►► Pontiac Grand Prix, 1967

dabei, die neuen Stahlkarosserien zu präsentieren, etwa indem sie die Autodächer höher erscheinen ließen und die Gürtellinie an den passenden Stellen mit Lichtreflexen schmückten.

Strike a blow for originality!
(Take the Mustang Pledge.)
Still the original and lowest-priced car of its kind with bucket seats.
MUSTANG
Ford

Vor allem Kredite und der Gebrauchtwagenmarkt trugen dazu bei, dass die USA rasch die weltweit größte Automobildichte verzeichneten. Ende der 1930er-Jahre besaßen 22,7 Prozent der Bevölkerung ein eigenes Auto; in Großbritannien waren es nur 5,4 Prozent, in Deutschland nur halb so viele wie in Großbritannien und in Italien sogar noch weniger. In Italien gab es lediglich rund zehn Autos pro tausend Einwohner, in der Sowjetunion indes weniger als fünf. Anders als in den USA waren Autos im Rest der Welt ein vergleichsweise seltener Anblick. Als die Verfilmung von John Steinbecks *Früchte des Zorns* in die europäischen Kinos kam, waren die Zuschauer ziemlich erstaunt: Die Joads brachen in einer alten Klapperkiste nach Kalifornien auf. Warum sollten sie arm sein? Sie besaßen doch schließlich ein Auto!

Der Depression fielen zahlreiche Luxusmarken wie Pierce-Arrow oder Duesenberg zum Opfer. Bisher an der Spitze der sozialen Leiter, wurde Packard durch Cadillac verdrängt, die sich als Teil von General Motors auf andere Marken stützen konnte. Packard sollte sich noch bis Mitte der 1950er-Jahre halten – mit protzigen Karossen, die ein schwacher Abglanz ihrer einstigen Eleganz waren.

In den 1950er-Jahren hatte die ab 1938 kommerziell genutzte Farbfotografie die Illustration in den Werbeanzeigen fast vollständig verdrängt, nicht aber in der Autowerbung. Zeichnerisch ließen sich nämlich Effekte erzielen, die in der prädigitalen Fotografie unmöglich waren. Autos konnten futuristisch dargestellt, verlängert oder verbreitert oder durch Betonen von Licht und Schatten und ihrer skulpturalen Eigenschaften romantisiert werden. Hierzu erhielten die Illustratoren streng geheime Fotos von den Autos des kommenden Jahres. Einige der führenden Werbe-Illustratoren arbeiteten zu zweit, wie Art Fitzgerald und Van Kaufman, die sich oft mit ihren Initialen auf den Nummernschildern verewigten. Bekannt wurden sie für ihre Bilder, die für Pontiacs „Breitspurigkeit“ werben sollten (der Pontiac wurde als niedrig und breit beworben, wohl mit Blick auf eine verbesserte Straßenlage). Zeichnerisch konnte man auch den Proportionen eines Autos schmeicheln und es länger oder größer erscheinen lassen. Bisweilen schnitt man Fotos entzwei und benutzte sie als

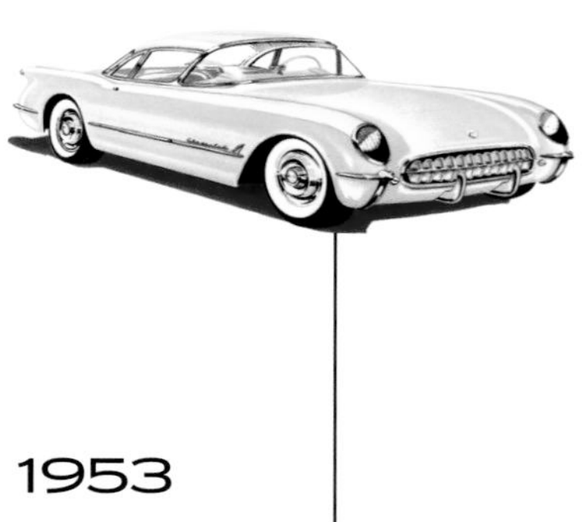

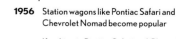

1953

1953 First fiberglass body released—Chevrolet's Corvette

Erste Glasfaser-Karosserie (Chevrolet Corvette)

Première carrosserie en fibre de verre pour la Chevrolet Corvette

1955 Chrysler's Forward Look design theme offers tail fins

Chryslers „Forward Look“ nun auch mit Heckflossen

Le look Forward de chez Chrysler se caractérise par ses ailettes arrière

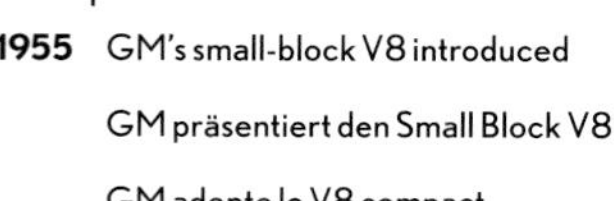

1955 GM's small-block V8 introduced

GM präsentiert den Small Block V8

GM adopte le V8 compact

1956 Station wagons like Pontiac Safari and Chevrolet Nomad become popular

Kombis wie Pontiac Safari und Chevrolet Nomad zunehmend beliebter

Les breaks comme le Pontiac Safari et le Chevrolet Nomad se popularisent

„ICH WERDE EINEN MOTORWAGEN FÜR DIE BREITE MASSE BAUEN … GEFERTIGT AUS DEN BESTEN MATERIALIEN VON DEN BESTEN MÄNNERN, DIE MAN BEKOMMEN KANN UND SO NIEDRIG IM PREIS, DASS JEDER, DER GUTES GELD VERDIENT, IHN SICH WIRD LEISTEN KÖNNEN …“

—HENRY FORD, FORD MOTOR COMPANY, 1908

Vorlage für „gedehnte“ Zeichnungen – mit Dächern, unter denen plötzlich auch ein Mann mit Hut Platz fand.

Mitte des Jahrhunderts war das Auto fest in die Alltagskultur integriert. Jack Kerouac setzte sich in einen alten Hudson und schrieb *Unterwegs* auf einer Blatt für Blatt zusammengeklebten, fast 40 Meter langen Rolle Pauspapier, die er der Legende nach wie die Straße selbst auf seinem Schreibtisch entrollte. Ike Turner schrieb 1951 den ersten Rock 'n' Roll-Song, benannt nach und inspiriert durch ein Auto: „Rocket 88“ verweist auf den neuen, hoch komprimierten V8-Motor von Oldsmobile. Dies war der Beginn einer Tradition, die Autos und Popmusik verband und sich über die Beach Boys bis zu Prince und Snoop Dogg fortsetzte. Wenn der Industriedesigner Raymond Loewy die US-Autos als „rollende Jukebox“ schimpfte – was war falsch daran, wo doch Elvis, Chubby Checker und Buddy Holly in der echten Jukebox steckten?

In den Eisenhower-Jahren veränderten Superhighways und Fernsehen das Leben – und das Auto. Heckflossenautos waren für den Dichter Robert Lowell wie Haie. Und sie bevölkerten die Welt von Sloan Wilsons Roman *Der Mann im grauen Flanell*. Das Magazin *Time* nannte Fords Chefdesigner Geoge Walker den „Cellini des Chrom“. Und Virgil Exner schuf Chryslers extremen „Forward Look“: „Plötzlich ist es 1960!“ Doch als Ford 1957 seinen Edsel lancierte, hatte die Rezession bereits Fahrt aufgenommen.

IM JAHR 1959 KONNTE DIE NEW YORKER WERBEAGENTUR DOYLE DANE BERNBACH DEN AUFTRAG für eine US-weite VW-Werbung an Land ziehen. Man startete die Kampagne „Think Small“, die unter Werbeprofis und Historikern als eine der besten Anzeigenkampagnen aller Zeiten gilt. Schlichte Schwarzweißfotos vom Käfer und VW-Bus, begleitet von ironischen Texten, zeugten von Understatement und Bescheidenheit. Die von Werbetexter Julian König und Artdirector Helmut Krone kreierten Anzeigen nahmen den alljährlichen Modellwechsel, all den glitzernden Chrom und den Ausstattungswahn der US-Modelle aufs Korn. „Eigentlich war dieses ‚Think Small‘ gar nicht so bescheiden“, schrieb der Werbehistoriker Bob Garfield. „Denn wer einen Käfer besaß, konnte damit prahlen, dass er nicht prahlen musste.“

In der Tat ging es bei den meisten US-Autos weiterhin darum, Eindruck zu schinden. Die USA waren 1960 auf der Höhe ihrer Macht und die Automodelle und Werbung spiegelten dies wider. Doch plötzlich stellten sich die Amerikaner Fragen nach der Sicherheit ihrer riesigen, PS-starken Autos. Das Buch *Unsafe at Any Speed* des Industriekritikers und Anwalts Ralph Nader avancierte zum Bestseller. Seine Aussagen vor diversen Kongress-Ausschüssen führten zu Gesetzen, die Sicherheitsgurte und weitere Verbesserungen vorschrieben.

Außerdem wünschten sich die Amerikaner persönlichere Autos. Auf der Weltausstellung in New York 1964 präsentierte man den Ford Mustang als das erste „persönliche“ oder zumindest „personalisierbare“ Auto – mit seinem kurzen Heck und der langen Motorhaube wurde er zum Spiegelbild der Minirock-Ära. Lee Iacocca, Generaldirektor von Ford, nannte ihn „den Wagen, den Sie selbst entwerfen“, und zwar dank einer langen Zubehörliste. Der Mustang wurde zum Symbol des jüngst emanzipierten jungen weiblichen Singles, wie ihn der Hit „Mustang Sally“ von Mack Rice verkörperte. Wilson Picketts Interpretation des Songs verkaufte sich allein im ersten Jahr über 400 000 Mal.

Während Detroit die Jugendrevolte und die um sich greifende Gegenkultur der 1960er-Jahre mit Slogans wie „Dodge Fever“ bewältigte, versuchte American Motors mit Bluejeans-Versionen die Jugend anzusprechen. Für Frauen gab es stark individualisierbare Pony-Cars wie den Chevy Camaro, für Männer ebensolche Muscle-Cars wie den Pontiac GTO.

Die 1970er-Jahre standen im Zeichen der Energiekrisen und der massiven Zunahme japanischer Importwagen. Im Oktober 1973 verhängte ein Bündnis Erdöl fördernder

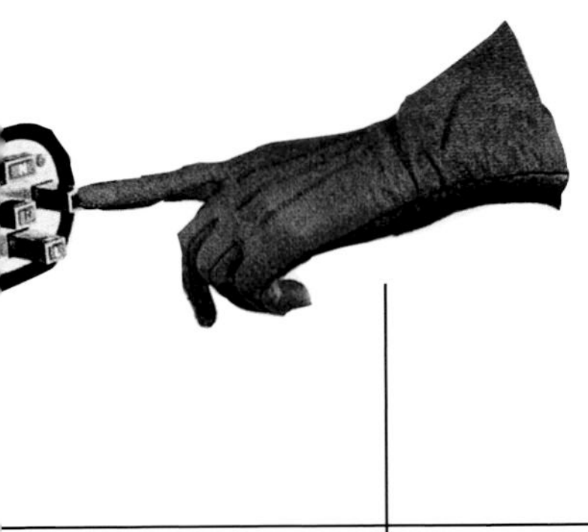

1956 Chrysler, DeSoto, Dodge, and Plymouth offer push-button transmission shifter

Chrysler, DeSoto, Dodge und Plymouth bieten Gangwechsel per Knopfdruck

Chrysler, DeSoto, Dodge et Plymouth proposent le bouton-poussoir de transmission automatique

1956 Federal-Aid Highway Act passed, mandating network of highways across U.S.

Federal-Aid Highway Act verabschiedet, um die gesamten USA mit einem Highway-Netz zu versorgen

Adoption de la loi américaine pour le développement du réseau autoroutier aux États-Unis

1957 Cadillacs offered in pink, recalling Elvis Presley's custom-painted 1955 Fleetwood

Cadillacs auch in Pink erhältlich, in Erinnerung an Elvis Presleys 1955er Fleetwood mit Speziallackierung

Les cadillacs sont disponibles en rose, comme la Fleetwood d'Elvis Presley, peinte sur mesure en 1955

1957 Ford introduces 1958 model Edsel; will fail within three years

Ford präsentiert den Edsel für 1958, der nach nur drei Jahren scheitert

Ford lance le modèle Edsel 1958 ; il disparaîtra trois ans plus tard

„WAS GUT IST FÜR UNSER LAND, DAS IST GUT FÜR GENERAL MOTORS, UND WAS GUT IST FÜR GENERAL MOTORS, DAS IST AUCH GUT FÜR UNSER LAND.“

—CHARLES WILSON, GENERAL MOTORS, 1955

Nahoststaaten einen Lieferboykott gegen jene Länder, die Israel im Jom-Kippur-Krieg unterstützten. Der Ölpreis kletterte auf zwölf Dollar pro Barrel. In den USA vervierfachte sich der Benzinpreis innerhalb weniger Wochen, gefolgt von Rationierungsmaßnahmen und der Einführung einer landesweiten Höchstgeschwindigkeit von 55 Meilen pro Stunde. Kleinwagen gingen weg wie warme Semmeln, doch Detroit hatte kaum etwas anzubieten. Ford, General Motors und Chrysler importierten daher hastig einige Modelle ihrer europäischen Niederlassungen und ihrer Tochterfirmen in Asien. Profitiert haben indes die japanischen Hersteller. Noch 1958 hatten alle japanischen Autobauer zusammen nicht einmal 1500 Wagen in den USA verkauft. Zehn Jahre später waren es bereits 150 000 und 1975 besaßen sie einen Marktanteil von zehn Prozent.

Der Toyota Corona und der Honda Civic erlangten durch Mundpropaganda rasch einen guten Ruf; Werbung hätte da nicht mithalten können. Der Datsun Z – die Reihe begann 1969 mit dem 240Z – fand als wirtschaftlicher Sportwagen junge Anhänger. Diverse Auszeichnungen, die ihm von Autozeitschriften verliehen wurden, festigten den guten Ruf der japanischen Autos. Mitte der 1970er-Jahre importierten die USA mehr Autos aus Japan als aus Europa. Trotz cleverer Werbung wie Renaults Kampagne „Le Car“ gingen die Importe aus Frankreich und Italien zurück. Auch VW wurde in Mitleidenschaft gezogen, nachdem der Käfer 1974 ausgelaufen war.

Gut zehn Jahre sollten vergehen, bis sich die großen Drei von Detroit auf die Veränderungen eingestellt hatten. General Motors lancierte 1989 die Marke Saturn mit dem Slogan „Saturn: eine andere Art von Unternehmen, eine andere Art von Auto“.

Neuartige Autos bedeuteten neuartige Werbung. Beim Minivan, 1983 von Chrysler als typisches Familienauto und Nachfolger des vertrauten Familienkombis mit Holzbeplankung entwickelt, rückte das Interieur in den Mittelpunkt. Und das SUV (Sport Utility Vehicle), ein Abkömmling von Jeep und Pick-up, nährte den Traum von der freien Fahrt.

Wenn Abertausende grundsolider Toyota Corollas und Honda Civics Henry Fords Versprechen eines bezahlbaren und zuverlässigen Automobils erneuerten, so bedeuteten die SUVs der 1990er-Jahre eine Rückbesinnung auf die markige Frühzeit des Automobils. Sie bargen das Versprechen, jedes Ziel erreichen zu können, mit oder ohne Straße. Und sie vermittelten das Gefühl der Sicherheit in einer gefährlichen Welt.

Die Historie des Automobils ist die Geschichte einer ganzen Industrie. Eng mit Mode, Kunst, Film und Musik verknüpft, ist das Auto eine maßgebliche kulturelle wie auch ökonomische Größe. Frühere Zeitalter trugen Namen wie Steinzeit oder Bronzezeit. In unserem Alltagsleben spielt das Auto eine derart tragende Rolle, dass man die Gegenwart durchaus das Zeitalter des Automobils nennen könnte.

1959 Firebird III concept car, "A Laboratory on Wheels," unveiled at GM Motorama

Concept-Car Firebird III („Ein Labor auf Rädern“) auf der GM Motorama gezeigt

La Firebird III, concept-car surnommée le « laboratoire ambulant », est dévoilée au Motorama de GM

1959 Recession boosts sales of Volkswagen, Renault, other small European cars in U.S.

Rezession beschleunigt den Absatz von Volkswagen, Renault und anderen europäischen Kleinwagen in den USA

La récession accroît les ventes américaines des Volkswagen, Renault et autres petites Européennes

1959 Doyle Dane Bernbach creates famed Think Small ad campaign for Volkswagen

Doyle Dane Bernbach kreiert für Volkswagen die berühmte Anzeigenkampagne „Think Small“

Doyle Dane Bernbach crée la célèbre campagne publicitaire Think Small pour Volkswagen

1959 Pontiac's Wide Tracks expand five full inches in width from previous models

Pontiacs „Wide Track“-Modelle bieten eine um gut zwölf Zentimeter größere Spurweite als ihre Vorgänger

Les modèles Wide Track de Pontiac gagnent treize bons centimètres de largeur sur leurs prédécesseurs

67-100

NO GAS
I'M SORRIER
THAN YOU ARE
RT-2585

« LA POÉSIE DU MOUVEMENT ! LA VRAIE FAÇON DE VOYAGER ! LA SEULE ! », s'exclame Crapaud dans *Le Vent dans les saules* (1908), un classique de la littérature pour enfants. C'est sans doute le premier hommage littéraire rendu à la fascination pour l'automobile, l'émergence du culte de la voiture. Les premiers modèles sont des jouets pour les riches. L'automobile sert moins à se déplacer pour se rendre au bureau ou faire les courses qu'à partir tranquillement en excursion le week-end. Les promenades en voiture sont l'apanage des plus fortunés, au même titre que la voile ou l'alpinisme, car ce passe-temps requiert un équipement particulier et, dans la plupart des cas, un personnel spécialisé, tels que chauffeurs et mécaniciens.

Les premières voitures sont faites sur mesure ; on commande une automobile comme on se fait faire un beau costume chez le tailleur ou une robe chez la couturière. En général, le châssis et le moteur sont vendus ensemble tandis que la caisse s'achète chez un fabricant différent, le carrossier, qui fournit le marché de l'attelage.

Parmi les premiers automobilistes figurent des personnalités telles que W.K. « Willy » Vanderbilt, héritier du magnat de l'industrie navale et des chemins de fer. L'enthousiasme de cet adepte des nouveautés technologiques égale celui de Crapaud. Il dépense sans compter pour acheter les toutes premières automobiles : une Stanley Steamer, une Daimler qu'il baptise « Fantôme blanc », et une Mercedes qu'il nomme « Diable rouge ». En 1904, Vanderbilt établit un record de vitesse à 148 km/h sur le sable à Ormond Beach, en Floride – à une époque où la plupart des voitures ne dépassent guère le 50 km/h à grand train.

LA PREMIÈRE PUBLICITÉ AUTOMOBILE, QUI PARAÎT AUX ÉTATS-UNIS EN 1896, promeut la première Américaine, construite par la Motor Wagon Company des frères Duryea. Au fil des décennies suivantes, la plupart des publicités seront réservées aux marques de grand luxe, comme Pierce-Arrow et Packard, ainsi qu'aux accessoires qu'elles proposent ; souvent, elles s'adressent plus aux personnes qui prennent soin des voitures qu'à leurs propriétaires. À l'époque, il faut changer l'huile et l'eau tous les quelques kilomètres. Les crevaisons sont fréquentes et comme les voitures sont ouvertes à tous les vents, elles nécessitent une garde-robe adaptée : lunettes de protection, écharpes et cache-poussière.

Parallèlement aux progrès de la technologie automobile et à l'essor de ce secteur industriel, la publicité et les médias modernes se développent. Outre la radio puis la télévision, les revues se multiplient : *Collier's*, le *Saturday Evening Post*, *Life*, *Fortune* et *Time* touchent à eux tous la quasi-totalité des foyers américains.

À vrai dire, les campagnes et slogans publicitaires les plus marquants du XXe siècle ont trait aux voitures. On peut ainsi citer la célèbre annonce intitulée « La sanction du plus fort », publiée par Cadillac en 1915. L'entreprise est alors fière de son excellence et de ses innovations techniques ; un de ses modèles présente toutefois certains défauts que Packard, sa rivale, s'empresse de souligner. Cadillac répond donc par une campagne générale destinée à redorer son blason. « Quand l'œuvre d'un homme devient la norme pour le monde entier, elle devient également la cible des flèches de quelques envieux », explique le grand publicitaire Theodore F. MacManus, sans mentionner ni modèle ni produit particuliers.

Cadillac sauve ainsi l'honneur, tout en asseyant la marque pour les cinquante ans à venir.

EN 1908, HENRY FORD COMMERCIALISE LE MODÈLE T ET FAVORISE AINSI L'ACCÈS DU GRAND PUBLIC À LA VOITURE. Il pense ainsi permettre aux pères de famille d'emmener leur maisonnée prendre l'air le week-end, loin des villes malsaines, mais la réalité dépasse largement son imagination : pour tous, la T incarne l'idée de l'automobile.

Ford promet de faire baisser le prix de la voiture jusqu'à ce que « tout travailleur gagnant un salaire décent soit en

1960 Photography begins dominating auto ad imagery, replacing illustration

Anstatt der Illustration wird die Fotografie zum dominierenden Bildgeber der Autowerbung

La photographie remplace l'illustration et commence à prédominer dans la publicité automobile

1963 Raymond Loewy's Studebaker Avanti debuts

Debüt von Raymond Loewys Studebaker Avanti

Lancement de la Studebaker Avanti de Raymond Loewy

1963 Front seat belts become increasingly popular in American cars

Sicherheitsgurte für Fahrer und Beifahrer in den USA zunehmend verbreitet

La ceinture de sécurité est de plus en plus répandue à l'avant dans les voitures américaines

1964 Ford introduces Mustang, first sporty "pony car," at New York World's Fair

Ford präsentiert den Mustang, das erste sportliche Pony-Car, auf der Weltausstellung in New York

Ford lance la Mustang, première voiture de sport dite « pony car », à la Foire internationale de New York

« CE QUI EST BON POUR LE PAYS EST BON POUR GENERAL MOTORS, ET CE QUI EST BON POUR GENERAL MOTORS EST BON POUR LE PAYS. »

—CHARLES WILSON, GENERAL MOTORS, 1955

mesure d'en posséder une ». L'avenir lui donne raison : en 1920, la voiture n'est déjà plus une nouveauté, et devient presque une nécessité.

Henry Ford est si convaincu que le modèle T – sa « voiture universelle » – se vendra sans difficulté qu'il renonce à en faire vraiment la publicité. « Chez Ford, la publicité ne cherche jamais à faire de l'esprit », se targue la firme en 1912. En fait, ce sont ses clients et adeptes qui se chargent de la vendre. Comme pour les produits actuels tels que l'iPod, le modèle T génère une base d'inconditionnels, une culture populaire et une industrie annexe. Il existe même des blagues sur le modèle T qui évoquent les blagues actuelles sur les blondes.

Cependant, lorsque le modèle T finit par céder la place au modèle A, en 1928, Ford engage l'agence N.W. Ayer, qui conçoit l'une des plus mémorables campagnes de l'époque : des voitures présentées dans un cadre familial rassurant, derrière les radieuses clôtures de planches blanches d'une petite ville. Ford ne peut plus se contenter de vanter ses prix bas. De plus en plus de gens achètent non seulement leur première, mais leur deuxième, voire leur troisième voiture.

Avec General Motors, également fondée en 1908, apparaît une autre approche pour promouvoir la voiture. L'entreprise, qui réunit plusieurs marques – dont Cadillac, Oldsmobile et Buick –, va miser sur la diversité offerte. « Une voiture pour chaque bourse et pour chaque usage », selon la formule d'Alfred Sloan, le patron de GM, dont les voitures se déclinent en quantité de styles et de degrés de sophistication différents. Les modèles changent chaque année. Pour Sloan, cette valse annuelle vise à « susciter de l'insatisfaction ». Cela devient un rituel pour toute l'Amérique, une sorte de fête, orchestrée par la publicité. À chaque rentrée scolaire en septembre, les petits Américains se collent contre les vitrines des concessionnaires pour repérer les nouveaux modèles.

Le modèle T est disponible dans « la couleur qu'on veut, du moment que c'est noir ». General Motors rend la chose vraiment possible et propose l'emploi des laques Duco à séchage rapide. D'abord uniquement disponibles pour le modèle Oakland en 1924, ces nouvelles peintures créées par le chimiste DuPont début 1920 permettent la production en série de modèles en couleur. La couleur prouve la volonté de General Motors d'offrir un choix toujours plus vaste au consommateur.

Pour rendre les nouvelles voitures plus attrayantes, Sloan se tourne vers Hollywood. Là-bas, les stars de cinéma et les metteurs en scène célèbres conduisent des voitures faites sur commande, devant lesquelles ils sont souvent photographiés dans un but publicitaire. On voit même apparaître les premiers ambassadeurs de marque. Nombre de ces voitures sur mesure sont l'œuvre d'un seul homme : Harley Earl. Ses clients comptent le producteur Cecil B. DeMille – son voisin direct – et les acteurs Mary Pickford, Tom Mix ou encore Fatty Arbuckle. Impressionné par la manière dont Earl conçoit chaque voiture d'un seul bloc, à partir de maquettes en terre, Sloan l'engage pour dessiner une nouvelle voiture : la LaSalle de 1927. Earl est aussi à l'origine du département Art et couleur de General Motors, chargé de concevoir de nouveaux modèles chaque année, comme dans la mode.

SI, DANS UN PREMIER TEMPS, LES FEMMES CONSTITUENT UNE CIBLE SECONDAIRE POUR LA PUBLICITÉ AUTOMOBILE, elles ne tardent pas à devenir le point de mire pour bien des modèles. La voiture fait irruption dans la vie des femmes, qui sont de plus en plus nombreuses à travailler, font les courses, etc. Transmission automatique, nouveaux coloris, bien des innovations s'adressent à la clientèle féminine ; les constructeurs placent d'ailleurs des encarts dans *Vogue*, *Good Housekeeping*, *Ladies Home Journal* et d'autres magazines féminins.

Dès 1930, le design des voitures joue un rôle important dans la vente ; il faut donc adapter la publicité au look des nouveaux modèles. Les peintres contribuent à mettre en valeur les nouvelles carrosseries en acier inoxydable ; ils

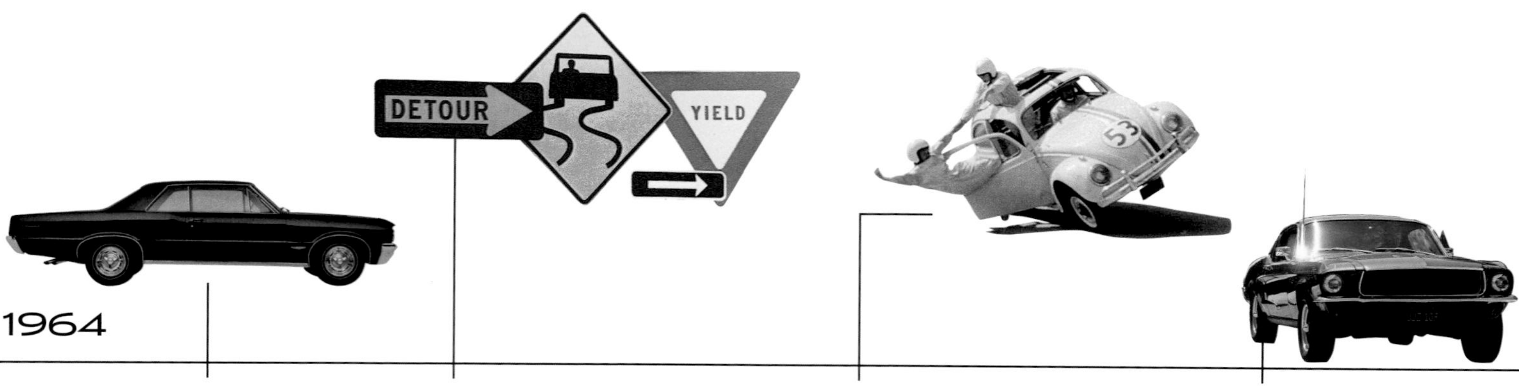

1964 Developed by John DeLorean, Pontiac GTO considered to be first muscle car

Der von John DeLorean entwickelte Pontiac GTO gilt als das erste Muscle-Car

La Pontiac GTO, mise au point par John DeLorean, est considérée comme la première grosse cylindrée

1965 Ralph Nader's book *Unsafe at Any Speed* inspires automobile-safety legislation

Ralph Naders Buch *Unsafe at Any Speed* führt zu strengeren Sicherheitsvorschriften

Ces voitures qui tuent, ouvrage écrit par Ralph Nader, inspire une législation pour la sécurité automobile

1968 *The Love Bug* stars VW Beetle named Herbie; "Beetlemania" ensues

Ein toller Käfer mit einem VW Käfer namens Herbie hat eine wahre Beetlemania zur Folge

Un Amour de coccinelle met en vedette une VW nommée Herbie ; la petite voiture suscite l'engouement

1969 Film's most memorable car chase to date in Steve McQueen's *Bullitt*

Steve McQueens *Bullitt* ist bis heute der Kinofilm mit der eindrucksvollsten Verfolgungsjagd

La plus mémorable poursuite en voiture du cinéma nous est offerte dans *Bullitt*, avec Steve McQueen

Volvo 164 E, 1974◄◄

Ford Bronco II, 1987

►► Volkswagen New Beetle, 1998

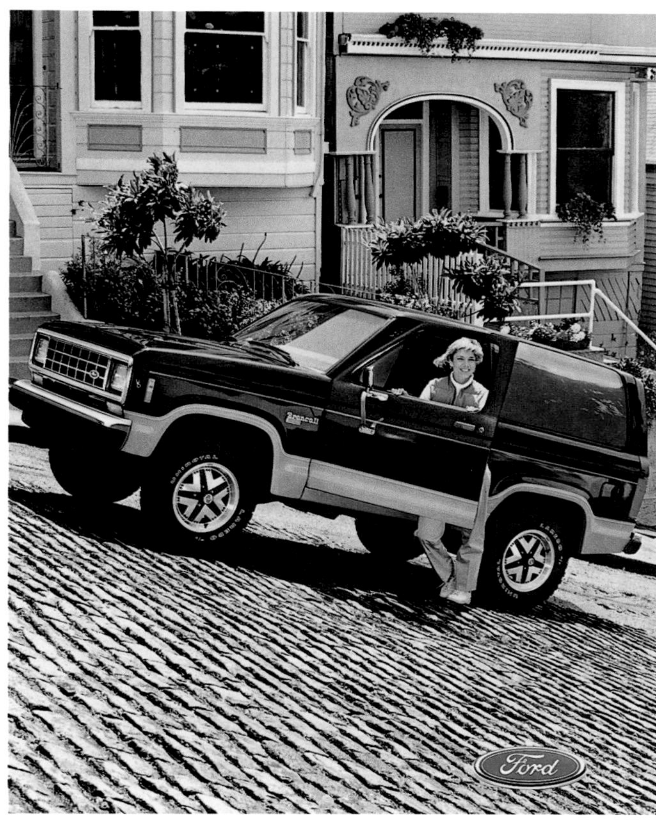

font paraître les toits plus hauts et veillent à ce que la lumière frappe au bon endroit, au niveau de la ceinture de caisse.

Grâce, en grande partie, à l'emprunt et au marché de l'occasion, les États-Unis prennent rapidement la place de leader mondial pour le nombre d'automobiles par habitant. Fin 1930, le pays affiche déjà un taux de 22,7 % de détenteurs de voitures, contre seulement 5,4 % au Royaume-Uni et moitié moins en Allemagne. En Italie, on compte seulement dix voitures pour mille habitants, chiffre qui tombe même à moins de cinq pour mille en Russie. La voiture est si répandue aux États-Unis, et comparativement si rare dans le reste du monde, que lors de sa sortie en Europe, le film de John Steinbeck *Les Raisins de la colère* déconcerte le public. En effet, on y voit la famille Joad se rendre en Californie dans une vieille guimbarde. Et on nous dit que cette famille est pauvre ? Les Européens restent incrédules. Elle a quand même les moyens d'avoir une voiture !

La Grande Dépression a anéanti, ou en tout cas gravement frappé, quantité de grandes marques de luxe, dont Pierce-Arrow et Duesenberg. La prestigieuse Packard se voit supplantée par la Cadillac, qui peut se reposer sur d'autres marques de sa maison-mère, General Motors. Packard se maintient tant bien que mal jusqu'aux environs de 1955, où elle propose des voitures démesurées qui ne sont plus que le pâle reflet de sa légendaire élégance.

Dans les années 1950, alors que la photographie couleur, commercialisée en 1938, a remplacé l'illustration dans la plupart des publicités imprimées, la peinture résiste dans la publicité automobile. Les peintres obtiennent des effets auxquels les photographes de cette ère prénumérique ne peuvent pas parvenir. Ils font paraître les voitures futuristes, ils en allongent et élargissent les lignes, en offrent une image romantique en jouant sur l'ombre et la lumière pour faire ressortir leurs qualités sculpturales. Pour leur faciliter la tâche, on fournit en secret aux illustrateurs des photos des nouveaux modèles de l'année suivante. Certains des grands peintres publicitaires travaillent en duo, comme Art Fitzgerald et Van Kaufman, qui insèrent souvent leurs initiales dans les plaques d'immatriculation des voitures qu'ils représentent. On leur doit notamment la promotion de l'image « plus large que nature » de Pontiac – la gamme est dotée d'un châssis à voie large très bas, soi-disant pour une plus grande stabilité de route. L'illustration permet en outre aux publicitaires de flatter les proportions des voitures en les faisant paraître plus longues ou plus

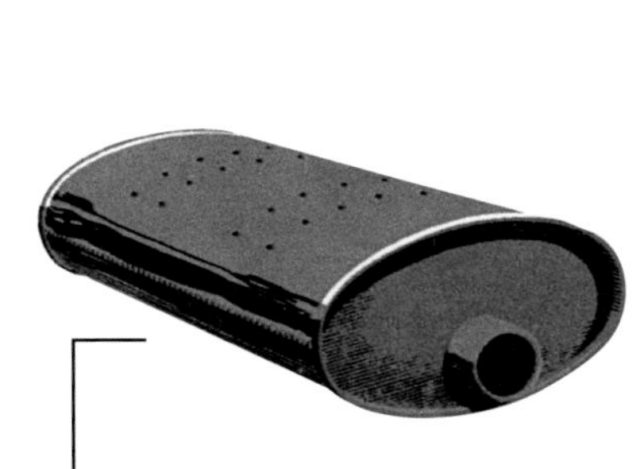

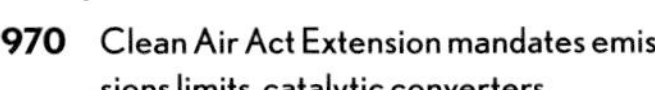

1970 Clean Air Act Extension mandates emissions limits, catalytic converters

Clean Air Act Extension schreibt Schadstofflimits und Katalysator vor

La législation limitant les émissions de gaz favorise les pots catalytiques

1971 Ford Pinto introduced

Präsentation des Ford Pinto

Lancement de la Ford Pinto

1971 Japanese car sales surpass European brands in U.S. market

In den USA erstmals mehr japanische Autos verkauft als europäische Modelle

Les ventes de Japonaises dépassent celles des marques européennes sur le marché américain

1973 Energy shortages lead to gasoline lines; will last for two years

Benzinrationierung führt zwei Jahre lang zu Schlangen an den Tankstellen

Pendant deux ans, la pénurie entraîne des files d'attente aux pompes à essence

0-60?

Yes.

©1998 Volkswagen. 1-800 DRIVE VW or WWW.VW.com

hautes. Parfois, on découpe des photos afin de s'en servir comme modèles pour réaliser des peintures « étirées » : les toits deviennent soudain assez hauts pour abriter un homme en chapeau.

Au milieu du siècle, la voiture fait partie intégrante de la culture américaine. C'est au volant d'une vieille Hudson que Jack Kerouac prend la route pour écrire son célèbre roman. Selon la légende, il tapera *Sur la route* sur ce qu'il

1975

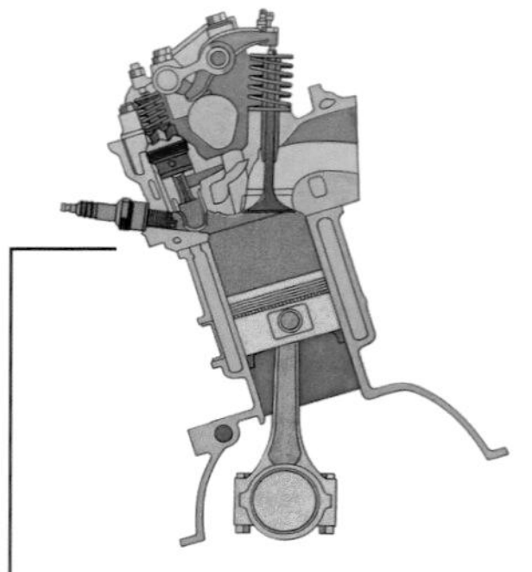

1975 BMW 3.0si billed as "Ultimate Driving Machine"; tagline will last for decades

BMW 3.0si als „ultimative Fahrmaschine" präsentiert – ein Prädikat, an dem man Jahrzehnte lang festhalten wird

La BMW 3.0si serait « l'ultime machine à conduire » ; le slogan perdurera plusieurs décennies

1975 Honda debuts CVCC engine; meets new U.S. emissions standards without catalytic converter

Hondas neuer CVCC-Motor erfüllt die neuen US-Emissionsnormen auch ohne Kat

Honda lance le moteur CVCC ; il répond aux nouveaux critères d'émissions américains sans recourir au pot catalytique

1977 Datsun's B-210 gets 50 miles per gallon on highway

Der Datsun B-210 erzielt auf dem Highway eine Reichweite von 21 Kilometer pro Liter

La Datsun B-210 permet d'effectuer 80 kilomètres sur autoroute avec 4 litres d'essence.

1977 Renaissance Center opens, Detroit, housing Ford (and, later, GM) headquarters

Einweihung des Renaissance Center in Detroit mit der Zentrale von Ford (und später GM)

Ouverture, à Detroit, du Renaissance Center, qui accueille le siège de Ford (et plus tard de GM)

« JE CONSTRUIRAI UNE VOITURE POUR LE GRAND PUBLIC … AVEC LES MEILLEURS MATÉRIAUX, LES MEILLEURS OUVRIERS … À UN PRIX SI PEU ÉLEVÉ QUE TOUT HOMME GAGNANT UN BON SALAIRE POURRA S'EN OFFRIR UNE … »

—HENRY FORD, FORD MOTOR COMPANY, 1908

nommera « le rouleau » – 38 m de feuilles de papier-calque scotchées bout à bout qu'il déroulera, comme la route elle-même, sur le bureau de son premier éditeur. La première chanson rock'n'roll, composée par Ike Turner, sort en 1951 sous un titre inspiré d'une voiture – *Rocket 88* se réfère en effet au nouveau moteur V8 à haute compression de chez Oldsmobile. C'est la naissance d'un lien devenu traditionnel entre voitures et musique pop, qui se perpétuera des Beach Boys à Snoop Dogg. Quel mal y a-t-il à ce que les voitures américaines ressemblent à des « juke-boxes ambulants », comme le regrette le concepteur de produits Raymond Loewy, alors qu'Elvis, Chubby Checker et Buddy Holly envahissent justement les juke-boxes ?

Sous Eisenhower, les autoroutes et la télévision modifient la vie et les voitures des Américains. Les modèles à ailettes arrière évoquent des requins au poète Robert Lowell, et traversent l'univers de *L'Homme au complet gris* de Sloan Wilson. Le magazine *Time* surnomme George Walker, designer en chef de Ford, le « Cellini du chrome », tandis que Virgil Exner crée le look extrême, « tourné vers l'avenir », de Chrysler, qu'accompagne le slogan : « Soudainement, nous voilà en 1960 ! » Le lancement de la marque Edsel par Ford en 1957, en pleine récession économique, marque cependant le sommet de la vague.

EN 1959, L'AGENCE DE PUBLICITÉ NEW-YORKAISE DOYLE, DANE & BERNBACH récupère le compte Volkswagen pour les États-Unis et lance la campagne « Penser petit », considérée par l'ensemble des professionnels et des historiens de la publicité comme une des meilleures de tous les temps. À l'aide de simples photos en noir et blanc représentant la Coccinelle et un bus, les publicités jouent l'euphémisme et la modestie avec beaucoup d'ironie. Conçues par le rédacteur Julian Koenig et le directeur artistique Helmut Krone, elles se moquent gentiment de la valse obligatoire des nouveautés annuelles, du chrome et du clinquant des modèles américains. « Penser petit, c'était en réalité penser en grand, explique l'historien Bob Garfield. Posséder une Coccinelle permettait de frimer en montrant qu'on n'avait pas besoin de frimer ».

La frime, c'est bien ce qui caractérise la plupart des Américaines. En 1960, l'Amérique est à l'apogée de son pouvoir, alors l'automobile et la publicité se doivent de refléter cette puissance. Pourtant, des questions commencent à se poser. Brusquement, les Américains réfléchissent à la sécurité des énormes et puissantes voitures qu'ils conduisent. L'ouvrage de Ralph Nader intitulé *Unsafe at Any Speed* (« Dangereuse à n'importe quelle vitesse »), très critique à l'égard de l'industrie, connaît un succès retentissant et le témoignage de l'auteur devant les commissions du Congrès conduisent à la mise en place d'une législation imposant, entre autres, la ceinture de sécurité.

Les Américains veulent aussi des voitures personnalisées. Lancée à la Foire internationale de New York en 1964, la Ford Mustang se présente comme le premier modèle « personnalisable ». Son arrière très court et son capot tout en longueur correspondent à la silhouette caractéristique de l'époque de la minijupe. Pour Lee Iacocca, responsable chez Ford, c'est « la voiture à concevoir soi-même », grâce à une longue liste d'équipements en option. Très vite, elle devient le symbole de la jeune célibataire libérée, incarnée par le tube *Mustang Sally* de Mack Rice, dont l'interprétation par Wilson Pickett dépassera les 400 000 exemplaires vendus dès la première année.

Pendant que Detroit déploie des slogans comme « La fureur Dodge » pour faire face à la « défection en masse des jeunes » et à la déferlante de la contre-culture des années 1960, American Motors propose des éditions bleu jean pour séduire les conducteurs débutants. Pour les femmes, on construit des modèles personnalisables comme la Mustang, à l'image de la Chevy Camaro, et pour les hommes des grosses cylindrées offrant moult options, comme la Pontiac GTO.

Avec les années 1970 et les crises pétrolières, les États-Unis connaissent une arrivée en force des importations

1980 Chrysler receives $1.2 billion bailout from U.S. government; releases K-cars

Chrysler erhält eine Staatsbürgschaft in Höhe von 1,2 Mrd. US-Dollar; Einführung der K-Cars

Chrysler perçoit 1,2 milliard de dollars du gouvernement américain et lance les modèles K

1983 Pop superstar Prince records "Little Red Corvette"

Pop-Ikone Prince nimmt den Song „Little Red Corvette"

Prince, la star de la pop, enregistre « Little Red Corvette »

1985 Toyota's popular Corolla first produced in U.S.

Toyotas populärer Corolla erstmals in den USA gefertigt

Première Toyota Corolla produite aux États-Unis

1989 Driver-side air bags become equipment in U.S.

Fahrer-Airbags werden in den USA zum Standard

L'airbag se répand côté conducteur aux États-Unis

japonaises. En octobre 1973, une alliance des pays pétroliers du Moyen-Orient déclare l'embargo sur les pays qui ont soutenu Israël pendant la guerre du Kippour et les prix du pétrole s'envolent. En quelques semaines, le prix de l'essence quadruple aux États-Unis ; on instaure le rationnement. Par ailleurs, le Congrès adopte la limitation de vitesse à 90 km/h sur tout le territoire. Les ventes de petites voitures montent en flèche, mais Detroit construit peu de petits modèles. Ford, General Motors et Chrysler importent en toute hâte de leurs branches européennes ou de leurs consœurs asiatiques des modèles qu'ils revendent sous un autre nom. Ce sont les constructeurs japonais qui en profitent. Alors qu'en 1958 ils vendaient moins de 1500 exemplaires à eux tous, dix ans plus tard, ce chiffre atteint 150 000 et en 1975, leurs ventes représentent 10 % du marché américain.

La Corona de Toyota et la Civic de Honda bénéficient rapidement du bouche à oreille, une publicité qu'aucune campagne organisée ne pouvait égaler. Les Datsun Z – à commencer par la 240 Z, en 1969 – plaît aux jeunes qui rêvent d'une voiture de sport économique. Les modèles Z remportent aussi les suffrages des revues spécialisées, qui plébiscitent les Japonaises. Vers 1975, les importations japonaises font déjà de l'ombre à leurs rivales européennes et, malgré d'habiles publicités comme la campagne de Renault pour « Le Car », les importations françaises et italiennes déclinent. Après avoir remplacé la Coccinelle, en 1974, Volkswagen dépérit à son tour.

Il faudra une bonne décennie pour que les trois géants de Detroit se décident à adopter les méthodes de leurs concurrents. En 1989, General Motors dévoile la marque Saturn, dont le slogan annonce : « Une firme différente, une voiture différente ».

De nouveaux types de véhicules font leur apparition dans des publicités d'un nouveau genre. Le monospace, conçu par Chrysler en 1983 pour succéder au traditionnel break bois, quintessence de la voiture familiale américaine, est présenté le plus souvent par des vues intérieures. C'est alors que survient le 4x4, descendant de la jeep militaire et du pick-up, qui perpétue le mythe de l'aventure hors des sentiers battus.

Si les solides Toyota Corolla et Honda Civic garées devant des millions de pavillons américains offrent une version actualisée de l'automobile bon marché, fiable et pratique promise par Henry Ford, le SUV des années 1990 représente un retour aux débuts de l'automobile. Il promet de pouvoir se rendre partout, qu'il y ait une route ou non ; il offre une sécurité symbolique dans un monde dangereux.

L'histoire de l'automobile est aussi l'histoire de l'économie industrielle. Aussi liée soit-elle à la mode, au monde de l'art, du cinéma et de la musique, l'automobile est une force à la fois culturelle et économique. La voiture joue un rôle tellement important dans notre vie que notre époque pourrait être qualifiée, comme il y eut l'âge de pierre ou l'âge de bronze, d'âge de l'automobile.

1994 NBC interrupts NBA finals to air O. J. Simpson's pursuit in white Ford Bronco

NBC unterbricht die NBA-Finals für die Live-Übertragung von O.J. Simpsons Flucht in einem weißen Ford Bronco

NBC interrompt la finale de la NBA pour retransmettre la poursuite d'O. J. Simpson au volant d'une Ford Bronco blanche

1995 Minivans account for 8.5% of overall vehicle sales in U.S.

Minivans erreichen in den USA einen Marktanteil von 8,5 Prozent

Les monospaces représentent 8,5 % de l'ensemble des ventes automobiles aux États-Unis

1998 Inspired by original Beetle, Volkswagen releases New Beetle

Volkswagen präsentiert den vom Käfer inspirierten New Beetle

Inspiré par la Coccinelle d'origine, Volkswagen lance la New Beetle

1999 MoMA, New York, previews Mini Cooper, Honda Insight, Toyota Prius

Das New Yorker Museum of Modern Art bietet eine Vorschau auf den neuen Mini, Honda Insight und Toyota Prius.

Le MoMA de New York expose en avant-première la Mini Cooper, la Honda Insight et la Toyota Prius

1935 500 K
1954 300 S
1955 300 SL
1971 280 SE
1981 380 SLC

THE FIRST CARS COULD INDEED HAVE BEEN CALLED "SPORT UTILITY VEHICLES," BECAUSE THEY WERE ESSENTIALLY DEVICES FOR OUT-DOOR ADVENTURE, NOT YET DEPENDABLE ENOUGH FOR REGULAR LIFE.

DIE ERSTEN AUTOS HÄTTE MAN IN DER TAT ALS „SPORT UTILITY VEHICLES" ODER SUVs BEZEICHNEN KÖNNEN, DENN SIE DIENTEN IN ERSTER LINIE DEM FREILUFTABEN-TEUER UND WAREN FÜR DEN ALLTAG EINFACH NOCH NICHT ZUVERLÄSSIG GENUG.

LES PREMIÈRES VOITURES PEUVENT ÊTRE QUALIFIÉES DE '4X4' CAR ELLES SONT AU FOND DESTINÉES À L'AVENTURE AU GRAND AIR ET MANQUENT ENCORE DE FIABILITÉ POUR LA VIE ORDINAIRE.

1900-

THE ORIGINAL SUVs
DIE ERSTEN SUVs
LES PREMIERS 4X4

-1909

THE LIBRARY OF COLUMBIA UNIVERSITY

Pierce Great Arrow, 1907 ◂◂

Pierce-Arrow, 1910 ◂

Ford Model A, 1902

FOR THE FIRST DECADES OF ITS LIFE, THE AUTOMOBILE WAS AN EXOTIC TECHNOLOGY, requiring technical knowledge and a willingness on the part of driver and passenger to endure the elements and frequent breakdowns. The automobile arrived with other modern wonders—the airplane, the wireless or radio, and household electrical appliances—but it remained a hobbyist's toy. The first cars could indeed have been called "sport-utility vehicles," because they were essentially devices for outdoor adventure, not yet dependable enough for regular life.

They required lots of attention and care, and early automobile advertising was often aimed more at people who took care of cars than at their owners. In those days, oil and water had to be changed every few miles. Flat tires were frequent; pumps and patches were important. So the tire industry brought us Bibendum, aka the Michelin Man, and the Fisk Tire Company offered up its sleepy boy and the slogan, "Time to Re-tire." The cars' bodies were not enclosed, requiring accessories and a special wardrobe—duster and goggles, bonnets, hats, gloves, and blankets.

The nascent auto-ad business hired such respected illustrators and painters as Thomas Cleland, who created elaborate architectural backgrounds behind Cadillacs, and James Montgomery Flagg, best known for his World War I Army-recruitment poster featuring Uncle Sam ("I want YOU for U.S. Army").

Standards were slow to develop. Electric, gasoline, or steam? (20 companies built and successfully marketed electric cars before World War I.) Right-hand, left-hand, or middle drive? Tiller or steering wheel? The first widely popular car had a tiller, not a wheel, but offered the luxury feature of a speedometer. Many of the major auto brands from those years, like Winton and Overland, are now forgotten.

Early manufacturers boasted of their cars' performance capabilities on long rallies and in races or climbing hills, and their exploits were shown in advertisements. Newspaper ads for Buick and Cadillac showed the cars climbing steps of public buildings to prove their toughness.

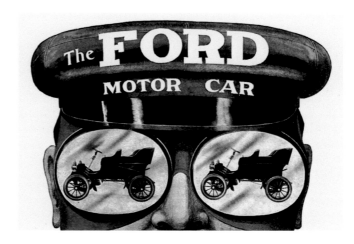

As cars became more dependable, thanks to better tires, batteries, and other equipment, trips could become longer. In 1903, auto enthusiast Dr. Horatio Nelson Jackson, his mechanic, Sewall Crocker, and a bulldog named Bud made the first road crossing of America, in a Winton touring car. Henry Joy, head of the Packard Motor Car Company, made a similar trip to promote his products. Henry Ford himself became a race driver to publicize his young company. In 1900, former bicycle builder Alexander Winton was known as a top builder of cars, especially racing cars. In 1901, Ford took him on and beat him in a famous 10-mile race that established Ford's reputation.

The Ford Model T began the true American automotive revolution and tied cars to every aspect of life. Henry Ford offered the simple, rugged T in 1908 as the "car for the great multitude." It established the idea and reality of universal automobility: Everyone should own a car.

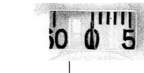

1900

1900 Open cars popularize elaborate garments to keep passengers warm and clean

Wer im Freien sitzt, greift gern zu einer speziellen Montur, die Wärme spendet und Schmutz abhält

Les voitures ouvertes popularisent une gamme de vêtements conçus pour maintenir les passagers au chaud et au propre

1901 First vehicle with original equipment speedometer offered in U.S.

Erstes US-Auto serienmäßig mit Tachometer ausgestattet

Apparition aux États-Unis du premier véhicule équipé d'un compteur

1901 Curved Dash Oldsmobile introduced

Curved Dash Oldsmobile vorgestellt

Lancement de l'Oldsmobile Curved Dash

1903 Horatio Nelson Jackson and dog Bud make first transcontinental car journey

Horatio Nelson Jackson und sein Hund Bud unternehmen die erste Autoreise quer durch die USA

Horatio Nelson Jackson effectue la première traversée des États-Unis en voiture, avec le chien Bud

IN SEINEN ERSTEN LEBENSJAHRZEHNTEN VERKÖRPERTE DAS AUTO EINE EXOTISCHE TECHNOLOGIE. Gefragt waren praktisches Wissen und die Bereitschaft von Chauffeur und Fahrgast, Wind und Wetter zu erdulden – und häufige Pannen. Das Auto betrat gemeinsam mit anderen technischen Wundern die Bühne, seien es Flugzeuge, Rundfunkempfänger oder elektrische Haushaltsgeräte. Doch Autos blieben zunächst ein Spielzeug des Hobbyisten. Die ersten Autos hätte man in der Tat als „Sport Utility Vehicles" (Sportnutzfahrzeuge) oder SUVs bezeichnen können, denn sie dienten in erster Linie dem Freiluftabenteuer und waren für den Alltag einfach noch nicht zuverlässig genug.

Da diese Wagen reichlich Zuwendung und Pflege erforderten, zielte die frühe Autowerbung eher auf das Wartungspersonal ab als auf die eigentlichen Besitzer. Damals musste noch alle paar Kilometer Öl und Wasser nachgefüllt werden. Luftpumpe und Flickzeug waren unentbehrlich, um die häufigen Reifenpannen zu beheben. Die Reifenindustrie bescherte uns das Michelin-Männchen namens Bibendum (oder kurz Bib). Fisk-Reifen brachte einen schläfrigen Knaben und dem doppeldeutigen Slogan „Time to Re-tire". Mehr oder weniger im Freien sitzend, benötigte man eine spezielle Kluft aus Staubmantel, Brille, Hut oder Haube, Handschuhen und Wolldecke.

Die noch in den Kinderschuhen steckende Branche der Autowerbung heuerte renommierte Illustratoren und Maler wie Thomas Cleland an, der den Cadillac vor kunstvollen architektonischen Hintergründen platzierte, oder James Montgomery Flagg, am besten bekannt für sein Poster mit Uncle Sam zur Anwerbung von Rekruten für den Ersten Weltkrieg („I want YOU for U.S. Army").

Verbindliche Standards setzten sich nur allmählich durch. So fragte man sich lange: Elektro, Benzin oder Dampf? (Vor dem Ersten Weltkrieg gab es zwanzig erfolgreiche Hersteller von Elektroautos). Lenkrad links, rechts oder in der Mitte? Lenkhebel oder Lenkrad? Das erste weitverbreitete Auto besaß in der Tat noch einen Lenkhebel, doch es bot den Luxus eines Tachometers. Zahlreiche bekannte Automarken jener Jahre wie Winton und Overland sind inzwischen vergessen.

Die frühen Konstrukteure rühmten in Werbeanzeigen die Leistungsfähigkeit ihrer Gefährte bei Ausdauer-Wettbewerben, Rennen oder Bergtouren. In den Zeitungen erschienen Anzeigen von Buick und Cadillac, in denen die Robustheit der Autos bewiesen werden sollte, indem sie die Stufen vor öffentlichen Gebäuden erklommen.

Als die Autos dank besserer Reifen und Batterien immer zuverlässiger wurden, konnte man schon längere Touren unternehmen. Dem Autoliebhaber Dr. Horatio Nelson Jackson gelang 1903 gemeinsam mit seinem Mechaniker Sewall Crocker und einer Bulldogge namens Bud in einem Winton Tourenwagen die erste Straßendurchquerung der USA. Henry Joy, Chef der Packard Motor Company, unternahm eine ähnliche Reise, um für seine Produkte zu werben. Und Henry Ford selbst wurde zum Rennfahrer, um die Werbetrommel für seine noch junge Firma zu rühren: Im Jahr 1900 galt der ehemalige Fahrradhersteller Alexander Winton als einer der besten Konstrukteure vor allem von Rennwagen. Ford nahm die Herausforderung an und besiegte ihn 1901 in einem berühmten Zehn-Meilen-Rennen.

Die wahre, sämtliche Lebensbereiche erfassende Autorevolution begann in den USA mit Fords Model T. Henry Ford offerierte den schlichten, unverwüstlichen T im Jahr 1908 als „Auto für die breite Masse". Damit war die Idee der universalen Automobilität zum Greifen nah, oder anders formuliert: Jeder sollte ein Auto besitzen.

1904

1904 First school for automobile mechanics opens in Detroit

Erste Schule für Automechaniker in Detroit eröffnet

Ouverture de la première école de mécanique automobile à Detroit

1905 Popular song "In My Merry Oldsmobile" celebrates Curved Dash Olds

Der Schlager „In My Merry Oldsmobile" zelebriert den Curved Dash Olds

La chanson populaire « In My Merry Oldsmobile » rend hommage à la Curved Dash

1906 Brush Runabout introduces new suspension system with shock absorbers

Brush Runabout präsentiert eine neue Federung mit Stoßdämpfern

Apparition d'un nouveau système de suspension doté d'absorbeurs de chocs

1907 Ford offers first mass-produced car with left-hand steering

Ford bietet das erste Großserienauto mit Linkslenkung an

Ford propose la première voiture de série à conduite à gauche

COPYRIGHTED
'04

Queen, 1905 ◄◄

Pierce-Arrow, 1910 ◄

►► Thomas-Flyer, 1907

PENDANT SES PREMIÈRES DÉCENNIES D'EXISTENCE, L'AUTOMOBILE RESTE UN OBJET TECHNOLOGIQUE EXOTIQUE, qui exige des connaissances techniques et suppose que le conducteur accepte de subir les éléments et des pannes fréquentes. L'automobile arrive au même moment que d'autres merveilles modernes : l'avion, la radio, les appareils ménagers électriques ... Elle demeure néanmoins un jouet pour amateurs éclairés – les premières voitures peuvent être qualifiées de « 4x4 », car elles sont au fond destinées à l'aventure au grand air, elles manquent encore de fiabilité pour la vie ordinaire.

Comme ces engins requièrent une grande attention et beaucoup de soins, les premières publicités s'adressent souvent davantage aux gens qui s'occupent des voitures qu'à leurs propriétaires. À cette époque, il faut changer l'huile et l'eau tous les quelques kilomètres. Les crevaisons sont fréquentes, il faut souvent pomper et poser des rustines. C'est pourquoi l'industrie du pneu nous présente un petit garçon ensommeillé pour Fiske, tandis que la naissance du Bibendum Michelin est saluée par le slogan: « Nunc est Bibendum – Le pneumatique boit l'obstacle ». Ouvertes à tous les vents, les voitures nécessitent des accessoires et une garde-robe adaptée : cache-poussière et lunettes de protection, serre-tête en cuir, foulards, gants et couvertures.

Aux États-Unis, la publicité automobile a recours à de grands illustrateurs comme Thomas Cleland, qui peint des Cadillac sur fond d'architectures complexes, et James Montgomery Flagg, auteur de la célèbre affiche pour la campagne de recrutement de l'armée américaine, pendant la Première Guerre mondiale, qui représente l'Oncle Sam le doigt tendu, clamant : « I want you ».

La standardisation progresse lentement. Électricité, essence ou vapeur? (Avant la Première Guerre mondiale, vingt constructeurs élaborent et écoulent avec succès des voitures électriques.) Conduite à droite, conduite à gauche ou au milieu? Poignée ou volant? La première voiture la plus répandue est équipée d'une poignée, et non d'un volant, mais elle offre le luxe d'un compteur. Quantité de grandes marques de cette époque, comme Winton et Overland, sont tombées dans l'oubli.

Les premiers constructeurs démontrent les performances de leurs voitures à l'occasion de longs rallyes, de courses de vitesse ou en côte, et leurs exploits sont vantés dans les publicités. Dans les journaux, on peut voir ainsi des Buick et des Cadillac prouver leur robustesse en gravissant les escaliers d'édifices publics.

Plus les voitures gagnent en fiabilité, grâce à l'amélioration des pneus, des batteries et d'autres équipements, plus les trajets rallongent. En 1903, le Dr Horatio Nelson Jackson, un passionné d'automobile, son mécanicien Sewall Crocker et un bulldog nommé Bud effectuent la première traversée des États-Unis par la route à bord d'un modèle de tourisme Winton. Henry Joy, directeur de la maison Packard, entreprend un voyage similaire pour promouvoir ses produits. Même Henry Ford se fait pilote de course pour assurer la publicité de la compagnie qu'il vient de créer. En 1900, Alexander Winton, l'ancien constructeur de bicyclettes, devient le plus célèbre constructeur automobile, spécialisé dans les voitures de course. En 1901, Ford le défie et le bat sur le circuit de Grosse Pointe, une victoire mémorable qui assiéra sa renommée.

Avec le modèle T de Ford, l'industrie automobile connaît une véritable révolution qui impose la voiture dans tous les aspects de la vie. En 1908, Henry Ford propose une « voiture pour les masses », simple et solide. La Ford T concrétise l'idée de l'automobile universelle : tout le monde doit pouvoir en posséder une.

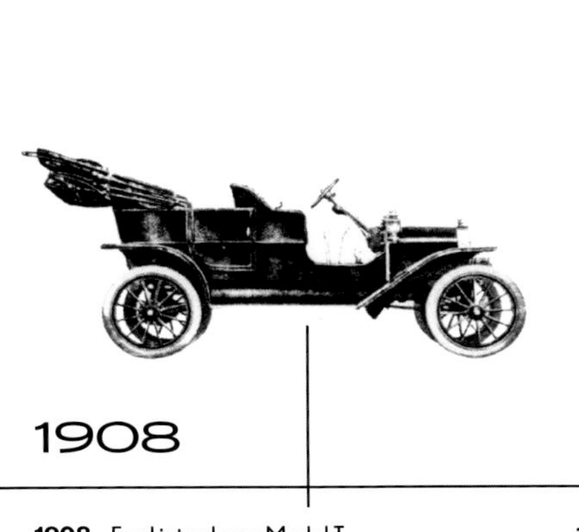

1908

1908 Ford introduces Model T

Ford lanciert das Model T

Ford lance le modèle T

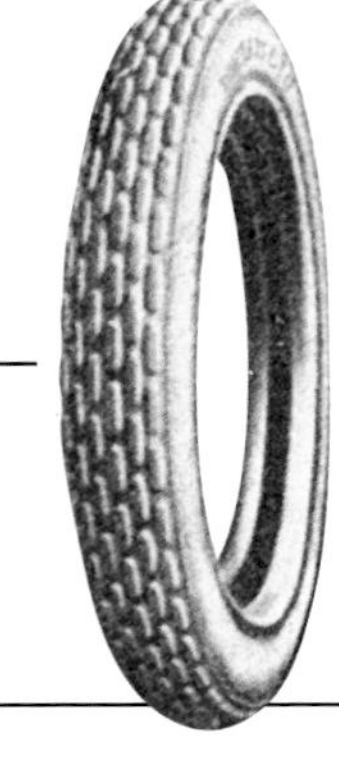

1908 Grooved tires improve road traction

Profilreifen verbessern die Traktion

Les pneus rainurés améliorent l'adhérence sur route

1908 Klaxon electric horn released

Elektrische Hupe von Klaxon

Apparition du klaxon électrique

1909 U.S. president Taft orders two Pierce-Arrows; first official White House car

US-Präsident Taft bestellt zwei Pierce-Arrows (erster Dienstwagen eines US-Präsidenten)

Le président américain Taft commande deux modèles Pierce-Arrow, qui devient la première voiture officielle de la Maison-Blanche

MORE THAN
LEVEL HEADED AM

THOMAS

A THOUSAND
RICAN BUSINESS MEN

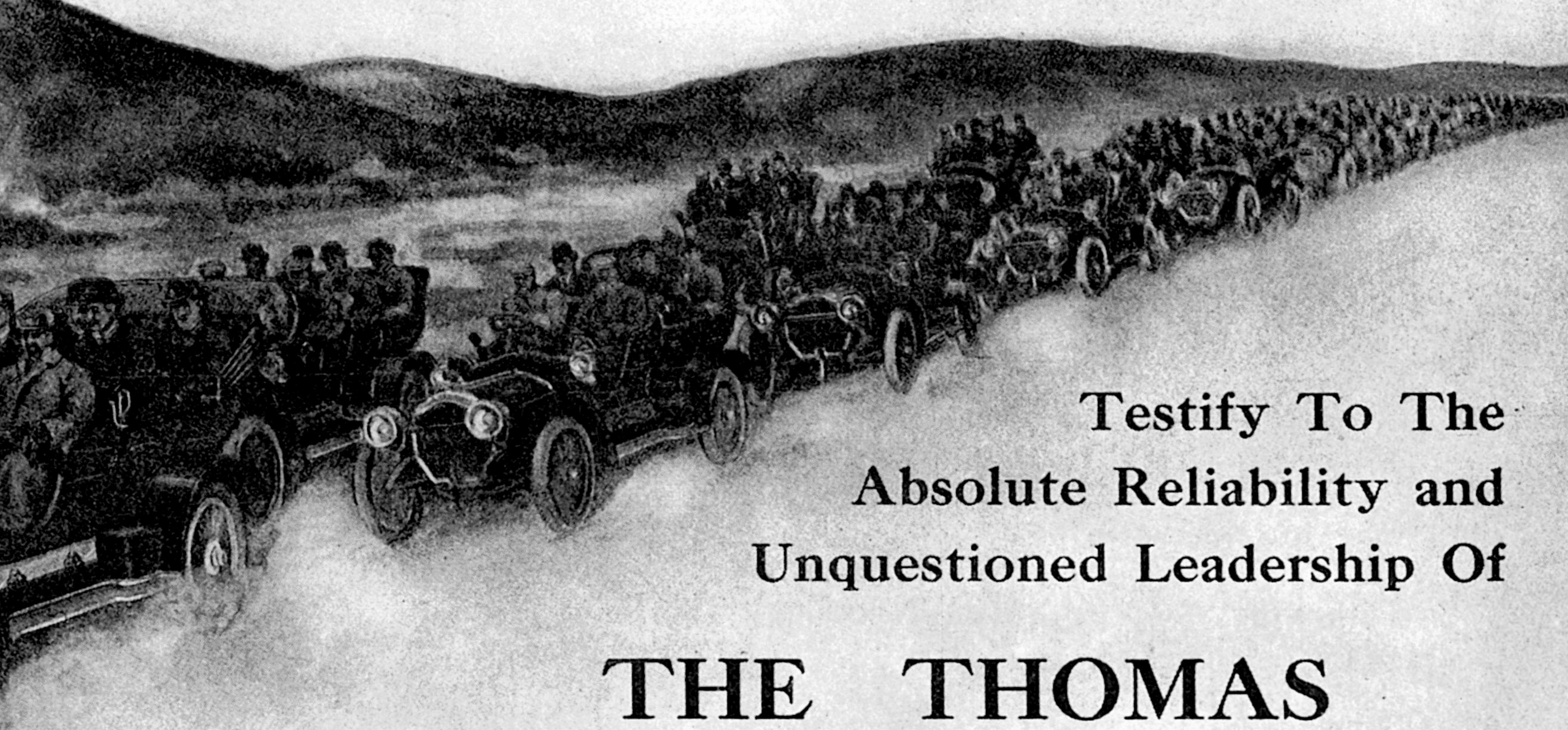

Testify To The Absolute Reliability and Unquestioned Leadership Of

THE THOMAS

Under Any And All Conditions. We Have Their Names. You May Have Them Too Upon Request. Meanwhile Send for the 1907 Catalogue. 60 H. P. Thomas Flyer $4,000. Factory. Thomas (40 H. P.) $2,750. F. O. B. Factory

THOMAS MOTOR CO. BUFFALO, N. Y.

Members Association Licensed Automobile Mfrs.

-FLYER

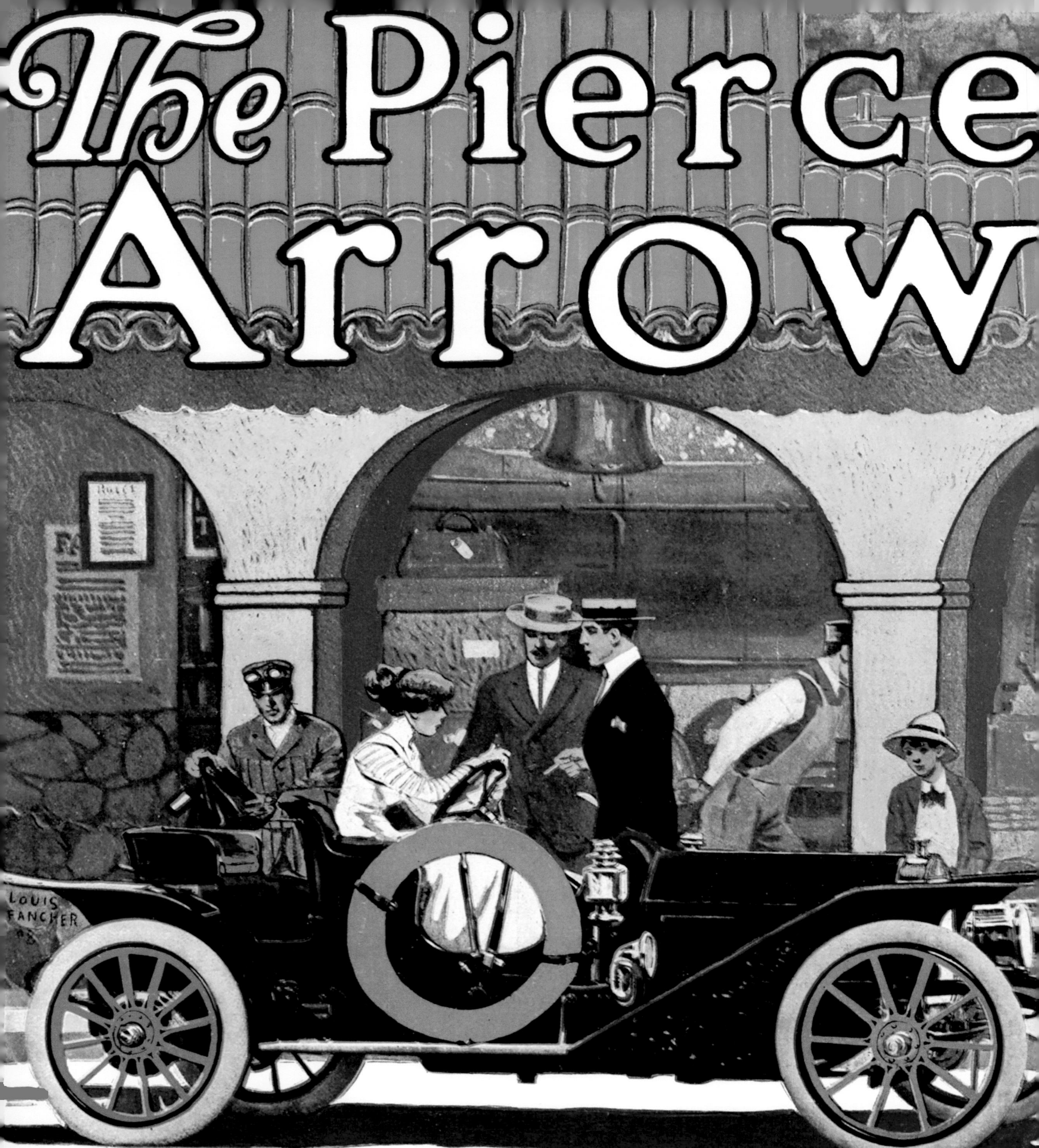

WITHOUT forgetting that, after all, a motor car is a piece of machinery, the Pierce Arrow ha never failed to offer its owner the highest luxury also. Here is the Pierce Runabout, the sam effective Pierce chassis, fitted with a smaller body, combining all of the efficiency of the Pierce engin with the convenience of a runabout.

Two Passenger Runabout, 24 H. P. $3,050 36 H. P. $3,700 Three Passenger Runabout, 24 H. P. $3,100 36 H. P. $3,750

Pierce Arrow Cars will be exhibited in New York only at the Madison Square Garden Show, January 16 to 23, 1909, and at the salesroom of our New York representatives, The Harrolds Motor Car Co., 233 W. 54th S

THE GEORGE N. PIERCE COMPANY (Members Association Licensed Automobile Manufacturers) **BUFFALO, N. Y.**

OLDSMOBILE

The Flowing Road

The joys of the flowing road are not confined to athletes and owners who employ chauffeurs. The simplicity and **roadability** of the Oldsmobile put the real pleasure of motoring within the reach of everyone. More money buys nothing better than the Oldsmobile, since your car has all the luxury and style of the most expensive car, plus the roadability, which is lacking in some of the complicated products manufactured for the reckless rich. That is what makes the Oldsmobile appeal to all ages and all classes who want ease of riding, substantial construction, stylish appearance and the one and only roadability that everybody concedes to the Oldsmobile. If you enjoy the pleasures of the open road you should examine the simple Oldsmobile. Duplicates of its most famous cars on sale at all agencies. There is but one quality and one performance in the Oldsmobile.

Member Association Licensed Automobile Manufacturers

OLDS MOTOR WORKS
Lansing, Mich., U. S. A.

Canadian Trade Supplied from Canadian Factory. Address Frederick Sager, St. Catherines, Ont.

Pierce-Arrow, 1909 ◂ Oldsmobile, 1907

SILENCE
COMFORT
Peerless
P
P

The Autocar
The Autocar 1907 Touring Type $3000
Five passengers — large, roomy tonneau 111-inch wheel base
Four-cylinder vertical motor. 30 horse-power. Direct shaft drive. Sliding-gear, roller-bearing transmission. Three speeds and reverse. Three-point suspension of motor, fly wheel, clutch and transmission as a unit. Extra long springs. The well-known Autocar clutch. Pressed steel frame. I-beam front axle. Autocar Control.
Reliability in every detail of construction and in every phase of performance assured by the most comprehensive system of factory tests employed anywhere in the world.
The Autocar will be exhibited in New York at the Madison Square Garden Show—Space 24, January 12 to 19, 1907. In Chicago at the Coliseum and First Regiment Armory Show, Space B 2, February 2 to 9, 1907.
The Autocar Company 17th Street Ardmore, Pa.
[Established 1897]
Member: Association Licensed Automobile Manufacturers
Write for The Autocar Book, illustrating and describing the 1907 models,—and explaining the system of factory tests assuring Autocar Reliability.
Reliability

Peerless, 1910 ◂

Many cars were luxury models and required employees. Frequently, the chauffeur (French words like *garage* and *chassis* were in favor among early motorists) sat in the open, while coachwork sheltered master and mistress.

Die zahlreichen Luxusmodelle erforderten Personal. Meist saß der Chauffeur im Freien, während die schützende Karosserie dem Herrn und seiner Dame vorbehalten blieb. (Die frühen Automobilisten hatten eine Vorliebe für französische Begriffe wie Garage und Chassis)

Bien des voitures sont des modèles de luxe qui requièrent du personnel. Souvent, le chauffeur est assis à l'extérieur tandis que ses maîtres sont abrités par la carrosserie.

Autocar, 1907

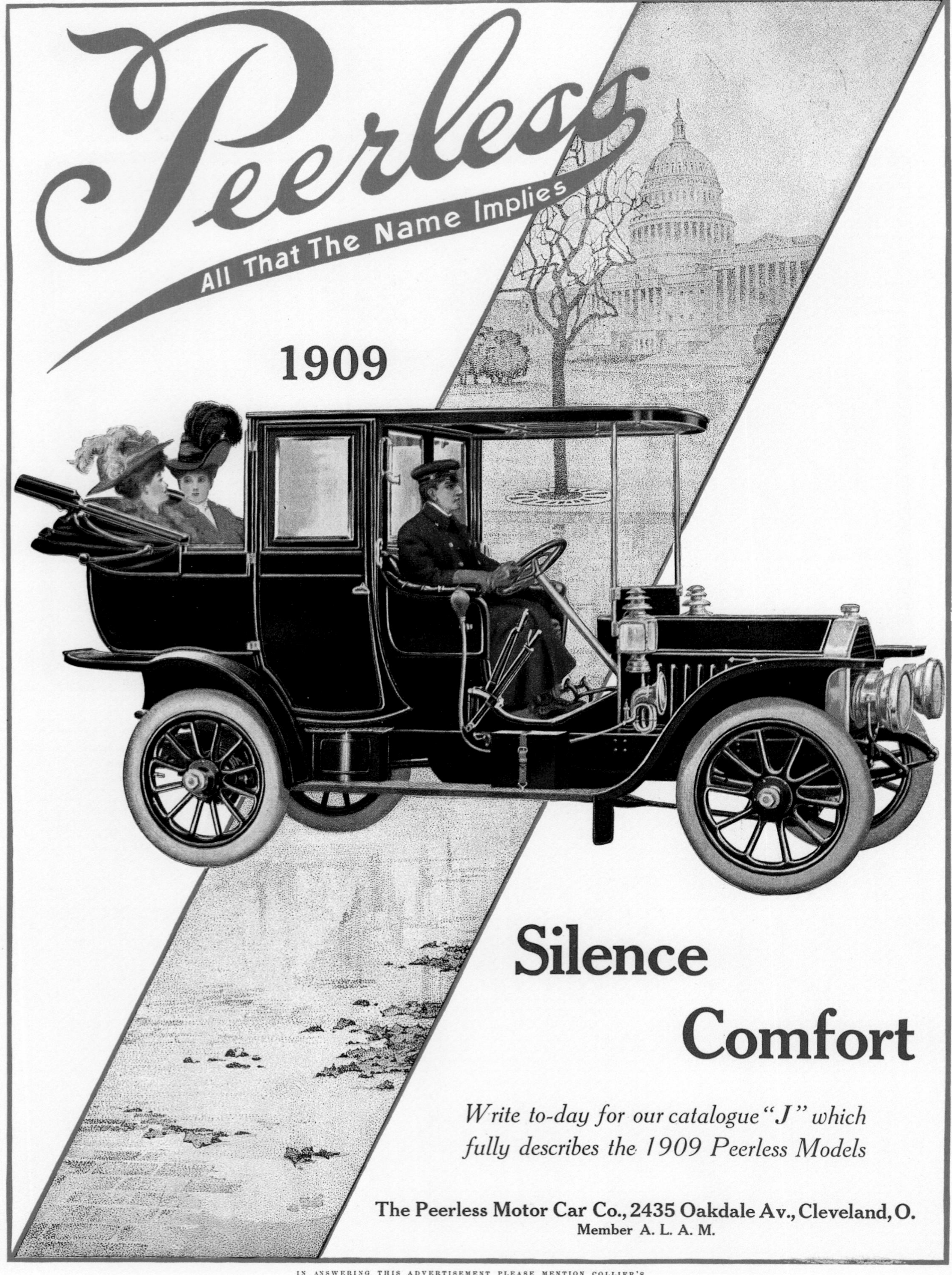
Peerless
All That The Name Implies
1909
Silence
Comfort
Write to-day for our catalogue "J" which
fully describes the 1909 Peerless Models
The Peerless Motor Car Co., 2435 Oakdale Av., Cleveland, O.
Member A. L. A. M.
IN ANSWERING THIS ADVERTISEMENT PLEASE MENTION COLLIER'S

Daimler, 1907

European models, like the English Daimler, the French Renault, and German Mercedes, were considered superior to most American brands in the early days of motoring.

In der Frühzeit des Automobils galten europäische Modelle wie der britische Daimler, der französische Renault und der deutsche Mercedes als den meisten amerikanischen Marken überlegen.

Dans les débuts de l'automobile, les modèles européens comme ceux du britannique Daimler, du français Renault et de l'allemand Mercedes sont considérés comme supérieurs à la plupart de ceux proposés par les marques américaines.

Peerless, 1909 ◂

MICHELIN

FRANCE, ENGLAND, ITALY, AMERICA

The high import duty and heavy trans-Atlantic transportation charges on Michelin tires have been removed by the establishment of our great American Michelin Factory.

YOU can now afford to equip your car with the tire which is universally recognized as the best in the world. Michelin durability is so universally appreciated that for years Americans have been heavy purchasers of the imported Michelins in spite of their high cost, because their unequalled wearing qualities resulted in a marked economy in the course of a year. This economy is now within your reach. The name Michelin has always stood for the greatest tire value that money could buy and now that it stands for reasonable cost also, the tire problem is solved.

THE tires made in our American factory are identical in the most minute particular with the outputs of our factories in France, England and Italy. They are the same famous Michelins which have been used on the winning cars in all the world's greatest races for the last six years and which made these victories possible.

Manufacturers of all classes of cars can now afford to equip with Michelins at no extra cost to you. The leading cars are making Michelins their standard catalogued equipment. Specify Michelin tires when purchasing your new car.

Exhibiting at Grand Central Palace, Gallery Space 129
Exhibiting at Madison Square Garden, Basement Space 209
Exhibiting at Chicago Coliseum, Annex Spaces 102 and 103

CLINCHER TYPE
Round, Flat and Anti-skid
American and Millimeter Sizes

QUICK DETACHABLE TYPE
Round and Anti-skid
American Sizes Only

All the above can be used on any of the well known Quick Detachable Rims

MICHELIN TIRE COMPANY
MILLTOWN, N. J., U. S. A.

Michelin Tires, 1907

Drivers of early cars had to get used to fixing tires every few miles and replacing them frequently. Batteries, oil, and water were other concerns.

Die Fahrer der ersten Autos mussten sich daran gewöhnen, alle paar Kilometer Reifen zu flicken und diese häufig auszutauschen. Batterien, Öl und Kühlwasser bereiteten ebenfalls Sorgen

Les premiers conducteurs doivent prendre l'habitude de réparer leurs pneus tous les quelques kilomètres et les remplacer fréquemment. Batterie, huile et eau leur causent également des ennuis.

► Pierce-Arrow, 1910

►► Locomobile, 1909

The Pierce Arrow
Adolph Treidler

15

TRAVEL BY AUTOMOBILE BECAME AN ALTERNATIVE TO THE TRAIN. AUTO ADVENTURE BECAME POPULAR, AND SOCIETIES LIKE THE LINCOLN HIGHWAY ASSOCIATION, FOUNDED IN 1913, AND THE DIXIE HIGHWAY ASSOCIATION, ESTABLISHED THE NEXT YEAR, PROMOTED NEW ROUTES…

DAS AUTO WURDE EINE ECHTE ALTERNATIVE ZUR EISENBAHN UND VIELE BEGEISTERTEN SICH DAFÜR. VEREINIGUNGEN WIE DIE 1913 GEGRÜNDETE LINCOLN HIGHWAY ASSOCIATION UND DIE IM JAHR DARAUF ENTSTANDENE DIXIE HIGHWAY ASSOCIATION WARBEN FÜR NEUE ROUTEN.

L'AUTOMOBILE DEVIENT UNE ALTERNATIVE AU TRAIN. L'AVENTURE AUTOMOBILE SE POPULARISE ET DES CLUBS FONT LA PROMOTION DE NOUVEAUX ITINÉRAIRES POUR TRAVERSER LE PAYS : LA LINCOLN HIGHWAY, QUI RELIE LES CÔTES EST ET OUEST OU LA DIXIE HIGHWAY, POUR SE RENDRE DU MIDWEST EN FLORIDE.

1910-

A CAR FOR EVERY PURSE AND PURPOSE

EIN AUTO FÜR JEDEN ZWECK UND GELDBEUTEL

UNE VOITURE POUR CHAQUE BOURSE ET POUR CHAQUE USAGE

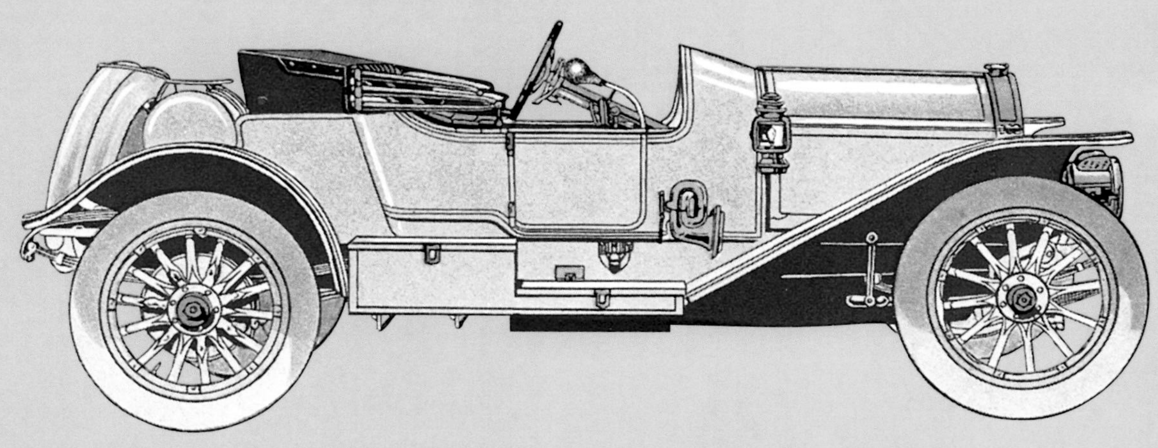

-1919

Milburn Light Electric, 1918 ◂◂

Packard 38 Limousine, 1914 ◂

Overland, 1916

THE EFFECTS OF FORD'S AFFORDABLE MODEL T WERE SO PROFOUND THAT TODAY WE BARELY EVEN NOTICE THEM. The car brought flexibility to shopping and employment that the railroad or life on foot could not. Advertisements pitched such accessories as tops, floor mats, and seat covers for the basic, no-roof Model T, and a whole industry grew around it, much as it has with such contemporary products as the Apple iPod.

Also in 1908, the year the T was introduced, General Motors was founded. Assembling such brands as Cadillac, Oldsmobile, and Buick, GM would become known for offering variety in models—"a car for every purse and purpose"—and frequency of updates (models would change each year, creating the "model year").

America decided the car was here to stay, and, with 1916 legislation from the Woodrow Wilson administration, began to build roads for it. Travel by automobile became an alternative to the train. Auto adventure became popular, and societies like the Lincoln Highway Association, founded in 1913, and the Dixie Highway Association, established the next year, promoted new routes: the Lincoln Highway, across the country from east to west, or the Dixie Highway, from the Midwest to Florida.

Among the wealthy, many accounts of auto adventure made "seeing the U.S.A." popular as an alternative to exploring Europe. Emily Post, the society matron and future bestselling author (*Etiquette in Society, in Business, in Politics, and at Home*), crossed the country by automobile and wrote a book about it in 1915. By the end of the decade, miles traveled by car approached those traveled by train; soon they would overtake. Rail travel peaked in 1920 at 1.2 billion passenger miles. By the end of the 1920s, while car ownership had tripled, train travel fell by one-fifth.

At the same time it grew, the car industry underwent a shakeout. According to automobile historian James Flink, this was a period of consolidation in the industry. From 253 companies in 1908, when the Model T arrived and General Motors was formed, the number fell to just 108 by

1920, and down to 42 by the end of the 1920s. Advertisements from the period memorialize many lost names: Haynes-Apperson, Peerless, Overland, Winton, Marmon.

GM took on Ford with its new low-price brand, the Chevrolet, named after racing driver Louis Chevrolet. The 1914 Chevrolet Royal Mail was pitched as "pleasing to the eye, coming and going." To compete with the Model T, Chevrolet's ads emphasized price. Its Model 490, released in 1915, was designed to be as cheap as the Model T, which at that time was priced at $500.

Henry Ford promised that by the time he finished lowering the price of a car, "No man earning a decent salary will be able to be without one." Thanks not just to his assembly line but to competition, his prophecy came true: By 1920, cars had moved from mere novelty to something close to necessity.

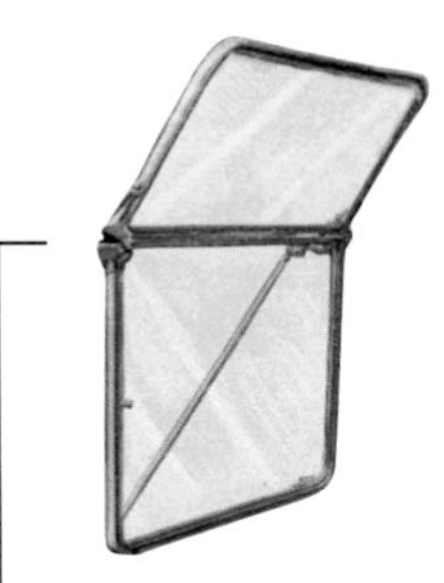

1910

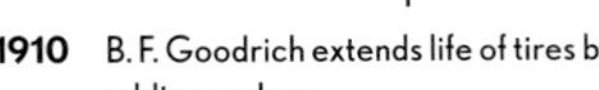

1910 B. F. Goodrich extends life of tires by adding carbon

B. F. Goodrich verlängert die Haltbarkeit von Reifen durch Zugabe von Kohlenstoff

B. F. Goodrich prolonge la vie des pneus en y ajoutant du carbone

1910 Plate glass windshields made available

Windschutzscheiben aus Tafelglas erhältlich

Apparition du pare-brise en verre blanc

1911 GM establishes Chevrolet brand with race-car driver Louis Chevrolet

GM etabliert die Marke Chevrolet mit dem Rennfahrer Louis Chevrolet

GM fonde la marque Chevrolet avec le pilote automobile Louis Chevrolet

1913 Boyce Moto-Meter temperature gauge patented; over 10 million units will sell

Boyce Moto-Meter Temperaturanzeige patentiert; über zehn Millionen Stück werden verkauft

Brevet déposé pour le thermomètre Boyce ; plus de 10 millions d'exemplaires vendus

FORDS BEZAHLBARES MODEL T HATTE TIEFGREIFENDE AUSWIRKUNGEN, DIE UNS HEUTE KAUM MEHR BEWUSST SIND. Dieses Auto brachte eine Flexibilität in Freizeit und Arbeitswelt, die weder mit der Eisenbahn noch zu Fuß zu erreichen war. Die Werbung konzentrierte sich auf Zubehör wie Verdecke, Fußmatten und Sitzbezüge für das spartanische, dachlose Model T. Der T bildete den Kern für eine ganze Zubehörindustrie; bei heutigen Produkten wie dem iPod verhält es sich nicht anders.

Das Jahr 1908, in dem der T präsentiert wurde, ist zugleich auch das Gründungsjahr von General Motors. Marken wie Cadillac, Oldsmobile und Buick vereinend, sollte GM für seine Modellvielfalt („ein Auto für jeden Zweck und Geldbeutel") und für die Regelmäßigkeit seiner Neuerungen (mit dem alljährlichen Modellwechsel entstand das „Modelljahr") bekannt werden.

Die Bürger der USA sagten Ja zum Auto. Den Startschuss für den Straßenbau bildeten die 1916 unter Präsident Woodrow Wilson erlassenen Gesetze. Das Auto wurde eine echte Alternative zur Eisenbahn und Viele begeisterten sich dafür. Vereinigungen wie die 1913 gegründete Lincoln Highway Association und die im Jahr darauf entstandene Dixie Highway Association warben für neue Routen wie den Lincoln Highway (quer durchs Land von Ost nach West) oder den Dixie Highway (vom Mittleren Westen bis Florida).

Unter den Wohlhabenderen sorgten zahlreiche Berichte vom Abenteuer Auto dafür, dass eine Rundfahrt durch die USA eine bedenkenswerte Alternative zur klassischen Europareise wurde. Emily Post, Salondame und spätere Autorin eines Etikette-Bestsellers, durchquerte das Land mit dem Auto und schrieb 1915 ein Buch darüber. Um 1920 reiste man mit dem Auto fast so viele Kilometer wie mit dem Zug; bald sollten es mehr sein. Das Transportmittel Zug erreichte seinen Spitzenwert 1920 mit 1,2 Milliarden Reisekilometern. Ende der 1920er-Jahre hatte sich die Zahl der Autobesitzer verdreifacht, während die Zugreisen um ein Fünftel zurückgegangen waren.

In dieser Wachstumsphase durchlief die Automobilindustrie zugleich einen Ausdünnungsprozess. Der Automobilhistoriker James Flink spricht von einer Zeit der Konsolidierung. Im Jahr 1908, als Fords Model T auf den Markt kam und General Motors gegründet wurde, gab es 253 Autohersteller, 1920 waren es nur noch 108 und Ende der 1920er-Jahre nur mehr 42. In alten Werbeanzeigen stößt man auf zahlreiche inzwischen vergessene Namen wie Haynes-Apperson, Peerless, Overland, Winton oder Marmon.

GM begegnete Ford mit einer im Tiefpreis-Segment platzierten und nach dem Rennfahrer Louis Chevrolet benannten Marke. Den 1914er Chevrolet „Royal Mail" pries man als „pleasing to the eye, coming and going". Um sich gegen das Model T zu behaupten, betonte man den Preis. Das Chevrolet Model 490 von 1915 sollte so preiswert sein wie das Model T, das damals 500 Dollar kostete.

Henry Ford versprach, dass nach Ende der stetigen Preissenkungen seiner Autos „kein Mann, der ein anständiges Gehalt verdient, ohne eines sein können" würde. Seinen Fließbändern, aber auch dem Wettbewerb ist zu verdanken, dass diese Prophezeiung wahr wurde: 1920 war das Auto keine bloße Neuheit mehr, sondern beinahe schon eine Notwendigkeit.

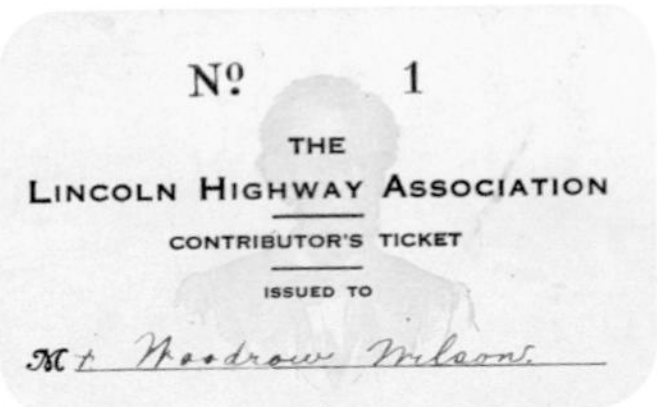

1913

1913 President Wilson co-founds Lincoln Highway Association

Präsident Wilson Mitbegründer der Lincoln Highway Association

Le président Wilson s'associe à la fondation de la Lincoln Highway Association

1914 First Dodge Brothers car; firm will become famous for all-steel body

Erstes Auto der Firma Dodge Brothers, die für ihre Ganzstahl-Karosserien berühmt werden sollte

Première voiture produite par les frères Dodge ; la firme se rendra célèbre par ses carrosseries tout acier

1914 Rear view and side mirrors offered

Seiten- und Rückspiegel erhältlich

Apparition des rétroviseurs intérieurs et extérieurs

1915 First stop sign erected, Detroit, Michigan

Erstes Stoppschild in Detroit (Michigan) aufgestellt

Installation du premier panneau stop à Detroit, Michigan

Pierce-Arrow, 1910 ◂◂

Studebaker Big-Six, 1919 ◂

▸▸ Overland Model 90, 1919

LE LANCEMENT PAR FORD D'UN MODÈLE AUSSI ABORDABLE QUE LA T A LAISSÉ UNE EMPREINTE SI PROFONDE DANS LA SOCIÉTÉ QU'ON LA REMARQUE À PEINE AUJOURD'HUI. La voiture permet une flexibilité pour faire les courses et se rendre au travail que n'offrent ni le chemin de fer ni les déplacements à pied. La publicité vante les accessoires du modèle de base sans toit : capotes, tapis de sol et couvre-sièges ; un tout nouveau secteur industriel se développe, comme c'est le cas aujourd'hui pour des produits tels que l'iPod d'Apple.

C'est également en 1908, année de création de la T, que naît la firme General Motors. Réunissant des marques comme Cadillac, Oldsmobile et Buick, GM va devenir célèbre pour sa variété de modèles – « Une voiture pour chaque bourse et pour chaque usage » – et la fréquence à laquelle elle renouvelle ses modèles (ils changent chaque année, d'où la notion nouvelle de « modèle année tant »).

L'Amérique décide que la voiture est faite pour durer ; c'est pourquoi, forte de la législation mise en place en 1916 par le gouvernement du président Wilson, elle entreprend la construction de routes. L'automobile devient une alternative au train. L'aventure automobile se popularise et des clubs font la promotion de nouveaux itinéraires pour traverser le pays : la Lincoln Highway, qui relie les côtes est et ouest ou la Dixie Highway, pour se rendre du Midwest en Floride.

Chez les riches, les récits d'aventures automobiles popularisent le tourisme local comme une solution alternative au voyage en Europe. Emily Post, reine des bonnes manières et de la bienséance, auxquelles elle consacrera un futur ouvrage, publie un livre sur sa traversée du pays en automobile en 1915. À la fin de la décennie, le nombre de kilomètres parcourus en voiture avoisine déjà celui du train ; il ne tardera pas à le dépasser. Les déplacements en train connaissent leur apogée en 1920, avec près de deux milliards de kilomètres parcourus. Dès la fin des années 1920, tandis que le nombre des propriétaires de voitures a triplé, le nombre de voyages en train a baissé de 20 %.

Malgré sa croissance, le secteur automobile connaît la crise. Selon l'historien James Flink, spécialiste dans ce domaine, cette branche industrielle traverse alors une période de consolidation. De 253 en 1908, année de l'apparition du modèle T et de General Motors, le nombre de constructeurs chute à 108 en 1920, et à 42 à la fin des années 1920. Les publicités de cette période nous remémorent des noms tombés dans l'oubli : Haynes-Apperson, Peerless, Overland, Winton, Marmon.

GM concurrence Ford sur le marché de la voiture à bas prix avec la Chevrolet, qui doit son nom au pilote de course Louis Chevrolet. En 1914, la publicité pour le modèle « Royal Mail » vante une voiture « agréable à l'œil, qui va et vient ». Pour concurrencer le modèle T, les réclames pour Chevrolet soulignent ses prix. Le modèle 490, commercialisé en 1915, est même conçu pour être aussi bon marché que la T, qui coûte à l'époque 500 $.

Henry Ford a promis de faire baisser le prix de la voiture jusqu'à ce que « tout travailleur gagnant un salaire décent soit en mesure d'en posséder une ». Grâce à sa chaîne de montage mais aussi à la concurrence, sa prophétie se réalise : en 1920, la voiture n'est déjà plus une nouveauté, mais une quasi-nécessité.

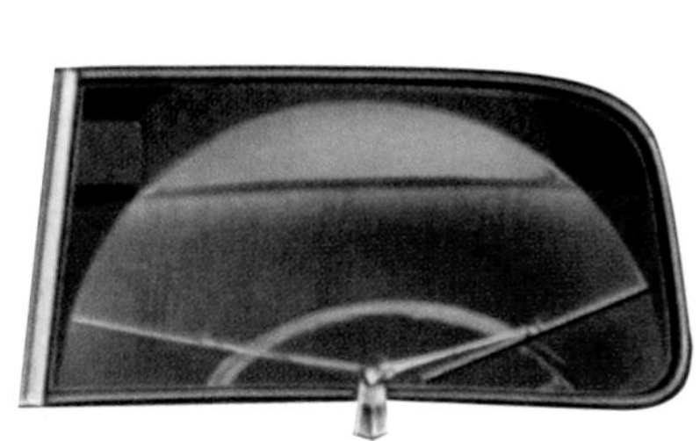

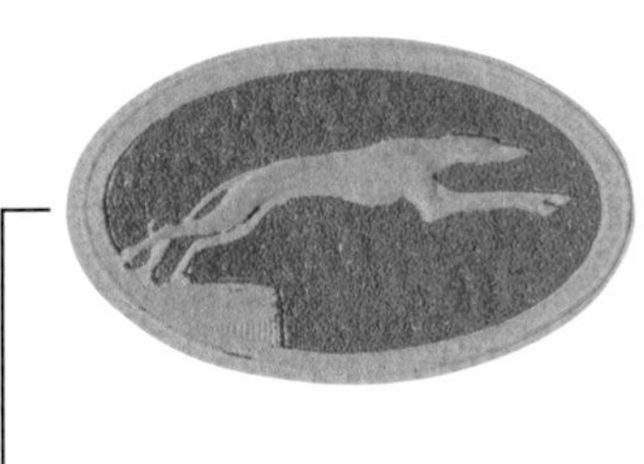

1915

1916 Invented in 1903, windshield wiper finally becomes standard for American cars

Der bereits 1903 erfundene Scheibenwischer wird bei US-Autos zum Standard

Inventé en 1903, l'essuie-glace finit par devenir standard sur les Américaines

1917 Henry M. Leland opens Lincoln Motor Company; first model released in 1921

Henry M. Leland gründet die Lincoln Motor Company; das erste Modell erscheint 1921

Henry M. Leland inaugure la Lincoln Motor Company ; le premier modèle est lancé en 1921

1919 Ford laminates windows and windshields, making them safer in accidents

Verminderte Unfallfolgen durch Fords Autoscheiben aus Verbundglas

Les vitres et les pare-brises mélaminés de Ford, moins dangereux en cas d'accident

1920 First three-color traffic-signal light erected, Detroit, Michigan

Erste dreifarbige Verkehrsampel in Detroit (Michigan) aufgestellt

Installation des premiers feux tricolores à Detroit, Michigan

FISK
31x4
2

FISK

Ford, 1919

The Ford Model T evolved in its nearly 20 years on the market, but the styling changes were far from dramatic. The first one did not even come with a top. As late as 1919, it was still considered to be a novel sales pitch to talk about a "closed car." And by the time the "Tin Lizzie" was retired in 1927, it was still only available in "any color that [the customer] wants so long as it is black."

Während der fast 20 Jahre, in denen es auf dem Markt war, entwickelte sich Fords Model T durchaus, wenngleich sich sein Styling nicht gerade dramatisch wandelte. Die erste Version besaß nicht einmal ein Dach. Noch 1919 glaubte man, mit der Werbung für ein „geschlossenes Auto" punkten zu können. Bis zur Einstellung der Produktion 1927 gab es die „Tin Lizzie" weiterhin nur „in jeder Farbe, sofern es Schwarz ist".

Durant la vingtaine d'années où elle reste sur le marché, la Ford T ne cesse d'évoluer, mais les changements de style sont loin d'être radicaux. Le premier modèle ne possède même pas de capote. Jusqu'en 1919, la « voiture fermée » reste l'argument de vente suprême. Lorsque « Tin Lizzie » se retire en 1927, la T reste disponible, dans « la couleur qu'on veut, du moment que c'est noir ».

► Overland, 1918

The Tudor Sedan

Not even a chilly all-day rain need upset the plans of the woman who has a Ford closed car at her disposal. Knowing it to be reliable and comfortable in all weathers, she goes out whenever inclination suggests or duty dictates.

The car is so easy to drive that it constantly suggests thoughtful services to her friends. She can call for them without effort and share pleasantly their companionship.

All remark upon the graceful outward appearance of her car, its convenient and attractive interior, and its cosy comfort. And she prides herself upon having obtained so desirable a car for so low a price.

TUDOR SEDAN, $590 FORDOR SEDAN, $685 COUPE, $525 (All prices f. o. b. Detroit)

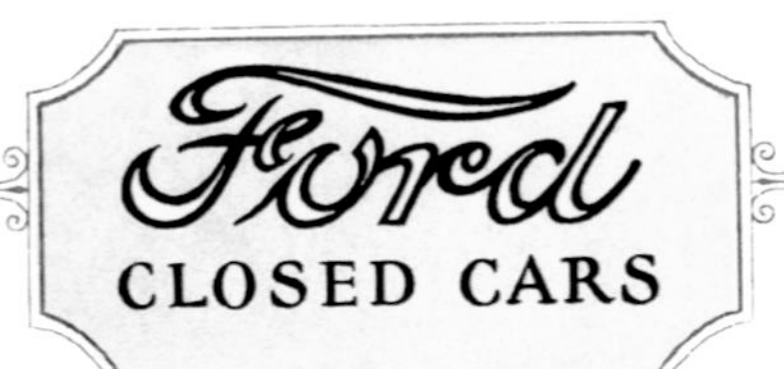

Overland
TRADE MARK REG.
The Thrift Car
Top-Notch Value—
Rock-Bottom Cost
SEE how satisfactorily this car meets all five of the requirements for complete satisfaction.
Its appearance commands admiration and its performance is equal to all demands.
The 32-horsepower motor is notoriously stingy with fuel, and liberal with power.
This car is simple to handle, has narrow turning radius, convenient control, Electric Auto-Lite Starting and Lighting and easy operating clutch that women drivers so appreciate.
It is exceedingly comfortable, with wide seats, deep upholstery, spacious interior, rear cantilever springs and large tires, non-skid rear.
Wherever you drive, expert Overland service facilities are available. Priced at its remarkably low figure, this Model 90 is truly a bargain.
All of these essentials for complete satisfaction cannot be bought for less.
Five points of Overland superiority:
Appearance, Performance, Comfort, Service and Price
Willys-Overland Inc., Toledo, Ohio
Willys-Knight and Overland Motor Cars and Light Commercial Cars
Canadian Factory, West Toronto, Canada
Light Four Model 90
Touring Car
"Show me where the highest valuation is put on brains and time, and I'll show you the greatest number of motor cars in service."
—John N. Willys

Overland
$1550
ELECTRICALLY
LIGHTED and STARTED
Lighting, starting, stopping, power and speed all easily controlled by the simple touch of a little electric button or lever. That's all.
All the comforts, conveniences and simplicity of a high priced storage battery electric, yet the cost is approximately one-half.
And in addition you have more power and unlimited mileage.
Send for our handsome catalogue—illustrated and very descriptive. This tells the whole story. It's gratis.
Also, see this car at the Overland dealer's in your town. Look him up today.
This coupe has a 35 horsepower motor, 114 inch wheel base, a jeweled Stewart Speedometer, Gray & Davis Electric Starter and Generator, electric lights and storage battery. Price $1550 complete with everything f. o. b. Toledo.
Literature on request. Please address Dept. 16.
The Willys-Overland Company
TOLEDO, OHIO.
Manufacturers of the famous Garford and Willys-Utility Trucks
Full Information on request

White Sixteen valve 4'

THE RUNABOUT BODY

THREE STAGES OF MOTOR DEVELOPMENT

In the first stage, higher power was obtained by building larger cylinders. In the second stage, greater flexibility was secured by adding cylinders. Both involve serious handicaps in a reciprocating engine. In the third stage, upon which gas engine design is now entering, a higher range of inherent capability has been developed—more power from existing plant. Simple and rugged, the sixteen-valve four draws straight from the source of high power and flexible performance: *valve efficiency.*

The White Company, Cleveland

67

White Sixteen-Valve 4, 1917

Overland, 1913 ◂

Baker
Electrics
SHAFT
DRIVEN
ORCHESTRA HALL

Baker Electrics, 1911◂

Thomas Edison was one of many who believed the future of the car lay in electric power, not gasoline or steam. Nearly two dozen companies, notably Baker and Brush, made electrics. Cleaner and easier to operate, electrics had special appeal to women. Most got about 40 miles per charge — a figure few current electrics have so far been able to exceed.

Thomas Edison glaubte wie viele andere auch, dass die Zukunft des Autos nicht im Benzinmotor oder Dampf, sondern im Elektroantrieb lag. Fast zwei Dutzend Firmen, darunter Baker und Brush, fertigten Elektroautos. Diese Gefährte waren sauberer und leichter zu bedienen, weshalb sie vor allem Frauen ansprachen. Die Reichweite betrug meist rund 65 Kilometer – ein Wert, den nur wenige heutige Elektroautos übertreffen.

Thomas Edison fait partie de ceux qui croient que l'avenir de l'automobile réside dans l'électricité et non dans l'essence ou la vapeur. Près d'une trentaine de constructeurs, dont Baker et Brush, proposent des modèles électriques. Plus propres et plus faciles à utiliser, ils séduisent en particulier les femmes. La plupart parcourent 65 km par charge – ce que peu de véhicules électriques actuels ont réussi à dépasser.

Rauch & Lang Electrics, 1919

Baker Electrics/Rauch & Lang Electrics, 1916

Mezger Automatic Windshield, 1910

Boyce Moto-Meter, 1919 Fisk Red Top Tires, 1917

Zerolene Oil, 1918 Klaxon Horns, 1910

REPUBLIC
STAGGARD Tread
The Tire Perfect
No skid to dread
With STAGGARD Tread
The Republic Rubber Company
Youngstown Ohio U. S. A.

Goodrich Tires, 1919

As late as World War I, motoring still carried an air of adventure, even danger. Capitalizing on their support of the war effort was common practice for advertisers, who also flattered drivers by associating them with the heroism of military aviators.

Noch im Ersten Weltkrieg verband man das Autofahren mit Abenteuer, ja sogar Gefahr. Die Werber zogen vielfach Nutzen aus der Kriegsunterstützung der Autohersteller – und sie schmeichelten dem Autofahrer, indem sie ihn mit den Heroen der Lüfte in Verbindung brachten.

À l'époque de la Première Guerre mondiale, la voiture évoque encore l'aventure, voire le danger. Les constructeurs ne manquent pas de capitaliser sur leur soutien à l'effort de guerre. Leurs publicités flattent les conducteurs en les comparant aux héroïques aviateurs de l'armée.

Republic Tires, 1911 ◂

Aces!
A whirring dash from behind the soft, cottony-whiteness of a giant cloud—
The hoarse death-rattle of a machine gun—
And Death traces a long flaming streak against the azure of Heaven as another Hun crashes to the earth.
Capt. Rickenbacher, erstwhile racing driver who has piloted Silvertowns to victory over the speedway, now leading ace with 22 planes downed — or Lt. Douglass Campbell, our own California boy, who has made his name a terror to German airman—
They are characteristic of the American birdman. They have that "Yankee Something"— intelligence, whirlwind attack and heart of oak — that *wins*. Victory has crowned their efforts.
God bless them all and bring them safely home to us.
THE B. F. GOODRICH RUBBER COMPANY
In San Francisco at 401 Mission Street
In Oakland - at 2550 Broadway
In Sacramento at 916 Eleventh Street
FACTORIES AKRON, OHIO
GOODRICH
· TIRES FOR PASSENGER CARS AND AIRPLANES ·

Everyman's Car $485

The Brush Runabout

AFTER six days of close application to your work—confined within four walls, perhaps—it is a blessing to be able to re-create your self on the seventh day—in the open air.

Thoughtful people are concerning themselves more and more with the problem of re-invigoration—the refreshing of one's vitality to meet the growing demands of the work-a-day world.

Practical people make producing hours more productive by this means.

The Brush Runabout is the ideal vehicle to carry one to that end.

For six days it will work as you work—go where you will, when you will—do for you what it is doing for thousands of Brush owners—become as essential to you as any aide in your business.

On the seventh day it will play as you play—whole-heartedly, with no discordant note, ever-ready, untiring, pleasing every sense—wholly satisfying. It is

This drawing is a reproduction of the cover design of a mighty interesting book that tells why the Brush is adaptable to your business—Send for it.

Everyman's Car Every Day

BRUSH RUNABOUT CO., 1230 Rhode Island Ave., Detroit, Mich.

Licensed under Selden Patent

Brush Runabout, 1911 ◄

A reborn carriage maker, Buick became one of the early auto-sales leaders and a cornerstone of General Motors. For a time, the Buick was known as the doctor's car, and was being pitched as a device for family dynamics – to protect children and keep the family together.

Aus dem einstigen Kutschenbauer Buick wurde einer der frühen Verkaufsführer und Grundpfeiler von General Motors. Eine Zeit lang galt der Buick als Ärztewagen und wurde als familienfreundlich beworben – die Kinder waren geschützt und die Familie blieb zusammen.

Née en 1903, la firme Buick devient un des premiers grands constructeurs et une des pierres angulaires de General Motors. Pendant un temps, c'est la voiture typique du médecin. On vante déjà les mérites de l'automobile pour le bien de la famille : elle permet de protéger les enfants et de resserrer les liens familiaux.

Buick Sedan, 1916

Buick Sedan, 1917

Paige, 1918 ▸ Lozier, 1913

LOZIER

The Quality Car
for Quality People

Touring Cars
Five Models
$5000

Limousines
Landaulets
$6500

G. W. Peters

LOZIER

241 Mack Ave. Detroit

Cozy
and
Happy
CHASE
CHASE
Plush
Motor Car
Robes
Made by Sanford Mills

Chase Motor Car Robes, ca. 1914 ◂

Since the first cars were open, like carriages, the automobile required its own wardrobe: goggles, scarves, and dusters. Women bound their large hats to their heads with tightly wrapped scarves, and, during the winter, passengers wrapped themselves in blankets like those made by Chase.

Da die ersten Autos kein Verdeck besaßen, bedurfte es einer speziellen Kluft aus Schutzbrille, Schal und Staubmantel. Die Frauen fixierten ihre großen Hüte mithilfe von Schals. Im Winter hüllte man sich in warme Decken wie diese von Chase.

Les premières voitures étant ouvertes, comme les attelages, l'automobile nécessite une garde-robe adéquate : lunettes, écharpe et cache-poussière. Les femmes vissent leur grand chapeau sur leur tête en nouant des foulards bien serrés et, l'hiver, tous les passagers s'emmitouflent dans des couvertures comme celles que propose la maison Chase.

Republic Tires, 1912

The Original Effective Non-Skid Tire

When you drive over wet, slippery pavements or in mud, the sturdy long studs of the Staggard Tread are always ready for the emergency, like an army of little rudders that hold the wheel true to its course, preventing skidding and giving powerful traction for quick starts and short stops without spinning or locking the wheels.

And when the center rows of studs are worn off (after thousands of miles of use) you still have the full-thickness plain tread of the ordinary tire and the two outer rows of studs which will prevent side-slipping for the life of the tire.

Write for our booklet giving description of this the original effective non-skid tire.

This booklet also describes the Republic Black-Line Red Inner Tube made cf the pure Para Rubber—the tube that gives 100% more riding comfort and wear than the ordinary tube.

THE REPUBLIC RUBBER COMPANY
YOUNGSTOWN, OHIO

Branches and Agencies in the Principal Cities

REPUBLIC STAGGARD TREAD TIRES

Republic Staggard Tread Pat. Sept. 15-22, 1908

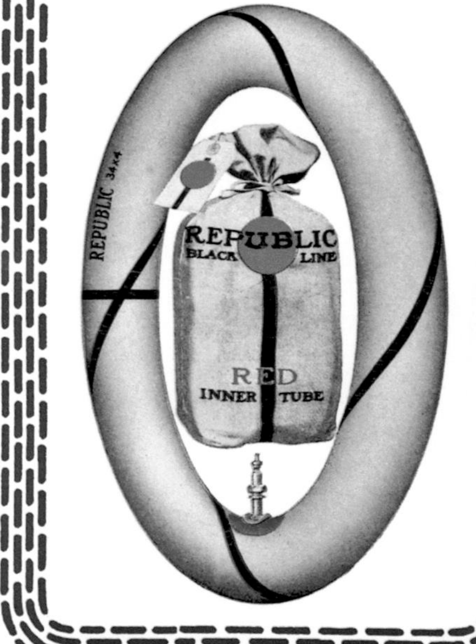

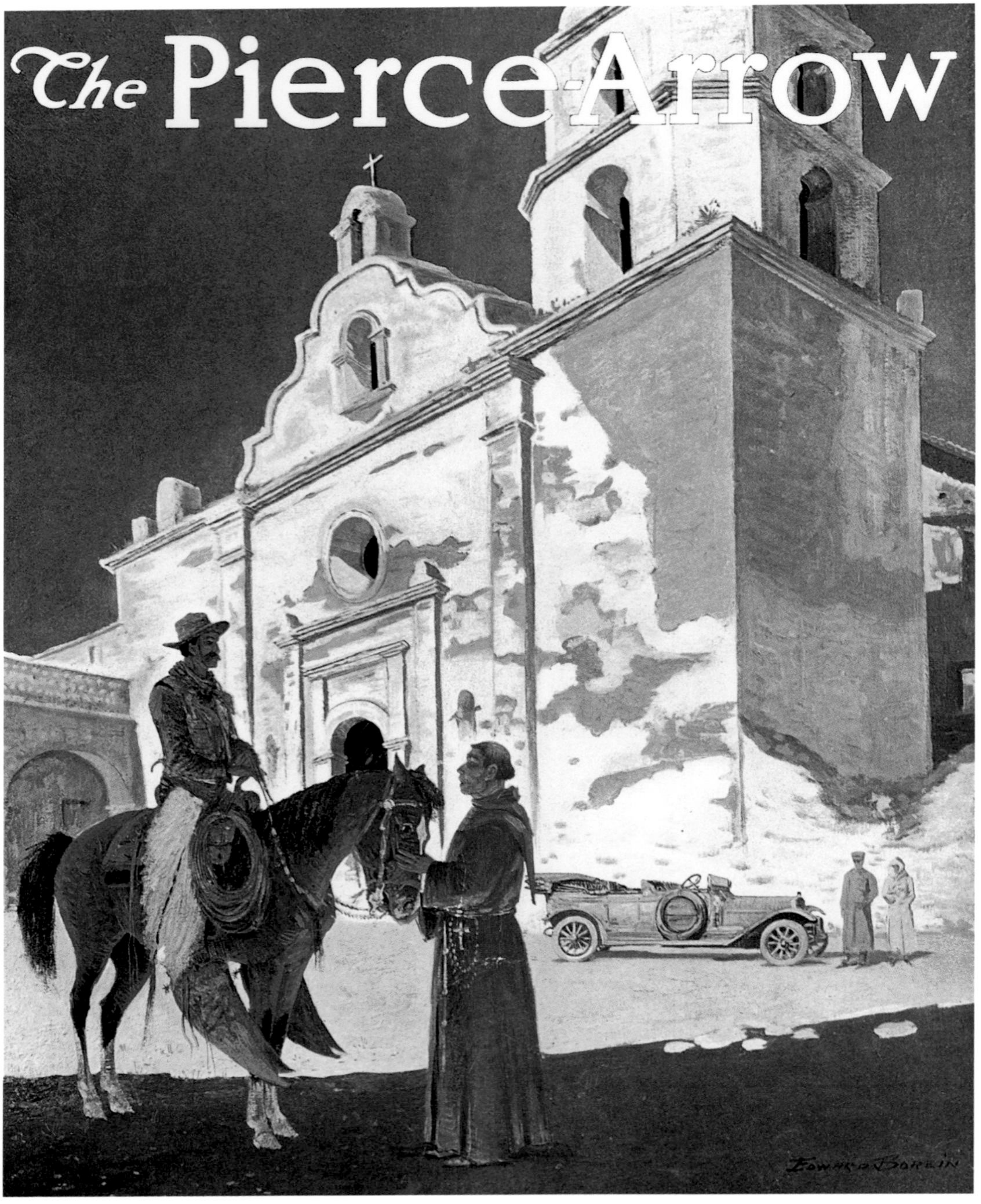

Pierce-Arrow, 1912

Before the automobile, it was easier to go from New York to Paris, France, than to Paris, Texas. Thanks to the car, seeing the distant corners of the U.S., especially the national parks, became a vacation alternative – though still for the wealthy – to the ocean liner to Europe or the train to the resort.

Als es noch keine Autos gab war es einfacher, von New York ins französische Paris zu reisen als nach Paris, Texas. Das Auto machte den Besuch der entlegenen Ecken der USA, speziell der Nationalparks, zu einer echten Alternative zu einer Schiffsreise nach Europa oder einer Zugfahrt in die Sommerfrische – wenngleich weiterhin nur für die Wohlhabenden.

Avant l'automobile, il était plus facile de se rendre de New York à Paris, en France, qu'à Paris, au Texas. Grâce à la voiture, les Américains – du moins les riches – peuvent prendre leurs vacances dans leur pays, et notamment visiter ses parcs nationaux, au lieu de traverser l'océan pour venir en Europe ou de prendre le train pour se rendre en villégiature.

► Firestone Tires, 1917

STRENGTH for the emergency, with the reserve power and endurance there to insure a long life of full service, that is the comfortable, confident feeling that belongs to those who ride on Firestone Tires.

In every country the name Firestone has come to mean tire satisfaction and economy. And now the standard is raised to even a higher plane by the remarkable service of Firestone Cord Tires.

With Firestone engineering ability applied to Cord Tires, motorists expect more. And they get more. The Firestone design, the Firestone standards of quality and care in materials, workmanship and inspection produce not only the safe, carefree, luxurious ride, but Most Miles per Dollar. Your dealer and the nearby Firestone Branch unite to give you prompt, economical service.

FIRESTONE TIRE & RUBBER COMPANY, AKRON, OHIO
Branches and Dealers Everywhere

Simplex

IN motors, as in clothes, the most admired and copied are those expressing the refinement and exclusiveness of the made to order. Simplex, Crane Model, 6 cylinder—Chassis $6000.

Bodies to Order

SIMPLEX AUTOMOBILE CO.
60 Broadway New York

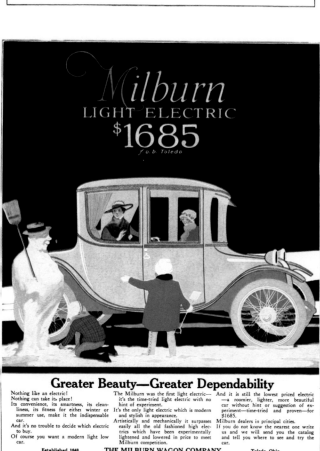

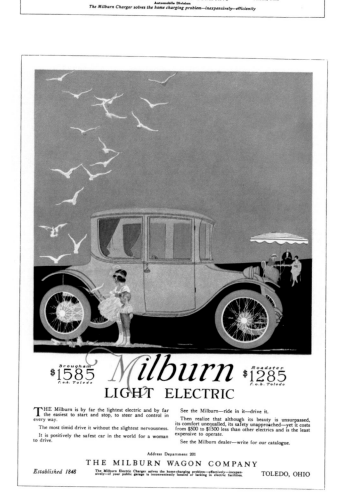

Milburn
LIGHT ELECTRIC
$1685
f. o. b. Toledo

Greater Beauty—Greater Dependability

Nothing like an electric!
Nothing can take its place!
Its convenience, its smartness, its cleanliness, its fitness for either winter or summer use, make it the indispensable car.
And it's no trouble to decide which electric to buy.
Of course you want a modern light low car.
The Milburn was the first light electric—it's the time-tried light electric with no hint of experiment.
It's the only light electric which is modern and stylish in appearance.
Artistically and mechanically it surpasses easily all the old fashioned high electrics which have been experimentally lightened and lowered in price to meet Milburn competition.
And it is still the lowest priced electric—a roomier, lighter, more beautiful car without hint or suggestion of experiment—time-tried and proven—for $1685.
Milburn dealers in principal cities.
If you do not know the nearest one write us and we will send you the catalog and tell you where to see and try the car.

Established 1848 THE MILBURN WAGON COMPANY Toledo, Ohio
AUTOMOBILE DIVISION
Write for catalog

The Milburn Town Car—outside driven—inside capacity four passengers—a beauty—$1995 f.o.b. Toledo

The Milburn Charger solves the home charging problem—inexpensively—efficiently

Brougham
$1585
f. o. b. Toledo
Milburn
Roadster
$1285
f. o. b. Toledo
LIGHT ELECTRIC

THE Milburn is by far the lightest electric and by far the easiest to start and stop, to steer and control in every way.

The most timid drive it without the slightest nervousness.

It is positively the safest car in the world for a woman to drive.

See the Milburn—ride in it—drive it.

Then realize that although its beauty is unsurpassed, its comfort unequalled, its safety unapproached—yet it costs from $500 to $1500 less than other electrics and is the least expensive to operate.

See the Milburn dealer—write for our catalogue.

Address Department 201

THE MILBURN WAGON COMPANY

Established 1848 The Milburn Electric Charger solves the home-charging problem—effectively—inexpensively—if your public garage is inconveniently located or lacking in electric facilities. TOLEDO, OHIO

Milburn Light Electric, 1917 Milburn Light Electric, ca. 1917

Milburn Light Electric, 1917 Milburn Light Electric, 1917 Simplex, 1916 ◂

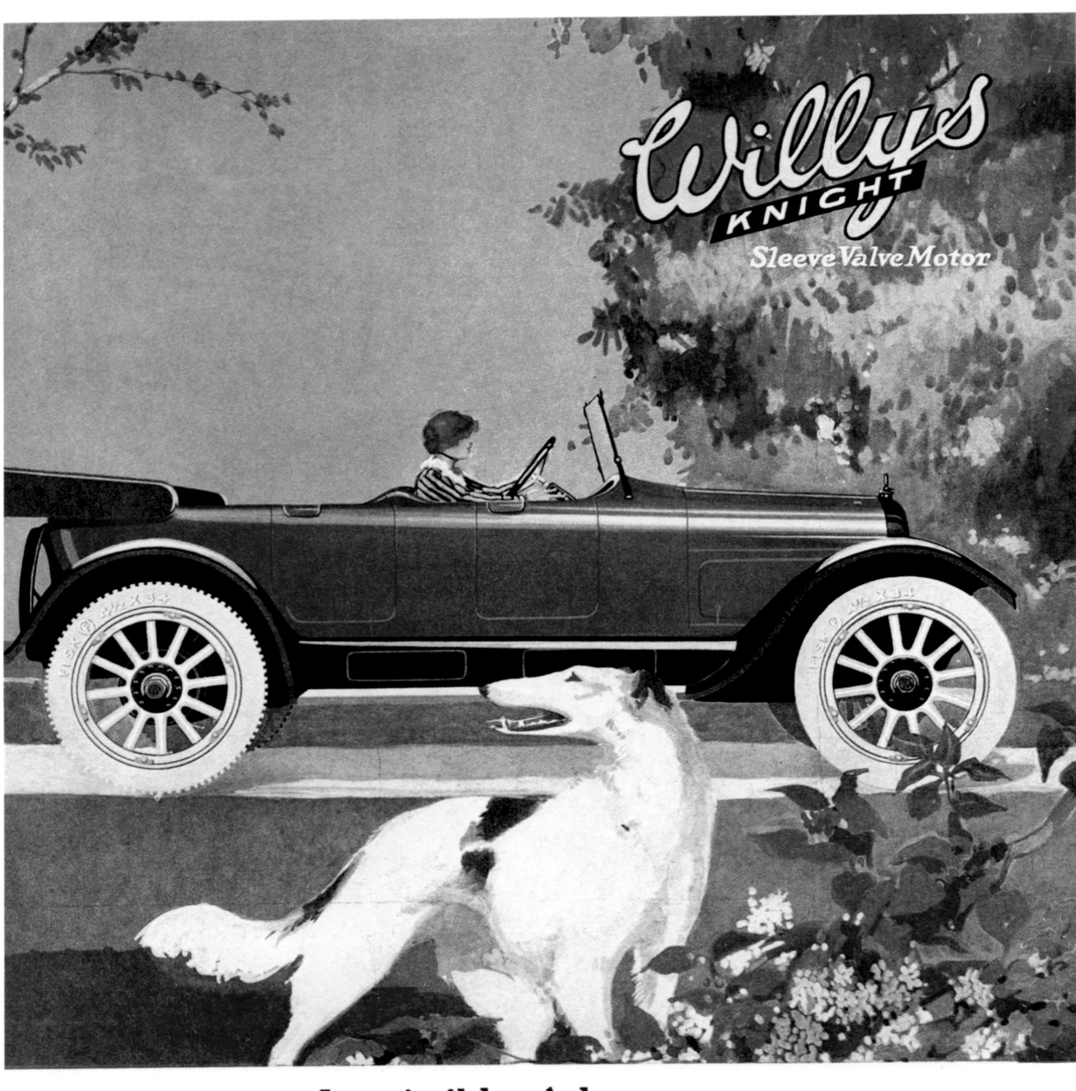

Irresistible Advantages

The Fours
Seven Passenger Touring

$1395

Four Passenger Coupe, $1650
Seven Passenger Touring-Sedan, $1950
Seven Passenger Limousine, $1950

The Eight
Seven Passenger Touring, $1950

All prices f. o. b. Toledo
Subject to change without notice

For sheer beauty the new Willys-Knight Four is captivating.

But even the charm of its beauty quickly yields to sorcery of its completely satisfying comfort.

Long forty-eight inch cantilever rear springs, seat cushions with every spiral separately encased so that it is air cushioned and checked against rebound, together with long 121 inch wheelbase, make it luxuriously comfortable even over rough roads.

Yet both its beauty and its comfort yield to the wizardry of its sleeve-valve motor.

We think you will consider this four-cylinder motor *even when new*, the equal in power, smoothness and flexibility of almost any six you ever drove.

And it actually and very noticeably *improves with use* because it is constantly revitalized by carbon, the very deadly element that devitalizes every other kind of motor.

This means more constant use without repair or adjustment, constant, instead of intermittent, efficiency and much longer life.

Let the Willys-Overland dealer tell you more of the advantages of the Willys-Knight motor.

The Willys-Overland Company, Toledo, Ohio
Manufacturers of Willys-Knight and Overland Motor Cars

Willys-Knight Four, ca. 1918

Willys, later known for its Jeep, began as a maker of elegant cars, with a factory in Toledo, Ohio. The bright artwork in this ad suggested fin de siècle prints; the borzoi was the favored dog breed of Art Nouveau.

Später durch seinen Jeep bekannt, begann Willys als Hersteller eleganter Wagen in Toledo, Ohio. Die Farbgebung dieser Anzeige erinnert an Lithographien aus dem Fin de Siècle; der Barsoi war eine beliebte Hunderasse der Jugendstil-Ära.

À ses débuts, Willys, connu plus tard pour sa Jeep, fabrique des voitures élégantes dans l'Ohio. Cette publicité aux couleurs vives évoque les affiches fin de siècle ; le barzoï est d'ailleurs la race de prédilection de l'Art nouveau.

► Marmon 34, 1918

1100 Pounds Lighter

Roominess is an outstanding Marmon excellence — wider seats and deeper sides than the custom is — and this notwithstanding that the Marmon is closer to the ground with lower center of gravity than other high-class cars that are working toward Marmon ideals. Long wheelbase, yet short turning radius, perfect lubrication, yet only four grease cups.

View this open model at the motor shows.

NORDYKE & MARMON COMPANY
Established 1851
INDIANAPOLIS

Leave it to Santa —"He knows"

Among discriminating motorists, their families and friends, the custom of giving Michelin Tires and Tubes for Christmas has grown in popularity year by year. No present could be more useful; none could better express appreciation of the rides you've had together or of favors you've received.

The universal recognition enjoyed by Michelins as *the* quality tires, gives them an unequalled gift-value which their moderate price makes doubly attractive to the giver.

For a gift costing a few dollars—A Michelin Inner Tube.
For a gift par excellence—A Michelin Universal Casing.

MICHELIN TIRE CO., Milltown, N. J.
Michelin Tire Co., of Canada, Ltd., 782 St. Catherine St. W., Montreal
Dealers in all parts of the world

MICHELIN

Fisk Tires, 1914

Drivers soon came to depend on their vehicles. More than horses, whose lives were short, cars could seem part of the family – friends, like the dog seen in this advertisement for tires.

Autos wurden bald zu einer emotionalen Angelegenheit. Mehr als einst das eher kurzlebige Kutschpferd konnte das Auto als Teil der Familie erscheinen, ja als Freund, wie dieser Hund in einer Reifenwerbung.

Très vite, les automobilistes deviennent dépendants de leur véhicules. Plus encore que le cheval, dont la longévité est courte, la voiture fait partie de la famille ; c'est une amie, au même titre que le chien représenté dans cette publicité pour pneus.

Michelin Tires, 1919 ◄

►► Willys-Knight Limousines 1916

Time to Re-tire?
(Buy Fisk)
4½ X 35
FISK
Faithful Service
Lasting Friendship
YOUR goodwill is of greatest value to us.
When you buy our product, you get more than tires. Every purchase includes our intention faithfully to fulfill our part of the contract.
Good tires, the will and the effort to see that your pleasure in them is such as to make you a satisfied and permanent Fisk user, *is our obligation.* We are meeting that obligation squarely and successfully with our thousands of satisfied users.
THE FISK RUBBER COMPANY
Factory and Home Office, Chicopee Falls, Mass.
18,000 Dealers and Fisk Branches in Principal Cities

FISK 4½X35

FISK

MANY NEW TECHNICAL FEATURES WERE OFFERED: BETTER BRAKES, POWERED WIND-SHIELD WIPERS, SAFETY GLASS; BUT COLOR, STYLE, AND PRICE BEGAN TO SUGGEST THAT YOU WERE WHAT YOU DROVE, AS MUCH AS YOU WERE WHAT YOU WORE.

ZAHLREICHE TECHNISCHE NEUERUNGEN HIELTEN EINZUG: BESSERE BREMSEN, ELEKTRISCHE SCHEIBENWISCHER, SICHERHEITS-GLAS. DOCH FARBE, STIL UND PREIS SUGGERIERTEN ZUNEHMEND, DASS NICHT NUR KLEIDER, SONDERN AUCH AUTOS LEUTE MACHEN.

NOMBRE DE NOUVELLES CARACTÉRISTIQUES TECHNIQUES VOIENT LE JOUR : PERFECTION-NEMENT DES FREINS, MOTORISATION DES ESSUIE-GLACES, VERRE SÉCURIT ; LA COULEUR, LE STYLE ET LE PRIX COMMENCENT À REFLÉTER LA PERSONNALITÉ DU CONDUCTEUR, UN PEU À LA MANIÈRE DES VÊTEMENTS.

1920

YOU ARE WHAT YOU DRIVE
AUTOS MACHEN LEUTE
DIS-MOI CE QUE TU CONDUIS, JE TE DIRAI QUI TU ES

Dodge, 1926 ◄◄

Nash, 1928 ◄

Chevrolet, 1930

THE ROARING TWENTIES, WE STILL CALL THESE YEARS, A DECADE SUMMED UP IN *THE GREAT GATSBY* CLICHÉS of flappers and raccoon coats, bathtub gin and Stutz Bearcats. But the '20s were also the decade in which the automobile market matured. Dozens of new models in an endless array of colors became available, and advertising expanded into the powerful new mass media of radio, film, and widely distributed magazines. Hollywood gave the automobile publicity as well, using the car's mobility as a way to bring movement to the camera, refining the "chase scene" into a staple of action film. Films brought visions of new models and luxury brands to the Main Street odeons of small towns, planting seeds of desire in rural America.

And, by the 1920s, social ranking was marked out by the type of car owned, as testified to by Sinclair Lewis in his novel *Babbitt* (1922), just as the ownership of carriages marked out socioeconomic status in novels by Jane Austen and Charles Dickens. Lewis's protagonist finds his own car just about perfect, thanks to a new gadget on its dash: a cigar lighter. "That makes a dandy accessory," Babbitt declared. The hero of another Lewis novel, *Dodsworth* (1929), was an automotive designer resembling the real-life Walter Chrysler.

Many new technical features were offered: better brakes, powered windshield wipers, safety glass; but color, style, and price began to suggest that you were what you drove, as much as you were what you wore. The automobile was becoming a personal statement, like fashion. More and more magazine advertisements appeared in color, and so did cars. Answering Ford's "any color you want as long as it is black," General Motors introduced a variety of colors, made possible by the new, fast-drying Duco paints.

Hollywood "designer to the stars" Harley Earl created the first "styled" car, the 1927 LaSalle. The next year, Earl established General Motors' Art and Color Section, whose job would be to design new cars for each new year. With Cadillac and Packard representing the top of the market and the Model T representing the bottom, a variety of new models were now aimed at the market in between. One was the Chrysler, which also offered the Dodge and Plymouth brands. The use of the company leader as spokesman began with a letter from Henry Ford introducing the new model in various advertisements. Walter Chrysler urged the public in ads to "Look at all three!" low-priced cars—Chevrolet's, Ford's, and his own Plymouth.

With the arrival of the electric starter, pioneered by Cadillac in 1912 and soon widely adopted, women became a key target of automobile advertising. Women would have a dramatic effect on automotive marketing, writes Virginia Scharff in *Taking the Wheel: Women and the Coming of the Motor Age* (1991). From new colors to automatic transmissions, many innovations were created with women buyers in mind. Car makers placed ads in *Vogue*, *Good Housekeeping*, *Ladies' Home Journal*, and other magazines, specifically to reach women.

1920

1920 Automobile travel miles overtake railroad travel miles in United States

Mit dem Auto werden in den USA erstmals mehr Kilometer zurückgelegt als per Bahn

Les Américains parcourent davantage de kilomètres en voiture qu'en train

1921 Model A Duesenberg first passenger car equipped with hydraulic brakes

Duesenberg Model A als erster Pkw mit Hydraulikbremsen ausgestattet

Modèle A Duesenberg, première voiture particulière équipée de freins hydrauliques

1921 Car hop service first offered at Pig Stand, Dallas, Texas

Pig Stand als erstes Schnellrestaurant für Autofahrer in Dallas (Texas) eröffnet

Ouverture du premier drive-in Pig Stand à Dallas, Texas

1921 Lincoln introduces turn signals as standard equipment

Serienmäßiger Fahrtrichtungsanzeiger von Lincoln eingeführt

Lincoln lance le clignotant installé en série

DIE „WILDEN ZWANZIGER JAHRE" – EIN JAHRZEHNT, wie es klischeehaft *Der große Gatsby* zusammenfasste: unabhängige junge Frauen, Waschbärmäntel, Badewannen voller Gin und schnittige Stutz Bearcats. Doch dies war auch eine Dekade, in der der Automobilmarkt reifte. Dutzende neuer Modelle in einer schier endlosen Farbpalette wurden angeboten. Und die Werbung hielt Einzug in die neuen, einflussreichen Massenmedien Radio, Film und in auflagenstarke Magazine. Auch Hollywood warb für das Auto, denn man nutzte dessen Mobilität für eine dynamische Kameraführung und machte die klassische Verfolgungsjagd zu einem Grundelement jedes Actionfilms. Auf Zelluloid gebannt, gelangten neue Modelle und Luxusmarken in die Lichtspielhäuser der Kleinstädte, womit auch im ländlichen Amerika die Saat der Begierde keimen konnte.

Wie Sinclair Lewis in seinem Roman *Babbitt* (1922) bezeugt, ließ sich die gesellschaftliche Stellung in den 1920er-Jahren vom Autotyp ablesen, ganz ähnlich dem Statussymbol Kutsche in den Romanen von Jane Austen und Charles Dickens. Lewis' Protagonist findet seinen Wagen so ziemlich vollkommen, dank einer Neuheit im Armaturenbrett, die er eines Dandys würdig erklärt: einen Zigarettenanzünder. Der Held seines 1929 veröffentlichten Romans *Dodsworth* ist ein Autokonstrukteur, der dem realen Walter Chrysler nachempfunden ist.

Zahlreiche technische Neuerungen hielten Einzug: bessere Bremsen, elektrische Scheibenwischer, Sicherheitsglas. Doch Farbe, Stil und Preis suggerierten zunehmend, dass nicht nur Kleider, sondern auch Autos Leute machen. Das Auto wurde allmählich zu einem persönlichen Statement, wie die Mode auch. Immer mehr Zeitschriftenanzeigen erschienen in Farbe und so auch die Autos. Als Antwort auf Fords in „jeder Farbe, sofern es Schwarz ist" führte General Motors, ermöglicht durch die neuen, schnell trocknenden Duco-Lacke, eine Vielzahl von Farben ein.

Harley Earl, der in Hollywood geborene „Designer für die Stars", kreierte mit dem 1927er LaSalle den ersten „durchgestylten" Wagen. Im Jahr darauf gründete er die Abteilung „Art and Color" von General Motors, die – wie in der Modewelt – jedes Jahr mit neuen Modellen aufwarten sollte. Während Cadillac und Packard das oberste Marktsegment repräsentierten und das Model T das unterste, erschienen diverse neue Modelle, die sich in der Mitte positionierten. Einer dieser Hersteller war Chrysler, der auch die Marken Dodge und Plymouth anbot. Dass der Firmenchef selbst als Sprecher auftrat, hatte mit einem Brief von Henry Ford begonnen, der sein neues Modell in diversen Anzeigen vorstellte. Walter Chrysler forderte den Leser nun auf: „Schauen Sie sich alle drei an!", nämlich die Tiefpreisautos von Chevrolet, Ford und seinen Plymouth.

Mit dem bereits 1912 von Cadillac eingeführten und schon bald weitverbreiteten Elektrostarter wurden die Frauen zu einer bedeutenden Zielgruppe der Autowerbung. Wie Virginia Scharff in ihrem Buch *Taking the Wheel: Women and the Coming of the Motor Age* (1991) schreibt, sollte die Vermarktung von Autos durch diese neue Zielgruppe nachhaltig beeinflusst werden. Zahlreiche Innovationen entstanden mit Blick auf weibliche Käufer, von neuen Farben bis zur Schaltautomatik. Und die Hersteller inserierten in Zeitschriften wie *Vogue*, *Good Housekeeping* oder *Ladies' Home Journal*, um Frauen gezielt anzusprechen.

1923

1923 First ethyl gasoline sold

Erstes Benzin mit Bleitetraäthyl als Antiklopfmittel angeboten

Première vente d'essence éthylique

1924 GM releases cars in range of Duco paint colors, starting with blue

GM präsentiert erstmals farbige Duco-Lackierungen, beginnend mit Blau

GM lance la couleur grâce aux laques Duco, en commençant par le bleu

1924 GM chief Alfred P. Sloan offers "a car for every purse and purpose"

GM-Chef Alfred P. Sloan bietet „ein Auto für jeden Zweck und Geldbeutel"

Alfred P. Sloan, directeur de GM, propose « une voiture pour chaque bourse et pour chaque usage »

1925 Walter P. Chrysler establishes Chrysler Corporation

Walter P. Chrysler gründet die Chrysler Corporation

Walter P. Chrysler fonde la Chrysler Corporation

Pierce-Arrow, 1920 ◂◂

Willys-Knight Great Six, 1930 ◂

▸▸ Chrysler Imperial 80, 1928

« LES ANNÉES FOLLES » : VOILÀ COMMENT NOUS QUALIFIONS ENCORE LA DÉCENNIE évoquée dans *Gatsby le Magnifique*, le fameux roman de Scott Fitzgerald peuplé de garçonnes, de manteaux en raton laveur, de gin de contrebande et de Stutz Bearcat. Ce sont aussi les années pendant lesquelles le marché de l'automobile arrive à maturité. L'offre repose sur des dizaines de nouveaux modèles – dans une palette infinie de couleurs – et la publicité gagne les puissants nouveaux médias de masse que sont la radio, le cinéma et les magazines à grand tirage. Hollywood fait également la promotion de l'automobile car sa mobilité lui permet de donner du mouvement à la caméra, et la « scène de poursuite » devient un passage obligé de tout film d'action. Le cinéma fait connaître les nouveaux modèles et les marques de luxe au grand public grâce à son réseau de salles dans les petites villes et suscite ainsi le désir dans l'Amérique profonde.

Comme en témoigne Sinclair Lewis dans son roman *Babbitt* (1922), le rang social est marqué à cette époque par le type de voiture qu'on possède, tout comme l'attelage définissait le profil socio-économique dans les romans de Jane Austen et de Charles Dickens. Le protagoniste de Lewis trouve sa propre voiture absolument parfaite, grâce à un nouveau gadget sur le tableau de bord : l'allume-cigare. « Voilà un accessoire épatant », déclare Babbitt. Le héros d'un autre roman de Lewis, *Dodsworth* (1929), est un concepteur d'automobiles qui ressemble au vrai Walter Chrysler.

Nombre de nouvelles caractéristiques techniques voient le jour : perfectionnement des freins, motorisation des essuie-glaces, verre sécurit ; la couleur, le style et le prix commencent à refléter la personnalité du conducteur, un peu à la manière des vêtements. L'automobile devient un objet personnel, soumis à la mode. Dans les magazines, la publicité est de plus en plus souvent en couleur et les voitures commencent également à être proposées en différents coloris. En réponse au slogan de Ford « la couleur qu'on veut, du moment que c'est noir », General Motors lance ses modèles dans un éventail chromatique rendu possible par les nouvelles laques Duco à séchage rapide.

À Hollywood, Harley Earl, le « designer des stars », crée le premier modèle « couture » : la LaSalle 1927. L'année suivante, Earl fonde le département Art et couleur de General Motors, dont la tâche consiste à dessiner de nouveaux modèles chaque année – comme dans la mode. Si Cadillac et Packard occupent le haut du marché et la Ford T le bas, désormais une grande variété de modèles existent entre les deux. Parmi eux figure Chrysler, qui propose également les marques Dodge et Plymouth. Les patrons de sociétés automobiles deviennent les ambassadeurs de leurs marques lorsque Henry Ford écrit une lettre ouverte, largement utilisée dans les publicités, pour le lancement du nouveau modèle Ford. Dans ses annonces, Walter Chrysler invite quant à lui le public à « comparer les trois » voitures à bas prix : la Chevrolet, la Ford et sa propre Plymouth.

Avec l'arrivée du démarreur électrique, introduit par Cadillac en 1912 et rapidement adopté, les femmes deviennent une des principales cibles de la publicité automobile. Les femmes auront un impact radical sur le marketing automobile, écrit Virginia Scharff dans son livre *Les Femmes et l'avènement de la société motorisée* (1991). Des nouveaux coloris à la transmission automatique, quantité d'innovations voient le jour dans le but de séduire les femmes. Les constructeurs font passer dans *Vogue*, *Good Housekeeping*, *Ladies Home Journal* et autres magazines féminins des annonces spécifiquement destinées aux femmes.

1926

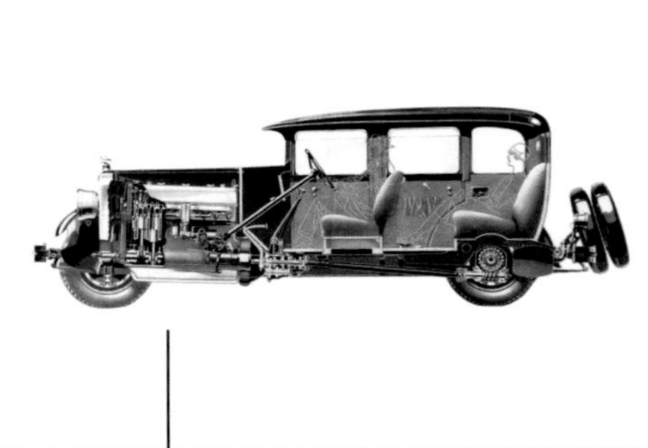

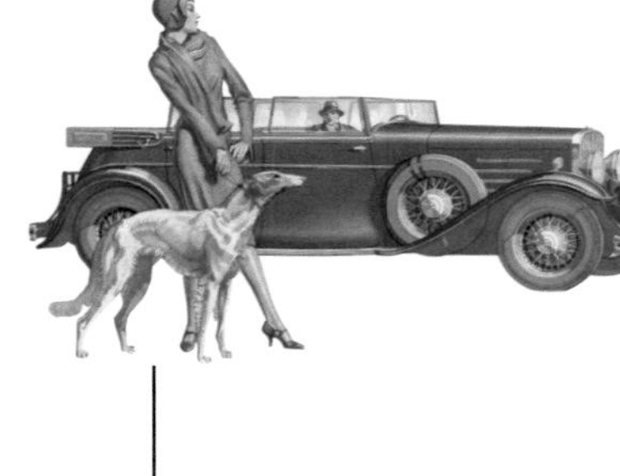

1926 Octane scale introduced

Einführung der Oktanzahl

Lancement du taux d'octane

1926 Safety glass first offered, making closed cars less dangerous in accidents

Sicherheitsglas reduziert die Verletzungsgefahr bei Unfällen in geschlossenen Wagen

Apparition du verre sécurit, qui limite les dangers en cas d'accident

1927 Ford introduces Model A for 1928 model year

Ford präsentiert das Model A für das Modelljahr 1928

Ford lance le modèle A, modèle de l'année 1928

1929 Great Depression begins; auto ads more formal, aimed at wealthy buyers

Beginn der Weltwirtschaftskrise; eher nüchterne Autowerbung zielt auf betuchte Käuferschichten

Début de la grande Dépression ; plus soucieuse des convenances, la publicité automobile cible une clientèle riche

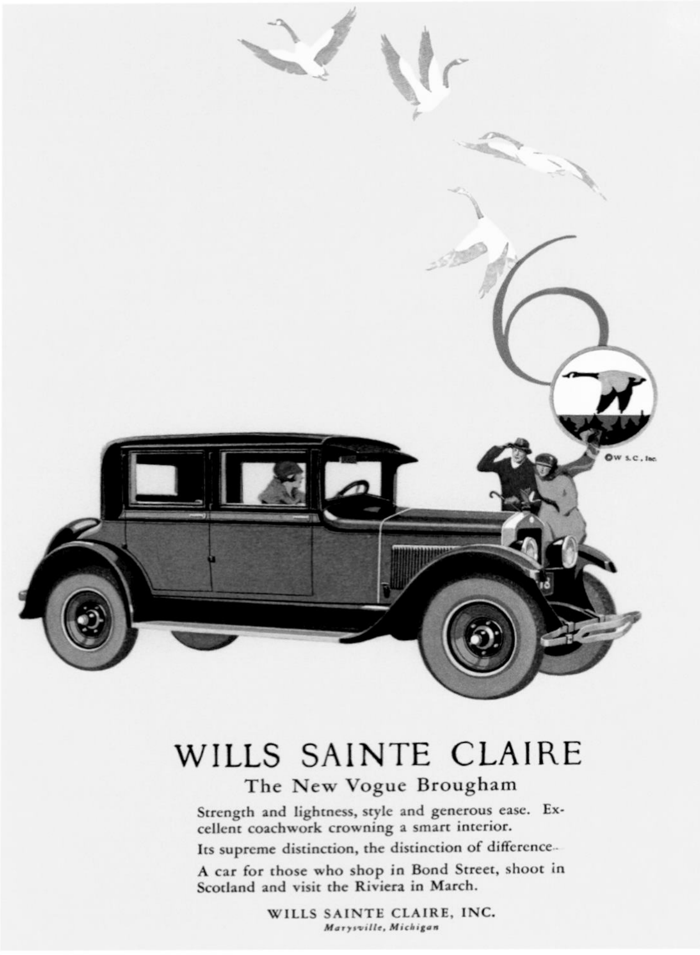

©W.S.C., Inc.
WILLS SAINTE CLAIRE
The New Vogue Brougham
Strength and lightness, style and generous ease. Excellent coachwork crowning a smart interior.
Its supreme distinction, the distinction of difference.
A car for those who shop in Bond Street, shoot in Scotland and visit the Riviera in March.
WILLS SAINTE CLAIRE, INC.
Marysville, Michigan

58 THE SATURDAY EVENING POST February 2, 1929

Long Hills? . . they're *made* for a Flying Cloud

If a hill makes you say, "Will she do it?"—you're in the wrong car. Hills should be the drama of touring, a quickened rhythm of excitement as the road rises—a long effortless sweep of power that carries you past the gear-shifters, the panting engines that haven't quite enough. The Flying Cloud has taken pet bad hills from Maine to California, from Canada to the Gulf. Show her the wickedest one in your neighborhood . . . and she won't be happy till she has the crest under her wheels. Then take her down, gunshot swift and safe as a church, and park her in front of the smartest hotel you know. Nothing can shake her *savoir faire*. She's a thoroughbred—from her engine out. REO MOTOR CAR CO · LANSING, MICHIGAN

REO
FLYING CLOUD
MATE MASTER

Now you can have a Reo Flying Cloud for less than ever before

1929 sees on the road Reo Flying Cloud *the Mate*—a car worthy, in every respect, to bear the name Reo Flying Cloud.

REO FLYING CLOUD *THE MASTER* IS PRICED FROM $1595 TO $1895

REO FLYING CLOUD *THE MATE* IS PRICED FROM $1375 TO $1520

102

► Hudson, 1928

Artistic, sophisticated imagery created an upscale image for one of the smaller carmakers. Hudson aimed to evoke an association with the upper class through images of the idle wealthy lounging in a drawing room or the elite world of horseback riding.

Hudson, einer der kleineren Hersteller, setzte auf künstlerische Raffinesse. Um mit der Oberschicht assoziiert zu werden, zeigte man Bilder von betuchten Müßiggängern im Salon oder aus der elitären Welt des Reitsports.

Grâce à une palette artistique sophistiquée, les publicitaires confèrent une image haut de gamme à ce petit constructeur. Pour se voir associé aux classes supérieures, Hudson met en scène de riches oisifs au salon ou à cheval.

Wills Sainte Claire, 1926

REO Flying Cloud, 1929

HUDSON

OAKLAND

Marmon, 1929

Unable to compete with the ad buys of the major manufacturers, it was left to the secondary automakers to compete by innovation in the pages of American magazines. Marmon, for example, relied on avant-garde influences, as seen in the dynamic graphics of their advertisements.

Da sie mit dem Anzeigenaufkommen der führenden Hersteller nicht mithalten konnte, suchte die zweite Riege mit Innovationen auf sich aufmerksam zu machen. Marmon etwa setzte auf Avantgardistisches, wie in der dynamischen Gestaltung seiner Anzeigen zu sehen war.

Incapables de concurrencer la publicité des grands constructeurs, les petits doivent faire preuve d'imagination dans les revues américaines. Marmon, par exemple, s'appuie sur des influences avant-gardistes, comme en témoigne le graphisme dynamique de ses annonces.

Oakland Landaulet, 1929 ◂

55710 M
for Economical Transportation
CHEVROLET
The
Outstanding Chevrolet
of Chevrolet History
-a Six in the price range of the four!
A new era dawns in personal transportation, for The Outstanding Chevrolet now makes available all the advantages of a truly luxurious Six in the price range of the four! To women drivers, in particular, it carries an irresistible appeal. It offers all the smoothness, quietness and reserve power of a marvelous six-cylinder valve-in-head motor. Its magnificent new Fisher bodies were created by master designers whose art has lent distinction to some of the world's finest automobiles. Its new silent four-wheel brakes and ball bearing steering gear insure safe and effortless handling. And it operates with an economy averaging better than twenty miles to the gallon of gasoline! If you have not yet seen and driven this remarkable new Six, visit your Chevrolet dealer today!
The Roadster, $525; The Phaeton, $525; The Coach, $595; The Coupe, $595; The Sedan, $675; The Sport Cabriolet, $695; The Convertible Landau, $725. All prices f.o.b. Flint, Mich.
CHEVROLET MOTOR COMPANY - DETROIT, MICHIGAN
Division of General Motors Corporation
QUALITY AT LOW COST

Chrysler, 1926

Walter Chrysler, former star executive at Buick, bought the Maxwell Motor Company and renamed it after himself. His success showed the presence of a diverse, mature market for cars. Through the years, Chrysler would offer technical innovations and value. Indeed, the slogan for the 1929 Knudsen offered "a six for the price of a four."

Walter Chrysler, einst strahlender Präsident von Buick, erwarb die Maxwell Motor Company und gab ihr seinen Namen. Sein Erfolg bewies, dass eine rege, breit gefächerte Nachfrage bestand. Chrysler sollte über Jahre hinweg für technische Neuerungen und Hochwertigkeit stehen. Den 1929er Knudsen offerierte man als „Sechser zum Preis eines Vierers".

Walter Chrysler, ancien responsable senior chez Buick, rachète la firme Maxwell et lui donne son nom. Sa réussite témoigne de la diversité et de la maturité du marché. Au fil des années, Chrysler offre innovation technique et bon rapport qualité/prix, comme l'annonce le slogan de la Knudsen 1929 : « Une six pour le prix d'une quatre. »

Chevrolet, 1929 ◂

BUICK dependability and low operating costs are mentioned with enthusiasm whenever motor cars are discussed. *There is* an inner circle of satisfaction among motor car owners and Buick owners belong to it.

The
BETTER
BUICK

109

Studebaker Commander, 1927

Studebaker Chancellor, 1927

◂ Buick, 1926

Cadillac Imperial, 1930

Cadillac became one of the world's ultimate status symbols by subtly advertising that a car said as much about its owner as did his home or clothing. Buyers chose from a book of coachbuilder's designs, like those in a luxury housing development.

Der Cadillac wurde weltweit zu einem der ultimativen Statussymbole, indem man subtil damit warb, dass ein Auto so viel über seinen Besitzer aussagt wie seine Einrichtung oder Kleidung. Wie bei der Planung einer Luxusbehausung konnten die Käufer aus einem Musterbuch auswählen.

Cadillac devient un des plus grands symboles de prestige social en faisant subtilement valoir dans ses publicités qu'une voiture en dit aussi long sur son propriétaire que sa maison ou ses vêtements. La marque met à disposition de sa clientèle un catalogue digne d'un promoteur de résidences de luxe.

► Cadillac, 1927

Hupmobile Eight, 1927 Franklin, 1929

Cadillac, 1929 Peerless Six-61, 1929

For Those Who Know and Appreciate the Finest in Motor Cars

ROAD MAP

CHRYSLER has wrought in the 112 h. p. Imperial "80" an entirely new kind of performance, style and appearance in the field of the finest cars . . . ¶ Its engine is unmatched for smooth power. It has an extraordinary reserve to achieve further marvels in speed, acceleration and hill-climbing . . . ¶ Its bodies are remarkable for their long, graceful lines, their fine upholstery and fittings, charm and diversity of chromatic colorings, and are indeed luxurious without even a hint of over-ornamentation . . . ¶ Ownership of a Chrysler Imperial "80" indicates appreciation of the finest in motor cars.

THE NEW 112 H.P. CHRYSLER IMPERIAL "80"

Open and closed custom-built body types by Chrysler, Dietrich, Locke and LeBaron, ranging in price from $2795 to $6795. All prices f. o. b. Detroit, subject to current Federal excise tax. Chrysler dealers are in position to extend the convenience of time payments.

Chrysler Imperial 80, 1928

► LaSalle, 1929

Marketed as a less-expensive sibling to Cadillac, the LaSalle was the first intentionally "styled" vehicle. Designed by Harley Earl – the first head of design at General Motors and the founding father of the profession – he adapted the look of high-end custom bodies, previously reserved for the wealthy, to mass production.

Als preiswerteres Pendant des Cadillac vermarktet, war der LaSalle das erste wirklich „durchgestylte" Fahrzeug. Sein Designer Harley Earl, erster Chefdesigner von General Motors und Begründer dieser Profession, adaptierte den Look der hochwertigen, bislang den Wohlhabenden vorbehaltenen Spezialkarossen für die Massenfertigung.

Présentée comme la petite sœur, moins coûteuse, de la Cadillac, la LaSalle est le premier véhicule « design ». Harley Earl – premier designer en chef chez General Motors et père fondateur de la profession – adapte à la production en série le look des carrosseries jusqu'alors réservées aux riches.

Stutz, 1927

Stutz, 1927

When Cadillac Makes Such A Statement You Know It Is So . .

Cadillac can honestly say that in twenty-three years it has never exaggerated or over-emphasized and Cadillac can still truthfully, honorably say: There are no motor car manufacturing plants in the world in which every other consideration is so completely set aside for the attainment of the highest possible quality and precision as the magnificent manufacturing laboratories in which Cadillac and La Salle are produced.

WITH the wealth of surpassing new engineering and manufacturing refinements in today's Cadillacs and La Salles, it becomes more obvious than ever before that if you want the kind of luxurious motoring that Cadillac provides, you simply must drive a Cadillac or La Salle. ✣ Three new safety features incorporated in both Cadillac and La Salle would, for themselves alone, lead you to these cars to the exclusion of everything else on the market: The new Cadillac-La Salle Syncro-Mesh Silent-Shift Transmission; the Duplex-Mechanical System of Four-Wheel Brakes; and Cadillac-La Salle Security-Plate Glass in all windows, doors and windshields. ✣ Prestige, beauty, long life, brilliant performance—these you know Cadillac and La Salle possess. Now have these newest features explained to you, and experience them for yourself Drive a Cadillac or La Salle, and see if you can find their equal elsewhere.

✣

La Salle is priced from $2295 to $2875; Cadillac $3295 to $3995; Fleetwoods up to $7000—all prices f. o. b. Detroit. Cadillac-La Salle dealers welcome business on the General Motors Deferred Payment Plan.

CADILLAC - LA SALLE

CADILLAC MOTOR CAR COMPANY • DIVISION OF GENERAL MOTORS • DETROIT, MICH. • OSHAWA, CAN.

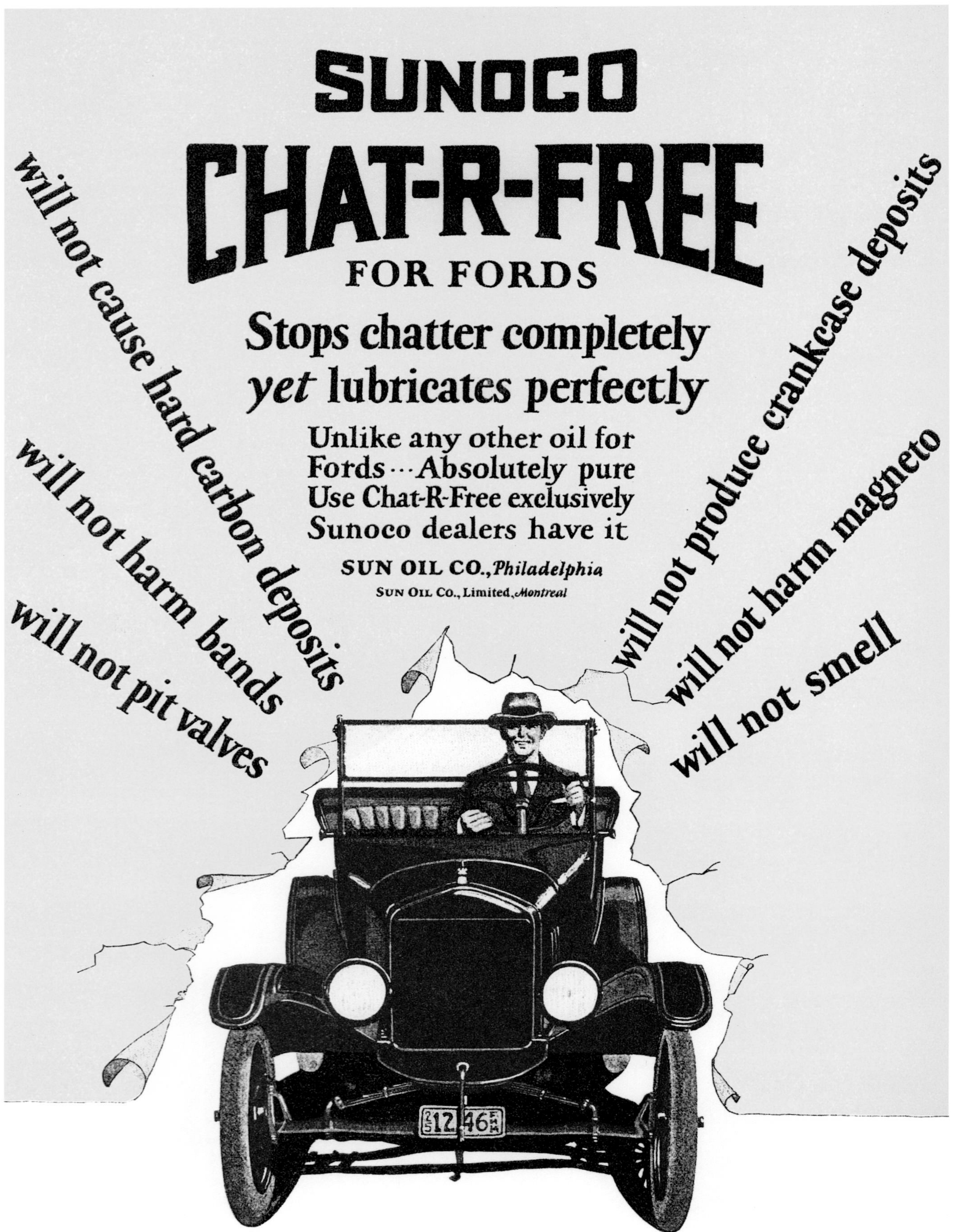
SUNOCO
CHAT-R-FREE
FOR FORDS
Stops chatter completely
yet lubricates perfectly
Unlike any other oil for
Fords···Absolutely pure
Use Chat-R-Free exclusively
Sunoco dealers have it
SUN OIL CO., Philadelphia
SUN OIL CO., Limited, Montreal
will not cause hard carbon deposits
will not harm bands
will not pit valves
will not produce crankcase deposits
will not harm magneto
will not smell

Sunoco Oil, 1925

▸ Michelin Tires, 1925

MICHELIN
COMFORT
BALLOON
Michelin is the oldest of the world's automobile tire makers. Always a leader, Michelin is now forging ahead faster than ever. Last year Michelin's sales grew three times as fast as those of the tire industry as a whole. To-day, 25,000 men are kept busy in Michelin factories to supply the great demand for Michelin Tires and Tubes.

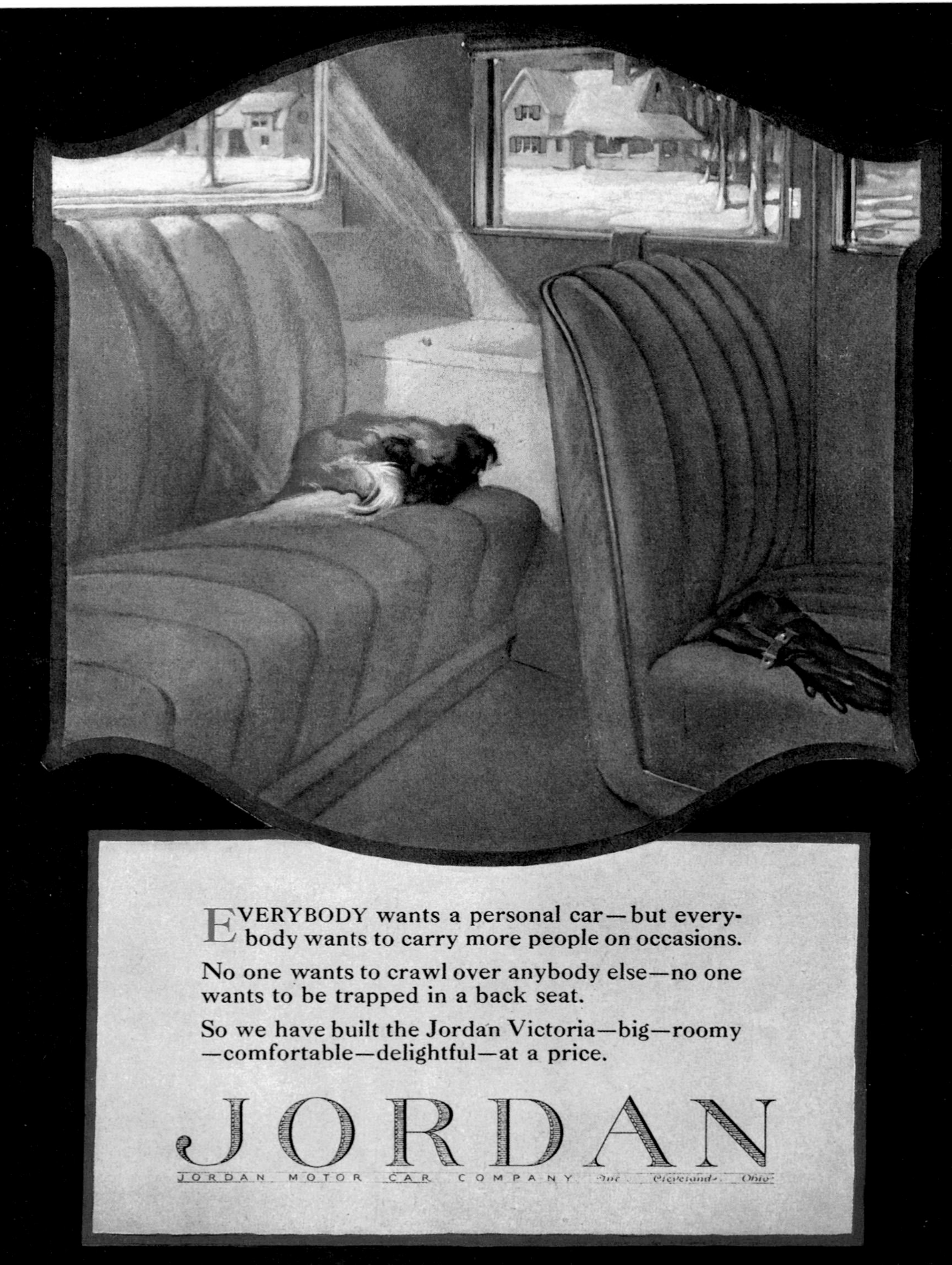

EVERYBODY wants a personal car—but everybody wants to carry more people on occasions.
No one wants to crawl over anybody else—no one wants to be trapped in a back seat.
So we have built the Jordan Victoria—big—roomy—comfortable—delightful—at a price.
JORDAN
JORDAN MOTOR CAR COMPANY

► Jordan Playboy, 1923

The Jordan Playboy is pretty much forgotten, but the ad for it in *The Saturday Evening Post* is perhaps the most famous automobile ad of all time. The company's owner, Edward "Ned" Jordan, was on a train ride through Wyoming "somewhere west of Laramie" when he spotted a woman on a horse through the window. He immediately associated her with his car – a "cross of the wild and the tame," wrote the ad and hired Fred Cole to illustrate it.

Den Jordan Playboy kennt heute kaum noch jemand, doch die in *The Saturday Evening Post* erschienene Anzeige ist vielleicht die berühmteste Autowerbeanzeige aller Zeiten. Firmenchef Edward „Ned" Jordan fuhr im Zug durch Wyoming, als er „irgendwo westlich von Laramie" eine Frau auf einem Pferd erblickte. Sofort assoziierte er sie mit seinem Auto (eine „Mischung aus wild und zahm"), verfasste den Werbetext und beauftragte Fred Cole mit der Illustration.

Aujourd'hui tombée dans l'oubli, la Jordan a sans doute bénéficié de la plus célèbre publicité automobile de tous les temps, qui fut publiée dans le *Saturday Evening Post*. Le patron de la société, Edward « Ned » Jordan, traversait le Wyoming en train quand, « quelque part à l'ouest de Laramie », il aperçut par la fenêtre une femme à cheval. Il associa aussitôt cette vision à sa voiture – « sauvage mais apprivoisée » selon son slogan, qu'il fit illustrer par Fred Cole.

Jordan Victoria, 1923

Somewhere West of Laramie

SOMEWHERE west of Laramie there's a broncho-busting, steer-roping girl who knows what I'm talking about. She can tell what a sassy pony, that's a cross between greased lightning and the place where it hits, can do with eleven hundred pounds of steel and action when he's going high, wide and handsome.

The truth is—the Jordan Playboy was built for her.

JORDAN

JORDAN MOTOR CAR COMPANY, Inc., Cleveland, Ohio

"Most Automobiles are like most Men
"They are either all right or all wrong, but seldom one or the other for long at a time."
"That's probably why they call this a Woman's Car, it's so consistent."
"Your intuition, my dear, is perfect. That's just it. You know, I used to call the last car we had, a 'Cook Four,' because it cost more than it was worth, consumed more than it earned, and was always quitting!"
"And what do you call this?"
"Oh, the Overland is like a first-rate cook — popular with the whole family! This is the first Saturday I've had this car to myself since—"
"Heavens, Helen, you went right into that mudhole!"
"Didn't jar you, did it?"
"No, not at all! But isn't it remarkable for so light a car?"
"Yes. Harry calls it a feather bed on wheels. It's some funny new spring they've invented that lets you down easy when the going's hard. How do you like the tan velour upholstery?"
"Just love it, Helen, it is so restrained. But how about gas?"
"That's restrained, too, my dear. Harry says we're averaging twenty-five miles to the gallon."
"Twenty-five miles?"
"Sounds as incredible as a woman's age, but it's true. In fact, I've only one complaint against this Overland Sedan — it's too useful!"
"Too useful?"
"Yes, too useful. So useful that it points a moral."
"For example?"
"Well, all you ever have to do with this Overland Sedan is to step on it. And that is the fate of all useful things and all useful people. Somebody is always stepping on them!"
"Helen, you talk like a Socialist."
"It's true. This little Overland Sedan is like a household drudge — always working and never through!"
"You'd better hurry, Helen, the train's in. We'll miss Harry."
"Don't worry. He'll wait. There he is now.... oh, Harry!"
"Hello, girls! Have you room for a few bundles and may a husband presume to ride home in his wife's car?"
WILLYS-OVERLAND, INC., TOLEDO, OHIO
Sedans, Coupés, Touring Cars, Roadsters
Willys-Overland, Limited, Toronto, Canada
The John N. Willys Export Corp., New York
Overland
TRADE MARK REG.

Overland, 1921 ◂

An early psychological appeal to women linked automobiles to mates. It proposed both offered the timeless trade-off between excitement and dependability.

Autos, so versuchte die Psychologie dieser frühen Anzeige den Frauen zu vermitteln, sind den Männern nicht unähnlich. Anscheinend boten doch beide einen zeitlosen Kompromiss aus Aufregung und Verlässlichkeit.

Très tôt, l'automobile séduit la femme, qui établit un lien psychologique entre la voiture et l'homme, qui semblent tous deux offrir un compromis entre « émotions fortes » et « fiabilité ».

Kelly Tires, 1924

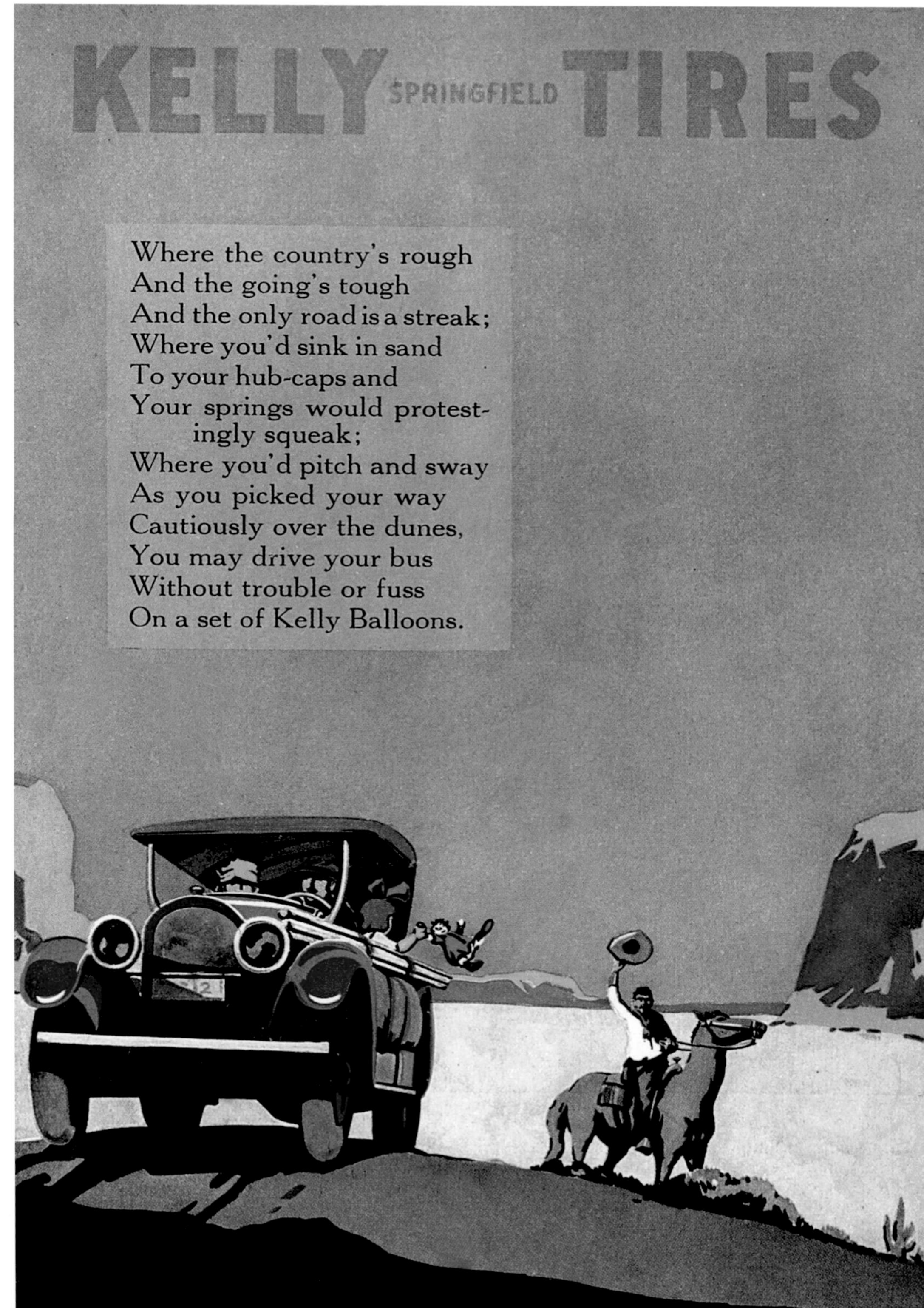
KELLY SPRINGFIELD TIRES
Where the country's rough
And the going's tough
And the only road is a streak;
Where you'd sink in sand
To your hub-caps and
Your springs would protest-
ingly squeak;
Where you'd pitch and sway
As you picked your way
Cautiously over the dunes,
You may drive your bus
Without trouble or fuss
On a set of Kelly Balloons.

LINCOLN
The Berline Landaulet
The goal of Lincoln builders is to build a motor car which shall reach today's peak of performance. Their next purpose is to beautify the car to the point where nothing is left undone to suit the most fastidious. ℭ How well they succeed is demonstrated by the action and beauty of this Berline Landaulet by Willoughby.
LINCOLN MOTOR COMPANY
Division of Ford Motor Company

LINCOLN
All-Weather Cabriolet
It has been so wisely said that minute attention to detail makes perfection. This truth is admirably illustrated in the Lincoln All-Weather Cabriolet. Even to the smallest detail this richly appointed car offers the very utmost in motoring satisfaction. Its interior fittings and appointments achieve a standard of comfort and convenience worthy of the satin-smooth performance of the precision-built Lincoln. The driver's compartment permits either Enclosed Drive or Town Car effect.
LINCOLN MOTOR COMPANY
Division of Ford Motor Company

LINCOLN
FOUR-PASSENGER TOWN SEDAN—By Willoughby
The fact that more Lincolns have been sold than any other car costing as much or more is convincing evidence that Lincoln value, quality and appearance are appreciated by those who buy fine cars.
Lincoln quality is beyond the measurement of price—in its balanced excellence it can be obtained only in the Lincoln—and measured only by the Lincoln standard; and because it can be obtained only in the Lincoln, there are no comparisons possible—at any price. ℭ That the Lincoln price for Lincoln quality happens to be low is due entirely to the economies made possible by the genius and resources of the Ford manufacturing organization which is known the world over for the great value it gives in all the products it makes. ℭ The exclusive distinction of Lincoln quality is expressed in Lincoln appearance—and everywhere admired by those who recognize unembellished fineness. For instance, the Four-Passenger Town Sedan above illustrated beautifully suggests the inherent fineness of Lincoln quality.
LINCOLN MOTOR COMPANY
Division of Ford Motor Company

LINCOLN
Club Roadster
Nowhere is the balanced excellence of Lincoln performance more appreciated than it is in this intimately personal car. As an open car the Club Roadster has the swift fleetness of Lincoln speed and Lincoln easy riding luxury for the all day distant trip. In performance—it is a Lincoln. As a closed car it is a beautifully distinctive coupe—a masterly design by a famous custom body builder. There is not a flaw in its expression of true quality and fineness—no compromise in any detail. Made for the most discriminating users of personally driven cars, its fittings and appointments are as fine as art and skill can fashion. In quality—it is a Lincoln!
LINCOLN MOTOR COMPANY
Division of Ford Motor Company

Lincoln Berline Landaulet, 1927 Lincoln All-Weather Cabriolet, 1928

Lincoln Four-Passenger Town Sedan, 1928 Lincoln Club Roadster, 1928

Seven-Passenger Sport Touring—by *Locke*

LONG, low and graceful in every line and curve, beautifully expressive of great power and inexhaustible speed . . . A motor as quiet and vibrationless as it is possible to make a superb piece of power machinery . . . Complete safety and effortless control even at the highest speeds . . . Equipment and appointments as fine as the quality-markets of the world affords . . . Spacious room for seven—even for the two passengers in the auxiliary seats. Restful touring comfort even across a continent. These are definite Lincoln qualities that make this a master-car among all fine open cars!

Aluminum body custom-designed by Locke—upholstered in soft, hand crushed Morocco in color to blend with the finish—a sport top of finest Burbank cloth with mahogany finished bows, nickel trimmed, compactly folding. Unlimited selection of color combinations. Six wire wheels—spares at the side or rear. Folding trunk rack.

LINCOLN MOTOR COMPANY

Division of Ford Motor Company

Lincoln Seven-Passenger Sport Touring, 1928

Wm Neu
8-88 Sedan $2195. Straight Eight, 130" Wheelbase, 80 M. P. H.
The Greatest Straight Eight
Power, comfort, ease of handling and long life, greater than you have ever known before. 6-66—$1095 to $1345. 8-77—$1395 to $1745. 8-88—$1995 to $2595. Freight, Tax and Equipment extra.
AUBURN AUTOMOBILE COMPANY, AUBURN, INDIANA
AUBURN

Auburn 8-88 Sedan, 1927

8-88 ROADSTER $1995
80 Miles Per Hour
130 Inch Wheelbase
Five Passenger Capacity
Door for Rear Seat
6-66. $1095 to $1345 8-77. $1395 to $1745 8-88. $1995 to $2595 Freight, Tax and Equipment Extra
AUBURN AUTOMOBILE COMPANY, AUBURN, INDIANA
Wm Neu-
AUBURN

Auburn 8-88 Roadster, 1927

at no extra cost

$695

AND UP AT FACTORY

ESSEX

Buyers of Essex the Challenger last month were supplied with more than 225 color combinations to their individual orders, and at no extra cost. Your own dealer is prepared to give you the same wide choice, and will forward your selection to the factory for prompt delivery. Orders are shipped from factory within 48 hours.

THE CHALLENGER

THE SUPREME INTERPRETATION OF COLOR HARMONIES
CREATED AND CARRIED ON BY DUCO

BUILDERS of motor cars are now, more than ever before, builders of beauty. The speed, the power, the endurance of the automobile are taken almost for granted. Familiar, too, the graceful lines of long, low-slung bodies. The present note, the new beauty, the last great forward step—is color.

The creation of Duco made possible this final expression of the vogue in motor car design. For in Duco, makers found at last a finish rich in tone, bright of hue. They learned that the sun and the rain and the snow could not fade its clear, vivid beauty.

But the challenge of beauty in motor car design finds du Pont still looking far ahead, toward a contribution that will give the modern vogue of color its highest interpretation.

The constant research of du Pont chemists has brought Duco to new heights of technical perfection. And through du Pont's association, in Paris and other European centers, with the sources of the changing modes, the owners of motor cars can now obtain the supreme interpretation of color harmonies, each season, on the leading cars in every price class, as well as on their present cars through a nation-wide chain of Authorized Duco Refinishing Stations.

Duco, which made possible the vogue of color, still dominates the color vogue today.

E. I. du Pont de Nemours & Co., Inc., Chemical Products Division, Parlin, N. J., Detroit, Mich., Chicago, Ill., San Francisco, Cal., Everett, Mass., or Flint Paint and Varnish Limited, Toronto, Canada

THERE IS ONLY *ONE* DUCO . . . *DU PONT* DUCO

Dupont Duco Paint, 1928

With the introduction of Duco paints in the mid-'20s, Henry Ford's basic black became a thing of the past. Oakland's True Blue, released in 1924, offered the first color choices for automobiles. Essex followed soon afterward with Algerian Blue.

Mit Einführung der Duco-Lacke Mitte der 1920er-Jahre landete Henry Fords schlichtes Schwarz in der Mottenkiste. Oaklands „True Blue" von 1924 brachte erstmals Farbe ins Spiel. Bald darauf folgte Essex mit seinem „Algerian Blue".

Avec l'arrivée des laques Duco vers 1925, le noir tout simple de Henry Ford passe aux oubliettes. La True Blue, lancée par Oakland en 1924 est la première voiture disponible en divers coloris. Peu après, Essex proposera le bleu algérien.

Essex The Challenger, 1929 ◂

There Is No Other Tire Like It

The new *Dual*-Balloon principle *alone* has been successful in combining greater mileage with regular balloon low-pressure — and with this low-pressure there is the extra advantage of the longer wearing, non-skid tread which will carry you through season after season of safety and assurance. ~ ~ In this day of speedy stop-and-go traffic a more effective and permanent non-skid is essential. The tire that will not wear prematurely "bald" holds every assurance of security for many seasons to come. ~ ~ On all roads you want trouble-free travel, without the annoyance of a moment's attention to the tires, without the tension of tire worry — the new experience of never having a puncture or a moment's delay because of your rubber. ~ ~ Whatever particular feature you most desire you can take in full measure from the *Dual*-Balloon. The General Tire and Rubber Company, Akron, Ohio.

128

"Viewing the Grand Canyon." Painted by Walter Klett for the General Tire and Rubber Co., Akron, Ohio.

The New GENERAL DUAL-BALLOON 8

—goes a long way to make friends

General Tires, 1929

With tire prices so low why be satisfied with anything less than the General

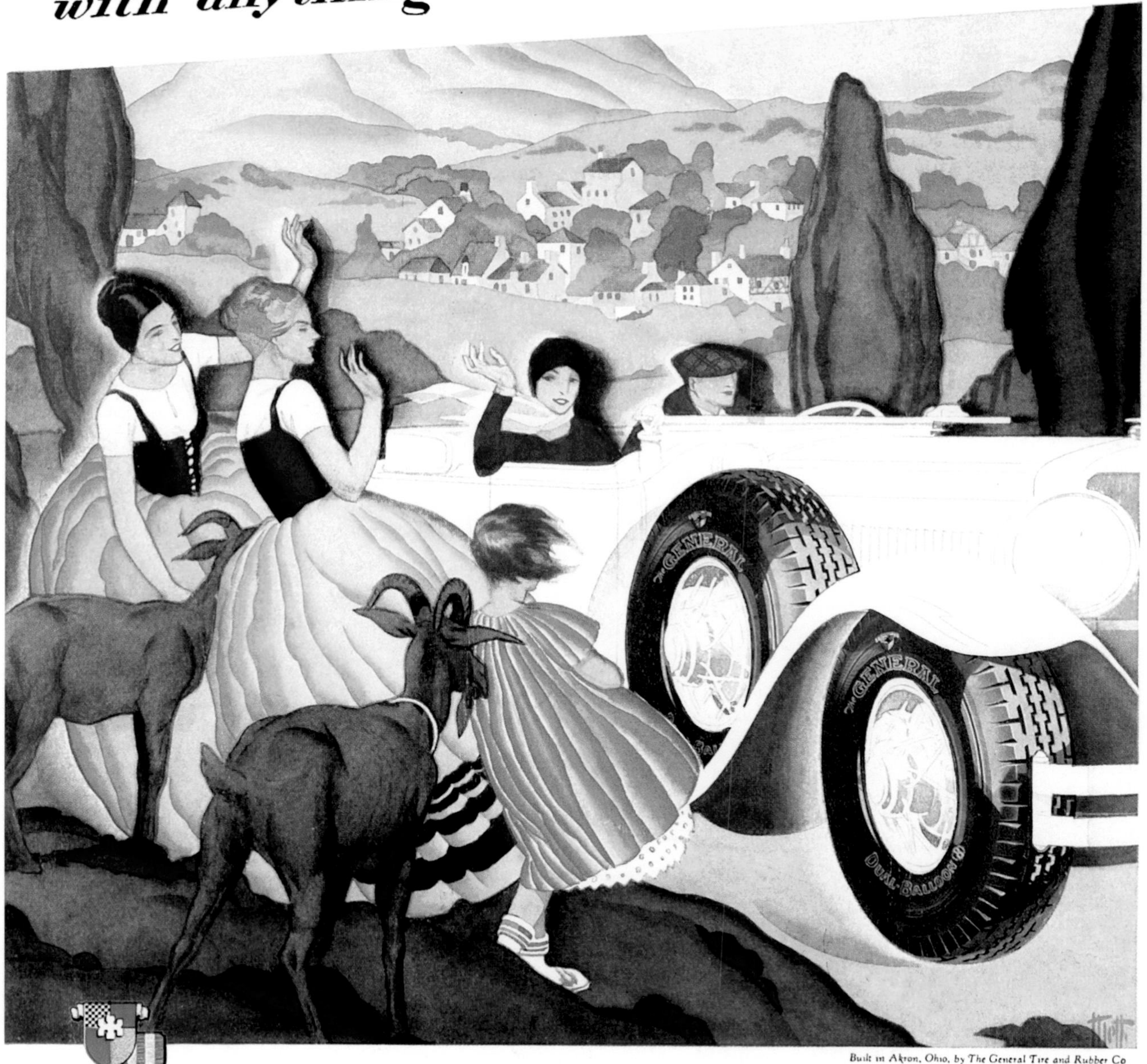

The New GENERAL DUAL-BALLOON 8

General Tires, 1929

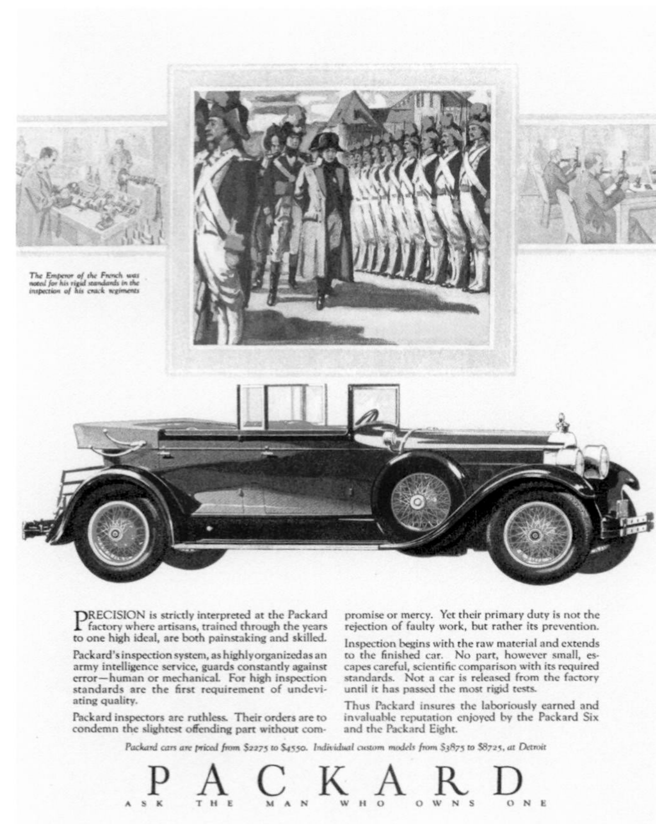

PACKARD

Ability and achievement have ever won permanent place in those organizations consecrated to one high ideal

Packard men bear the imprint of the Packard organization. They are selected and schooled for but one quality of work and service. It shows, and it pays—both them and Packard.

From skilled machinist to designing engineer, Packard cars are produced by men who know and love fine things—men brought up in the interpretation and application of quality ideals. From suburban dealer to manager of sales, Packard's clientele is served by men who uphold the Packard principles—men who know that the patronage of the discriminating brooks no compromise with quality either in product or in service.

For a single standard of high quality is ever uppermost in the minds of the Packard management—and the Packard organization is the guardian of a priceless reputation.

ASK THE MAN WHO OWNS ONE

Packard, 1928

Packard, 1929

▸ LaSalle, 1928

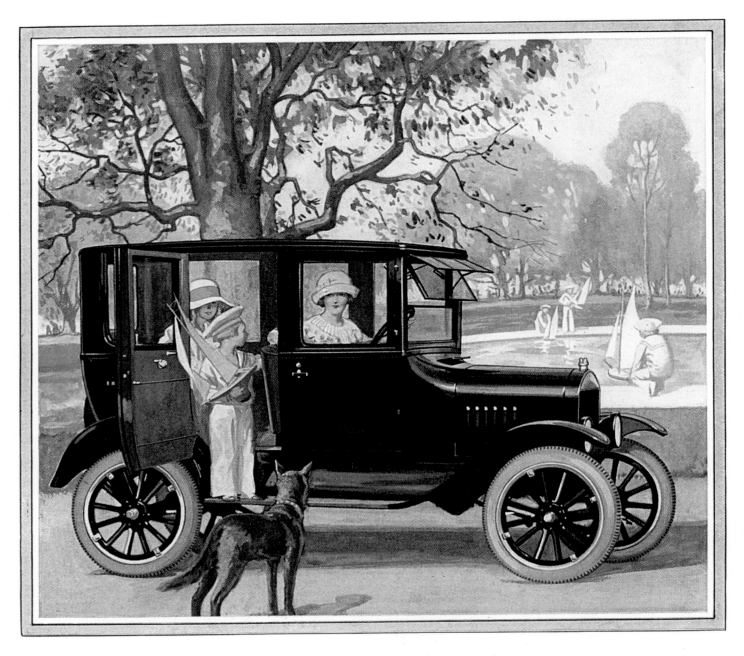

AS COOL in summer, as it is snug and weatherproof in winter, the Ford Closed Car has an unfailing appeal to women and children, who appreciate its many features of comfort.

Furnishings and equipment of the Sedan are of the highest order, including soft, durable cushions, revolving type window lifts, windshield visor, cowl ventilator, rugs, dome light, door locks, electric starting and lighting equipment.

And the Ford Closed Car costs so little to own and operate that mother and children can use it daily for every errand of business or pleasure.

TUDOR SEDAN, $590 FORDOR SEDAN, $685 COUPE, $525 (All prices f. o. b. Detroit)

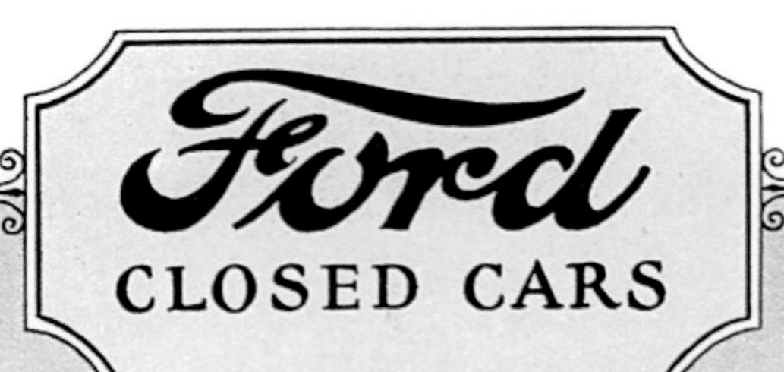

Chevrolet, 1926

Chevrolet competed with Ford's Model T not by trying to match the low price — an impossibility — but by offering more for the money. By the mid-'20s, it caught up in sales.

Um sich gegen Fords Model T behaupten zu können, versuchte Chevrolet erst gar nicht, preislich gleichzuziehen. Vielmehr bot man mehr fürs Geld. Mitte der Zwanziger hatte man aufgeholt.

Chevrolet concurrence la Ford T, non pas sur le prix (c'est impossible), mais sur le rapport qualité/prix. Vers 1925, les ventes des deux modèles se valent.

Ford, 1924 ◂

N. W. Ayers campaign for the Model A showed it as America's car, set in front of white fences, beside bungalows and on small town main streets, with active families all about.

Die Agentur N. W. Ayer präsentierte den Ford als das US-Auto, sei es vor weiß gestrichenen Zäunen, neben Bungalows oder in kleinstädtischen Hauptstraßen, stets umgeben von aktiven Familien.

La campagne de N. W. Ayer pour Ford vante « la » voiture de l'Amérique, représentée devant des clôtures blanches, à côté de petites maisons ou dans la rue principale d'une petite ville, avec des familles qui s'activent tout autour.

▸▸ Franklin, 1929

STONER

THIS WAS THE DECADE OF STREAMLINING, WITH AERODYNAMIC SHAPES, SPEED LINES AND STREAMLINES. THE BOLD NEW DESIGNS SEEMED DEVISED AS MUCH TO CUT THOUGH THE WIND AS TO CUT THROUGH THE ECONOMIC DRAG OF THE DECADE.

DIES WAR DAS JAHRZEHNT DER STROMLINIENFORM. DIE NEUEN GEWAGTEN ENTWÜRFE WAREN OFFENBAR EBENSO DAFÜR GEDACHT, SICH GEGEN DEN WIND WIE DIE ALLGEMEINE WIRTSCHAFTSFLAUTE ZU BEHAUPTEN.

LA DÉCENNIE EST ÉGALEMENT MARQUÉE PAR L'AFFINEMENT DES LIGNES ET L'AVÈNEMENT DE FORMES AÉRODYNAMIQUES POUR UNE VITESSE ACCRUE. LES AUDACIEUX NOUVEAUX MODÈLES SEMBLENT CONÇUS POUR DÉFIER LE VENT AUTANT QUE LE RALENTISSEMENT ÉCONOMIQUE.

STREAMLINING HITS THE STREETS
STROMLINIENFORM AUCH AUF DER STRASSE
L'AÉRODYNAMISME GAGNE LA RUE

-1939

Lincoln, 1931 ◂◂

Packard Eight Deluxe, 1932 ◂

Riverside Batteries, 1931

1932 SAW THE ARRIVAL OF FORD'S REASONABLY PRICED FLATHEAD V8 ENGINE, PROBABLY THE MOST SUCCESSFUL ENGINE OF ALL TIME. The infamous criminal couple Bonnie Parker and Clyde Barrow wrote to Henry Ford in 1934 to express their appreciation for the acceleration the engine afforded. But it was not quite good enough: The pair were shot by police in their Ford V8 a few months later. While the handwriting of the letter has never been authenticated, Henry Ford was nonetheless quick to capitalize on the pair's appeal and widely publicized the document.

Until the 1930s, car bodies included many wooden parts, and most roofs were constructed from wood. Only by the middle of the decade did GM introduce the steel "Turret Top." It would be a few more years until metal bodies, made of parts stamped out by huge machines, became standard. This was also the decade of streamlining, with aerodynamic shapes, speed lines, and streamlines. The bold new designs seemed devised as much to cut though the wind as to cut through the economic drag of the decade.

The Depression meant not only the end of many small companies but of such famed coachbuilders as Dietrich and LeBaron, as well as great luxury marques like Pierce-Arrow and Duesenberg. Cadillac survived in part by opening sales to African Americans; Packard, meanwhile, began its steady decline in prestige until it too died, in the 1950s.

The designs of the cars themselves had become an important part of the sales process, and modern ads and promotions came with the territory. World's Fairs in Chicago, in 1933, and New York, in 1939, showed off visions of the cars of the future from Norman Bel Geddes, Raymond Loewy, Walter Dorwin Teague, as well as other designers. Streamliners such as Chrysler's Airflow and Lincoln's Zephyr and Continental claimed aircraft-style construction and body shape. "Look out for the clouds!" intoned an ad for the Zephyr. Associating cars with airplanes and flying, ads depicted the Chrysler Airflow and the Lincoln Zephyr beside aircraft. The 1938 Cadillac Sixty Special was featured in ads in front of a Boeing Clipper.

In 1938, the last year of his life, the great Mississippi blues singer Robert Johnson had his only hit with "Terraplane Blues," inspired by the fast Hudson Essex Terraplane automobile. "In the air, an airplane," went the car's slogan. "In the water, a hydroplane. On the earth, a Terraplane." Many other car songs would follow—as would car advertising jingles for radio and television ads. The automobile had become thoroughly interwoven with pop culture in song, story, and film, a fact advertisers would take advantage of.

Due largely to its financial credit structure, which allowed for buying on time, and its expanding used-car market, the United States quickly became the world leader in cars per capita. In 1939, France registered only 51 cars per thousand residents; Italy registered just 11, and Russia fewer than 5. The United States had 227 cars per thousand residents—and, more importantly, almost everyone also aspired to own one.

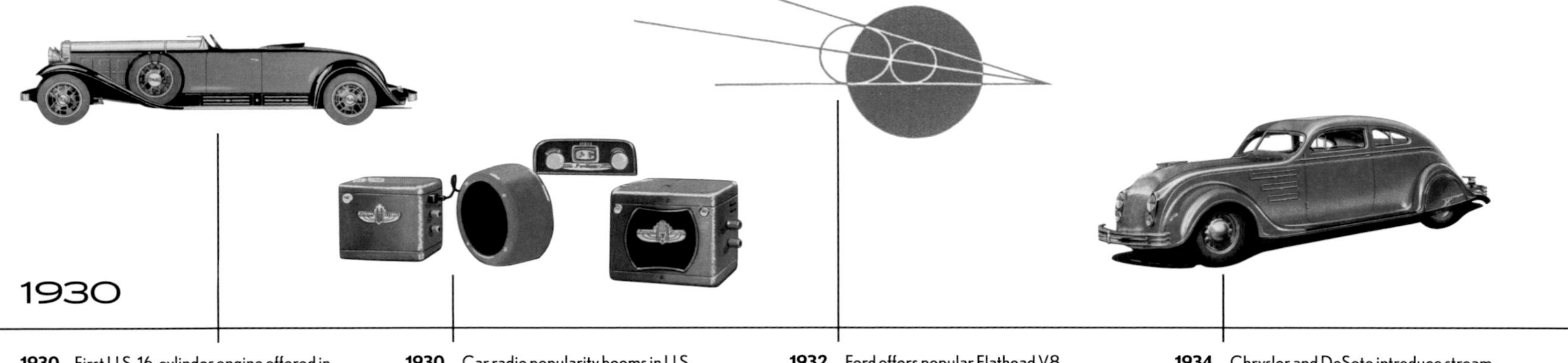

1930

1930 First U.S. 16-cylinder engine offered in Cadillac

Cadillac präsentiert das erste US-Modell mit 16-Zylinder-Motor

Premier moteur 16 soupapes proposé aux États-Unis par Cadillac

1930 Car radio popularity booms in U.S.

Autoradios in den USA en vogue

La popularité de l'autoradio croît en flèche aux États-Unis

1932 Ford offers popular Flathead V8

Ford findet Anklang mit dem Flathead V8-Motor

Ford lance le populaire V8 à culasses plates

1934 Chrysler and DeSoto introduce streamlined unibody Airflow models

Chrysler und DeSoto stellen ihre stromlinienförmigen Airflow-Modelle (Monocoque) vor

Chrysler et DeSoto proposent des modèles Airflow aux lignes aérodynamiques

FORD PRÄSENTIERTE 1932 MIT SEINEM RECHT PREISWERTEN FLATHEAD-V8-MOTOR DEN VERMUTLICH ERFOLGREICHSTEN AUTOMOTOR ALLER ZEITEN. Das berüchtigte Gaunerpaar Bonnie Parker und Clyde Barrow äußerte 1934 in einem Brief an Henry Ford seine Wertschätzung für die gute Beschleunigung. Doch diese sollte nicht ausreichen, denn beide wurden in ihrem Ford V8 ein paar Monate später von der Polizei erschossen. Auch wenn die Handschrift des Briefs niemals überprüft wurde, zögerte Henry Ford nicht, die von dem Gaunerpaar ausgehende Faszination zu nutzen und ließ das Schriftstück wiederholt veröffentlichen.

Bis in die 1930er-Jahre hinein bestanden die Autokarosserien vielfach aus Holzelementen. Erst Mitte des Jahrzehnts präsentierte GM das Ganzstahldach „Turret Top". Es sollten noch einige Jahre vergehen, bis sich Metallkarosserien durchsetzten, deren Einzelteile von gewaltigen Stanzen ausgespuckt wurden. Zugleich war dies das Jahrzehnt der Stromlinienform. Die neuen gewagten Entwürfe waren offenbar ebenso dafür gedacht, sich gegen den Wind wie die allgemeine Wirtschaftsflaute zu behaupten.

Die Depression bedeutete nicht nur das Ende vieler kleiner Firmen, sondern auch berühmter Karosseriebauer wie Dietrich und LeBaron sowie Nobelmarken wie Pierce-Arrow und Duesenberg. Cadillac überlebte unter anderem, weil man sich der afroamerikanischen Klientel öffnete. Packard verlor bis zum Ende in den 1950er-Jahren zunehmend an Prestige.

Das Design der Autos war zu einem bedeutenden Verkaufsaspekt geworden, begleitet von moderneren Anzeigen und Werbekampagnen. Auf den Weltausstellungen 1933 in Chicago und 1939 in New York präsentierten Designer wie Norman Bel Geddes, Raymond Loewy und Walter Dorwin Teague ihre Visionen von den Autos der Zukunft. Stromlinienautos wie Chryslers Airflow und die Modelle Zephyr und Continental von Lincoln orientierten sich technisch und optisch am Flugzeug. „Achten Sie auf die Wolken!", heißt es in einer Anzeige für den Zephyr. Autos sollten mit Flugzeugen und dem Fliegen assoziiert werden, weshalb der Chrysler Airflow und der Lincoln Zephyr in den Anzeigen zusammen mit einem Flugzeug abgebildet wurden. Der 1938er Cadillac Sixty Special wurde vor einer Boeing Clipper präsentiert.

Robert Johnson, der große Sänger des Mississippi Blues, hatte 1938, in seinem letzten Lebensjahr, mit „Terraplane Blues" seinen einzigen Hit. Pate stand der flotte Hudson Essex Terraplane, dessen Slogan lautete: „In the air, an airplane. In the water, a hydroplane. On the earth, a Terraplane." Viele weitere Autosongs sollten folgen – wie auch Jingles für die Autowerbung in Rundfunk und Fernsehen. Das Auto war zu einem wichtigen Bestandteil der Populärkultur geworden, sei es in Liedern, Prosa oder Spielfilmen – ein Umstand, den die Werbung nicht ungenutzt ließ.

Die Möglichkeit der Ratenzahlung sowie der expandierende Gebrauchtwagenmarkt trugen maßgeblich dazu bei, dass die USA rasch die weltweit höchste Automobildichte verzeichneten. In Frankreich gab es 1939 nur 51 Autos pro tausend Einwohner, in Italien zehn und in der Sowjetunion nicht einmal fünf. In den USA waren es 227 Autos pro tausend Einwohner und, wichtiger noch, fast jeder wollte eines besitzen.

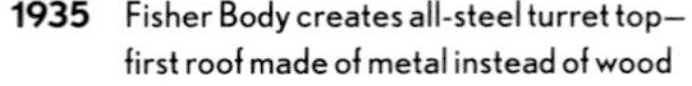

1935

1935 Fisher Body creates all-steel turret top—first roof made of metal instead of wood

Fisher Body präsentiert das Ganzstahldach „Turret Top" als erstes Autodach aus Metall anstatt Holz

Fisher Body crée le toit tout acier – premier toit en métal et non en bois

1936 Streamlined Lincoln Zephyr released

Vorstellung des aerodynamischen Lincoln Zephyr

Lancement de l'aérodynamique Lincoln Zephyr

1936 Mercedes offers first production diesel model

Mercedes präsentiert das erste serienmäßige Diesel-Modell

Mercedes propose sa première collection de modèles diesel

1938 Buick releases first cars with electric turn signals

Buick fertigt die ersten Autos mit elektrischem Fahrtrichtungsanzeiger

Buick propose ses premiers modèles à clignotants électriques

Pierce-Arrow, 1930 ◄◄

Buick Eight, 1934 ◄

►► Oldsmobile, 1933

L'ANNÉE 1932 VOIT L'ARRIVÉE DU MOTEUR V8 À CULASSES PLATES, COMMERCIALISÉ PAR FORD À UN PRIX RAISONNABLE, et sans doute le moteur le plus répandu de tous les temps. En 1934, le tristement célèbre couple Bonnie Parker et Clyde Barrow écrit à Henry Ford afin de le remercier pour la capacité d'accélération de ce moteur. Pourtant, cela ne suffira pas à sauver ces bandits : ils seront abattus par la police dans leur Ford V8 quelques mois plus tard. L'écriture sur le courrier n'a jamais été authentifiée, mais Henry Ford ne pouvait manquer l'occasion de miser sur ce témoignage, qu'il diffusa largement.

Jusque dans les années 1930, la carrosserie comprend maints éléments en bois. Il faudra attendre le milieu de la décennie pour que GM lance le « Turret Top », un toit d'une seule pièce en acier. Quelques années plus tard, les carrosseries en métal, composées d'éléments découpés par des machines gigantesques, deviendront à leur tour la norme. La décennie est également marquée par l'affinement des lignes et l'avènement de formes aérodynamiques pour une vitesse accrue. Les audacieux nouveaux modèles semblent conçus pour défier le vent autant que le ralentissement économique.

La Grande Dépression condamne une multitude de petites entreprises mais aussi de célèbres constructeurs comme Dietrich ou LeBaron et de grandes marques de luxe, telles Pierce-Arrow et Duesenberg. Cadillac survit en partie grâce à une ouverture au marché afro-américain ; Packard perd régulièrement de son prestige, jusqu'à disparaître à son tour dans les années 1950.

Le design des voitures elles-mêmes joue désormais un rôle important dans la vente, tandis que les annonces promotionnelles se modernisent. Les Foires internationales de Chicago en 1934 et de New York en 1939 offrent une vision des voitures du futur telles que les imaginent Norman Bel Geddes, Raymond Loewy, Walter Dorwin Teague et autres concepteurs. Les modèles aérodynamiques comme l'Airflow de Chrysler ou les Zephyr et Continental de Lincoln revendiquent un style de construction et une forme de carrosserie dignes de l'aéronautique. « La tête dans les nuages ! » clame une publicité pour la Zephyr ; l'Airflow de Chrysler et la Zephyr de Lincoln sont présentées aux côtés d'un avion. Dans les publicités, la Cadillac Sixty Special 1938 se tient aussi devant un Boeing.

En 1938, dernière année de sa vie, le grand chanteur de blues du Mississippi Robert Johnson connaît son unique succès avec *Terraplane Blues*, hommage à la rapide Hudson Essex Terraplane (« l'avion de terre »). « Dans les airs, un avion. Dans l'eau, un hydravion. Sur terre, une Terraplane », clame le slogan publicitaire pour cette voiture . La voiture inspirera quantité d'autres chansons et jingles publicitaires pour la radio et la télévision. L'automobile fait désormais partie intégrante de la culture pop, tant sur le plan musical que littéraire et cinématographique, et les publicitaires en tirent parti.

Grâce en grande partie au crédit qui facilite les « achats impulsifs » et à l'expansion du marché de la voiture d'occasion, les États-Unis occupent le premier rang mondial en termes de nombre de voitures par habitant. En 1939, la France ne compte que 51 voitures pour mille habitants, l'Italie 11 et la Russie moins de 5, contre 227 pour les États-Unis – et, surtout, tout le monde aspire à en posséder une.

1939

1939 Ford debuts new line, Mercury

Ford präsentiert seine neue Marke Mercury.

Ford lance une nouvelle gamme : la Mercury

1939 Lincoln Continental unveiled

Lincoln Continental vorgestellt.

Présentation de la Lincoln Continental

1939 Chrysler introduces Fluid Drive transmission driveline combination

Chrysler stellt sein halbautomatisches Getriebe „Fluid Drive" vor.

Chrysler inaugure la transmission Fluid Drive

1939 GM Futurama and Ford Pavilion show "cars of the future" at New York World's Fair

GM Futurama und Ford-Pavillon zeigen „Autos der Zukunft" auf der Weltausstellung in New York.

Le Futurama de GM et le pavillon Ford présentent les « voitures du futur » à la Foire internationale de New York

148

ANNOUNCING
The Reo-Royale
CONVERTIBLE COUPE
A distinguished sport vehicle, convertible for open or closed driving, and in every detail a car of Reo character.
Folding snugly into a special well, the top, when collapsed, perfectly preserves the car's aerodynamic streamlining.
125 horsepower. 135-inch wheelbase. One-shot chassis lubrication. Reo Silent-Second Transmission.

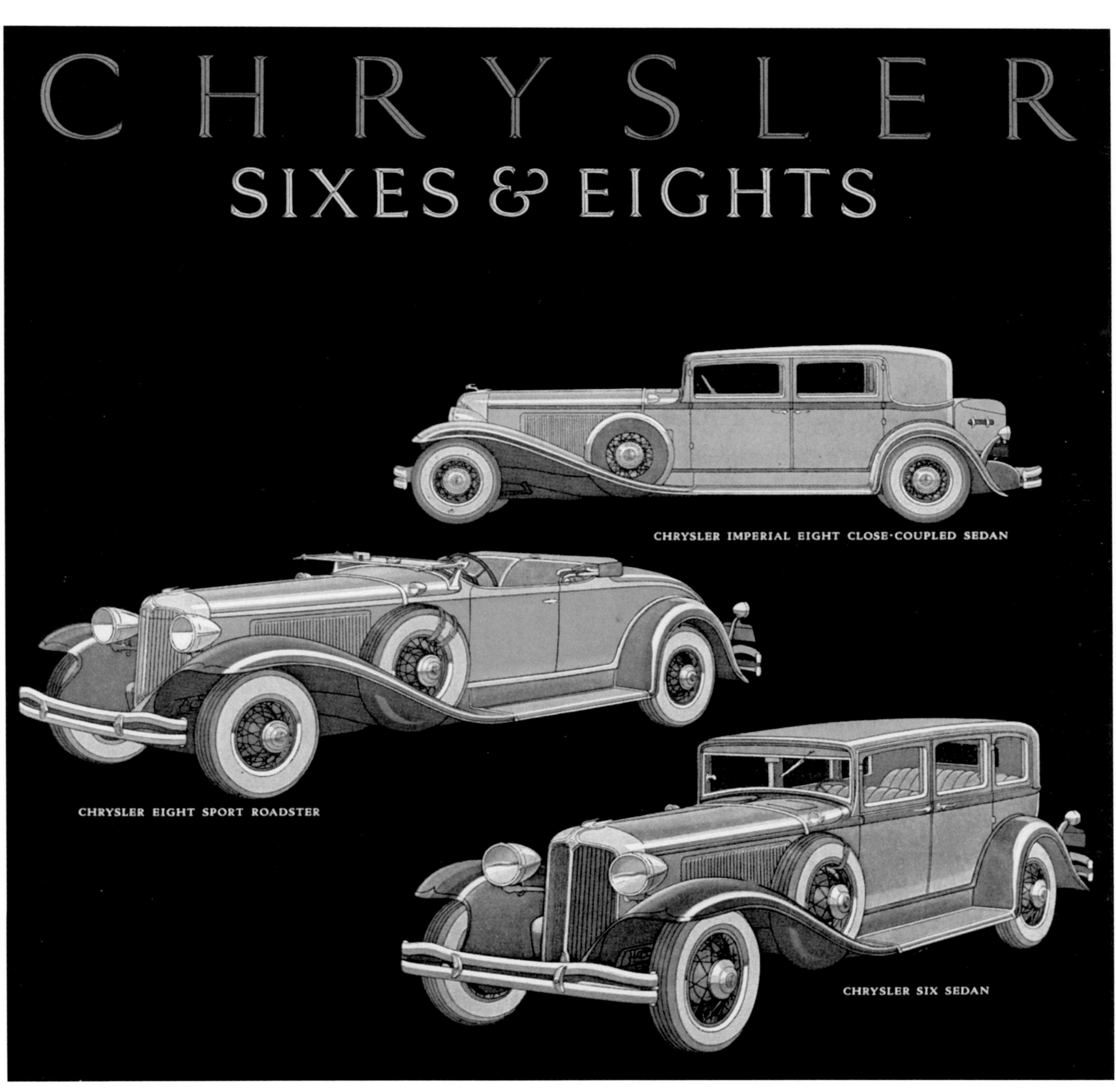

CHRYSLER
SIXES & EIGHTS
CHRYSLER IMPERIAL EIGHT CLOSE-COUPLED SEDAN
CHRYSLER EIGHT SPORT ROADSTER
CHRYSLER SIX SEDAN

Chrysler, 1931

Reo-Royale, 1931 ◂

STARRING IN

Standing out prominently and proudly among the new cars—*starring in style*—is Chevrolet for 1937. It proves, once and for all, that beauty in a car depends on *design* rather than on dollars, and that true distinction springs from *car-personality* rather than from price. Outstandingly beautiful, this new Chevrolet is also outstandingly fleet and spirited, and, of course, outstandingly thrifty. It is *the complete car, completely new,* and it is causing a complete revision in the buying habits of many families that formerly paid much more money for their motor cars.

CHEVROLET MOTOR DIVISION
General Motors Sales Corporation
DETROIT, MICHIGAN

CHEVROLET

Pontiac, 1931 Pontiac, 1932

Chevrolet Master DeLuxe, 1937 ◂

Refinement Evident in Every Detail

BUICK GIVES MORE AND BETTER MILES
—its record provides the proof

After all, when it comes to choosing a motor car, you want *proof* of value, instead of claims. And there is ample proof that *Buick gives more and better miles* in the acts of the car itself. You have only to drive a Buick Eight a short distance to know that it gives *better* miles. Its long wheelbase means a far smoother ride; its size and weight assure real comfort and security at all speeds; the performance of its Valve-in-Head Straight Eight Engine is the kind of performance you've always wanted in a car. And Buick gives *more* miles, too. Witness the number of Buicks that have travelled 200,000 miles and more—and that are still serving with true Buick reliability after five, ten, even fifteen years of use. You can't go wrong buying a Buick—you never could. It's a wise, economical investment.

• • •

The twenty new Buick models are offered at moderate prices on liberal and convenient G. M. A. C. terms. All are Buicks through and through. They have new Bodies by Fisher, Valve-in-Head Straight Eight Engines, and new Fisher No Draft Ventilation, Individually Controlled. All are fine, economical motor car investments.

THE CROIX DE GUERRE

Buick Red Cross ambulance . . . served during entire period of World War . . . bears Croix de Guerre and three citations awarded units to which it was attached . . . now among permanent exhibits in the American Red Cross museum in Washington.

"CAR THAT TIME FORGOT"

"The Car That Time Forgot" . . . Buick Sedan owned by Mr. John Erickson, 727 South 6th Street, Minneapolis, Minnesota . . . 370,000 miles of service and still running . . . a typical example of Buick's ability to give more and better miles.

THE DESERT MAIL

Buick . . . steadily, faithfully carrying the Desert Mail from Beirut to Bagdad . . . five hundred miles through the mountains and across the Syrian Desert . . . making the thousand-mile round trip without adding a drop of water to the radiator.

CIRCLING THE GLOBE

A "Round-the-World" Buick . . . Route: New York City across the Atlantic to London, Paris, Cairo, Calcutta . . . thence through the Australian bush to New Zealand, Honolulu, San Francisco and back to New York. World-wide reliability—that's Buick.

MEDAL OF AWARD

Chicago's forthcoming "Century of Progress" . . . (be sure to attend!) . . . reminiscent of the great Panama-Pacific Exposition . . . where the International Jury of Awards presented a Gold Medal to Buick in recognition of its quality and reliability.

WHEN BETTER AUTOMOBILES ARE BUILT, BUICK WILL BUILD THEM . . . A GENERAL MOTORS VALUE

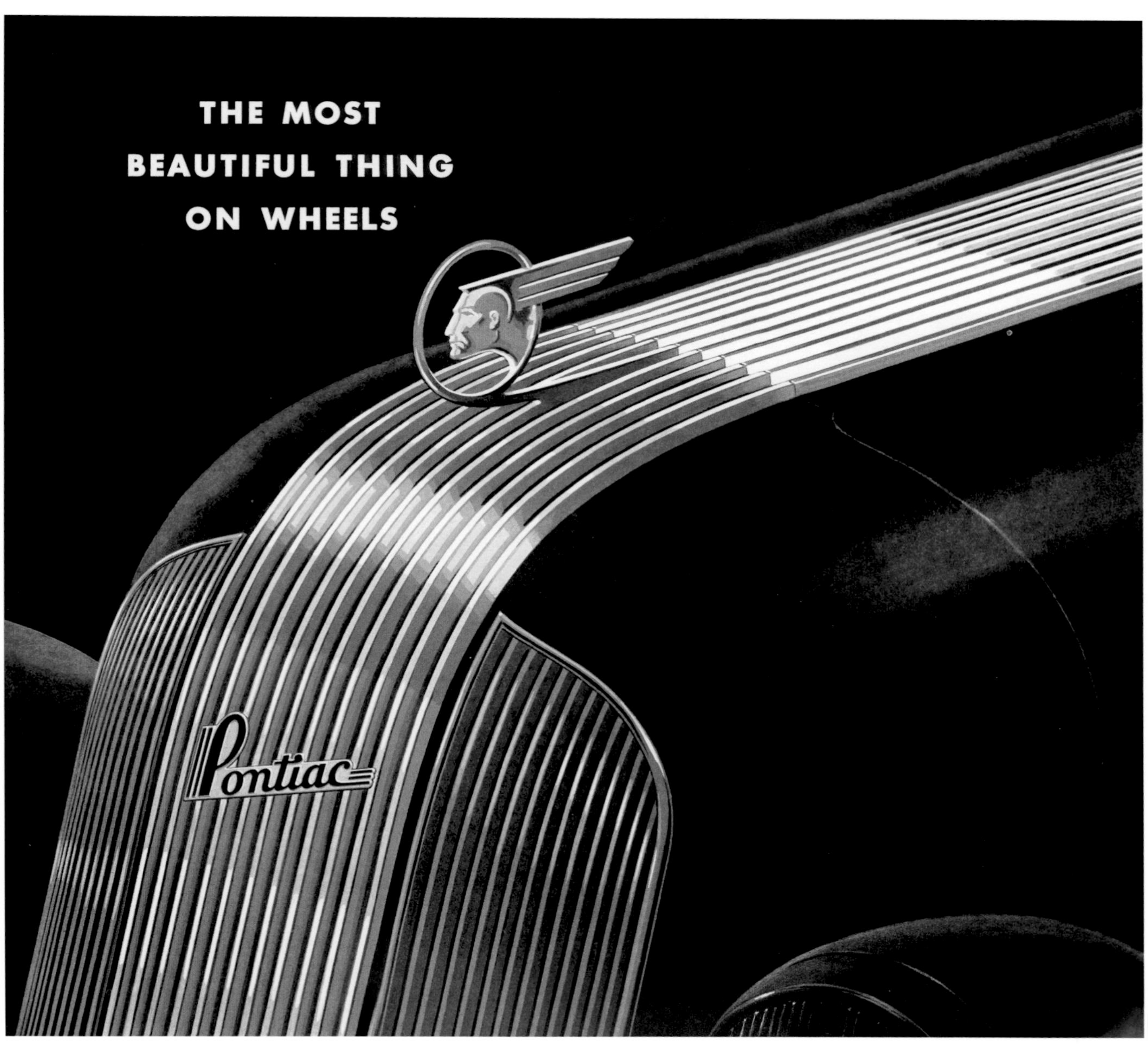
THE MOST
BEAUTIFUL THING
ON WHEELS
Pontiac

Pontiac, 1935

During the Machine Age, the parallel patterns of Art Deco motifs were transmuted into streamlines. Parallel lines were rendered in chrome on refrigerators and toasters as well as automobiles.

Im Maschinenzeitalter wurden die Parallelmuster des Art déco zu Stromlinien. Parallele Linien aus Chrom zierten neben Kühlschränken und Toastern auch Autos.

Au siècle des machines, les lignes parallèles caractéristiques de l'Art déco se traduisent par des lignes aérodynamiques soulignées de chrome, sur les automobiles comme sur les réfrigérateurs ou les grille-pains.

Buick, 1933 ◂

154

Marmon Big Eight, 1930

Marmon Big Eight, 1930

► Jordan Playboy, 1930

A Charming Something with lithe and youthful lines—a thoroughbred descendant of a roving race—inspired with the verve of modern youth—and dressed up like nobody's business—in short ready to go somewhere—and going. That's the new Jordan Playboy.

JORDAN

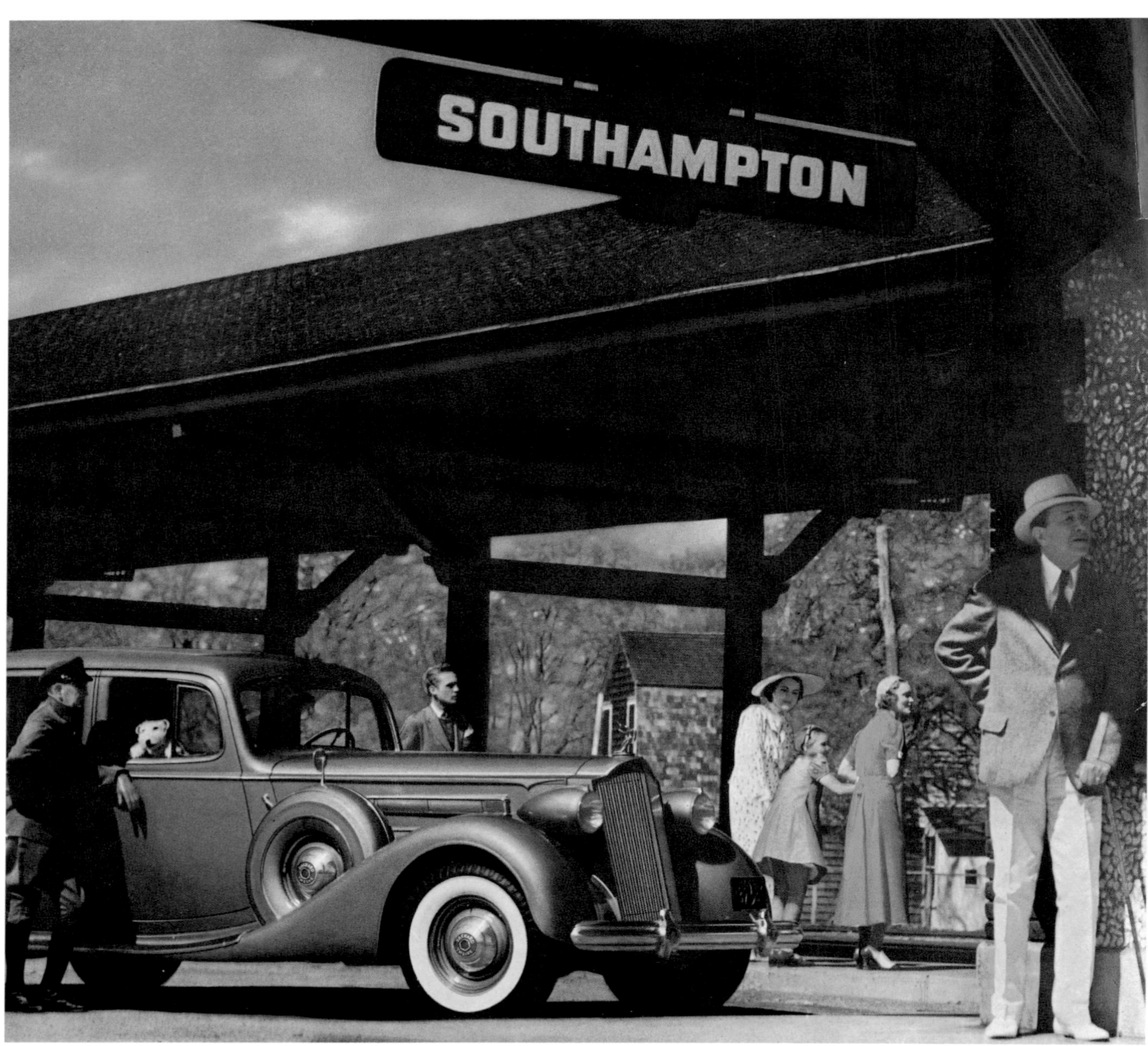

Packard, 1937

Packard was still socially at the top of the market in the late '30s. Its snob appeal is hinted at in this ad's prominent railroad sign denoting a posh destination on Long Island, New York.

Packard war in den späten 1930er-Jahren immer noch eine Nobelmarke. Einen Hinweis auf die anvisierte Zielgruppe gibt das auffällig platzierte Ortsschild, das auf einen angesagten Treffpunkt auf Long Island, New York verweist.

À la fin des années 1930, Packard occupe encore le haut du marché, comme le laisse entendre cette publicité, où le panneau de la gare indique une destination très chic sur Long Island, près de New York.

► Nash, 1933

Standard of the World
A man is known by his automobile
Of all those material possessions which bespeak a man's place among his fellow men—none is more instantly recognized than his automobile. Wherever he goes and whatever he does, his car has come to be accepted as a symbol of his tastes, his standing and his business success. Because of this, there has grown up about Cadillac and LaSalle a degree of respect which is unusual in America's business life. Men who have given the problem serious thought will have no other automobile; for here is the "Standard of the World"—the car which has stood, for thirty years, as the emblem of all that is fine. They know, when they drive a Cadillac or La Salle, that they have the masterpiece itself—and that it is given the recognition which a masterpiece always inspires. LaSalle prices range from $2395, Cadillac from $2795, f. o. b. Detroit.
CADILLAC
V 8 12 16

The Cadillac V-8 Two-Passenger Coupé

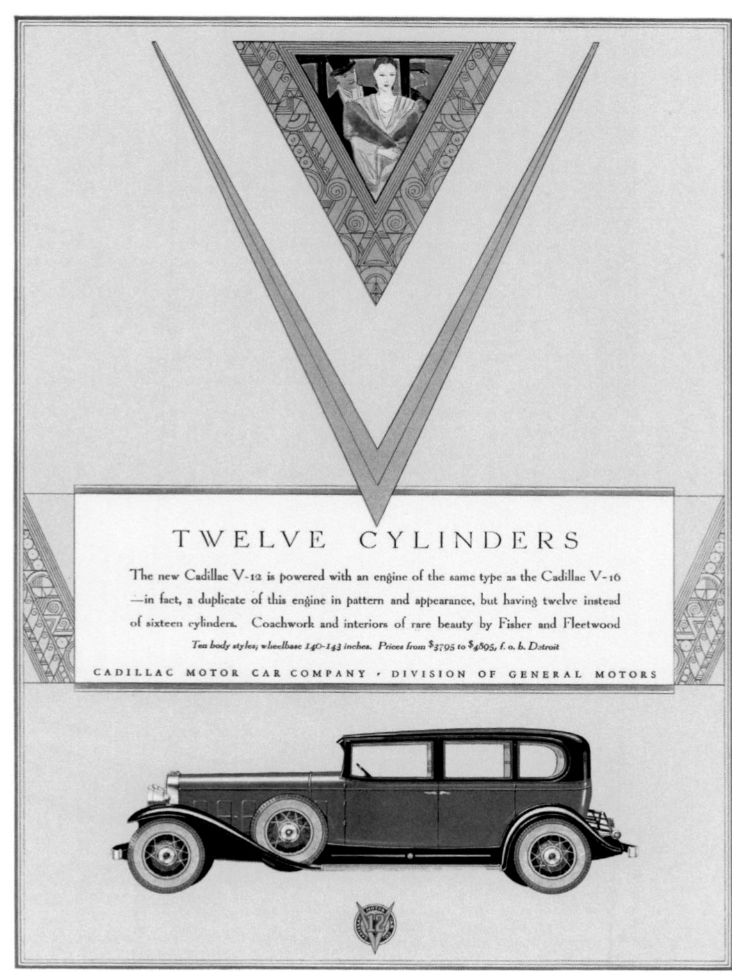

Cadillac, 1931

Cadillac, 1931

Cadillac, 1932 ◂

Yesterday's tiresome journey

IS JUST A REFRESHING JAUNT!

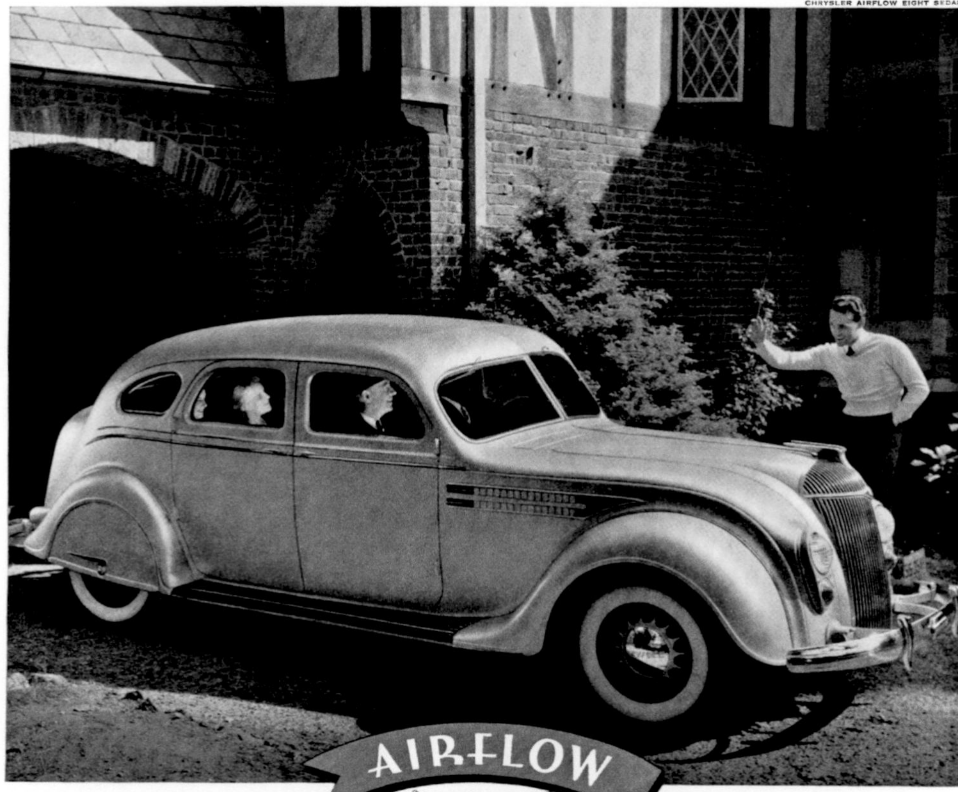

To people who haven't experienced it before, the effortless ease of riding in an Airflow Chrysler is nothing short of astonishing.

As you ride, you are conscious, of course, that the trip is smooth. But after 500 miles, you'll be downright amazed at the lack of fatigue you feel.

The reason is purely scientific . . . the effect of a rhythm which scientists know is most pleasing to human nerves. All the little jiggles and jounces are gone. The car takes the big bumps in long, easy glides . . . so slowly and softly that your nerves are scarcely conscious of the motion at all.

To this magnificent ride is added the magic of Chrysler's Automatic Overdrive† which cuts engine speed one-third at road speeds over 40. It's a sensation as smooth and silent as sailing . . . and you actually get as much as 5 more miles from every gallon of gas.

Your nearby Chrysler dealer cordially invites you to get acquainted at first hand with the greatest luxury in travel today . . . the spacious roominess, the scientific economy, the unmatched safety, the glorious ease and comfort of the world's most modern motor car. Accept his invitation to ride in an Airflow Chrysler.

☆ Chrysler Six . . . 93 horsepower, 118-inch wheelbase, $760 and up.

☆ De Luxe Eight . . . 105 and 110 horsepower, 121 and 133-inch wheelbase, $925 and up.

☆ Airflow Eight . . . 115 horsepower, 123-inch wheelbase All models, $1345.

☆ Airflow Imperial . . . 130 horsepower, 128-inch wheelbase. All models, $1475.

☆ Airflow Custom Imperial . . . 130 horsepower, 137-inch wheelbase, $2475 and up.

†Standard on Airflow Imperial. Available on all 1936 Chryslers at slight additional cost.

All prices list at factory, Detroit; special equipment extra.

Ask for the Official Chrysler Motors-Commercial Credit Company Time Payment plan. Available through all Chrysler Dealers.

Chrysler's on the Air! . . . Big Star Program . . . Every Thursday, 8 P. M., Eastern Daylight Saving Time . . . Columbia Network. You're invited to listen.

Chrysler Airflow, 1936

Introduced in 1934, the stylistically and technologically novel Airflow was ahead of its time, but it suffered teething troubles and never quite caught on with buyers.

Der 1934 präsentierte Airflow war seiner Zeit stilistisch wie technisch voraus. Kinderkrankheiten hatten indes zur Folge, dass er nie so recht ankam.

Lancé en 1934, le modèle Airflow, révolutionnaire sur les plans esthétique et technologique, est en avance sur son temps mais il ne surmontera jamais vraiment ses difficultés initiales.

► Buick Eight, 1935

In Warner Bros.' "GOLD DIGGERS OF 1935," Buick is featured with Dick Powell and the Berkeley Girls. Warner Bros. consistently choose Buick for shots of lavish musical revue display, and for those depicting people in the modern manner. Today's Buick is exquisitely styled. It harmonizes perfectly with the advanced and newly created styles which Warner Bros. productions display.

Hollywood — *Creator of Style* — *Chooses* BUICK *for Its Own*

In brilliant Hollywood — where picture directors and stars create the styles for a nation — Buick plays the star style part. A world once ruled by Paris now looks to Hollywood; and there Buick is the featured car. In production after production, for the hit pictures of the year, Buick is chosen . . . just as it is favored by those who value the prestige of modish, modern design. ¶ All you have ever known or heard of Buick size and roominess . . . of Buick quality and dependability . . . luxury, performance and economy . . . is now surpassed. To see Buick today is to feast your eyes upon aristocratic, sparkling style. To drive it is to gratify your enthusiasm for unsurpassed performance and to enjoy the unprecedented ease and simplicity of the newest automatic operating features. To ride is to know the finest of all fine motoring. ¶ Twenty-five beautiful models, in four series. Four popular price groups, \$795 to \$2175, list prices at Flint, Mich. Prices subject to change without notice. Special equipment extra. Favorable G.M.A.C. terms.

\$795
and up, list prices at Flint.

BODY BY FISHER . . . A GENERAL MOTORS PRODUCT

WHEN BETTER AUTOMOBILES ARE BUILT—BUICK WILL BUILD THEM

MILLIONAIRES WILL BUY IT!

But you can easily afford it . . .
Actually, it costs you but little more than the low-priced cars!

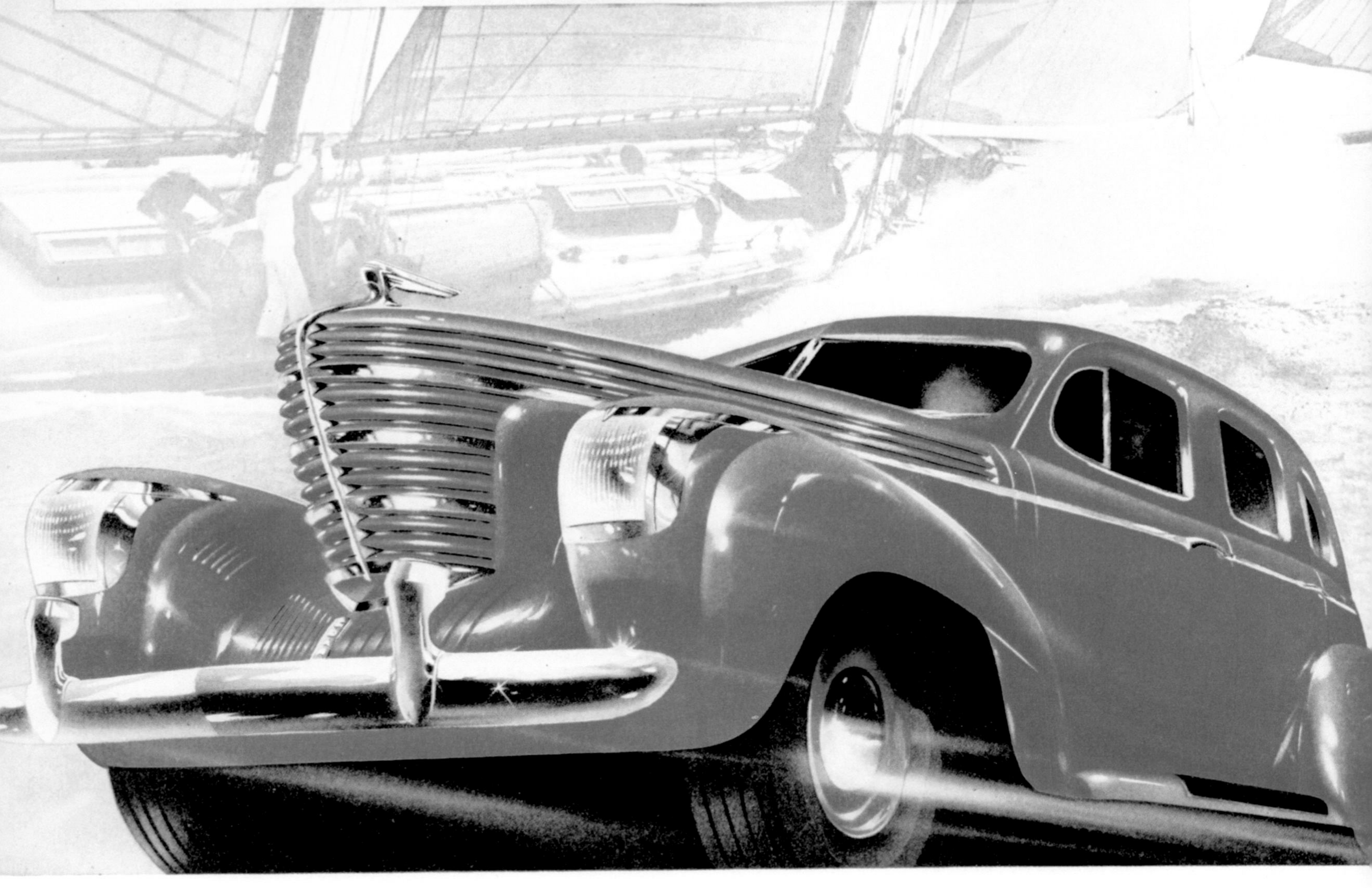

Eager Throngs Crowd Graham Showrooms — Thousands Say It's The Only New Car In A Year When So Many Cars Have That "Warmed-Over" Look

Just look at the racy, rakish lines of that handsome big car in the picture. See that distinguished hood . . . the built-in headlights . . . the forward pitch of those fenders! There's movement, motion in every line of this car. It looks like it's going . . . when it's standing still.

And wait till you drive a SUPERCHARGER! Take this high-spirited car out on the highway. Put its nose into the wind—and GO! You'll hear a new song coming from beneath that hood . . . the Song of the Supercharger! A new motoring miracle! A brand new kind of performance. Amazing power and pick-up. On any road—you're boss!

Graham brings you luxurious size. Every car in the line—from lowest priced to Supercharged models—has a 120-inch wheelbase. 57-inch wide seats. More headroom, legroom. Vacuumatic Gear Shift (optional at slight extra cost) clears the front compartment. No wonder people *think* Graham is high-priced.

We honestly believe Graham is the safest car on the highway. Lower center of gravity, wider rear tread, for extra safety. Oversized hydraulic brakes. Sound-proofed all steel body. Gyrolator Sway Eliminator. Recessed instrument panel controls. Safety-Doors. Safety-Step running boards. Safety Headlights.

And Graham leads in economy. A big, full-sized car . . . yet, in official tests, Graham has proved its economy—23.95 miles on a gallon of gasoline with supercharger. Fram Oil Filter is standard equipment on all Supercharged models. You need change oil only twice a year. Think of the saving that means.

Go see this exciting new car that everybody's talking about. Let your dealer show you how easy it is to own.

ONLY A LITTLE MORE THAN LOW-PRICED CARS
Ask your dealer for the price of the big 120-inch wheelbase Graham *delivered right in your own town.* You'll be amazed. Now just a little more than low-priced cars! Easy payment plans. Overdrive Transmission now optional at slight extra cost on all models.

SUPERCHARGE

A Sensational Engineer Development — Drastic Cuts Fuel Costs

An engineering marvel pioneered 5 years ago by Graham! Proved in over 100 million miles of service! Only the Supercharger can offer you the combination of **1. SUPER-ACCELERATION!** Far faster pick-up at all speeds—even from 50 m.p.h. and up, where ordinary engines become sluggish. **2. LOW FUEL CONSUMPTION!** Burns more air—less gasoline. A proved record of 23.95 miles on a gallon of gasoline in official tests, sanctioned and supervised by the A. A. A.

Again Graham, who has consistently led the industry in pioneering important automotive developments, achieves another victory!

GRAHAM NOW ON DISPLAY AT ALL GRAHAM SHOWROOMS

Pontiac, 1936

Graham, 1938 ◂

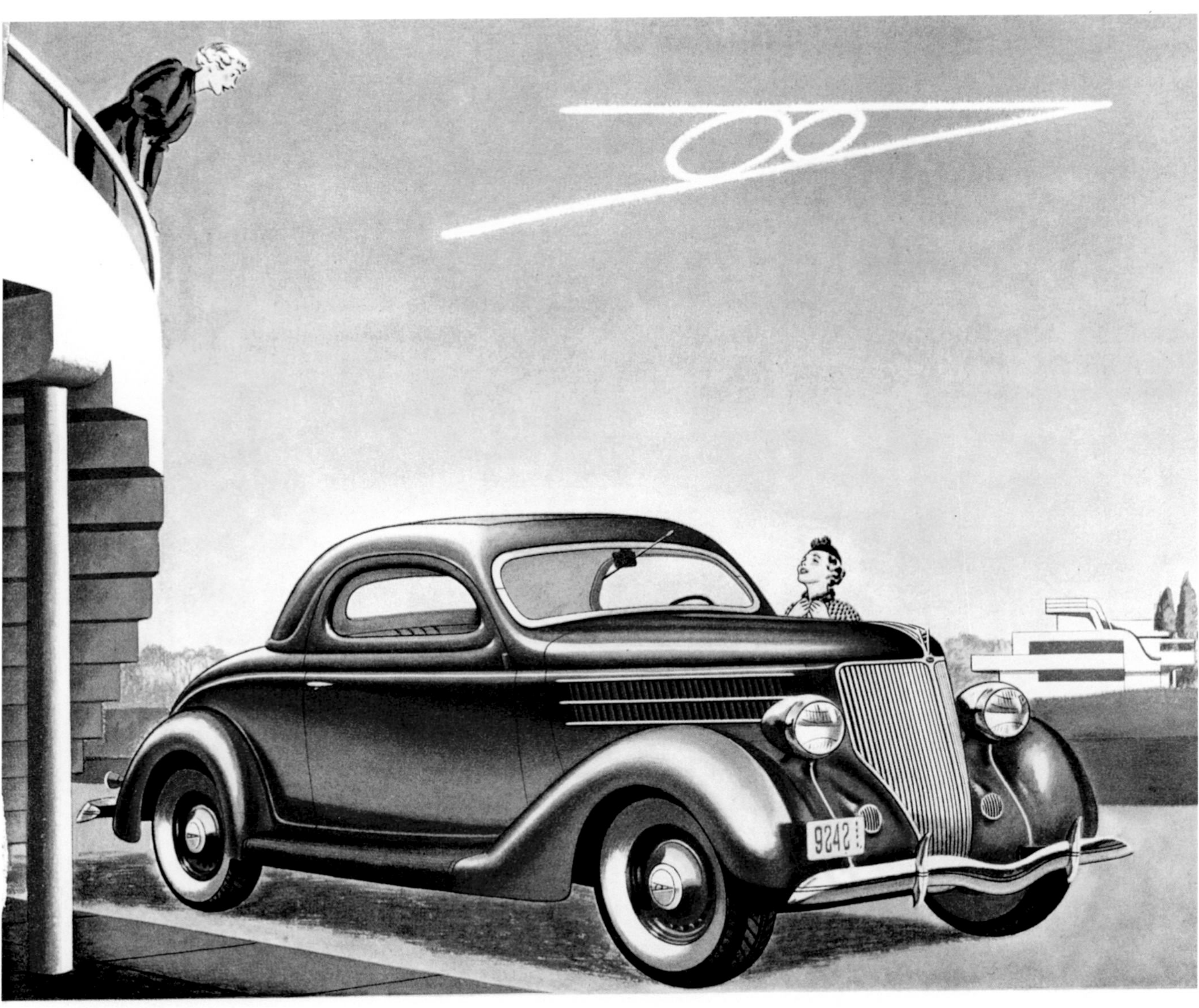

THE NEW FORD V·8 FOR 1936

The New Ford V-8 for 1936 is beautifully timed for these modern days. It is personable without being pretentious—as up-to-date in performance as in appearance. . . . The V-8 engine maintains its leadership in power, acceleration, smoothness and all-round efficiency—gives you many advantages formerly available only in high-priced cars. This V-8 engine is an important reason why the Ford is such a satisfying car to drive. . . . You will find, too, that there is something equally outstanding about the safety, comfort and roominess of the 1936 Ford V-8. . . . You drive with unusual security because of ease of handling, the welded steel body, big powerful brakes that stop the car with ease and certainty, and Safety Glass (all around in all Ford body types at no additional cost). . . . The compact design of the V-8 engine means extra inches of body room and makes the Ford a really big car inside. Center-Poised seat position contributes to easy riding comfort on every type of road—in the back seat as well as in the front. . . .You will like everything about the New Ford V-8 for 1936. For it has everything you would like to have in a modern motor car.

Ford V-8, 1936

Ford succeeded by giving customers a V8 engine, previously restricted to luxury makes like Packard and Cadillac. The Ford V8 brought power to the masses, including, most famously, the Depression-era gangsters Bonnie and Clyde.

Fords Erfolg basierte auf seinem V8-Motor. Zuvor auf Nobelmarken wie Packard und Cadillac beschränkt, brachte der Ford V8 Power für alle, so auch für das berüchtigte Gangsterpaar Bonnie und Clyde.

Ford parvient à proposer à sa clientèle le moteur V8, auparavant réservé aux marques de luxe comme Packard et Cadillac. Avec la Ford V8, le grand public – ainsi que Bonnie et Clyde, célèbre couple de gangsters de la Grande Dépression – accède à la puissance.

► Lincoln Zephyr, 1936

LINCOLN ZEPHYR V12

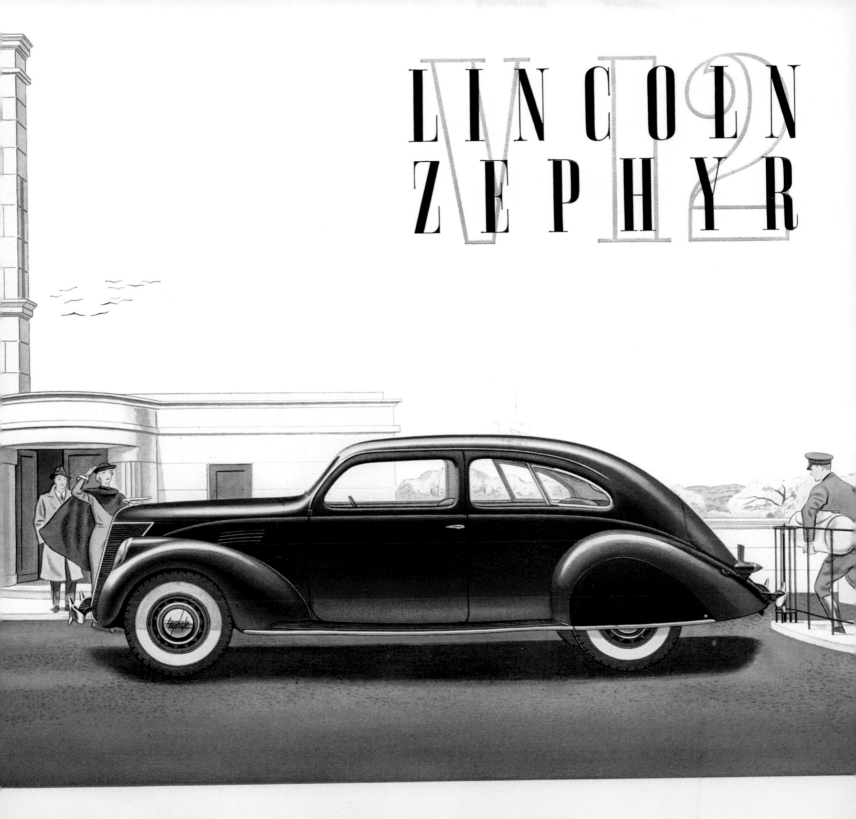

TWELVE CYLINDERS POWER THIS NEW CAR OF MANY-SIDED APPEAL

THE first person who bought a LINCOLN-ZEPHYR was the president of a railroad. A fair cross-section of owners reveals, also, eminent physicians . . . executives who travel much . . . society matrons with children of school age. Their reasons for buying this car are varied and practical. Underlying them all, typical of them all, is this: "It is a new *kind* of car. It offers a new kind of value!"

It is an unusual idea to place a 12-cylinder engine in a car of medium price. The engine itself is new. Designed by Lincoln, built by Lincoln, it is the culmination of years of research and experiment. It develops 110 horsepower. Because of its exclusive design; because of its great power and flexibility; because it pulls a car low in weight for its size, *owners are getting 14 to 18 miles a gallon!*

It is a *new* idea to streamline a car as fully as this car is streamlined. But the graceful, flowing contours simply grow out of the body structure beneath. Steel trusses form a rigid bridge over which steel panels are welded—top, sides, bottom. Six passengers, or one, are gently cradled in the framework, and poised forward of the rear axle. You ride near the center even when in the back seat.

It is a *new* idea, finally, to provide so much power, size, comfort in a car selling for $1275.

But a conviction of the builder is that engineering experience, precision methods, and vast resources, applied intelligently, can do what otherwise could not be done. This car combines Ford ability to give great value at low cost with the Lincoln tradition to build without regard to cost. It does for the medium-price field what these other cars do for their own fields.

Learn, today, what outstanding value Lincoln has built into a car new in idea, new in *performance!*

PRICED FROM $1275 F. O. B. DETROIT

Available in Two Sedan Body Types

"We arrived in New York at Midnight...and the Lincoln-Zephyr knows all about traffic"

THIS new kind of car conquers all roads, all circumstances of travel. In city or country, on roads good and bad, the LINCOLN-ZEPHYR rolls up new records of performance.

Ask, as you consider this car, what it offers that other cars in its price field do not. The LINCOLN-ZEPHYR has a 12-cylinder engine—the V-type. Twelve cylinders mean greater smoothness . . . greater flexibility. And twelve cylinders, here, *mean 14 to 18 miles per gallon!*

The LINCOLN-ZEPHYR has a unique body structure. *This is the only car of its kind.* Body and frame are one, welded together. You ride surrounded by steel. And you ride amidships. This car flows along like a sloop in a favoring breeze.

The LINCOLN-ZEPHYR has extra roominess. It is a big car. The wheelbase is 122 inches. The engine is compact, and interiors thus longer. There are no conventional running boards; seats, like divans, are wider. Three may sit comfortably on the front seat or the back. THE LINCOLN-ZEPHYR, finally, has the Lincoln background. It is built in the Lincoln plant. Lincoln precision methods are LINCOLN-ZEPHYR precision methods. Mechanical standards for the one are mechanical standards for the other.

Prices now are lower. Convenient terms can be arranged through Authorized Universal Credit Company Finance Plans. *Lincoln Motor Company, builders of the Lincoln and Lincoln-Zephyr.*

LINCOLN-ZEPHYR V·12

THIS IS THE CAR THAT IS PRICED BELOW ITS SPECIFICATIONS

Cadillac Sixty Special, 1938

The first car without running boards, Cadillac's sleek Sixty Special model was compared with airliners, such as the transoceanic Pan Am Clipper long-range flying boat.

Cadillacs schnittigen Sixty Special, das erste Auto ohne Trittbrett, verglich man mit einem Verkehrsflugzeug wie dem transatlantischen Flugboot Pan Am Clipper.

Première voiture sans barres de frottement, la très épurée Sixty Special est comparéeaux paquebots volants de la Pan Am qui traversent les océans.

Lincoln Zephyr, 1937 ◂

Two New Beauties!
BETTER Engineered ... BETTER Made!
CHRYSLER Royal
MORE FOR THE MONEY IN THE LOW-PRICED FIELD!
Chrysler for 1938
CHRYSLER Imperial
PHENOMENAL PERFORMANCE AT A REMARKABLE PRICE!

BIGGER . . . and a beauty. That's the new Chrysler Royal for 1938. Three inches more wheelbase than the 1937 Royal which invaded the low-priced field with such spectacular success.

Look at that proud, commanding radiator . . . the jewel-like modeling of the radiator grille . . . the graceful union of hood and fenders and streamlined headlamps.

Inside, beauty greets you again. The instrument panel sets the keynote . . . rich, smart, luxurious . . . blending in color harmony with the striking new steering wheel and its ring-type horn control . . . complementing the superb upholstery in new short-nap mohair or broadcloth.

A new, larger 95 horsepower Gold Seal engine . . . amazingly thrifty . . . silky smooth with Floating Power.

Glorious roominess! 119 inches of wheelbase. 96¼ inches from windshield to rear window! A 49 inch rear seat! The most spacious luggage capacity you ever saw!

High-priced riding comfort! Safety *All-Steel* Bodies . . . time-tested hydraulic brakes . . . finger-touch steering . . . toe-touch stopping . . . synchronized gear-shifting. A big, beautiful, luxurious car that tops everything in the low-priced field.

The Luxurious Imperial

The beautiful, high-powered Chrysler Imperial for 1938! More fine car for the money than America has ever seen!

Long famous as Chrysler's top-ranking car, the magnificent Imperial is now in the medium-priced field.

The proud, commanding beauty that comes from added length and size! Wheelbase increased to 125 inches . . . for low-swung smartness and grace . . . for the roominess of true fine-car luxury.

Deep, wide, chair-high seats! Beautiful appointments! Matchless riding ease . . . the buoyant, gliding smoothness of longer wheelbase . . . balanced weight distribution . . . independently sprung front wheels . . . slow-recoil springs and Aero Hydraulic Shock Absorbers.

Under that long, impressive hood, the electrifying response of 110 horsepower . . . cradled by Floating Power.

The safety and reliability of Chrysler's great engineering features . . . all at their finest expression. Safety *All-Steel* Bodies . . . hydraulic brakes . . . steering and gear-shifting perfection that makes this big, powerful car as effortless as the breeze.

See this great, new Imperial . . . you'll thrill to its beauty . . . marvel at its price.

★ ★ ★

Easy to buy on convenient terms with the official Commercial Credit Company plan.

☆ **NEW 1938 ROYAL** . . . 95 horsepower, 119-inch wheelbase. Ten body types.

☆ **NEW 1938 IMPERIAL** . . . 110 horsepower, 125-inch wheelbase. Six body types.

☆ **NEW 1938 CUSTOM IMPERIAL** . . . 130 horsepower, 144-inch wheelbase. Three body types.

Tune in on Major Bowes, Columbia Network, every Thursday, 9 to 10:00 P. M., E. S. T.

★ **CHRYSLER SWEEPS ON IN THE LOW-PRICED FIELD!**

Chrysler Royal and Imperial, 1938

► Nash, 1937

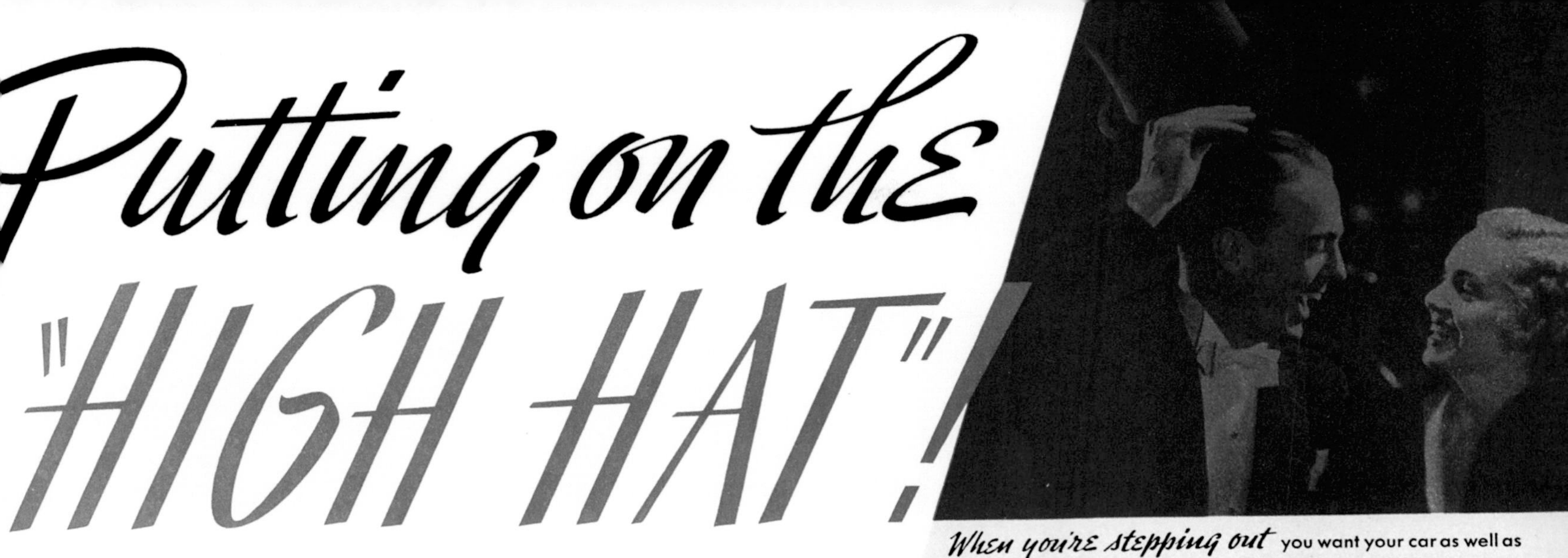

When you're stepping out you want your car as well as your clothes to be in good taste. That's why Nash is winning thousands. It's *conservatively smart* without being "tricky" or "freakish".

n actual photograph of Nash Ambassador Six 4-Door Sedan with trunk

Extra room! You get extra headroom, egroom and extra wide seats in all Nash cars. The finest upholstering. No Draft Ventilation.

Get out of the Small Car Class! You can get a great big Nash for just a few dollars more than small cars cost.

It's fun to go "high hat" when the cost is so low . . . thousands changing to these bigger, more luxurious Nash cars this year!

Hundreds are getting out of the "small car" class. They're changing to the new Nash LaFayette-"400". It's a great big 117-inch wheelbase car. Much bigger than any of the "all three" cars in the same price class. But compare prices on 4-door sedans. *Nash costs just a few dollars more!* ℭThe Nash Ambassador Six is a big 121-inch wheelbase car . . . the Ambassador Eight, on a 125-inch wheelbase, is as big a car as anyone would want to own. Both have the famous Nash "Twin-Ignition" valve-in-head engine. All Nash cars give you oversized hydraulic brakes, the strongest type of steel bodies, extra headroom, seat room—plus vital engineering features you'd expect to find only in the most expensive cars. *Nash gives you more for your money!* See Nash first!

NASH MOTORS DIVISION
NASH-KELVINATOR CORPORATION
KENOSHA . . . . WISCONSIN

NASH

DELIVERED PRICES throw a new light on the remarkable value Nash is offering. For example, on the big 117-inch wheelbase Nash LaFayette-"400", monthly payments run as low as $28. Ask about new Nash C. I. T. Budget Plan. Automatic Cruising Gear available on all models at slight extra cost.

BUY WITH YOUR EYES OPEN . . . SEE THE X-RAY SYSTEM! Only complete summary of all the facts about all the cars! Reveals some astonishing differences in cars of same price.

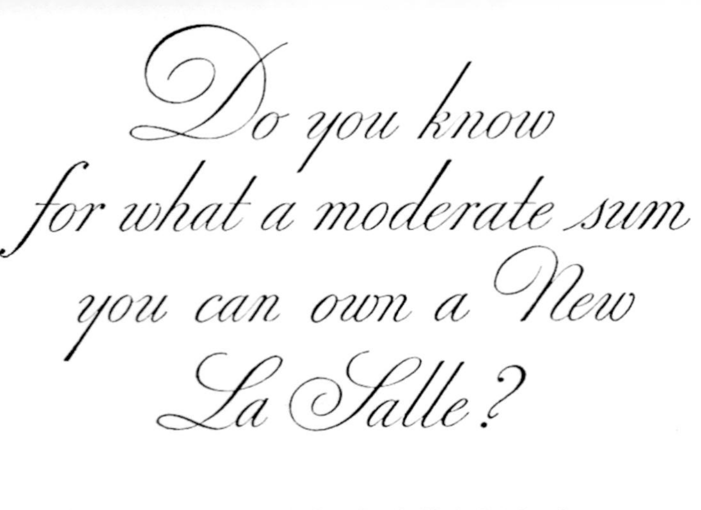

Do you know
for what a moderate sum
you can own a New

Because of their deep regard for La Salle's high place among the fine cars of the world, many people do not realize that La Salle is *not* a costly car to own. The initial expenditure is very little more than the price of many automobiles of less distinguished character. As a result of the thorough quality Cadillac creates with its fine design and precise craftsmanship, the expense for La Salle's operation and maintenance is surprisingly small. And, finally, La Salle's faultless style and faithful performance inspire an unusual span of ownership. One is happy to keep a La Salle over a much greater length of time and drive it a great deal farther than a lesser automobile. In fact, the actual figures often prove that many who are now driving lower-priced cars might very *profitably* be enjoying the prestige and satisfaction of owning a LaSalle. Why not get the facts from your Cadillac-LaSalle dealer today? LaSalle prices from $2395, Cadillac from $2795, f.o.b. Detroit.

LA SALLE

V EIGHT

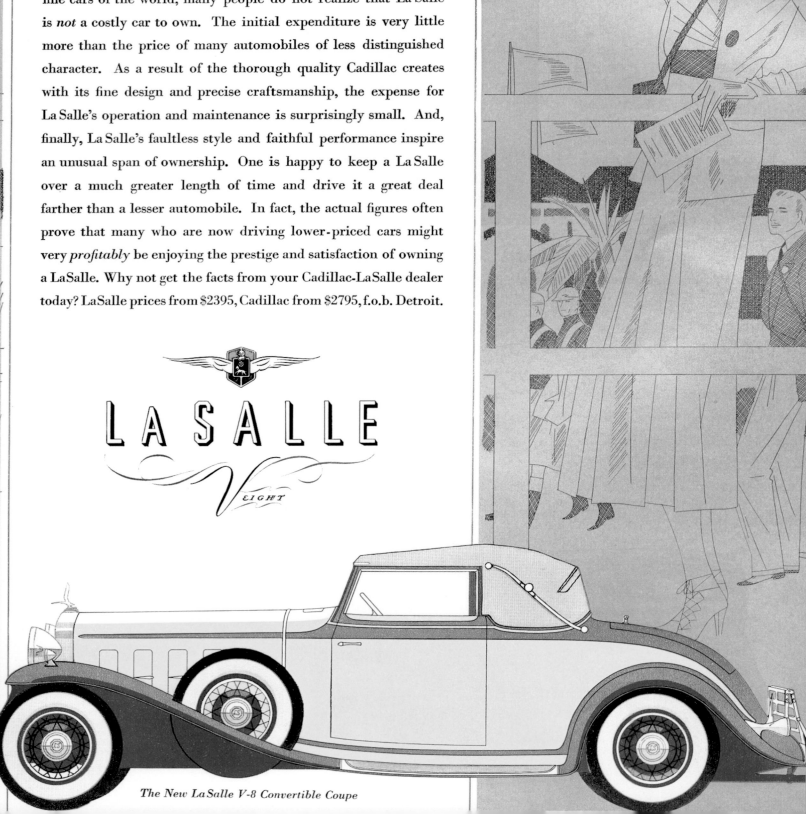

The New La Salle V-8 Convertible Coupe

The silent, smooth performance of La Salle V-8 is admirably reflected in the long, flowing lines of the 2-Passenger Coupe, with body by Fisher, illustrated below. La Salle V-8 prices range from $2195, f. o. b. Detroit. G. M. A. C. terms available on all body styles.

So completely is the ideal of fine workmanship ingrained at the Cadillac plant that, no matter whether it be for Cadillac or for La Salle, every detail of design and manufacture is approached with the same meticulous care. There is only one standard of excellence, regardless of the task to be done. As a result, the La Salle V-8 provides a degree of quality and a type of performance far beyond those suggested by its moderate price—for it is built with the same exactitude as Cadillac itself.

LA SALLE V-8

Illustrated below is Fleetwood's interpretation of the Roadster—mounted on the V-12 chassis. In the smartness of its lines and appointments, no less than in the capabilities of its 12-cylinder power plant—it is one of the most distinguished creations to have borne the Cadillac name. Cadillac V-12 prices range from $3795, f. o. b. Detroit G. M. A. C. terms available on all body styles

To ride in the Cadillac V-12 is to know at once why it is ranked so highly among the fine cars of the world—for the appeal of its 12-cylinder performance is well-nigh irresistible. Even those who are accustomed to the foremost automobiles, are finding in the V-12 a new conception of motoring luxury. In fact, a V-12 demonstration, almost without exception, makes conventional cars seem commonplace.

CADILLAC V8 12 16

LaSalle, 1931

Cadillac, 1931

LaSalle, 1931 ◂

FULL PROTECTION at 400°F !

saves your Engine !

But quick starting alone is not enough. Many so-called "winter oils" may give you easy starting. But they can't stand up. They are not *double-range* winter oils.

Mobiloil Arctic is the unique *double-range* winter oil. You not only get a quick start below zero but a few minutes later, when engine temperatures may run up to 400° F. you get *full, rich protection.*

Mobiloil Arctic does not thin out dangerously when you need its protection most. It stands up! It maintains its rich lubricating quality.

The world leaders in scientific lubrication have chosen crudes and refining processes that give Mobiloil Arctic its unique ability to stand up. You will find no other winter oil like it, because no other winter oil is made in just the same way!

Your Mobiloil dealer is ready to drain your crankcase and refill with Mobiloil Arctic. See him today. While you are there, insure easy gear-shifting by having him put Mobiloil "CW" in your gears.

We invite you to listen to the Mobiloil Concert, broadcast coast to coast each Wednesday evening from WEAF and 53 associated N. B. C. stations at 9:30, Eastern Standard Time.

Mobiloil Arctic

Duplate Safety Glass, 1935

Many safety innovations now taken for granted were huge breakthroughs when first introduced. Safety glass brought an end to the carnage rendered by jagged glass in accidents, replacing deadly edges with a shower of small, considerably less dangerous chunks.

Viele sicherheitstechnische Innovationen, die wir heute nicht weiter beachten, verkörperten bei ihrer Einführung einen gewaltigen Durchbruch. Dank seiner erhöhten Bruchfestigkeit und der geringeren Splitterwirkung setzte das Sicherheitsglas den verheerenden Auswirkungen umherfliegender Glassplitter ein Ende.

Nombre d'innovations pour la sécurité, aujourd'hui tenues pour acquises, devinrent populaires dès leur lancement ; ce fut le cas du verre sécurit, qui mit fin au carnage causé par les bords coupants des vitres cassées lors des accidents.

Mobiloil Arctic, 1932 ◂

▸▸ U.S. Royal Tires, 1935

Don't GAMBLE
with their Safety!

WHAT man would knowingly jeopardize the safety of his family? Yet many men thoughtlessly permit their wives and children to ride behind car windows of ordinary, easy-to-break glass . . . despite the fact that Duplate Safety Glass is so much safer, and the extra cost of it, thanks to car manufacturers, almost negligible. For the sake of your family's greater security, insist on Duplate Safety Glass in every window of the next car you buy. Pittsburgh Plate Glass Company, 2267 Grant Bldg., Pittsburgh, Pennsylvania.

YOUR FAMILY RIDES IN GREATER SECURITY BEHIND WINDOWS OF DUPLATE SAFETY GLASS

To replace glass in your present car with Duplate, look for the name of your nearest Duplate dealer in the "Where to Buy It" section of your local Telephone Directory under "Glass . . . Safety"

Duplate
Safety

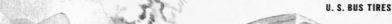

EXPERIENCE
U. S. TRACTOR TIRES
U. S. BICYCLE TIRES
U. S. VENTILATING WINDOW FRAMES
U. S. PNEUMATIC TRUCK TIRES
U. S. INDUSTRIAL SOLIDS
U. S. FISHING BOOTS
A CROWNING ACHIEVEMENT
in tire dependability . . . by the company
with an unparalleled knowledge of rubber
U. S. INDUSTRIAL PNEUMATIC TIRES
Day by day experience with the most diversified family of rubber products has given "U. S." an unparalleled knowledge in the rubber field...and has enabled "U. S." Engineers to vastly improve U. S. Tires.
They have acquired perfect balance in tire building...they know the type of construction which prevents dangerous blow-outs...they know the kind of rubber which makes the toughest, longest-wearing tread...they know the tread design which gives maximum protection against skidding.
Profit by this "U. S." experience. Buy U. S. ROYALS. Get extra miles for your tire dollars!
Manufactured by
UNITED STATES RUBBER PRODUCTS, INC.
1790 Broadway New York, N. Y.
U. S. RUBBER COATS—BOOTS—FIRE HOSE
U. S. ROYAL FLEETWAY "15"
U. S. WATER TOYS
U. S. RAYNSTERS—GAYTEES
U. S. RUBBER SWIM SUITS, CAPS AND SHOES
U. S. NOBBY TRACTION TIRES
U. S. RUBBER LINED TANKS
KEDS
SPUN-LATEX U. S. ROYAL GOLF BALLS
U. S. INDUSTRIAL HOSE
U. S. TRANSMISSION BELTING
U. S. ROYAL HEELS
USKIDE SOLES
United States Rubber Company
U. S. SHEET PACKINGS

CAROLE LOMBARD TELLS WHY SHE PICKED DE SOTO

MY STORY

Carole Lombard

"I wanted a Smart Car that was easy to drive and economical to own —I chose De Soto."

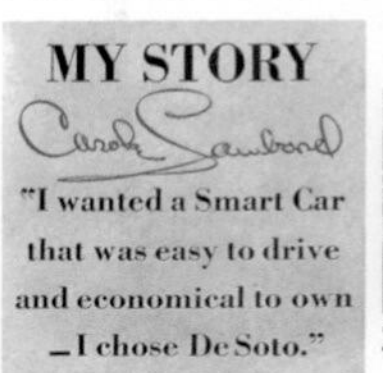

2 "STYLE COMES FIRST with me. I like De Soto's Streamline design, the fascinating headlamps...thank heavens, there's no old-fashioned trunk bustle.

3 "THEN I DISCOVERED De Soto's new Handy-Shift—simplest gear shift I've ever used. It's mounted right on the steering post. More room in front.

4 "FRONT AND BACK, the seats are wide as sofas. Room for six people. That Streamlined Luggage Locker has plenty of room, too.

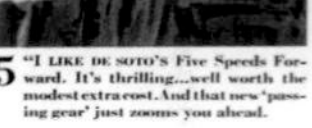

5 "I LIKE DE SOTO'S Five Speeds Forward. It's thrilling...well worth the modest extra cost. And that new 'passing gear' just zooms you ahead.

6 "I LIKE DE SOTO'S economy, Safety-Steel body and hydraulic brakes; my friends say I used good judgment getting such a dependable car.

7 "I WATCH my check stubs. De Soto's low price is good news." *De Soto Division of Chrysler Corporation*, Detroit, Mich.

SEE YOUR

DE SOTO DEALER

FOR A GREAT CAR... FINE SERVICE & A SQUARE DEAL

THEODORA GOES WILD [ABOUT HER NEW DE SOTO]

Irene Dunne Demands Value and Economy— She Gets Both in this GREAT DE SOTO!

LOOK AT these two big reasons why smart car buyers are choosing De Soto: (1) VALUE—you get more for your automobile dollar. (2) OPERATING ECONOMY —De Soto fits in with today's budgets!

Think of it! You get faster pick-up with De Soto's 93-h.p. "Economy Engine." Greater safety, too, with its deeper, stronger frame and bigger, GENUINE hydraulic brakes. Greater comfort...with independent front wheel springing and airplane-type shock-absorbers that smooth even the roughest roads.

Chrysler Corporation engineering gives you complete sound-proofing...Floating Power engine mountings...effortless handling—DOZENS of FINE-CAR features that all add up to EXTRA VALUE!

De Soto is smart to LOOK AT and smart to OWN. This BIG car is now priced just above the lowest... costs no more to run than most SMALL cars! Investigate De Soto's EXTRA VALUE today! DE SOTO DIVISION OF CHRYSLER CORPORATION, Detroit, Michigan.

IT'S AMERICA'S SMARTEST LOW-PRICED CAR

QUICK FACTS: 1. "Lightning-fast" pick-up...Improved 93-h.p. "Economy Engine." 2. Patented Floating Power engine mountings. 3. Longer wheelbase...119 inches. 4. Bigger hydraulic brakes. 5. Easier shifting. 6. Safety-steel body rubber-mounted on a bigger, stronger frame. 7. Luxurious Safety Interior. 8. "Cushioned" ride with airplane-type shock-absorbers. 9. Easier steering...no "road-shock." See De Soto today —discover how easy it is to own this smart car.

TUNE IN MAJOR BOWES' AMATEUR HOUR—COLUMBIA NETWORK—THURSDAYS, 9 TO 10 P. M., E.S.T.

SEE YOUR DE SOTO DEALER

FOR A **GREAT CAR, FINE SERVICE** AND A **SQUARE DEAL**

DeSoto, 1939

DeSoto, 1938

► Nash 400, 1935

THE WHOLE TOWN'S TALKING

about the "Newest New Car in Years!"

NEW NASH "400"

675

p, f. o. b. factory. There are six "400" body types—ix-passenger victorias, with and without trunk; two ssenger sedans, with and without trunk; a three-nger coupe and a five-passenger coupe. Prices sub-o change without notice—special equipment extra.

MONITOR-SEALED MOTOR • RAPID SERVICE HOOD • AEROFORM DESIGN • STEEL TOP, ALL-STEEL BODY • BALANCED WEIGHT SYNCHRONIZED SPRINGING • MIDSECTION SEATING • CLUTCH-PEDAL STARTING • SUPER-HYDRAULIC BRAKES • LUGGAGE COMPARTMENT IN EVERY MODEL • ROOMIEST CAR AT THE PRICE

A DISTINGUISHED OLD NAME ON A BRILLIANT NEW CAR:

NEW HUPMOBILES FOR 1938! A Six and a Custom Six—each on a 122″ wheelbase, each powered by another famous Hupp engine, of 101 hp. A bigger, more luxurious Custom Eight—on a full 125″ wheelbase, with a rugged, responsive, 120-horsepower, eight-in-line engine. Smooth, flashing performance and owner-satisfying economy reach new highs in these brilliant new Hupps. Safe, all-steel bodies, double-action hydraulic brakes, extra-roomy interiors, and super-width doors feature every model.

"HUPP HAS ALWAYS BUILT A GOOD CAR"

STEP UP WITH HUPP The 1938 Hupmobiles are *now* on display in Hupp dealers' showrooms everywhere! And these new cars, like all their famous forebears, will be enthusiastically welcomed by *their own* public—those for whom Hupmobiles are especially designed and built.

For no Hupmobile was ever planned like a variety show—to please everybody—to meet every purse. Hupmobiles have always had a distinctive clientele. Hupp builds for those who want a bigger car, one more luxurious in its roominess and appointments, modern without being extreme in its body lines, built to last for years and yet modestly priced in the middle brackets.

The 1938 Hupmobiles are for those people. If you are one of them—if you are tired of the cars that the millions drive—if you can't recognize your own in a parking lot without reading the license number—see and drive the *distinctive* 1938 Hupmobile. Or if you are tired of paying fancy prices for the power and weight and room and precision-built excellence you demand, and yet want a *fine* car with a famous name, see and drive the *big* 1938 Hupmobile.

These brilliant new cars are better looking, better performing and more comfortable, safe and enduring than any previous Hupmobile. Anyone who *ever* owned a Hupp will tell you that is saying a great deal!

HUPP MOTOR CAR CORPORATION, DETROIT, MICHIGAN

THE 1938 **HUPMOBILE**

SIXES and EIGHTS

MEET HUDSON FOR 1938

HUDSON *Terraplane* • HUDSON *Six* • HUDSON *Eight*

117-INCH WHEELBASE . . . 96 AND 101 HORSEPOWER — 122-INCH WHEELBASE . . . 101 AND 107 HORSEPOWER WITH SIX STAR MOTOR — 122 AND 129-INCH WHEELBASE . . . 122 HORSEPOWER

3 Brilliant New Cars

That cost you *less* for what you *get* than any other cars in the world!

BIGGER ★ ROOMIER ★ WITH NEW LUXURY ★ NEW DRIVING EASE

Today, Hudson proudly announces three really unusual new automobiles . . . all under the Hudson banner.

With prices starting close to the very lowest, these new Hudsons have been designed from the ground up with the one idea of giving you more for your money than you can get anywhere else. Each of them, we believe, tosses overboard every previous idea as to what its price should buy.

Each brings you brilliant new style and luxury, and more size and room than ever . . . backed by performance, economy and long life hard to match no matter how much more you might pay.

And, in a year when automatic gear shifting is the brand new feature of other cars, Hudson's Selective Automatic Shift Transmission . . . made greater still for 1938 . . . stands alone as the only automatic shift that has proved itself in three years of use, by over 150,000 owners and more than a billion miles of driving.

When you meet the three new Hudsons for 1938, at any of thousands of Hudson showrooms, it is our confident belief that you will meet cars unequalled anywhere for downright *value*. Then *drive* Hudson for the biggest, happiest surprise of your motoring life. And . . . best of all . . . see how little it costs to *own* a Hudson. America's No. 1 Cars!

Complete line of new 1938 Hudson Terraplane Business Cars also on display

IT'S "BARGAIN YEAR" IN HUDSON SHOWROOMS

NEW LUXURY INTERIORS *and* A STYLE IDEA NEVER SEEN BEFORE!

1938's GREATEST DRIVING FEATURE . . NEW SELECTIVE AUTOMATIC SHIFT TRANSMISSION

(Optional at low extra cost . . . conventional gear shift available at no cost if desired)

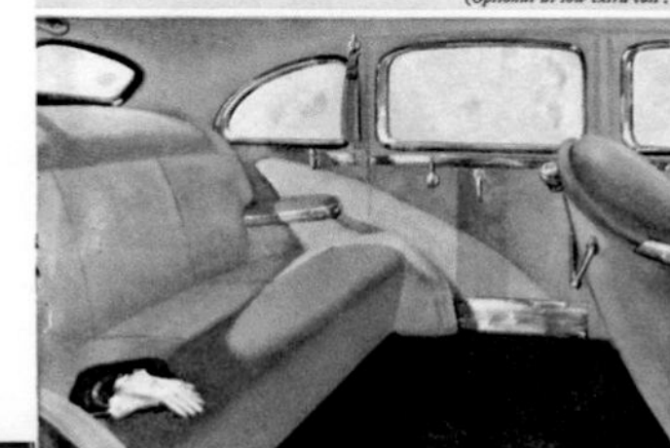

(LEFT) A hint of the ultra modern style . . . with contrasting chromium trim . . . in Hudson Six and Eight models . . . while the Hudson Eight Custom series and the big Country Club Sedan present an even more luxurious style design. Again, in Hudson Terraplane . . . new and different luxury interiors! The art of leading designers has been at work on every detail of every model . . . seat widths, leg and head room, fabrics, finish, fittings . . . combining beauty with thoughtful attention to your comfort and convenience.

(RIGHT) Shift by merely flicking a finger up at the wheel and lifting your toe from the accelerator. You never need to use the clutch pedal. Yet shift to any gear you want, at any car or engine speed. Enjoy a clear floor in front . . . no gear or brake levers to stumble over.

Hudson, 1938

To accentuate the automobile's similarity to the airplane, carmakers not only adopted names from aviation but suggested flight with winged hood ornaments and body shapes that suggested airliner engine cowls.

Um die Ähnlichkeit des Autos mit dem Flugzeug hervorzuheben, griff man bei der Namensgebung auf die Luftfahrt zurück. Typisch waren auch geflügelte Kühlerfiguren und Frontpartien, die an Triebwerksverkleidungen erinnerten.

Pour accentuer les similitudes entre l'automobile et l'avion, les constructeurs adoptent des noms issus de l'aviation et suggèrent la traversée des airs en ornant capots et carrosseries d'ailettes qui évoquent l'empennage des avions.

Hupmobile, 1938 ◂

YOU'LL BE HAPPIER WITH A CHRYSLER

THIS IS THE LIFE!

MAYBE it's because convertible cars have a particular swank; maybe it's because they have two-in-one utility—in either case, or both, it is obvious that convertible sedans and coupes are strongly in vogue.

The increasing popularity of these smart and useful body types finds Chrysler in the forefront, with convertibles meeting every desire. Chrysler has created outstanding convertible sedans and coupes in four different chassis sizes—ranging all the way from $935 to $3595.

The convertible sedan pictured above is that of the Chrysler Imperial Eight, listing at $2195. Wheelbase, 135 inches; engine, 125 horsepower . . . a magnetic and magnificent motor car. Just to look at it makes you want to drive it.

Together with all the style and luxury of Chrysler's new convertibles, and of all other Chrysler models, there is an entirely new sensation in Chrysler performance. New results due to Floating Power engine mountings. Smoothest, quietest power you have ever experienced. Not the slightest engine tremor at any car speed. Not the slightest suggestion of engine effort.

The most refreshing of all cars to drive. Shock-proof steering. Effortless gear shifting. Squeak-proof springs. Strongest, safest bodies. Surest, safest brakes. Chrysler's unrivaled Hydraulic Brakes are always self-equalizing, and have Centrifuse drums that give *five times* the wear of ordinary brakes.

There's everything about a Chrysler to make you like it—and keep on liking it. There's just no equaling Chrysler engineering or Chrysler results.

A new Chrysler Imperial Custom Eight, six body models, $2895 to $3595 · a new Chrysler Imperial Eight, three body models, $1925 to $2195 · a new Chrysler Eight, five body models, $1435 to $1695 · a new Chrysler Six, five body models, $885 to $935 F. O. B. Factory · (On Sixes, the Automatic Clutch is optional at $8 extra and Oilite Squeak-Proof Springs are optional at $10 extra) · Duplate Safety Plate Glass standard on Custom Eights. Obtainable on Six and Eight Sedans, $17.50; on Imperial Sedans, $20 · all 2-passenger Coupes, $9.50. All closed models wired for PHILCO-TRANSITONE RADIO.

FLOATING POWER · AUTOMATIC CLUTCH · SILENT GEAR SELECTOR · FREE WHEELING · INTERNAL HYDRAULIC BRAKES · OILITE SQUEAK-PROOF SPRINGS · DOUBLE-DROP GIRDER-TRUSS FRAME

CHRYSLER
IMPERIAL
WITH PATENTED
FLOATING POWER

Tune in on CHRYSLER MOTORS RADIO PROGRAM "Ziegfeld Radio Show" personally conducted by Flo Ziegfeld—Columbia Coast-to-Coast Network; every Sunday evening

A FINER AND FAR MORE DISTINGUISHED LA SALLE
. . . at an even more moderate price

It was an occasion for great rejoicing among men and women who admire fine possessions when the new La Salle V-Eight appeared upon the American scene a few weeks ago. For here was something they had been seeking. Here was a motor car of proud lineage, enriched throughout in its quality—yet offered at prices in perfect keeping with the current economic scheme. . . . No need to question the correctness of the youthful grace which is the dominating note in its appearance—for the style of the new La Salle was created by the most accomplished designers at the command of the Fisher studios. No need to wonder about its mechanical fitness or the nature of its performance—for La Salle is the product of the same skilled craftsmen who build those magnificent motor cars, the Cadillac V-Eight, V-Twelve, and V-Sixteen. . . . The new La Salle is powered by the 115-horsepower Cadillac V-type eight-cylinder engine. Throughout chassis and body are many refinements and developments of major importance, including the new Fisher No-Draft Ventilation system, individually controlled. Yet the standard five-passenger sedan is now reduced to $2245, f.o.b. Detroit—a price most attractively reasonable for a car of Cadillac design, Cadillac construction, and genuine Cadillac quality.

A GENERAL MOTORS VALUE

180

MEETING · THE · NEW · TIMES
WITH GREATER HUPMOBILE SIXES AND EIGHTS
26 MODELS . . . . $795 AND UP AT THE FACTORY

Two views of the Cabriolet-Roadster. Note how top completely disappears, leaving just a smooth expanse of gleaming metal.

LE BARON CONVERTIBLE ROADSTER

THE LINCOLN

The Lincoln appeals first to the sophisticated motorist. Those who know the most about motor cars, who need not compromise with price, are its loyal adherents. They have owned four, six, or ten Lincolns. . . . Even more than its predecessors, the new Lincoln merits the allegiance of owners, old and new. This year, the powerful V-12 cylinder engine is placed forward several inches in the frame. As a result, the luxurious body becomes roomier, and rear-seat passengers ride poised ahead of the axle, rather than directly over it. Thus the new Lincoln is a more comfortable car than ever before. . . . And it is an easier car to handle. It surges lightly, swiftly ahead with a touch of the accelerator. Shifting is smoother. Springs are more flexible. . . . Modern beauty has been achieved without the sacrifice of the dignity traditional with Lincoln. Eighteen body types designed to meet every motoring requirement, formal or informal, are available.

Chrysler Imperial, 1932 LaSalle, 1933

Hupmobile Cabriolet-Roadster, 1932 Lincoln Convertible Roadster, 1935

▸ Packard Twelve, 1934

A FAMOUS SLOGAN GOES TO WORK

FOR MORE than 30 years, Packard advertising has carried the slogan—Ask the man who owns one.

● Now this slogan has gone to work. It is helping motorists select their next fine car.

This is how it can help you. We have prepared an unusual little book which your Packard dealer will gladly send you. This book contains the names of people in your community—many of them friends and neighbors of yours — who have purchased Packards. The book contains, too, a list of questions covering every phase of motor car performance and upkeep.

● From this book, choose any number of those "who own one." Ask them the questions given, and any others you may think of. Then follow their verdict.

● If it's unfavorable, dismiss Packard from your mind. But if it's what we're sure it will be, phone your Packard dealer and have him bring one of the new Packards to your door. Drive it—see how thrillingly it lives up to what its owners say about it. Notice, too, that in appearance, as in performance, this car is unmistakably a Packard . . . one American fine car that has maintained its individuality and distinction.

PACKARD

ASK THE MAN WHO OWNS ONE

182

—WITH MORE THAT'S NEW—MORE THAT'S GOOD AND MORE THAT SAVES YOU MONEY!

OWNERS SAY, "18 TO 24 MILES PER GALLON"

Thousands of owners certify that Pontiac, despite its size, matches economy records with any car on the road. It is a money-saving marvel on gas, oil and upkeep.

When someone asks you "what's new" here's your answer—*the new, low-priced Pontiac Six*, with 51 basic advancements, with improvements in every department of motoring—distinctive in styling, brilliant in performance, safe, comfortable, roomy, as no low-priced car has ever been before! Take your choice of check-ups on this statement—talk to owners, or impartial engineers, carefully compare Pontiac with other cars feature by feature, or take a trial ride. You'll find that the only low-priced car with Safety Shift Gear Control*—*the great advancement that clears the front floor and speeds up shifting*—rules the low-price field in everything that counts! What's more—you'll find that you can easily afford it. Pontiac's big, new six is priced near the lowest!

PONTIAC MOTOR DIVISION, *General Motors Sales Corporation*, PONTIAC, MICHIGAN

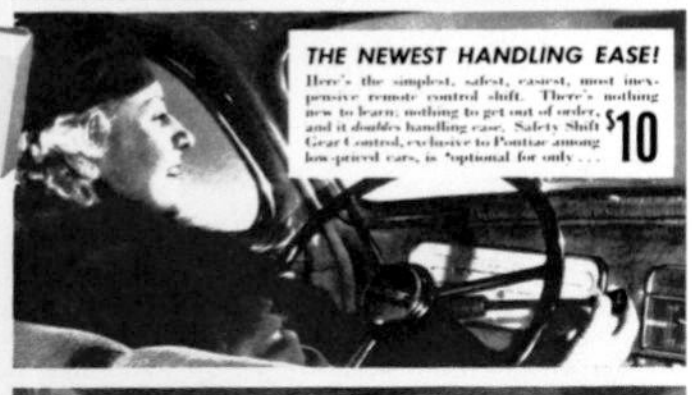

Pontiac Six, 1938

► Auto-Lite Spark Plugs, 1937

BOTH HAVE
Rhythm
AND PERFECT
PERFORMANCE . . .
AUTO-LITE

The world applauds the perfect performance. Perfect performances don't "just happen." For twenty-five years, the Electric Auto-Lite Company has been the foremost builder of Starting, Lighting and Ignition systems for the leading motor cars of America. . . . With this record of knowledge and experience, Auto-Lite engineers now introduce the perfected spark plug —the final link in perfect ignition performance—the Auto-Lite Spark Plug, Ignition Engineered by Ignition Engineers. Now you can get the most out of motoring — Greater Economy, Increased Acceleration and —Perfect Performance. Replace with Auto-Lite Spark Plugs today. Merchandising Division, The Auto-Lite Company, Toledo, Ohio.

AUTO-LITE SPARK PLUGS

Ignition Engineered by Ignition Engineers

To be a dozen places in a day . . . as you often are; to keep going with good grace and an eye on the clock . . . you need wings on your ankles or a Mercury 8 at your door!

The Mercury 8 is the fine new Ford-built motor car priced between the Ford V-8 and the Lincoln-Zephyr.

There's a serene elegance about this car that is thoroughly satisfying. It *looks* unhurried yet moves forward with fleet V-8 power. It's long and low . . . as streamlined as a ribbon in the wind. And it's luxuriously large inside . . . completely cushioned for lounging . . . remarkably silenced for rest.

And *driving* this "Eight" is sheer delight! A Californian writes that "my wife is particularly pleased with the steering . . . makes the car so easy to park. On our first trip, we did better than 20 miles to the gallon of gasoline . . . in traffic, have not fallen below 17 miles to the gallon." The Mercury has money-sense along with style! As a lady of action, you'll phone for a demonstration.

MERCURY FEATURES SUMMED-UP

Streamlined length: more than 16 feet over all on 116-inch wheelbase . . . Very wide, deep seats . . . Scientific soundproofing . . . Balanced weight and center-poise design for smooth riding . . . A 95-horsepower V-type 8-cylinder engine . . . Hydraulic brakes . . . Large and accessible luggage locker.

FORD MOTOR COMPANY—FORD, MERCURY, LINCOLN-ZEPHYR AND LINCOLN MOTOR CARS

MERCURY EIGHT

Mercury, 1939

Ford added the Mercury line to compete with GM's Buick and Pontiac.

Ford brachte den Mercury heraus, um sich gegen GMs Buick und Pontiac behaupten zu können.

Ford lance la gamme Mercury pour concurrencer les Buick et Pontiac de GM.

► Cook Paint, 1930

►► De Soto, 1937

COROC

GAVE MOTOR CAR MANUFACTURERS A DISTINCTIVE FINISH FOR DISTINGUISHED MODERN CARS

COROC

IS THE TRADE-NAME OF A VARIETY OF FINISHES FOR SPECIFIC USES, PLEDGED ALWAYS TO DO EXACTING JOBS PERFECTLY . . . AND ECONOMICALLY

COOK'S products have solved some of the most difficult finishing problems in aviation and in the automobile industry, as well as in many other industries which are exacting in their demands for finishes that stand up longest under the most trying conditions. ¶ Such a product is COOK'S COROC maroon finish, which for the first time provides a sturdy, durable, solid-covering **maroon finish** needing no special ground coats, as formerly required, and fewer finishing coats than previously necessary. Thus a manufacturer can now offer a model in maroon finish at no higher price than for ordinary colors. ¶ The COOK'S COROC label appears on a variety of special finishes, each pledging to solve a particular industrial finishing problem well.

A NEW MAROON FINISH

DIFFICULT AS THE REQUIREMENTS WERE, **COOK'S COROC MAROON FINISH** HAS SOLVED A DIFFICULT AUTOMOTIVE PROBLEM . . . JUST AS OTHER **COROC** FINISHES HAVE SATISFIED A VARIETY OF USERS

COOK

PAINT AND VARNISH COMPANY

Cook's paints, enamels, varnishes and lacquers long have proved **Best for Wear and Weather,** particularly to exacting industrial buyers requiring greatest serviceability, permanence and economy.

FACTORIES IN CINCINNATI, DETROIT, ST. LOUIS, KANSAS CITY, HOUSTON AND FORT WORTH ◆ ◆ ◆ BRANCHES IN PRINCIPAL CITIES

DE SOTO

AFTER THE WAR, WITH YEARS OF PENT-UP CONSUMER DEMAND TO BE TAPPED AND THE ECONOMY BACK IN THE UPSWING, THE AUTOMAKERS WHO GOT THEIR NEW MODELS OUT FIRST DID WELL. IT WAS A SELLER'S MARKET.

NACH DEM KRIEG PROFITIERTEN ANGESICHTS DER JAHRELANG UNBEFRIEDIGT GEBLIEBENEN NACHFRAGE UND DEM NEUERLICHEN WIRTSCHAFTSAUFSCHWUNG JENE HERSTELLER, DIE IHRE NEUEN MODELLE ALS ERSTE PRÄSENTIEREN KONNTEN.

APRÈS LA GUERRE, EN RAISON DE LA REPRISE ÉCONOMIQUE ET DES ANNÉES DE DEMANDE REFOULÉE À RATTRAPER, LES PREMIERS CONSTRUCTEURS À SORTIR LEURS NOUVEAUX MODÈLES SONT COURONNÉS DE SUCCÈS. LE MARCHÉ EST FAVORABLE AU VENDEUR.

1940

LOOKING TO THE SKIES
DER BLICK GEN HIMMEL
TOURNÉS VERS LE CIEL

-1949

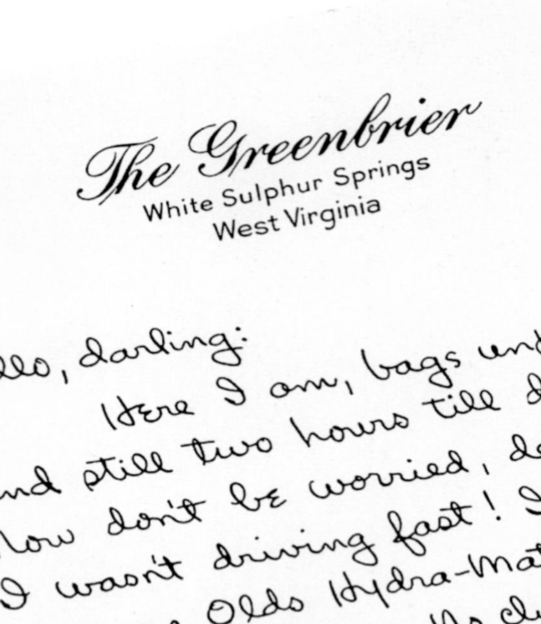

The Greenbrier
White Sulphur Springs
West Virginia

Hello, darling:

Here I am, bags unpacked and still two hours till dinner. Now don't be worried, dear — I wasn't driving fast! It's simply that an Olds Hydra-Matic cuts down driving time. No clutch to press and no gears to shift saves delays in going through cities. And the special pick-up gear makes it easy and safe to gain time on mountain roads. I'm certainly glad we have Hydra-Matic Drive in our Oldsmobile. It's the greatest thing that ever happened to make driving safe and easy for a woman.

Love,
Sue

DeSoto, 1947 ◄◄

Oldsmobile, 1941 ◄

Packard One-Sixty Engine, 1940

AUTOMOBILE PRODUCTION IN THE U.S. SHUT DOWN ALMOST IMMEDIATELY AFTER THE JAPANESE ATTACK AT PEARL HARBOR, ON DECEMBER 7, 1941. Dodge and Studebaker trucks were shipped overseas to help Allied troops. By 1942, assembly lines that had been turning out cars quickly shifted to producing tanks and fighter planes. But advertising continued, as companies boasted of their contributions to the war effort and sought to keep customer enthusiasm alive for postwar sales. In one ad, Oldsmobile even compared its promised future models to the Douglas B-19 bomber.

Earlier, Willys-Overland Motors had won a competition to build a new vehicle for the Army. Thanks to the work of legendary engineering boss Delmar G. "Barney" Roos, the little truck, eventually called the Jeep, was severely slimmed down to meet military weight requirements.

The Allison division of General Motors produced aircraft engines for such fighter planes as the P-38 Lightning and P-51 Mustang. In *Life* magazine, General Motors ran ads celebrating its role in the war effort and hailing the P-51 by another nickname: "Cadillac of the skies." Ironically, Ford would borrow the fighter's Mustang name for its sports car of the mid-1960s. And another fighter, the twin-tailed P-38, would inspire designers to deploy the first tail fins, which resembled the P-38's, on the 1948 Cadillac.

After the war, with years of pent-up consumer demand to be tapped and the economy back in the upswing, the automakers who got their new models out first did well. It was a seller's market. Studebaker found success with its novel "coming and going" style — the windshield and back window were so much alike that some joked they could not tell which way the car was going. Willys brought the Jeep home from the war and out to the ranches and even suburbs, with the Jeepster.

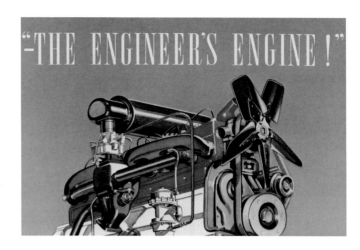

New entrepreneurs entered the market as well. Henry Kaiser, who turned out hundreds of wartime Liberty ships to transport goods to embattled Europe, turned to carmaking. Preston Tucker, who believed he could build a technologically innovative car, attempted to break into the ranks of Detroit carmakers. (His efforts would later be mythologized in the film *Tucker*, directed by Francis Ford Coppola.) But thanks in part to the importance and cost of advertising to create a brand image, the cost of entry into the car market had become much higher than these entrepreneurs had estimated. Both Kaiser and Tucker failed in a matter of a few years.

A few oddball manufacturers struggled on: Nash offered the small Metropolitan and quirky little Ambassador. With its Wasps and Hornets, Hudson advertised its novel "step down" bathtub styling and an infamous built-in seat bed, which Nash also pushed. Eventually, in 1954, Nash and Hudson joined to form American Motors. Instead of growing, in fact, the number of automakers shrank again. Americans would have to look overseas for additional choices.

1940

1940 U.S. government mandates sealed-beam headlights

Monoblock-Scheinwerfer in den USA behördlich vorgeschrieben

Le gouvernement américain recommande les phares scellés

1940 Willys begins Jeep delivery

Auslieferung der ersten Willys Jeeps

Willys livre ses premières Jeeps

1940 U.S. carmakers begin to support war effort; P-51 fighter called "Cadillac of the Skies"

US-Autobauer beginnen mit der Produktion kriegswichtiger Güter; Jagdflugzeug P-51 als „Cadillac der Lüfte" bezeichnet

Les constructeurs américains soutiennent l'effort de guerre ; Le chasseur P-51 est baptisé « la Cadillac des airs »

1942 Wartime gas and rubber rationing begin in U.S.

Beginn der kriegsbedingten Rationierung von Benzin und Gummi in den USA

Rationnement de l'essence et du caoutchouc aux États-Unis en raison de la guerre

DIE ZIVILE AUTOPRODUKTION KAM FAST UNMITTELBAR NACH DEM ANGRIFF DER JAPANER AUF PEARL HARBOR AM 7. DEZEMBER 1941 ZUM ERLIEGEN. Nun wurden Trucks von Dodge und Studebaker zur Unterstützung der alliierten Truppen nach Übersee verfrachtet. Fließbänder, auf denen bisher Autos produziert wurden, wurden bereits 1942 auf Panzer und Kampfflugzeuge umgestellt. Geworben wurde jedoch weiterhin, denn die Firmen rühmten sich ihres Beitrags zur Landesverteidigung und suchten die Begeisterung des Kunden mit Blick auf den Nachkriegsabsatz lebendig zu erhalten. Oldsmobile verglich seine versprochenen künftigen Modelle in einer Anzeige sogar mit dem Douglas B-19 Bomber (dem Prototyp eines großen Langstreckenbombers).

Willys-Overland Motors hatte die Ausschreibung für die Fertigung eines neuen Armeefahrzeugs gewonnen. Dem legendären Chefkonstrukteur Delmar G. „Barney" Roos ist zu verdanken, dass der kleine Truck, später „Jeep" genannt, stark abspeckte, um die militärische Gewichtsnorm zu erfüllen.

Die Allison-Abteilung von General Motors produzierte Triebwerke etwa für Jagdflugzeuge vom Typ P-38 Lightning und P-51 Mustang. General Motors schaltete Anzeigen in der Zeitschrift *Life*, in denen man den eigenen Beitrag zur Landesverteidigung zelebrierte und der P-51 einen neuen Spitznamen verpasste: „Cadillac der Lüfte". Ironischerweise sollte sich Ford Mitte der 1960er-Jahre für die Namensgebung seines Mustang bei dem gleichen Flugzeugmodell bedienen. Und die P-38 mit ihrem Gabelschwanz sollte die Designer beim 1948er Cadillac zu den ersten Heckflossen inspirieren.

Nach dem Krieg profitierten angesichts der jahrelang unbefriedigt gebliebenen Nachfrage und dem neuerlichen Wirtschaftsaufschwung jene Hersteller, die ihre neuen Modelle als Erste präsentieren konnten. Erfolg erntete Studebaker mit dem neuartigen „coming and going"-Stil – Front- und Heckscheibe sahen sich zum Verwechseln ähnlich; manche scherzten, man wisse gar nicht, wo vorne und hinten sei. Willys brachte seinen Jeep von den Kriegsschauplätzen auf die Ranches und den Jeepster sogar in die Vorstädte.

Neue Unternehmer betraten die Bühne. Henry Kaiser, der seine Liberty-Frachter zu Hunderten in das umkämpfte Europa geschickt hatte, wurde zum Autobauer. Preston Tucker, der überzeugt war, ein technologisch innovatives Auto bauen zu können, versuchte zu den etablierten Autoherstellern von Detroit aufzusteigen. (Einen verklärten Blick auf sein Werk gab später Francis Ford Coppolas Film *Tucker*). Um ein Markenimage aufzubauen, bedurfte es jedoch auch umfassender, aufwendiger Werbung. So lag der Preis für den Eintritt in den Automarkt schließlich viel höher als man geschätzt hatte – mit der Folge, dass Kaiser wie auch Tucker nach wenigen Jahren am Ende waren.

Doch ein paar Verrückte bemühten sich weiter: Nash präsentierte den kleinen Metropolitan und den kleinen Ambassador. Und Hudson warb mit seinen Wasps (Wespen) und Hornets (Hornissen) für die neue, wannenartige „step down"-Karosserie und seine unerhörten Liegesitze. Nash und Hudson schlossen sich 1954 zu American Motors zusammen. Doch anstatt zu wachsen, ging die Zahl der Autohersteller erneut zurück. Um die Auswahl zu vergrößern, mussten die Amerikaner nach Übersee blicken.

1945 Ford establishes Lincoln-Mercury Division

Ford gründet die Lincoln-Mercury Division

Ford fonde la division Lincoln-Mercury

1947 Studebaker Starlight, with similar front and back, dubbed "coming and going" model

Studebaker Starlight wegen seiner gleichartigen Front- und Heckpartie als „coming and going"-Modell bezeichnet

La Studebaker Starlight, dont l'avant et l'arrière se ressemblent, est surnommée la « va et vient »

1948 In-N-Out hamburger offers "drive thru" service; customers order through speaker

In-N-Out Hamburger bietet „drive thru"-Service mit Wechselsprechanlage

In-N-Out hamburger propose le service au volant ; les clients passent commande par interphone

1948 Cadillac gives birth to "fishtail," later to become tail fin

Cadillac präsentiert mit den ersten „Fischschwänzen" die später populären Heckflossen

Cadillac crée la « queue de poisson », qui deviendra l'ailette

DEER
LODGE
25 MI
DEER
LODGE
1 MI

Whether you need gasoline or not...
You're Welcome!
REGISTERED
REST
ROOM
A TEXACO DEALER SERVICE

Chrysler New Yorker, 1946 ◂◂

Texaco Oil, 1941 ◂

▸▸ Pontiac, 1948

LA PRODUCTION AUTOMOBILE S'EFFONDRE PRESQUE AUSSITÔT APRÈS L'ATTAQUE DES JAPONAIS SUR PEARL HARBOR LE 7 DÉCEMBRE 1941. Dodge et Studebaker envoient des camions aider les troupes alliées en Europe. Dès 1942, les chaînes de montage n'accouchent plus de voitures mais de tanks et d'avions de combat, ce qui n'empêche pas les constructeurs de continuer à faire de la publicité. Ils se targuent de contribuer à l'effort de guerre et préparent ainsi les esprits à la reprise des ventes après-guerre. Dans une réclame, Oldsmobile compare même ses futurs modèles au bombardier Douglas B-19.

Un peu plus tôt, la société Willys Overland Motors a remporté un appel d'offre pour construire un nouveau véhicule militaire. Œuvre du légendaire ingénieur en chef Delmar G. « Barney » Roos, cette petite camionnette, finalement baptisée « Jeep », a subi un sérieux dégraissage pour satisfaire aux exigences de l'armée concernant son poids.

Allison, filiale de General Motors, produit des moteurs pour les avions de chasse tels que le P-38 Lightning et le P-51 Mustang. Dans le magazine *Life*, GM glorifie sa contribution à l'effort de guerre à travers ses publicités et surnomme le P-51 la « Cadillac du ciel ». Comble de l'ironie, c'est à ce Mustang que Ford empruntera son nom pour sa voiture de sport du milieu des années 1960. Un autre avion de combat, le P-38 à double queue, inspire aux designers les premières ailettes arrière – qui rappellent les empennages de l'appareil – sur la Cadillac 1948.

Après la guerre, en raison de la reprise économique et des années de demande refoulée à rattraper, les premiers constructeurs à sortir leurs nouveaux modèles sont couronnés de succès. Le marché est favorable au vendeur. Studebaker fait un tabac avec son nouveau style « coming and going » (littéralement « va et vient ») – le pare-brise et la lunette arrière se ressemblent tant que certains plaisantins prétendent qu'on ne peut distinguer dans quelle direction la voiture roule. De la guerre, Willys rapporte la Jeep qui séduit les propriétaires de ranch, et mêmes les banlieusards s'enthousiasment pour le modèle Jeepster.

De nouveaux entrepreneurs arrivent sur le marché. Henry Kaiser, qui a produit des centaines de cargos pour ravitailler l'Europe pendant la guerre, se tourne vers l'automobile. Croyant pouvoir construire une voiture à partir d'une technologie nouvelle, Preston Tucker tente de se faire une place à Detroit. (Ses efforts seront portés à l'écran par Francis Ford Coppola dans le film *Tucker*). Mais créer une image de marque est devenu non seulement coûteux mais crucial, et il devient financièrement beaucoup plus difficile de pénétrer le marché automobile. Kaiser comme Tucker échouent en l'espace de quelques années.

Une poignée d'excentriques refusent néanmoins de déposer les armes. Nash propose deux petits modèles : la Metropolitan et l'Ambassador, plus excentrique. Avec ses Wasps et ses Hornets, Hudson fait valoir son nouveau style « baignoire retournée » et son célèbre « lit dans l'auto », également proposé par Nash. En 1954, Nash et Hudson finissent par s'unir pour former American Motors. Au lieu d'augmenter, le nombre de constructeurs diminue de nouveau. Les Américains doivent se tourner vers l'étranger pour avoir un choix plus vaste.

1948

1948 Buick introduces Dynaflow, first torque converter–style automatic transmission

Buick entwickelt mit Dynaflow das erste Automatikgetriebe nach dem Prinzip des Drehmomentwandlers

Buick lance la boîte de vitesses Dynaflow, première transmission automatique à convertisseur de couple hydraulique

1949 Cadillac and Oldsmobile introduce high-compression V8s that use high-octane fuel

Cadillac und Oldsmobile präsentieren hoch komprimierte V8-Motoren für hoch oktanigen Kraftstoff

Cadillac et Oldsmobile adoptent le V8 à haute compression, qui utilise un taux d'octane élevé

1949 Newly styled Mercury coupe released; will become favorite car for customizers

Vorstellung des im Design überarbeiteten Mercury-Coupés, das zum Lieblingsauto der Kunden werden sollte

Lancement du coupé Mercury redessiné ; il deviendra le chouchou des amateurs de sur mesure

1950 Nash Rambler debuts

Der Nash Rambler wird eingeführt

Débuts de la Nash Rambler

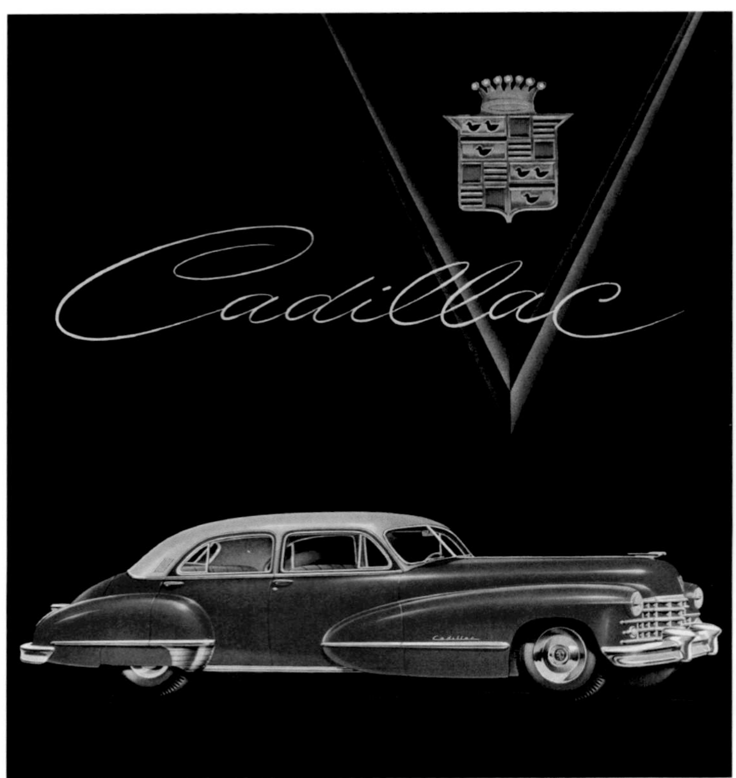

An indefinable something—more than luxurious appearance, or superlative craftsmanship, or matchless performance—places Cadillac in that restricted category reserved for products which are beyond all serious competition. Even the casual observer can sense this quality; but the full measure of its meaning comes only to those who possess a Cadillac. In essence, it is expressed in the owner's unmitigated satisfaction—in his unqualified assurance that here is personal transportation in its nearest approach to perfection. Perhaps you are one of the many so eagerly awaiting delivery of new Cadillacs. If so, we wish to assure you that everything possible, consistent with Cadillac's standards, is being done to get your car into your possession. But despite our best efforts, some delay in delivery is still inevitable. We feel confident, however, that you will wait with patience —because you are waiting for a Cadillac!

* CADILLAC MOTOR CAR DIVISION * GENERAL MOTORS CORPORATION *

At the top of the automotive world stands General Motors—the leader from every conceivable standpoint. And at the top of the General Motors quality list stands Cadillac—the world-wide symbol of all that is fine and distinguished in an automobile. It took forty-four years of conscientious effort to bring the present model Cadillac into being . . . forty-four years of progressive engineering, ever-finer craftsmanship, and cumulative experience. In no other way could it have been produced. For like every other superior creation, a superb motor car is a *development* —the sum of a long series of progressive advancements. That is why there is not—and never can be—another car like Cadillac. For no other motor car is built against such a background of quality—and experience.

* CADILLAC MOTOR CAR DIVISION * GENERAL MOTORS CORPORATION *

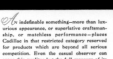

▸ Cadillac Series 62 Convertible, 1948

An outsize logo resembling a coat of arms and script typeface that seemed to be borrowed from an engraved invitation to a dress ball were staples of Cadillac advertising. Its new style included "fish tails," soon to be called tail fins.

Ein übergroßes, wappenartiges Logo und eine Schrift, die einer Einladung zu einem Kostümball entlehnt schien – dies waren gängige Elemente der Cadillac-Werbung. Die neuartigen „Fischschwänze" sollten bald als „Heckflossen" bekannt werden.

Un logo de taille démesurée aux allures de blason et une typographie semblant empruntée à un carton d'invitation mondain, voilà les bases de la publicité pour Cadillac. Le nouveau modèle arbore des ailettes à l'arrière.

Cadillac Sixty Special, 1947

Cadillac Sixty Special, 1946

Cadillac
White Sidewall Tires available at additional cost.

TODAY'S Cadillac is the most beautiful ever built—and the new Cadillacs you see on the streets and highways are the most popular in Cadillac history. ☆ ☆ ☆ America's first look at these smart new cars was enough to win instant approval for their uncommon beauty—heralding, as it does, all that is best in modern motor car design. ☆ ☆ ☆ But beauty is only *half* the story of the great new Cadillacs—for the exterior smartness is matched completely by the new mechanical goodness. In all the things that make a motor car a joy to possess and a pleasure to drive—here, indeed, is the car of cars. ☆ ☆ ☆ Small wonder that thousands who have previously been content with lesser cars are turning to Cadillac—determined, once and for all, to be done with compromise. ☆ ☆ ☆ We feel sure you would enjoy a careful inspection of the car by which all others are measured and adjudged. You will be welcome at your Cadillac dealer's showrooms at any time.

★ CADILLAC MOTOR CAR DIVISION ★ GENERAL MOTORS CORPORATION ★

Biggest Thrills **of Motoring have been the Self-Starter, 4-Wheel Hydraulic Brakes, Safety-Steel Body, High-Speed Engine. Now, Latest and Greatest is De Soto with Fluid Drive and Simplimatic Transmission! For all Normal Driving, You Needn't Shift or Use the Clutch! Try This De Soto!**

YOU'LL GET A THRILL when you step into the Custom De Soto! Every knob and panel, all upholstery—in glorious new Two-Tones!

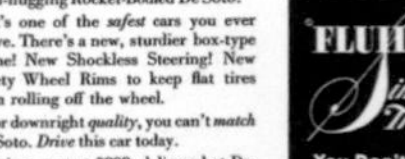

Of course you want the most important single advance of the decade. And when you can get perfected No-Shift Driving in a car like *this*, you simply mustn't miss it!

Just look at De Soto. If you think it's beautiful in the picture, wait till you *actually* see its rich new body colors with harmonizing interiors!

And what a kick you'll get out of its full 105 horsepower—the way it whips you out and around other cars. Curves—you can take them with all the confidence in the world in that long, low, road-hugging Rocket-Bodied De Soto!

It's one of the *safest* cars you ever drove. There's a new, sturdier box-type frame! New Shockless Steering! New Safety Wheel Rims to keep flat tires from rolling off the wheel.

For downright *quality*, you can't *match* De Soto. *Drive* this car today.

Prices start at $898, delivered at Detroit. Transportation, state, local taxes, are extra. De Soto Division of Chrysler Corporation, Detroit, Mich. *Prices subject to change without notice.*

MAJOR BOWES, C.B.S., THURS., 9-10 P.M., E.S.T.

De Soto De Luxe 6-Passenger Sedan, $965 at Detroit (white sidewall tires extra).

Slip **behind De Soto's wheel...relax in an interior "tailored" in every detail! Smart plastic-trimmed fittings, richly-grained mouldings, wide "bolster" seats—all *harmonize* with your choice of body color! Yes, you've 12 to choose from—8 solid colors, 4 superbly blended 2-tones!**

IT'S TAILORED! De Soto's Custom Brougham Interior features a new center armrest ... deep Airfoam cushions ... 2-tone colors!

MAJOR BOWES, C.B.S., THURS., 9-10 P.M., E.D.S.T.

Everyone likes to express his personality—in the clothes he wears, the car he drives! That's the beauty of De Soto...it gives you practically custom tailoring at low cost!

Inside that Rocket Body, note the use of plastics in tan, green, or blue to blend with your upholstery! And you have a choice of smooth broadcloth or rich, deep pile fabric. Every detail says "quality"!

And beneath this smart appearance is a *real performer!* That high-compression engine delivers 105-horsepower (10 to 15 more than other cars near the price)! A new Box-type Frame, Ride Stabilizers front and rear, Aero-type Shock Absorbers—all combine to give you a *Miracle Ride!*

And, for all its bigness, De Soto with 121½" wheelbase is delightfully easy to drive. The most effortless steering you've ever known takes the work and strain out of traffic, parking!

Ask for a demonstration today! There's a De Soto Dealer right near you. De Soto Division of Chrysler Corporation, Detroit, Michigan.

FLUID DRIVE WITH Simplimatic Transmission
You Don't Have To Shift Or Use The Clutch For Normal Driving
*AVAILABLE ON ALL MODELS AT MODERATE ADDITIONAL COST

$898 for De Luxe Coupe Illustrated, at Detroit. Federal taxes included. White sidewall tires, transportation, state, local taxes extra. Prices subject to change without notice.

No-Shift Driving
AT ITS BEST!
TRY IT IN THE
New De Soto

The Year's Newest **New Car Offers 1941's Newest Driving Thrill! Stop—Start—Go—For All Normal Driving You Don't Have to Shift or Use the Clutch. De Soto has famous Fluid Drive with a New Simplimatic Transmission that shifts gears for you whenever you need it! By All Means, Try this Exciting Car Today!**

Model Illustrated is De Luxe 2-Door Sedan—$965 at Detroit.

WHAT A BEAUTIFUL BACK! Under those sleek lines is a *10-bag* luggage locker, with a counterbalanced lid for easy opening!
TUNE IN MAJOR BOWES' HOUR, C.B.S., THURSDAYS, 9-10 P.M., E.S.T.

Imagine—No-Shift Driving in this new Rocket Body car! De Soto is full 17 feet long...with that "certain something" in styling that makes people turn and look twice. It's *rich-looking*, inside and out!

And talk about ride! This car "hugs" the road—smooths out bumps—takes curves without a sway. Shockless Steering keeps road shocks away from your hands—and the big 105-horsepower engine gives almost limitless power! See your De Soto Dealer ... drive this car now!

Prices start as low as $898 delivered at Detroit, federal taxes included. Transportation, state and local taxes, if any, extra. De Soto Division of Chrysler Corporation, Detroit, Michigan. *Prices subject to change without notice.*

1941 DeSoto

Enjoy **(1) De Soto Fluid Drive with (2) Simplimatic Transmission—Automatic Shifting for all normal driving! (3) Low-slung Rocket Bodies! (4) New 2-Tone Interiors! (5) Chrysler Corporation Quality, Economy!**

ROCKET BODIES have spacious leg room, elbow room—deep, luxurious new Form-Rest Seats.

"BUILT BY CHRYSLER CORPORATION" MEANS QUALITY

Fluid Drive
Formerly only on high-priced cars, now combined with Simplimatic Transmission, gives you Automatic Shifting for all normal driving
ASK FOR A DEMONSTRATION TODAY!

De Soto!...that's the name to remember—the car to watch—this year! It's a *big* car—a *wide* car—*a long, rakish, low-slung* car...with lines that are all action and beauty.

You can *see* and *feel* its quality...in the way it is designed and fitted throughout, in the velvety smoothness with which it handles.

It has every new and worth-while feature for '41. Drive it, and you'll see!

With Fluid Drive, you can stop, start, go all day without shifting or touching the clutch! A wonderful smooth surge of power at the getaway...flashing acceleration in traffic or on hills. Always that feeling of effortless, limitless power! And this beauty hugs the road ... literally *smooths out* the rough spots. It gives you that solid, steady-riding "feel" you want.

Stop in today and see this big, impressive, 1941 De Soto. Take it out on the road and try it. You'll find a rich, luxurious, wonderfully easy-handling car ...priced surprisingly low.

There are thirteen body styles—eight new solid colors...four beautiful two-tone combinations.

You have a choice of fine upholstery fabrics—two-tone interior color schemes. De Soto Division of Chrysler Corporation, Detroit, Michigan.

TUNE IN MAJOR BOWES, C.B.S., THURS., 9 TO 10 P.M., E.S.T.

DeSoto, 1941 DeSoto, 1941

DeSoto, 1941 DeSoto, 1941

► LaSalle, 1940

The Chassis Comes **First** !

LASALLE is invariably the choice of the man who looks under the hood when buying a car.

He buys LaSalle because LaSalle's superiority is so readily discernible in its chassis construction; because Cadillac's standards of craftsmanship and materials are so evident in every part of the LaSalle chassis.

And, as you know, on the chassis are almost entirely dependent the essential qualities of performance, of economy, and of riding comfort. In fact, the very life of the car is built in its chassis.

That is why it is *important* for you to know the LaSalle chassis is designed and built by Cadillac engineers and craftsmen—the men who build the magnificent Cadillac-Fleetwood.

That is why you should know that LaSalle is powered with a Cadillac V-8 engine, and that the same exacting standards are applied equally to Cadillac and LaSalle chassis construction and materials.

It is no wonder that LaSalle buyers remain enthusiastic LaSalle owners through the years—for they *enjoy* the advantages of driving a medium-priced car built on a Cadillac foundation.

Your Cadillac-LaSalle dealer would be pleased to have you drive this exceptional car. Then you can prove to your own satisfaction that no other car in its price class equals LaSalle.

Cadillac Motor Car Division—builder of LaSalle, Cadillac and Cadillac-Fleetwood cars.

$1240 *for the Series Fifty Coupe, delivered at Detroit. Sedan prices start at $1280. Transportation based on rail rates, state and local taxes (if any), optional equipment, accessories—extra. Prices subject to change without notice.*

and so-o-o to bed

There's a spot in the hills where the big bass bite and the air is cool with pine.

Get in a new Nash "600" and you'll be there tonight. Just snuggle down in the big soft seat and watch the road start flying backwards.

Look—!

The curves straighten out and the bumps unwrinkle up ahead. The hills lie down and the stuffy day turns sparkling fresh.

Look—your speedometer shows you're getting an incredible 25 to 30 miles on a gallon of gas at moderate highway speed!

Hey—what's happened anyway?

Where's the dust and the noise? The swaying—and the wheel tugging?

A *lot* has happened—since you last bought an automobile. And it's all happened here in the Nash "600."

This car is built a new way. *Welded* (not bolted together)—a single unit body and frame, free of dead weight and noise-making joints.

New, easier steering is here . . . and coil springing on all four wheels . . . new soundproofing . . . and the famous Nash Weather-Eye automatic "Conditioned Air" System! And a Nash can even sleep you tonight with Convertible Bed equipment. Just yawn . : : and so-o to bed!

Is it any wonder the swing today is to Nash? Smart people *like* this new kind of car—and the new kind of solid, friendly dealer who sells it. See him today about the brilliant new Nash "600" and the Nash Ambassador.

You'll be ahead with Nash

NASH MOTORS DIVISION NASH-KELVINATOR CORP., DETROIT

Nash Ambassador, 1947

The Nash's roomy cab, complete with a bed that could be used for camping, could also be put to other purposes; parents and teachers were not amused with the innovation.

Der geräumige Nash besaß ein Bett, das man zum Camping, aber auch anderweitig nutzen konnte. Eltern und Lehrer waren nicht eben begeistert über diese Neuerung.

Avec sa spacieuse cabine et son concept de « lit dans l'auto », elle peut servir à camper – comme ici – mais aussi à d'autres activités : cette innovation ne plaît guère aux parents et aux enseignants.

► Oldsmobile Custom 8 Cruiser, 1940

Most Modern Car in the World!

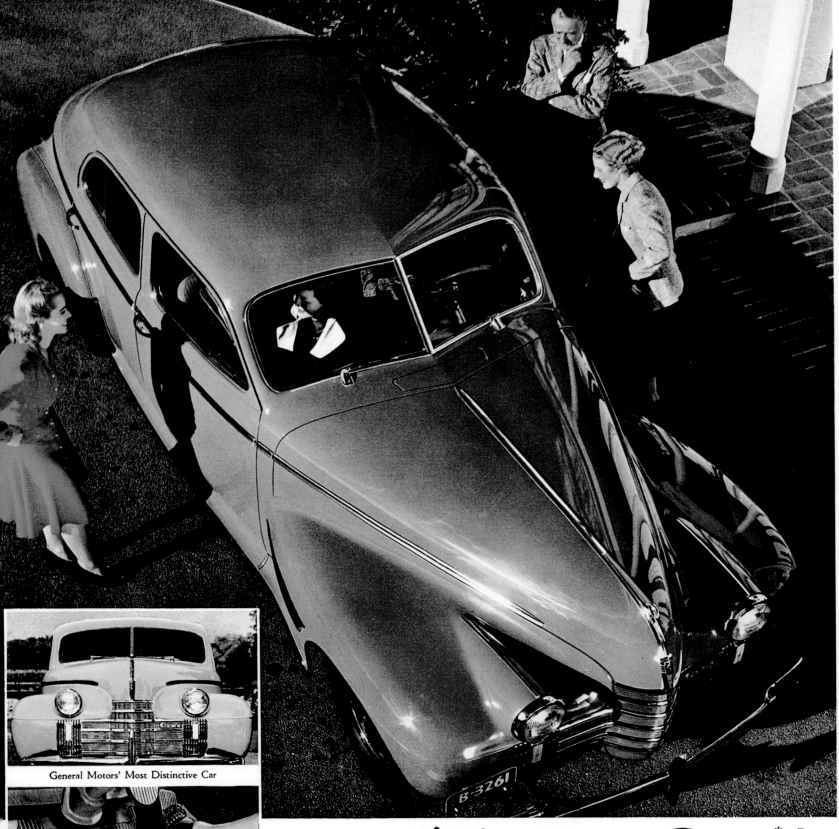

General Motors' Most Distinctive Car

ONLY OLDS OFFERS THE *Hydra-Matic Drive*!*

OLDSMOBILE'S magnificent 110 H. P. Custom 8 Cruiser stands in its own right as America's super-luxury car of moderate price. Add Oldsmobile's exclusive Hydra-Matic Drive and you have the *most modern car in the world.* With Hydra-Matic Drive, you have *no gears to shift—no clutch to press.* You get smoother, more dynamic performance and you save on gasoline. Visit your Oldsmobile dealer today and try the one BIG new motoring advance of the year!

*Optional at only $57 extra on *all* 1940 Olds models.

OLDSMOBILE "CUSTOM 8 CRUISER"

A GENERAL MOTORS VALUE

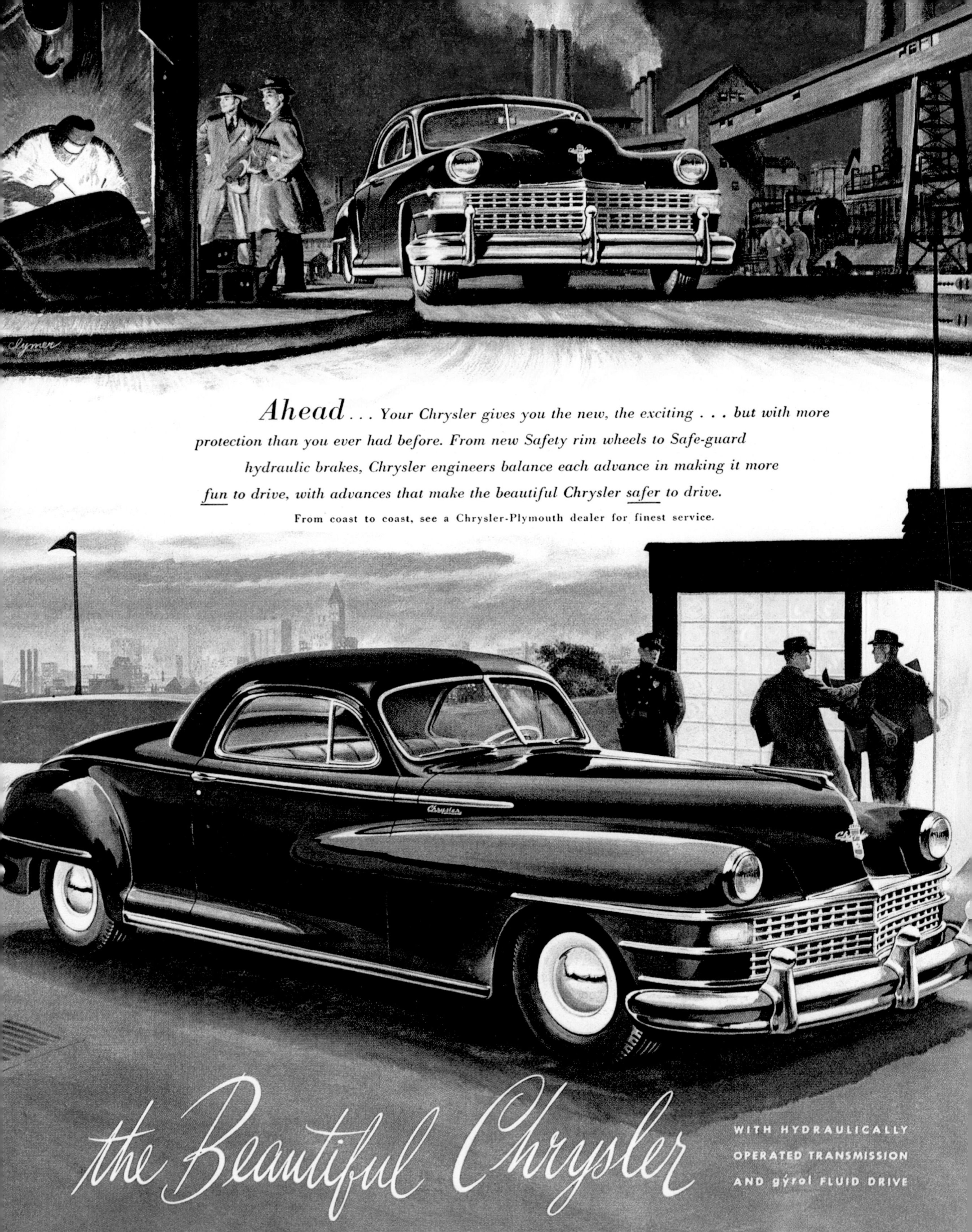
Clymer
Ahead . . . Your Chrysler gives you the new, the exciting . . . but with more protection than you ever had before. From new Safety rim wheels to Safe-guard hydraulic brakes, Chrysler engineers balance each advance in making it more fun to drive, with advances that make the beautiful Chrysler safer to drive.
From coast to coast, see a Chrysler-Plymouth dealer for finest service.
Chrysler
the Beautiful Chrysler
WITH HYDRAULICALLY OPERATED TRANSMISSION AND gyrol FLUID DRIVE

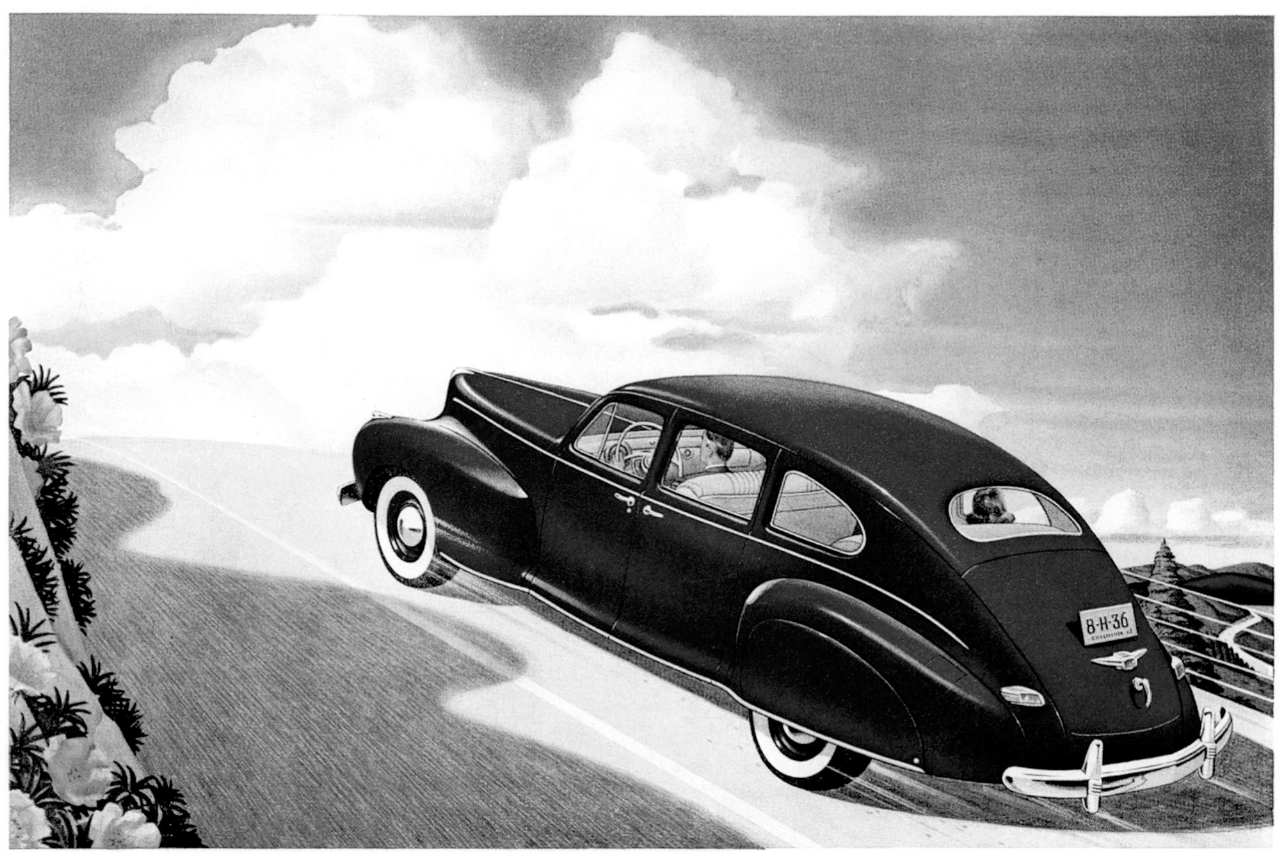

Look Out For Those Clouds!

You're skimming straight for the horizon! A warm wind softly fans your face as you soar to the crest of the hill. And stretching below you are ribbons of roads and trees that dwindle to pencils . . . *Watch out*—or you'll bump into one of those big, billowy clouds! You're driving a new Lincoln-Zephyr, mister, and that means you're *riding high!*

Up through giant valleys, packed with dusk and hush, this glorious V-12 whisks you quickly and quietly to the carefree top of the world. For it's a sleek-lined new beauty, triple-cushioned in rubber to give you a ride as smooth as glider flight! You settle back and delight in the restful luxury of lavishly deep, wide chair-high seats . . . and in the magnificent, road-hugging, low-gravity balance of the car, cushioned on slow-motion Lincoln cradle springs.

So vital and live and packed with gallant *go* is this exciting traveler that you can't stay still when you own one. Streamlined from the inside out, it gives you more fun per gallon than any car you've ever had! And a staunch unit body-and-frame in closed types surrounds you with a welded-steel framework of protection.

Pause awhile before you pay less—*for less.* Remember, these Lincoln-Zephyrs are built to a watch-like nicety in the Lincoln precision plant. Small wonder they are so strikingly *different* in engine—design—and basic construction.

Why not ask your nearest Lincoln-Zephyr dealer for a demonstration? Drive this eager car . . . and you'll feel irresistible new realms of motoring adventure opening wide and limitless before you!

• For utmost motoring enjoyment try the new *Lincoln Automatic Overdrive!* It makes driving smoother and easier than ever before . . . reduces engine revolutions by 30% . . . prolongs engine life . . . reduces fuel and oil costs! Factory-installed at moderate extra cost. Be sure to get a demonstration.

LINCOLN MOTOR CAR DIVISION, FORD MOTOR COMPANY

Builders also of the Lincoln-Continental, Cabriolet and Coupe; the Lincoln-Custom, Sedan and Limousine

Lincoln Zephyr, 1941

Chrysler Windsor, 1946 ◂

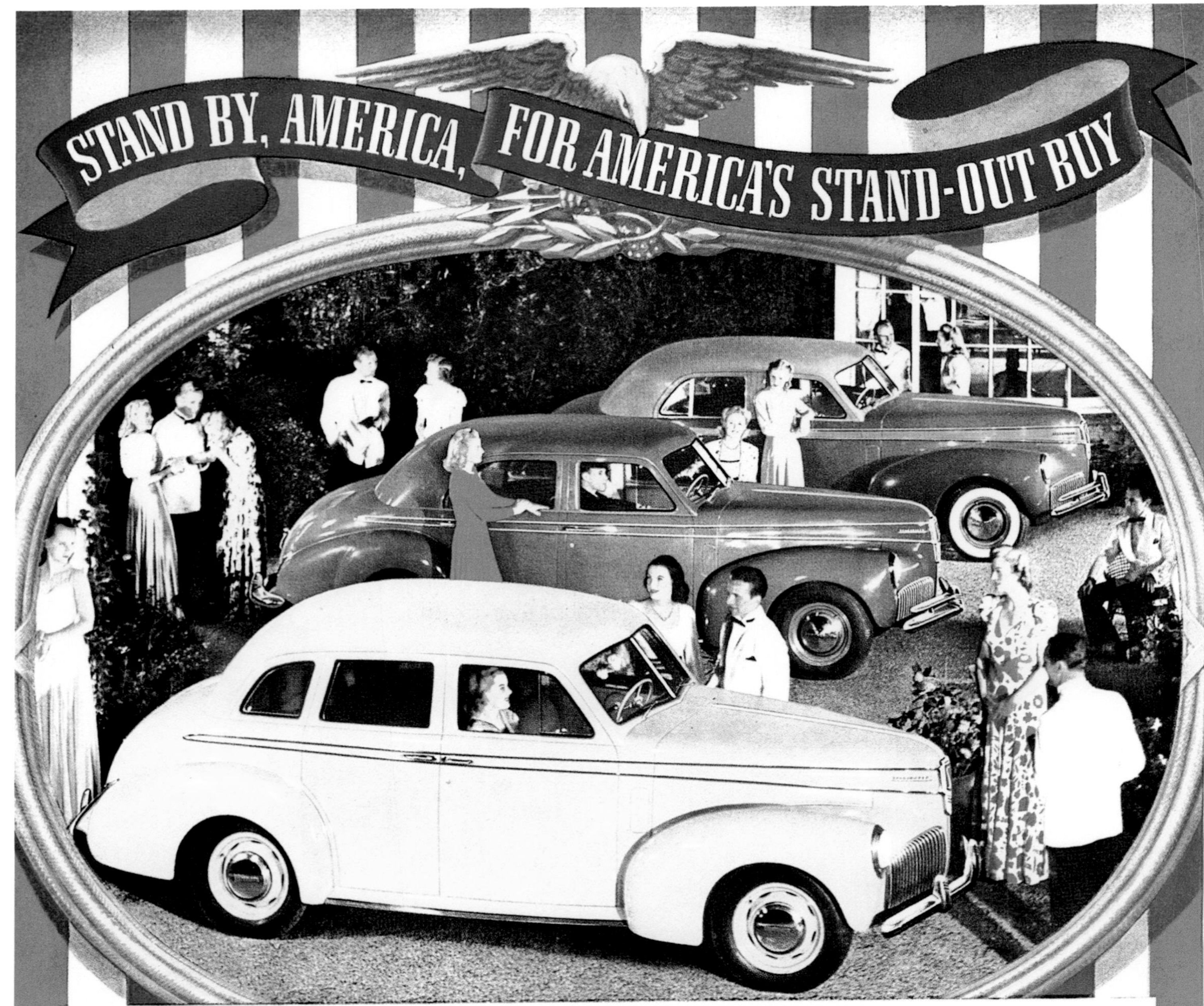

208

Announcing 1941 Studebakers

A Big New Studebaker Champion in the Lowest Price Field!
Distinctive New, Luxury-Laden Studebaker Commander and President!

RIDING the crest of Studebaker's spectacular 1940 success come these three dramatically distinctive, brand-new Studebakers for 1941 . . . a bigger, longer, wider, roomier, new Studebaker Champion in the lowest price field—a glamorously beautiful new Studebaker Commander Six—a richly finished, luxury-laden, new Studebaker President Eight.

These new 1941 Studebakers are slipstream styled in an exciting new aero mode by famous Raymond Loewy, designer of the smart interiors of the Boeing Stratoliners. Their advanced torpedo-type bodies come in your choice of single-tone, or exquisite, contrasting-color Delux-tone, exteriors and interiors.

Every model is a marvel of sound, solid, long-lasting Studebaker craftsmanship.

Remarkable gas economy

These safe, sure-footed, easy-handling new Studebakers for 1941 are engineered to equal or excel the sensational records of the Studebakers of 1940 in gas economy.

And the 1940 Studebakers defeated all other cars in the Gilmore-Yosemite Sweepstakes—the Champion averaging 29.19 miles per gallon, the Commander 24.72 miles per gallon, the President 23.40 miles per gallon with low extra-cost-overdrive.

See your local Studebaker dealer now and go for a revealing Studebaker drive. Prices begin on a level with the three other large-selling lowest price cars. Low down payment. C.I.T. budget plan terms.

Tucker "Torpedo", 1948

With its offbeat, three-headlight face, the Tucker represented a romantic dream. Preston Tucker tried to join the big boys in Detroit, only to find it was too late and too expensive. Just 50 Tuckers were built, but the car's legend would later be immortalized in a film directed by Francis Ford Coppola.

Mit seiner ungewöhnlichen dreiäugigen Front verkörperte der Tucker einen romantischen Traum. Preston Tucker versuchte es den Großen von Detroit gleichzutun, doch es war bereits zu spät und zudem zu teuer. Nur 50 Tucker wurden gebaut, doch später sollte ein Film unter der Regie von Francis Ford Coppola diesem Namen ewigen Ruhm bescheren.

Avec son avant original ponctué de trois phares, la Tucker incarne un rêve romantique : celui du constructeur Preston Tucker, qui tenta d'entrer dans la cour des grands de Detroit. Hélas, l'effort fut trop tardif et trop coûteux. Seule une cinquantaine de Tucker furent construites, mais la légende fut immortalisée à l'écran par Francis Ford Coppola.

Studebaker, 1941 ◂

Only One is Number One

Only CHEVROLET IS FIRST!

America's biggest money's worth!

Yes, you'll find people everywhere agreeing: Of all cars, only *one* is Number One, only Chevrolet for 1948 is first, because it alone gives BIG-CAR QUALITY AT LOWEST COST—*stepped-up in style and value!* That's why *more people* drive Chevrolets—and *more people* want Chevrolets—than any other make of car, according to official nation-wide registration and seven independent nation-wide surveys.

CHEVROLET MOTOR DIVISION, GENERAL MOTORS CORPORATION, DETROIT 2, MICHIGAN

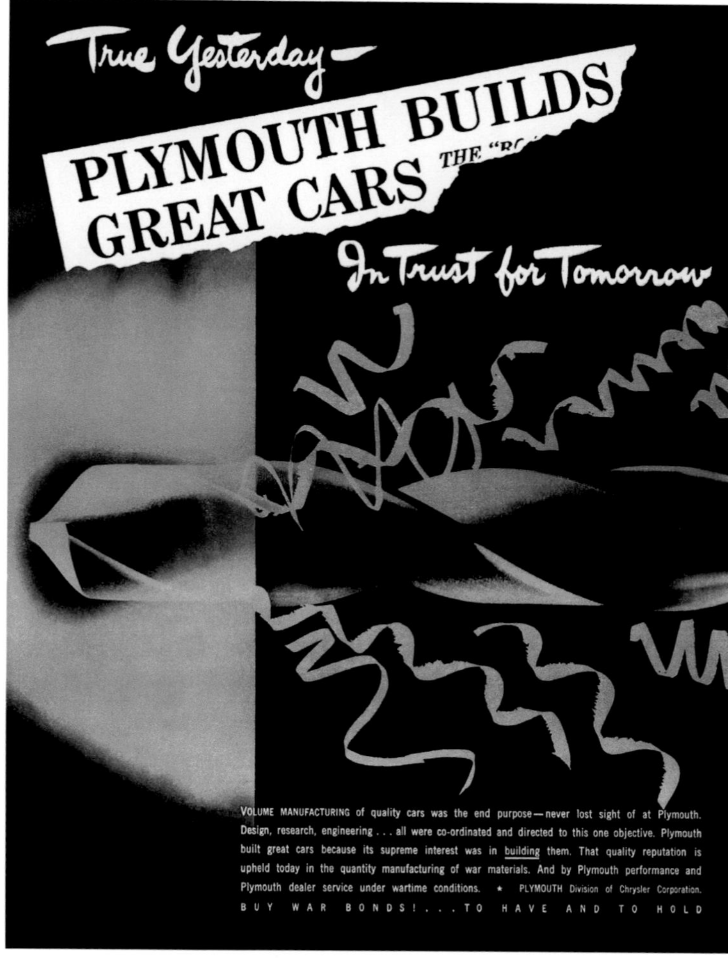

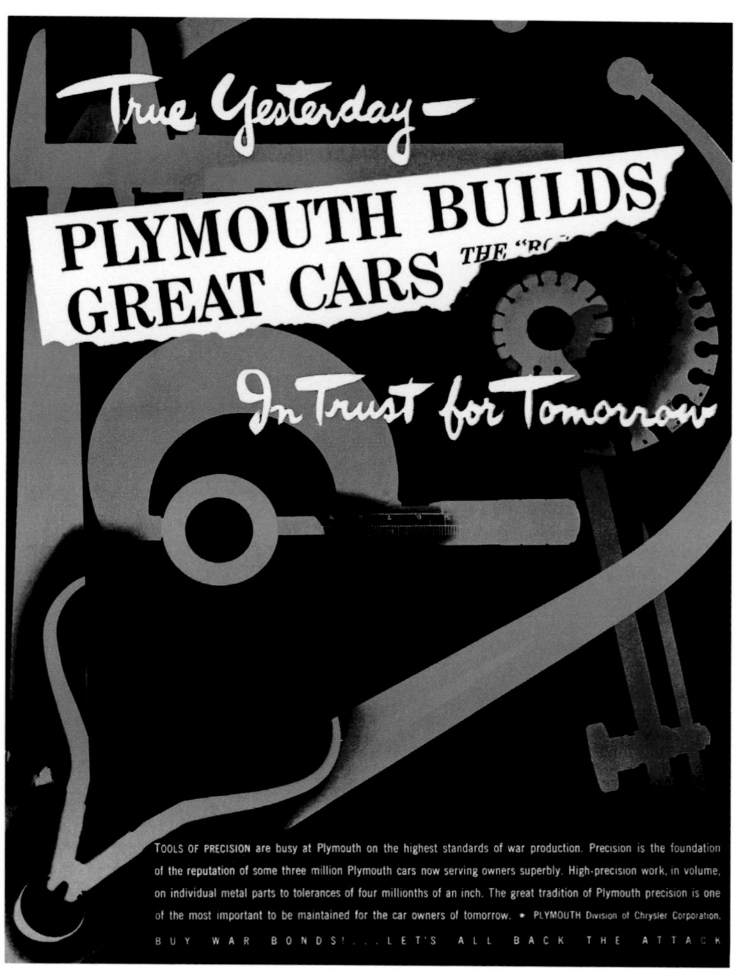

Plymouth, 1944

Companies continued to advertise during World War II to remind customers of their contributions to the war effort and to keep their names before the public in anticipation of a postwar sales boom.

Auch während des Zweiten Weltkriegs schalteten die Unternehmen Anzeigen, um die Kunden an ihren Beitrag zur Verteidigung zu erinnern und um in Erwartung eines Nachkriegsbooms in Erinnerung zu bleiben.

Pendant la Seconde Guerre mondiale, les constructeurs continuent à faire de la publicité pour rappeler à leurs clients qu'ils contribuent à l'effort de guerre et maintenir leur nom dans les esprits en prévision d'une flambée des ventes après la guerre.

Plymouth, 1944

Chevrolet Stylemaster, 1948 ◂

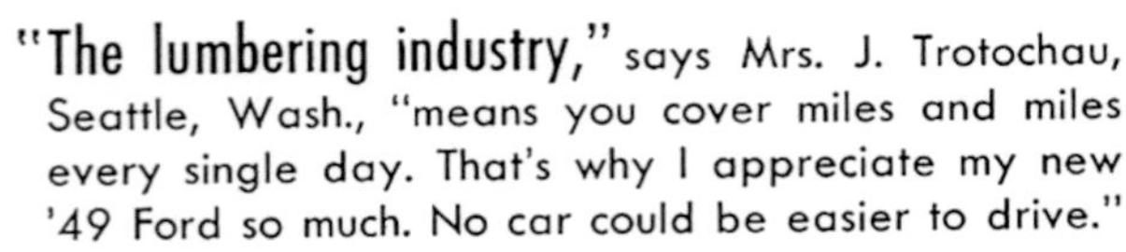

"**The lumbering industry,**" says Mrs. J. Trotochau, Seattle, Wash., "means you cover miles and miles every single day. That's why I appreciate my new '49 Ford so much. No car could be easier to drive."

(A few reasons for that, Mrs. Trotochau, are Ford's new "Arrow-Straight" Steering and new "Magic Action" King-Size Brakes that are 35% easier to apply.)

MRS. J. TROTOCHAU, Seattle, Washington

OUT FRONT with All America ...'49 FORD

"**With some 50,000 head of cattle** on approximately 900,000 acres to look after, the '49 Ford is a welcome addition to the Ford family. I can drive mine all day without fatigue," says Mr. Richard M. Kleberg, Jr. of Kingsville, Texas.

(Thanks, Mr. Kleberg. We're glad you like our new "Hydra-Coil" Front Springs and our new "Para-Flex" Rear Springs. They're what make our new "Mid Ship" Ride so smooth on all kinds of roads.)

MR. RICHARD M. KLEBERG, JR.
King Ranch, Kingsville, Texas

The Fine Car of its Field!

There's a New Ford in your future

"I taxi my family 25 miles a day," says Mrs. Robert E. Prescott, Jr. of Quincy, Mass., "so you can guess why I like my new Ford. It feels so safe—something a mother appreciates."
(That's because our new "Lifeguard" body combined with the 5-cross member, box-section frame is actually 59% more rigid! And those big "Picture Windows" give you more visibility, too—a great safety factor.)
MRS. ROBERT E. PRESCOTT, JR.
Quincy, Massachusetts
"Straight as an arrow, even when the wind blows across the road, is the way my new Ford goes. It handles like a much more expensive car," says Mrs. Bruce Montgomery, Jr. of Atlanta, Georgia.
(There's a reason, Mrs. Montgomery. The new steering linkage, front wheel suspension and low center of gravity combine to give the '49 Ford real fine-car roadability.)
MRS. BRUCE MONTGOMERY, JR.
Atlanta, Georgia
ly Ford's a fine storeroom for the various metal products carry—with plenty of room for overnight luggage," says Ar. Wright Yount, Detroit, Michigan. "And traveling 750 miles week, I'm sold on the extra gas mileage, too!"
(Yes, Mr. Yount, there's lots more space in the new "Deep Deck" Luggage ocker. And that extra gas saving—up to 10%—results from improvements ıch as the new "Deep Breath" Manifolding and new "Equa-Flo" Cooling.)
MR. WRIGHT YOUNT, Salesman
Detroit, Michigan
"Color sense must be the middle name of Ford designers," says Mrs. Richard M. Kleberg, Jr. of Kingsville, Texas. "I've never seen a better green, for example—and those wide, wide seats inside! I just love my '49 Ford."
(Thanks, Mrs. Kleberg. Ford's ten new colors are right and they stay right because they're baked-on. And those seats—they really are wide—57 inches in the front, 60 in the rear!)
MRS. RICHARD M. KLEBERG, JR., Kingsville, Texas
FORD
ord Custom
White side wall tires, optional at extra cost.

THE SATURDAY EVENING POST December 15, 1945

● Have you actually seen it? The new Mercury is new in style, ride, thrift! From imposing grille to rear bumper—a beauty . . . Step inside for more newness. Rich fabrics—faultlessly tailored. Smartly designed instrument panel. Colorful trim . . . Comfort? Room all around you. Wide, deep seats—and soft. . . . Improved springing for a smooth, level ride. Brakes are new, too. Extra-big, self-centering hydraulics. Quick-acting—and silent . . . Under the hood, there's a full 100 horse-power in the improved 90-degree V-8 engine. Definitely easy on gas and oil . . . Some new cars available now. Will be even more plentiful soon. See your Mercury dealer. He'll keep you posted!

A DIVISION OF FORD MOTOR COMPANY

Time to stop—
look and whistle!

STEP OUT WITH MERCURY

MERCURY
EIGHT

Tune in . . . THE FORD SHOW . . . CBS, Tuesdays, 10-10:30 P.M., E.S.T. THE FORD SUNDAY EVENING HOUR . . . ABC, Sundays, 8-9 P.M., E.S.T.

Ford, 1949 ◄◄

This hugely popular car, with its "prop spinner" nose resembling earlier Studebakers, saved the company during a time of labor unrest.

Dieser ungemein populäre Wagen mit seiner an ältere Studebaker erinnernden „Propeller-hauben-Nase" rettete die Firma in einer Zeit der Arbeitskämpfe.

L'immense popularité de ce modèle, orné d'une boule au centre de la calandre comme les anciennes Studebaker, sauvera la firme de graves troubles sociaux.

Mercury, 1946

► Pontiac, 1945

FINEST OF THE FAMOUS

"Silver Streaks"

This is the new Pontiac—a car that adds new luster to a fine old name. It carries to an even higher level the tradition of quality that began when the first Pontiac "Silver Streak" was introduced a decade ago. If you are a Pontiac owner you know what that statement means—because four years of wartime driving have <u>proved</u> that Pontiac quality pays great dividends in owner satisfaction. And if you have never owned a Pontiac, we believe you will be greatly impressed by this fine new car. In appearance, in all-around performance, in comfort—*in everything that stands for quality*—it is the finest of the famous "Silver Streaks."

NEW PONTIAC

PONTIAC MOTOR DIVISION • GENERAL MOTORS CORPORATION

More of everything you want with Mercury

One day in the life of your Mercury Station Wagon shows you why it's just about the most useful car you ever owned!

You pick up week-end guests at the station. There's a whole lot more luggage than you

More fashionable — wherever you go

expected, but it all fits easily—*and* your friends do, too! Eight people ride comfortably—with plenty of leg room and elbow room for everyone. And the clear, full vision in all directions is a treat for the passengers as well as the driver.

More room — whenever you need it

You take your guests to the beach—and its room again comes in mighty handy. Nice part of it is—your Mercury Station Wagon is the *smartest* car *wherever* you go—at the beach, the club, the local playhouse or even in town. The body is made of beautifully grained hard woods fashioned with the finest of craftsmanship—built to last!

More practical — for every purpose

What's more, this handsome spacious station wagon has all the famous pickup and liveliness that makes Mercury more fun to drive —*plus* gas and oil economy unusual in such a big, powerful car.

For *more of everything you want*—get to know the Mercury Station Wagon.

MERCURY—DIVISION OF FORD MOTOR COMPANY

White sidewall tires at extra cost, when available

Willys-Station Wagon, 1948

After World War II, military vehicles modified for domestic sales to residents of ranches and suburbs would later serve as prototypes for the sport-utility vehicle.

Nach dem Zweiten Weltkrieg fanden modifizierte Militärfahrzeuge neue Kunden auf Farmen und in Vorstädten. Später sollten sie als Prototyp des SUV dienen.

Après la guerre, des véhicules militaires américains, modifiés pour le marché civil et la clientèle vivant dans les ranchs et les banlieues résidentielles, servent de prototypes au futur SUV.

Mercury Station Wagon, 1946 ◂

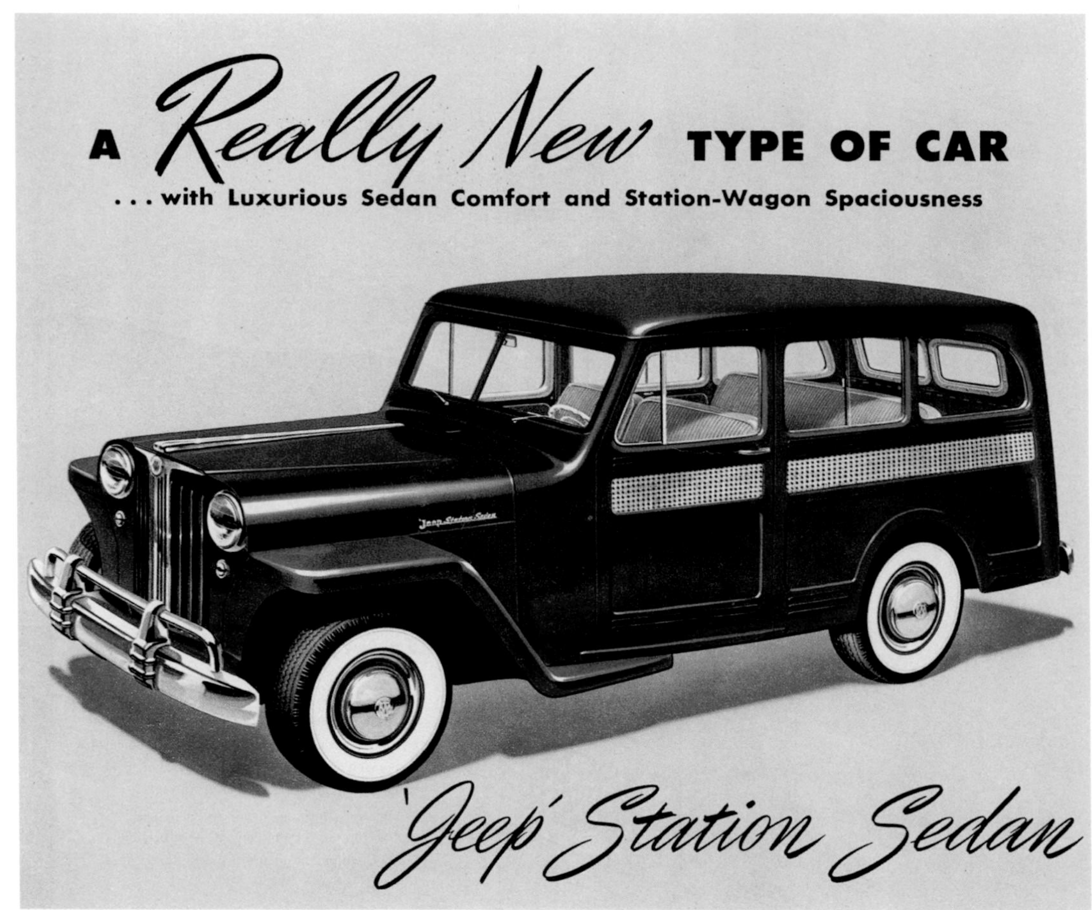

A Really New TYPE OF CAR
. . . with Luxurious Sedan Comfort and Station-Wagon Spaciousness
'Jeep' Station Sedan

More Usable Space in the 'Jeep' Station Sedan's all-steel body for parcels and luggage . . . accessible from interior or through rear doors . . . protected from dust and weather. You'll welcome this large, convenient load room whether you're packing for a trip or only going shopping. And if you must transport something large, the sturdy bottom door can be left open.

The New Willys-Overland "6" Engine delivers smooth power and surging pickup . . . yet it is outstanding for economy of operation and upkeep. And for extra gas mileage, the 'Jeep' Station Sedan has an overdrive which travels the car 42% farther down the road for every turn of the engine!

Designed For Driving Ease: Better vision all around—you see the road right in front of the bumper. Independent front-wheel suspension levels rough roads. Easier to park. You turn in a tenth less space than other standard sedans.

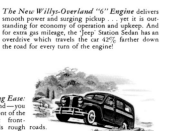

WILLYS-OVERLAND MOTORS
TOLEDO, OHIO
MAKERS OF AMERICA'S MOST USEFUL VEHICLES

Really Spacious Inside . . . more head and leg room than you ever had in ordinary sedans. Doors are wide and tall, easy to enter without knocking off your hat! Luxuriously finished interior, with fabric-upholstered seats, two dome lights, armrests, ash trays. In every way...comfort, distinctive styling and economy . . . the 'Jeep' Station Sedan is a grand buy. See it now!

WHERE DO THEY ALL COME FROM?

Wherever you look it seems as though a new Dodge has just been delivered.

People admire them, talk freely about them, demand them as though a million or more had been built.

The answer is simple. They are sharply and freshly attractive. They stay in the mind and the eye. A few in any community give the impression of many.

First chance you get take a drive or a ride in this car that has stolen the show.

Behind the style and appearance are power and performance that never came so smoothly before.

It's our thanks for your patience, a rich reward for your waiting.

MOTHER OF INVENTION

Why do you find Dodge way out in front with more performance features than any other car in its price class?

Why do you find it outstanding among all cars for its economy?

Why is the public more interested and enthusiastic about the present Dodge than any other car in the market?

Necessity may not have been the mother of these things, but Dodge standards of design, and Dodge resources in engineering ability may have had something to do with it.

The proof of this leadership is everywhere, for you to observe and act upon.

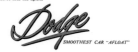

Dodge
SMOOTHEST CAR "AFLOAT"

FAMILY RIFT

There's a rift in many a family.

There are flaws between husbands and wives.

There are brawls among the youngsters. Grandparents are often involved.

What's the reason? Dodge is the reason, and the feuds concern "who gets the car."

Dodge
SMOOTHEST CAR "AFLOAT"
Lowest Priced Car with Fluid Drive

SAFE PASSAGE—And Another Look

There's no let up in the interest people take in the New Dodge car.

And there's no slack in the huge demand for it either.

Remember,—behind the good looks is a smoothness of performance never known before.

No other car like it at any price.—and remember Dodge gives you All-Fluid-Drive.

Dodge Custom, 1947   Dodge Custom, 1947

Dodge Custom, 1947   Dodge Custom, 1947

▸ Ford Super DeLuxe, 1946

Young looking ... with lots of "hustle"

Any way you look at it—this new 1946 Ford has what it takes! New comfort. New economy. New beauty. And under the hood, new stepped-up power to match its eager, youthful look . . . Inside, you'll find the accent is on smartness. Colorful fabrics and trim in distinctive two-tone combinations. Seats that are wide and deep . . . For a smooth and level ride, this car has new multi-leaf springs—long and slow-acting. While extra-large hydraulic brakes of a new design assure you quick, soft stops . . . Two great engines to choose from: the V-8, now increased from 90 to 100 horsepower—the 90 horsepower Six . . . See this smartest, most powerful Ford car ever built—at your Ford dealer's today.

FORD MOTOR COMPANY

THERE'S A

Ford

IN YOUR FUTURE

TUNE IN . . . THE FORD SHOW . . . CBS, Tuesdays. 10-10:30 P.M., E.S.T. THE FORD SUNDAY EVENING HOUR . . . ABC, Sundays. 8-9 P.M., E.S.T.

Ford

KAISER
KAISER
SPECIAL
PRODUCT OF KAISER-FRAZER
BODY STYLING BY
Darrin

220

TRAIL BLAZERS IN POSTWAR STYLING!

BUILT AT WILLOW RUN

ONLY ONCE in a decade comes a distinctly new trend in motor car styling—a trend so clearly in accord with public preference that it is only a matter of time until all manufacturers fall into line. The KAISER SPECIAL and the FRAZER, America's first 1947 motor cars, have set a trend in body styling, passenger comfort and driver convenience that will be reflected in other automobiles in the years to come. You can see *these* cars at your dealer's showroom now.

BODY STYLING BY
Darrin
FRAZER
PRODUCT OF
GRAHAM-PAIGE
FRAZER

Oldsmobile B-44, 1942

Comparing a sedan with a B-19 bomber hinted at the stylistic influences that would arrive after the war, when airplane-inspired shapes became common.

Der Vergleich einer Limousine mit dem B-19 Bomber gibt einen Vorgeschmack auf die stilistischen Einflüsse der Nachkriegszeit mit ihrer Formgebung, die sich an Flugzeugen orientierte.

Cette berline aux faux airs de bombardier B-19 donne une idée des influences stylistiques qui émergent après la guerre, quand les formes inspirées de l'aviation se répandent.

Oldsmobile B-44, 1942

Kaiser Special and Frazer, 1946 ◂

ICE CREAM
BAR-B-Q

One out of *Two*
knows this
to be *True*!

*The Sixty Special, as illustrated, $2115**

THE NEW CADILLAC SIXTY SPECIAL

ONLY TWO YEARS have passed since the first Sixty Special appeared—scarcely time, you would think, for a car to get far in the world. Yet, today, in the field above $2,000, *the Sixty Special is the choice of one out of two!* ¶ You don't need to look far to discover the reason—no farther than the nearest owner. For it is he, and his fellow-owners, who have won the Sixty Special its great following, by spreading the simple truth about this car. ¶ He'll tell you—and *prove* it—that the Sixty Special does more things to warm an owner's heart than any other car built today. No other duplicates its comfort, vision and roominess. And this dynamic car is just as inimitable in the way it runs, handles, and rides. ¶ Take the word of owners—once you drive a Sixty Special nothing else will do. If you want first-hand evidence of this fact, just call your Cadillac dealer. He'll gladly let you and the Sixty Special settle the matter between you.

Have you seen the lowest-priced Cadillac —the new Sixty-Two? It's a great car and a great value!

*The Cadillac Motor Car Division builds LaSalle, Cadillac and Cadillac-Fleetwood cars. Prices begin at $1240 for the LaSalle Series Fifty Coupe *delivered at Detroit. Transportation based on rail rates, state and local taxes (if any), optional equipment, accessories—extra. Prices subject to change without notice.*

The Sixty Special, as illustrated, $2090★

THE NEW CADILLAC SIXTY SPECIAL

A FRIEND ONCE ASKED an owner of this gorgeous Cadillac-Fleetwood, "Why do they call it the Sixty *Special?* What has it got that other cars haven't?" ¶ We pass on to you the owner's reply because it answers, in two words, every question *you* might ask. The owner said, "Drive it," and that's what we suggest to you. For the Sixty Special, more than any car, must be driven to be appreciated at its full worth. The reason is that no other car handles, rides, and performs with the easy brilliance of this dynamic beauty. ¶ The ride is not just smooth—it's the steadiest, easiest motion on four wheels. Driving isn't merely easy—it's the next thing to automatic. And engine performance is beyond belief. Power-dive acceleration—and smooth, effortless action at every speed—put you in a holiday mood each time you take the wheel. ¶ Try it. You'll find that driving a Sixty Special is the most glorious experience in motoring!

Have you seen the lowest-priced Cadillac —the new Sixty-Two? It's a great car and a great value!

The Cadillac Motor Car Division builds LaSalle, Cadillac and Cadillac-Fleetwood cars. LaSalle prices begin at $1240 for the Series Fifty Coupe. Cadillac prices start at $1685 for the Series Sixty-Two Coupe ★delivered at Detroit. Transportation based on rail rates, state and local taxes (if any), optional equipment, accessories—extra. Prices subject to change without notice.

Gulf Oil, 1946 ◂

A leisurely trip to a new, round, drive-in restaurant. The late '40s marked the rise of drive-ins and theaters – as well as Holiday Inn hotels, and many fast-food chains – all of which shared interests with automobile manufacturers.

Entspannte Fahrt zu einem der neuen runden Drive-in-Restaurants. Die zahlreichen neuen Drive-ins, Autokinos, Holiday Inn Hotels und Fastfood-Ketten der späten Vierziger verfolgten teils die gleichen Interessen wie die Autohersteller.

La fin des années 1940 est marquée par l'avènement de la culture du drive-in. Chaînes de motel et de restauration rapide, cinémas en plein air et constructeurs automobiles voient leurs intérêts converger.

Cadillac Sixty Special, 1940

Cadillac Sixty Special, 1940

224

FIBBER McGEE and MOLLY
FIBBER IS TAKEN FOR A RIDE
HAVE YOU POLISHED OUR CAR, McGEE ?
WELL, MOLLY - I JUST BET DOC GAMBLE HERE I CAN DO IT WITH MY EYES SHUT.

YES SIR, ARROWSMITH — I MAY BE "IN THE DARK," BUT THIS IS WHERE BOTH ME AN' THE CAR SHINE.
YOUR GAGS "GAG" ME, McGEE. WATCH YOUR STEP NOW - RIGHT THIS WAY.

NO SIR, NO NEED TO SEE WITH JOHNSON'S CARNU. JUST RUB IT ON AND LET IT DRY. HOW'M I DOIN', BONE-BENDER ?
FOR ONCE, McGEE, I AM OVERCOME WITH ADMIRATION. DIDN'T THINK YOU HAD IT IN YOU !

NOW WE RUB HER UP LAZY-LIKE AND THERE SHE IS - GLEAMIN' LIKE A DIAMOND. DO I WIN THAT BET, DOC ?
WIN YOU DO, AND THANKS, FIBBER. JOHNSON'S CARNU SURE DOES A SWELL JOB. I HAVEN'T SEEN MY CAR SO BEAUTIFUL IN YEARS!

YOUR CAR !!! WHY, DAD RAT THE DAD-RATTED — OF ALL THE LOW-DOWN, DOUBLE-CROSSIN' —
NOW, NOW, McGEE. IT'S EASY WITH CARNU, YOU CAN DO OUR CAR RIGHT NOW !

HEAVENLY DAYS, WHAT A HEAVENLY GLAZE YOU GET WITH **JOHNSON'S CARNU!** REMEMBER, FOLKS, WHEN YOU GO SHOPPING, GET **CARNU** FOR YOUR CAR

To preserve the beautiful finish CARNU gives your car, give it a coat of JOHNSON'S AUTO WAX

Yes—here's the really *easy* way to restore that original showroom shine to your car. Johnson's Carnu is a liquid, wax-fortified polish that cleans *and* polishes in just one application. No hard rubbing. Just apply and let dry to a white powder. Wipe off—and dirt and road grime disappear as if by magic—leaving a sparkling, waxy shine that makes your car look *new* again. Try Johnson's Carnu yourself today—you'll be mighty pleased you did.

Tune in Fred Waring!
The Johnson Summer Show every Tuesday Night—NBC

Your car looks like new when you use CARNU*
Made by the makers of Johnson's Wax

*Trademark Registered

Johnson's Wax, 1946

▸ Firestone Tires, 1940

Firestone
CHAMPION TIRES
FOR 21 CONSECUTIVE YEARS FIRESTONE TIRES HAVE BEEN ON ALL THE WINNING CARS IN THE 500-MILE INDIANAPOLIS RACE
Firestone CHAMPION
FLASHING down the straightaways at speeds as high as 160 miles an hour, Wilbur Shaw streaked to victory in this great race to become a three-time winner and the only man ever to win two consecutive victories at Indianapolis.
500 miles of grinding, pounding, torturing speed — and not one tire failed! Here's proof of Safety—Proof of Blowout Protection—Proof of Tire Superiority—backed, not by claims, but by performance.
Patented construction features in the Firestone Tires used by these great drivers on the speedway are incorporated in the Firestone Champion Tires you buy for the highway.
For greater safety, economy and dependability, equip your car with a set of these wonderful tires today. Easy terms on the Firestone Budget Plan if you desire.
Listen to the "Voice of Firestone," Monday evenings, N.B.C. Red Network.
See Firestone Champion Tires made in Firestone Factory and Exhibition Building at the New York World's Fair
THE ONLY TIRES MADE THAT ARE SAFETY-PROVED ON THE SPEEDWAY FOR YOUR PROTECTION ON THE HIGHWAY

Daily News LOS ANGELES, CALIFORNIA TUESDAY, JANUARY 27, 1948 13

★ ★

You saw it at the Pasadena Tournament of Roses...
You read about it in LIFE... in thousands of magazines and newspapers

Four American Airlines Stewardesses demonstrate the roomy comfort of the new Davis

Now!
SEE THE DAVIS IN ACTION!

SEE IT spinning at high speeds backwards and forwards in a thirteen foot circle....
SEE IT "stopping on-a-dime"....
SEE ITS amazing "painless parking" in less space than needed by other full-sized cars

FREE PUBLIC DEMONSTRATIONS FOR 10 DAYS!

You are cordially invited to the First Open House Demonstration of the new Davis 3-Wheeler—at our Assembly Plant, 8055 Woodley Avenue, Van Nuys.

Demonstrations every hour on the hour from 9 A.M. to 9 P.M. —rain or shine—starting Tuesday, January 27th, through February 5th—Saturday and Sunday included.

MOTORCAR COMPANY
8055 Woodley Ave., Van Nuys • Phone:-STate 5-3156

226

Davis, 1948

Inventors and entrepreneurs in the 1940s still dreamed of making their fortunes with radically new visions of the automobile. One of these was Gary Davis, who built 15 examples of his odd-pod three-wheeled Davis Divan model in an old aircraft factory in Van Nuys, California. Billed as "the car of tomorrow today," it seated four in a single bench seat.

Erfinder und Unternehmer träumten auch in den 1940er-Jahren noch davon, mit einer grundlegend neuen Vision des Automobils ihr Glück zu machen. Einer von ihnen war Gary Davis, der in einer alten Flugzeugfabrik in Van Nuys, Kalifornien 15 Exemplare seines skurrilen dreirädrigen Davis Divan baute. „Das Auto von morgen schon heute" besaß eine durchgehende Sitzbank für vier Personen.

Dans les années 1940, inventeurs et entrepreneurs rêvent encore de fortunes bâties sur une vision totalement nouvelle de l'automobile ; c'est le cas de Gary Davis, qui construit quinze exemplaires de son drôle de modèle à trois roues dans une ancienne usine d'avions à Van Nuys, en Californie. Annoncée comme « la voiture de demain, aujourd'hui », elle accueille quatre passagers sur une seule banquette.

► Plymouth, 1941

►► Packard Clipper Custom Sedan, 1946

VOTED: "MOST LIKELY TO SUCCEED"

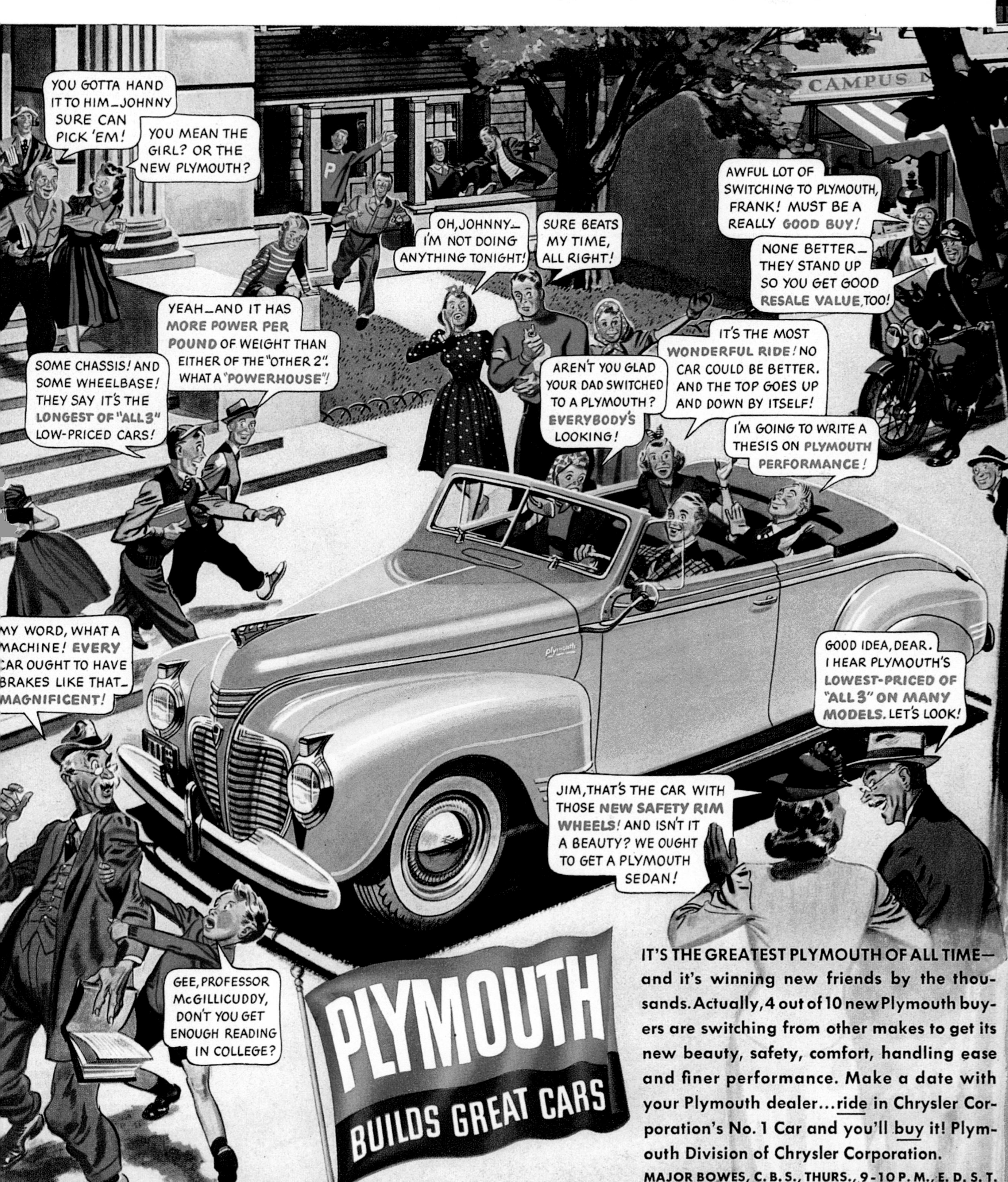

Clipper

THE GOLDEN AGE OF ROCK 'N' ROLL COINCIDED WITH PEAK YEARS OF AUTO DESIGN AND AUTO ADVERTISING. ELVIS PRESLEY LOVED CADILLACS SO MUCH HE BOUGHT A PINK ONE FOR HIS MOTHER. PRESIDENT EISENHOWER RODE TO HIS 1953 INAUGURATION IN ONE OF THE VERY FIRST CADILLAC ELDORADOS.

DAS GOLDENE ZEITALTER DES ROCK 'N' ROLL WAR ZUGLEICH DIE HOCHZEIT VON AUTODESIGN UND AUTOWERBUNG. ELVIS PRESLEY LIEBTE DIE CADILLACS SO SEHR, DASS ER SEINER MUTTER EIN PINKFARBENES EXEMPLAR SCHENKTE. UND PRÄSIDENT EISENHOWER FUHR 1953 IN EINEM DER ALLERERSTEN CADILLAC ELDORADOS ZU SEINER AMTSEINFÜHRUNG.

L'ÂGE D'OR DU ROCK'N'ROLL COÏNCIDE AVEC L'APOGÉE DU DESIGN ET DE LA PUBLICITÉ AUTOMOBILES. ELVIS ADORE LES CADILLAC, À TEL POINT QU'IL EN OFFRE UNE ROSE À SA MÈRE. EN 1953, LE PRÉSIDENT EISENHOWER SE REND À SA CÉRÉMONIE D'INVESTITURE AU VOLANT D'UNE DES TOUTES PREMIÈRES CADILLAC ELDORADO.

1950

DREAMING IN CHROME
EIN TRAUM IN CHROM
LE TOUT CHROME

Mobilgas
Mobilgas
Mobiloil

obilubrica

Mobilgas, 1950 ◂◂

Plymouth Cranbrook Sedan and Savoy, 1953 ◂

Lukens Steel Company, ca. 1954

THE FIRST ROCK 'N' ROLL SONG APPEARED IN 1951, AND IT WAS NAMED AFTER AND INSPIRED BY A CAR — "Rocket 88" took its title from Oldsmobile's new high-compression V8 engine, which used high-octane fuel. Written by Ike Turner (who owned a Buick) for Jackie Brenston and the Delta Cats, the song boasted of its "V8 motor and this modern design," and promised that "gals will ride in style." The golden age of rock 'n' roll coincided with peak years of auto design and auto advertising. Elvis Presley loved Cadillacs so much he bought a pink one for his mother. President Eisenhower rode to his 1953 inauguration in one of the very first Cadillac Eldorados. These were the expansive years of Eisenhower prosperity, when television was reshaping American life. New sports models like the Chevrolet Corvette and Ford Thunderbird were introduced. Ads touted new engines and comfort features, always with trademarked names, like Ultramatic or Powerglide. Air conditioning came to cars, as did better radios and even record players! When darkness fell, Cadillac's Twilight Sentinel feature turned on the headlights automatically and dimmed them again for oncoming drivers.

Powerful new engines, like Chrysler's Hemi and Chevrolet's small-block V8, provided more muscle for new highways, as the country committed itself, in 1956, to a massive interstate highway program. "What's good for General Motors is good for America," a GM president famously proclaimed in the 1950s. "See the U.S.A. in your Chevrolet," sang Dinah Shore of her sponsor, on her popular television show. Never before and never again would the dream of the automobile and the American dream seem so perfectly in sync, and ads exploited this to the hilt.

The station wagon often figured in family scenes, in front of swimming pools or baseball fields. The Chevrolet Nomad and Pontiac Safari implied the adventures of travel, even if the travel boiled down to taking the kids to school and a two-week summer road trip.

Cars were painted or photographed in front of modern buildings to show how advanced their design and technology

was: a flat-roofed glass house, for instance, or Frank Lloyd Wright's circular Guggenheim Museum in New York.

Tail fins grew in popularity. The 1948 Cadillac's big fins were passed down, a few seasons later, to the Chevrolet, then imitated by Chrysler, reaching their peak in the Cadillacs and Chryslers of the late 1950s. Chrome became more popular, layered on grilles and taillights as if with a trowel, and derided by critics as "gorp." But when Ford tried to create a whole new brand, with the Edsel, in 1958, the American public wasn't buying it.

The nation's tastemakers weren't buying American cars in general. In 1953, when the Museum of Modern Art in New York assembled a group of cars for a design exhibition, the only contemporary model was a Raymond Loewy-designed Studebaker; the rest were prewar models. In college towns and wealthy resorts, in movies and fashion shoots, Triumphs, Fiats, Mercedeses, and Porsches showed up — and even odd models like the three-wheeled BMW Isetta. What Americans increasingly were interested in were European cars — a small minority of the market, but growing.

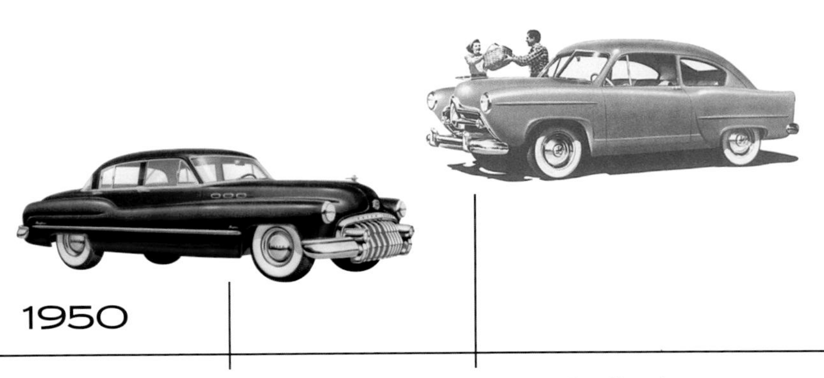

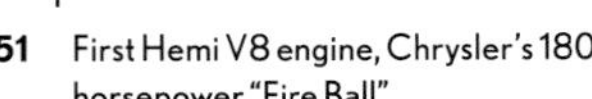

1950

1950 Buick offers tinted glass

Buick bietet getönte Scheiben an

Buick propose le verre teinté

1950 Kaiser introduces Henry J car

Kaiser lanciert das Modell Henry J

Kaiser lance le modèle Henry J

1951 First Hemi V8 engine, Chrysler's 180 horsepower "Fire Ball"

Erster Hemi V8-Motor, Chryslers „Fire Ball" mit 180 PS

Premier moteur V8 Hemi, la « boule de feu » à 180 chevaux de Chrysler

1951 Chrysler makes power steering optional feature in select new models

Optionale Servolenkung in ausgewählten neuen Modellen von Chrysler

Chrysler propose la direction assistée, en option, sur une sélection de nouveaux modèles

DER ERSTE ROCK 'N' ROLL-SONG ERSCHIEN 1951: „ROCKET 88" GEHT ZURÜCK AUF DEN DAMALS NEUEN V8-MOTOR VON OLDSMOBILE, ein hoch verdichteter Motor, der Kraftstoff mit einer höheren Oktanzahl verlangte. Für Jackie Brenston and the Delta Cats von Ike Turner geschrieben, der selber einen Buick besaß, schwärmt der Song von dem „V8-Motor und diesem modernen Design" und verspricht den „Bräuten eine stilvolle Tour". Das goldene Zeitalter des Rock 'n' Roll war zugleich die Hochzeit von Autodesign und Autowerbung. Elvis Presley liebte die Cadillacs so sehr, dass er seiner Mutter ein pinkfarbenes Exemplar schenkte. Und Präsident Eisenhower fuhr 1953 in einem der allerersten Cadillac Eldorados zu seiner Amtseinführung. Dies waren die expansiven Wohlstandsjahre unter Eisenhower, in denen das Fernsehen dem Leben der Amerikaner eine neue Prägung gab. Neue Sportwagen wie die Chevrolet Corvette und der Ford Thunderbird betraten die Szene. Werbeanzeigen priesen neue Motoren und Komfortfeatures, stets verknüpft mit geschützten Bezeichnungen wie „Ultramatic" oder „Powerglide". Klimaanlagen hielten Einzug in die Autos, ebenso bessere Radios und sogar Plattenspieler! Bei einbrechender Dunkelheit sorgte der „Dämmerungswächter" von Cadillac dafür, dass die Scheinwerfer selbsttätig angingen und bei Gegenverkehr abblendeten.

Kraftvolle neue Motoren wie der Hemi von Chrysler oder der V8 Small Block von Chevrolet lieferten genügend Power für die neuen Highways, als die USA 1956 ihr massives Interstate-Highway-Programm auflegten. „Was gut für General Motors ist, das ist gut für Amerika", verkündete ein GM-Präsident in den 1950er-Jahren. „See the USA in your Chevrolet", warb Dinah Shore in ihrer beliebten Fernsehshow singend für ihren Sponsor. Nie zuvor und nie wieder stimmten der Traum vom Auto und der amerikanische Traum wohl so perfekt überein – ein Umstand, den die Werbung voll auskostete.

Kombis wurden in Familienszenen vor einem Swimmingpool oder vor Baseballfeldern präsentiert. Modelle wie der Chevrolet Nomad oder der Pontiac Safari suggerierten das Abenteuer Reise, auch wenn dies in der Praxis bedeutete, die Kinder zur Schule zu fahren und mit dem Auto im Sommer eine zweiwöchige Tour zu unternehmen.
Um die Fortschrittlichkeit von Design und Technologie zu bekunden, zeichnete oder fotografierte man die Autos vor modernen Gebäuden, etwa einem gläsernen Bungalow oder dem schwungvollen New Yorker Guggenheim Museum von Frank Lloyd Wright.

Heckflossen erfreuten sich wachsender Beliebtheit. Die mächtigen Heckflossen des 1948er Cadillac wurden ein paar Modelljahre später zunächst an Chevrolet weitergereicht, dann von Chrysler nachgeahmt, um bei den Cadillacs und Chryslers der späten 1950er-Jahre ihre volle Blüte zu entfalten. Auch Chrom wurde immer beliebter – vor allem rund um Kühler und Heckleuchten aufgetragen – und von Kritikern als „gorp" geschmäht. Doch als Ford 1958 den Versuch unternahm, mit dem Edsel eine neue Marke zu etablieren, gab es kaum Käufer.

Und die Geschmackspäpste übten sich gegenüber den US-Autos allgemein in Zurückhaltung: In der vom New Yorker Museum of Modern Art 1953 präsentierten Design-Ausstellung landete mit einem von Raymond Loewy entworfenen Studebaker nur ein einziges zeitgenössisches Modell; die übrigen Autos stammten aus der Vorkriegszeit. Was sich in Universitätsstädten und teuren Urlaubsorten, in Kinofilmen und auf Modefotos zeigte, waren Marken wie Triumph, Fiat, Mercedes und Porsche – und sogar Skurriles wie die dreirädrige BMW Isetta. In der Tat bekundeten die Amerikaner ein zunehmendes Interesse an europäischen Autos – ein Nischenmarkt mit Wachstumspotenzial.

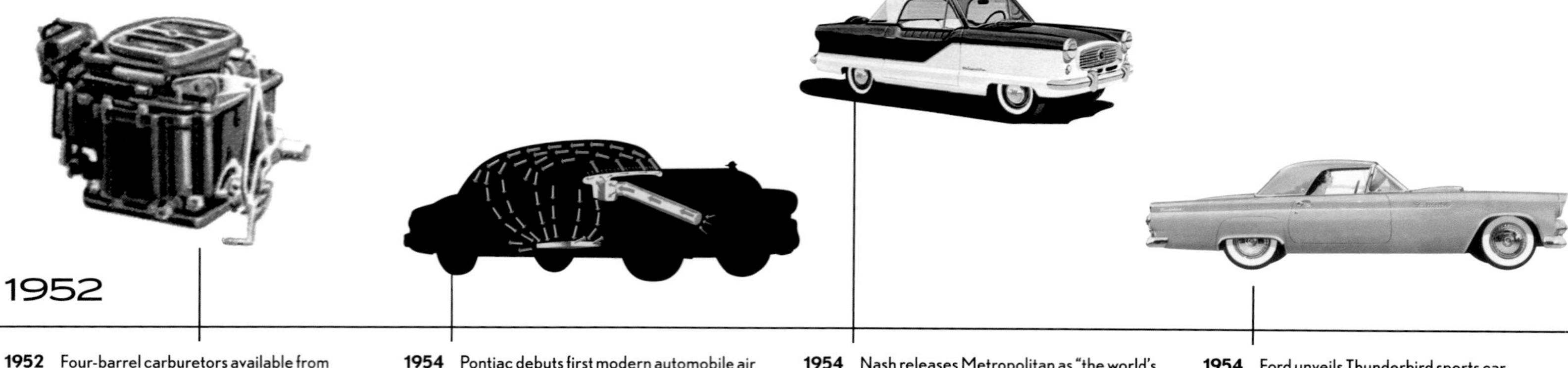

1952 Four-barrel carburetors available from Buick, Oldsmobile, and Cadillac

Vierfachvergaser bei Buick, Oldsmobile und Cadillac erhältlich

Carburateurs quadruple corps disponibles chez Buick, Oldsmobile et Cadillac

1954 Pontiac debuts first modern automobile air conditioning system

Pontiac präsentiert die erste moderne Autoklimaanlage

Pontiac lance le premier système de climatisation automobile

1954 Nash releases Metropolitan as "the world's smartest smaller car"

Nash präsentiert den Metropolitan als den „pfiffigsten Kompaktwagen der Welt"

Nash lance la Metropolitan, la « plus intelligente des plus petites voitures au monde »

1954 Ford unveils Thunderbird sports car

Ford stellt den sportlichen Thunderbird vor

Ford dévoile sa Thunderbird, une voiture de sport

DODGE

Dodge Coronet, 1957 ◄◄

Ford Thunderbird, 1959 ◄

►► Oldsmobile Starfire 98, 1957

LA PREMIÈRE CHANSON ROCK'N'ROLL NAÎT EN 1951, ET SON TITRE REND HOMMAGE À UNE VOITURE – *Rocket 88* se réfère en effet au nouveau moteur V8 à haute compression d'Oldsmobile, qui utilise un carburant à forte teneur en octane. Composée par Ike Turner, lui-même propriétaire d'une Buick, pour Jackie Brenston et les Delta Cats, le morceau vante le « moteur V-8 et son design moderne » qui permet de « sortir les filles avec style ». L'âge d'or du rock'n'roll coïncide avec l'apogée du design et de la publicité automobiles. Elvis adore les Cadillac, à tel point qu'il en offre une rose à sa mère. En 1953, le président Eisenhower se rend à sa cérémonie d'investiture au volant d'une des toutes premières Cadillac Eldorado. Ce sont des années prospères, durant lesquelles la télévision transforme la vie en Amérique. De nouveaux modèles de sport voient le jour, notamment la Corvette de Chevrolet et la Thunderbird de Ford. Les publicités insistent sur les nouveaux moteurs et les éléments de confort, toujours associés à des marques comme Ultramatic ou Powerglide. La climatisation fait son apparition dans les voitures, tout comme des radios plus performantes et même des électrophones ! Quand la nuit tombe, la « sentinelle du crépuscule » (Twilight Sentinel) de Cadillac allume automatiquement les phares et passe en code chaque fois qu'elle croise un autre véhicule.

De nouveaux moteurs puissants – le Hemi de Chrysler et le petit V8 compact de Chevrolet, par exemple – permettent de savourer les joies des nouvelles autoroutes dont le pays se dote dans le cadre d'un vaste programme mis en place en 1956. Un président de GM proclame dans les années 1950 que « ce qui est bon pour General Motors est bon pour l'Amérique » ; à la télévision, Dinah Shore chante « Visite les États-Unis au volant de ta Chevrolet ». Jamais le rêve automobile n'a été et ne sera aussi parfaitement conforme au rêve américain ; une symbiose que la publicité exploite sans réserve.

Le break est souvent présenté dans des scènes à caractère familial, au bord de la piscine ou sur un terrain de base-ball. La Chevrolet Nomad et la Pontiac Safari évoquent l'aventure et les voyages, même si le voyage se résume à conduire les enfants à l'école et à partir quinze jours l'été.

Les voitures sont représentées ou photographiées devant des bâtiments modernes pour faire valoir l'aspect novateur de leur design et de leur technologie : une maison tout en toits-terrasse et baies vitrées, par exemple, ou le musée Guggenheim dessiné par Frank Lloyd Wright à New York.

Les ailettes arrière remportent un franc succès. Les grandes ailettes de la Cadillac 1948 font leur apparition quelques saisons plus tard chez Chevrolet, avant d'être imitées par Chrysler et de connaître leur apogée chez Cadillac et Chrysler à la fin des années 1950. Également apprécié, le chrome gagne les grilles et les feux arrières ; certains en abusent tellement que les critiques finissent par dénoncer ces excès. En revanche, lorsque Ford tente de créer une toute nouvelle marque avec l'Edsel, en 1958, le public américain ne suit pas.

Ceux qui font et défont les modes dans le pays n'achètent en général pas d'Américaines. En 1953, lorsque le musée d'Art moderne de New York réunit un ensemble de voitures pour une exposition sur le design, le seul modèle contemporain est une Studebaker dessinée par Raymond Loewy ; tous les autres datent d'avant la guerre. Les Triumph, Fiat, Mercedes et Porsche apparaissent de plus en plus dans les villes universitaires et les stations chics, au cinéma et sur les photographies de mode – sans oublier quelques modèles un peu originaux comme l'Isetta à trois roues de BMW. Les Américains s'intéressent toujours plus aux Européennes, qui représentent une petite mais croissante part du marché.

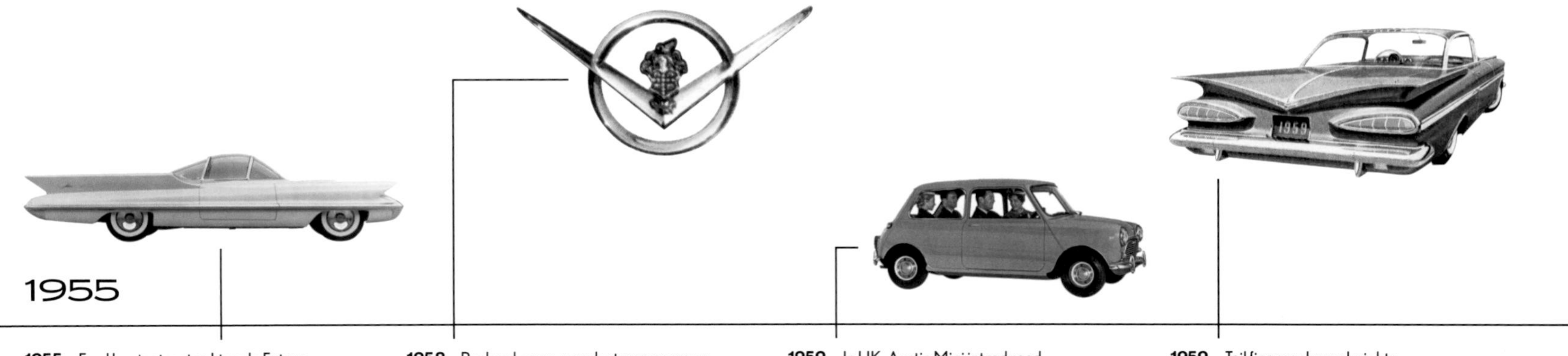

1955

1955 Ford begins touring Lincoln Futura bubble-top concept car

Ford startet eine Tournee mit der Designstudie Lincoln Futura

Ford présente la Lincoln Futura, un concept-car avec toit bulle

1958 Packard, once grandest name among American automobiles, ceases production

Packard, einst der klangvollste Name unter den US-Autobauern, stellt die Produktion ein

Packard, autrefois un des plus grands noms de l'automobile américaine, cesse sa production

1959 In UK, Austin Mini introduced

Vorstellung des Austin Mini in Großbritannien

Lancement de l'Austin Mini au Royaume-Uni

1959 Tail fins reach new heights

Heckflossen erreichen ungeahnte Ausmaße

Les ailettes arrière battent de nouveaux records

Ninety Eight
1957

Cadillac
Cadillac presents
the greatest advancements it has ever achieved
in motor car styling and engineering !

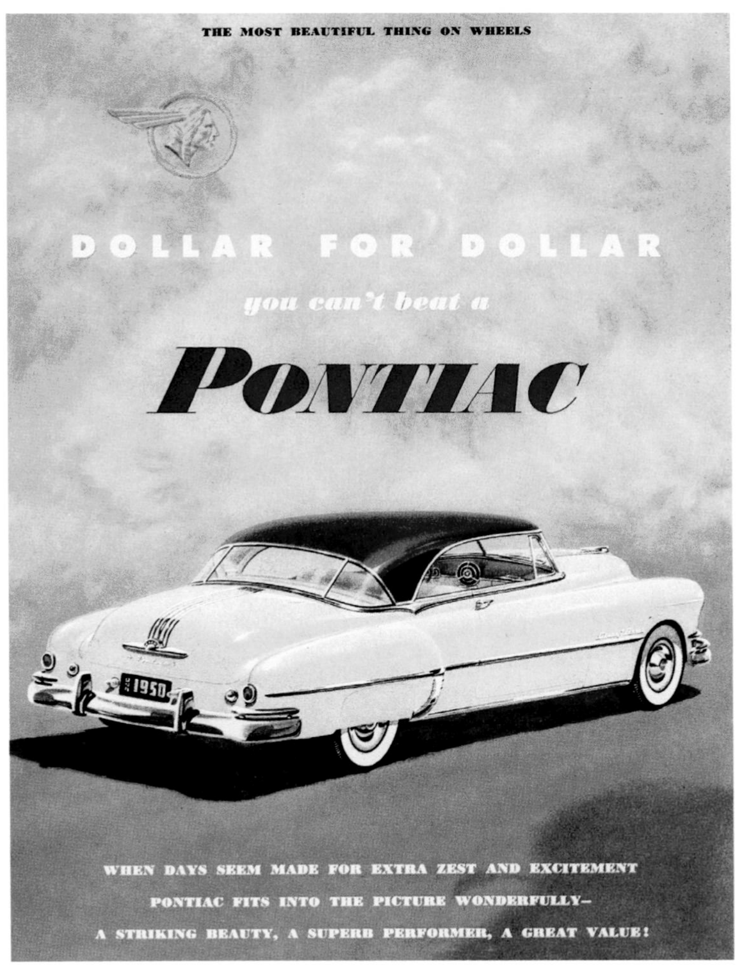

Pontiac Chieftain Super DeLuxe Catalina, 1950

Pontiac Chieftain Super DeLuxe Catalina, 1950

Cadillac Series 62 Eldorado Biarritz, 1957 ◂

1957 IMPERIAL PRICES RANGE FROM ABOUT $4763 TO $6996, DEPENDING ON MODEL AND EQUIPMENT, LOCAL TAXES, DELIVERY AND TRANSPORTATION CHARGES.

Congratulations to the man who drives the exclusive Imperial

IMPERIAL

Finest expression of The Forward Look

Six months ago, when the magnificent new Imperial swept on the scene, buyers of vision—like yourself—instantly recognized a great car. You, who own or have ordered or will order Imperials, are the leaders in a remarkable switch in America's fine car tastes.

Now the car of your choice is the most sought-after and talked about of all the fine cars. Its beauty and power and flawless engineering have excited a nation . . . and have set a historic new high in month-to-month sales records. You knew it would. We knew it would. Now all the world knows it did. Congratulations!

IMPERIAL . . . FINEST PRODUCT OF CHRYSLER CORPORATION

The most distinguished motorcar of our time...
CONTINENTAL
Mark IV

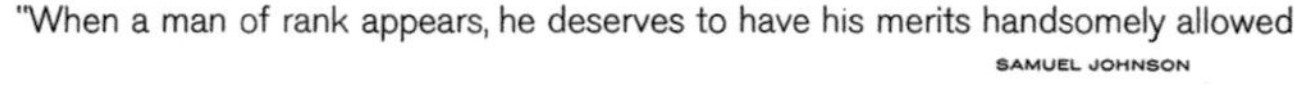

LINCOLN DIVISION • FORD MOTOR COMPANY
"When a man of rank appears, he deserves to have his merits handsomely allowed"
SAMUEL JOHNSON

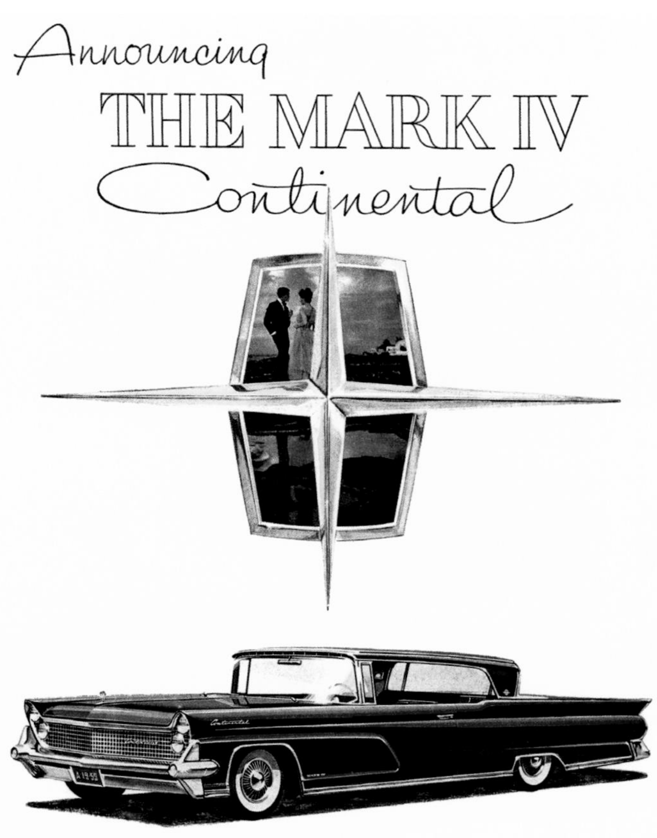

Announcing
THE MARK IV
Continental
The fourth and finest in the Distinguished Series of the world's most admired car.
LINCOLN DIVISION • FORD MOTOR COMPANY

Imperial, 1957 ◂

Chrysler's Virgil Exner became famous for the extreme tail fins of his "forward look," which, for the first time, put a scare into dominant design leader General Motors. Dramatic rooflines and taillights ran from the top-of-the-line Imperial down to the Dodges and Plymouths at the lower end of the market.

Virgil Exner, der für Chrysler arbeitete, wurde berühmt für die extremen Heckflossen seines „Forward Look", was bei General Motors, der bisherigen Speerspitze in puncto Design, für Unruhe sorgte. Imposante Dachlinien und Heckleuchten gab es vom Topmodell Imperial bis zu den Dodges und Plymouths im unteren Marktsegment.

Virgil Exner, de chez Chrysler, devient célèbre grâce au caractère extrême des ailettes de son look « tourné vers l'avenir », qui suscite pour la première fois la frayeur chez General Motors, leader incontesté du design depuis des décennies. Les lignes de toit et les feux arrière spectaculaires se retrouvent sur toute la gamme, de la très chic Imperial à la simple Plymouth, en passant par la Dodge.

Lincoln Continental Mark IV, 1959

Lincoln Continental Mark IV, 1959

In the market for a car that's sweet, smooth, and sassy?

Chevy's got 20 to pick from!

Here's the whole beautiful line-up of '57 Chevrolets. And every last one — from the "One-Fifty" 2-Door Sedan to the dashing new Corvette — brings you a special, spirited way of going that's Chevy's alone!

The "One-Fifty" Utility Sedan.
The "Two-Ten" Beauville.
The "Two-Ten" Townsman.
The "Two-Ten" 4-Door Sedan.
The "One-Fifty" 2-Door Sedan.
The Bel Air 4-Door Sedan.
The "Two-Ten" Sport Sedan.
The "One-Fifty" Handyman.
The "Two-Ten" 2-Door Sedan.
The "One-Fifty" 4-Door Sedan.
The Bel Air Nomad.
The "Two-Ten" Sport Coupe.
The Bel Air Convertible.

14. The Bel Air 2-Door Sedan.
15. The "Two-Ten" Handyman.
16. The "Two-Ten" Delray Club Coupe.
17. The Corvette Sports Car.
18. The Bel Air Sport Sedan.
19. The Bel Air Sport Coupe.
20. The Bel Air Townsman.

See your favorite "number" at your Chevrolet dealer's. . . . Chevrolet Division of General Motors, Detroit 2, Michigan.

CHEVROLET

1 USA
'57 CHEVROLET

Here is excitement on wheels . . .
the newest, freshest thing you ever laid eyes on.
And it's even more exciting to drive
than to look at!

the motoramic Chevrolet for 1955!

Take a good look and you'll know that the Motoramic Chevrolet is far more than just a new model. Take the wheel and you'll realize that it's more, even, than a completely new car!

For this is the Chevrolet that began with a whole new idea—the idea that a low-priced car can be made to look, ride and perform like the very finest and highest-priced automobiles.

Big order? You bet! So big that only the world's leading car builders could have filled it. Chevrolet and General Motors alone have the resources and the facilities it takes to put this great new idea on wheels.

Everything's new in the Motoramic Chevrolet—from its tubeless tires to its lower top! Your Chevrolet dealer will be happy to show it to you. . . . Chevrolet Division of General Motors, Detroit 2, Michigan.

GREAT NEW V8—TWO NEW 6's! New "Turbo-Fire V8" delivers 162 h.p. with an ultra-high compression ratio of 8 to 1. Two new 6's, too—the new "Blue-Flame 136" with Powerglide (optional at extra cost) and the new "Blue-Flame 123."

SWEEP-SIGHT WINDSHIELD WITH FOUR-FENDER VISIBILITY! Chevrolet's new Sweep-Sight Windshield curves around to vertical corner pillars. And you can see all four fenders from the driver's seat!

OVERDRIVE JOINS THE POWER TEAMS! Take your choice. There's new Overdrive teamed with the new V8 or the new "Blue-Flame 123." There's Powerglide teamed with the new V8 or the new "Blue-Flame 136." (Powerglide and Overdrive are extra-cost options.) And there's a new standard transmission teamed with the new V8 or the "Blue-Flame 123."

WONDERFUL NEW GLIDE-RIDE FRONT SUSPENSION! New spherical joints flex freely to cushion road shocks. New Anti-Dive Braking Control, exclusive with Chevrolet, assures "heads up" stops.

A VENTILATING SYSTEM THAT REALLY WORKS! Chevrolet's new High-Level Ventilating System takes in air at hood-high level, away from road heat, fumes and dust.

NEW OUTRIGGER REAR SPRINGS! Rear springs are longer—and they're attached at the outside of the frame to give you greater stability in cornering.

EVEN AIR CONDITIONING, IF YOU WISH! Air is heated or cooled by a single highly efficient unit. This is only one of the wonderful extra-cost options you can get!

MORE THAN A NEW CAR . . .
A NEW CONCEPT OF LOW-COST MOTORING

Chevrolet, 1957 ◂◂

Chevrolet's array of coupes, sedans, and station wagons exemplified the huge variety of General Motors models in the 1950s. With names like Nomad and Safari, these suburban wagons suggested adventure, but most were used for domestic pursuits.

Chevrolets Palette von Coupés, Limousinen und Kombis steht beispielhaft für die gewaltige Modellvielfalt bei General Motors in den 1950er-Jahren. Namen wie Nomad oder Safari suggerierten Abenteuer, wenngleich die meisten Vorstadtkombis lediglich Alltagszwecken dienten.

La diversité des coupés, berlines et breaks de Chevrolet illustre le large éventail de modèles offert par General Motors dans les années 1950. Avec des noms comme Nomad et Safari, les breaks de cette période suggèrent l'aventure, même si la plupart n'ont qu'un usage domestique.

Chevrolet Bel Air, 1955

▸ Kaiser DeLuxe, 1951

This year it's clear...

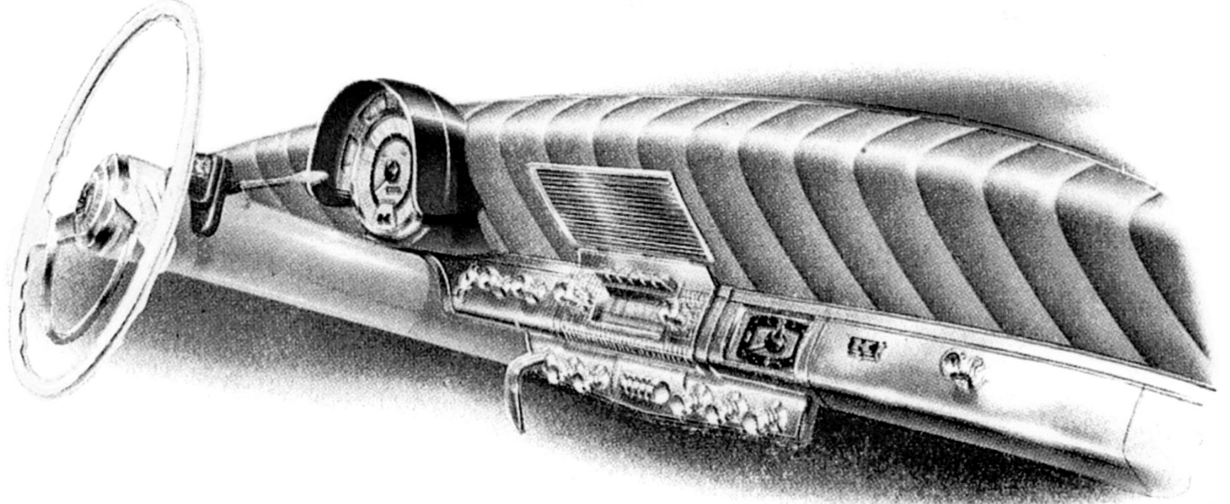

Kaiser's the car!

1951 Kaiser DeLuxe 4-door sedan... one of 6 body styles and 12 models. Hydra-Matic Drive available in all models at extra cost. Styled by DARRIN

1951 Kaiser... the only car with Anatomic Design!

1951 Kaiser sedan Wins World's Highest Honor

Grand Prix D'Honneur at Cannes, France

From the sensational new Safety-Cushion Padded Instrument Panel to the smart, continental High-Line rear Fenders, the beautiful KAISER is the *all-new* car for 1951.

You look out through the biggest of all windshields, unhampered by thick corner posts, for the widest vision in any car. Wide doors, curving high into the roof, let you step in without knocking off your hat. The Tuck-Away Tire Well gives you extra trunk space because the spare tire is stored under the luggage compartment... not in it!

The great Kaiser Supersonic Engine is the most efficient engine on the highway today. Inside and out, Kaiser's the *all-new* car for 1951. See it—drive it at your Kaiser-Frazer dealer's today!

Built to Better the Best on the Road!

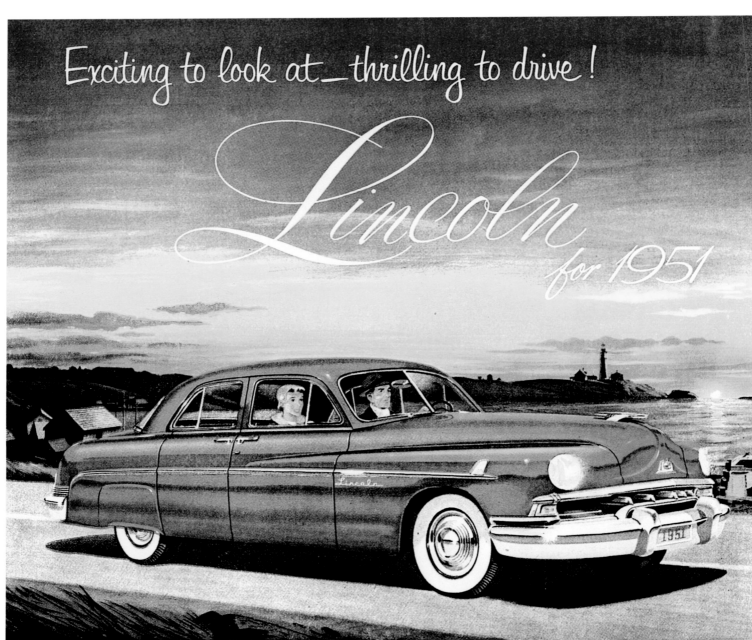

Exciting to look at—thrilling to drive!

Lincoln for 1951

*All Lincoln cars equipped with improved HYDRA-MATIC transmission at extra cost.

250

There's a new and exciting Lincoln for you to see! A sleek, debonair car with the look of an adventurer . . . with a giant heart and a gypsy spirit . . . as your first ride will prove!

For under its gleaming hood is the great Lincoln V-type 8-cylinder engine, eager as a thoroughbred colt! Anxious to take you places.

And how you *will* go places. With this mighty Lincoln engine coupled with HYDRA-MATIC*, you've got the freedom and power of an eagle in soaring flight—right under your very toe!

And *inside* this dramatically new Lincoln, there's exciting news as well! Tailor-fashioned upholsteries . . . a new kind of smart and modern motorcar decor . . . and Fiberglas soundproofing. Yet all of this car luxury costs less than you imagine!

Arrange with your Lincoln dealer for your personal driving experience in a glamorous new Lincoln or the magnificent new Lincoln Cosmopolitan, finest of 1951's fine cars. These cars enhance the great and growing Lincoln reputation for creating the best of everything in automobiles. If you've looked forward to the day when your car will be the one most exciting to look at—most thrilling to drive—the new Lincolns await your inspection.

Lincoln Division • Ford Motor Company

Lincoln—Nothing could be finer

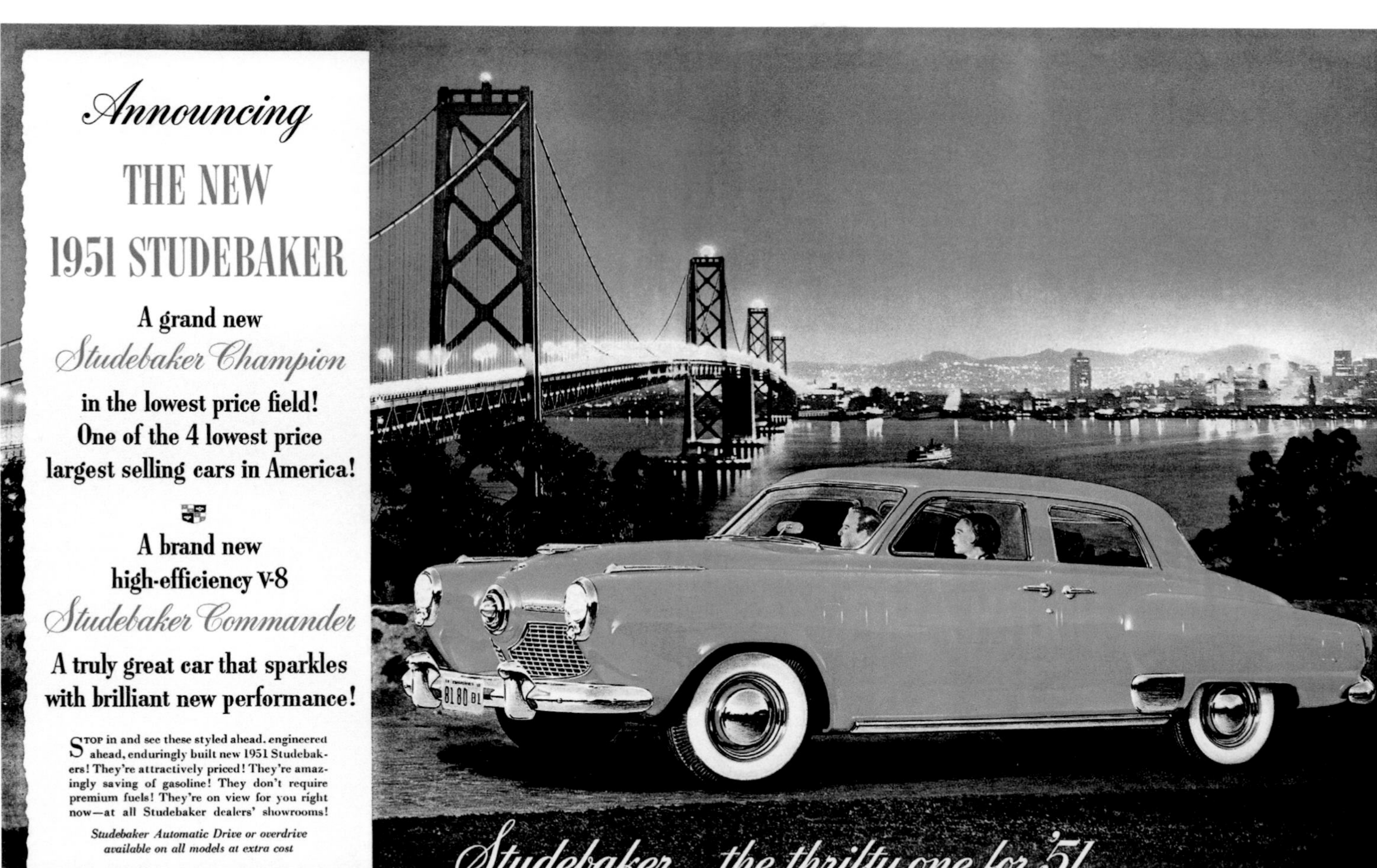

Announcing
THE NEW
1951 STUDEBAKER
A grand new
Studebaker Champion
in the lowest price field!
One of the 4 lowest price
largest selling cars in America!
A brand new
high-efficiency V-8
Studebaker Commander
A truly great car that sparkles
with brilliant new performance!
STOP in and see these styled ahead, engineered ahead, enduringly built new 1951 Studebakers! They're attractively priced! They're amazingly saving of gasoline! They don't require premium fuels! They're on view for you right now—at all Studebaker dealers' showrooms!
Studebaker Automatic Drive or overdrive available on all models at extra cost
Studebaker... the thrifty one for '51

Studebaker Champion, 1951

The onetime wagon maker Studebaker beat out Detroit's Big Three to get its cars on the market first after the end of World War II. That promptness, along with its so-called "coming and going" styling, helped Studebaker prosper for several years.

Nach Ende des Zweiten Weltkriegs brachte der einstige Waggonbauer Studebaker seine Autos noch vor den „großen Drei" aus Detroit auf den Markt. Auch dank des so genannten „coming and going"-Stils ermöglichte dies einige Jahre lang ansehnliche Verkaufszahlen.

À la fin de la Seconde Guerre mondiale, Studebaker, l'ancien constructeur de charrettes, est le premier à envahir le marché, devant les trois grands de Detroit. Cette rapidité, ainsi que le style dit « coming and going » (du va et vient), va contribuer à la prospérité de Studebaker pendant plusieurs années.

Lincoln, 1951 ◂

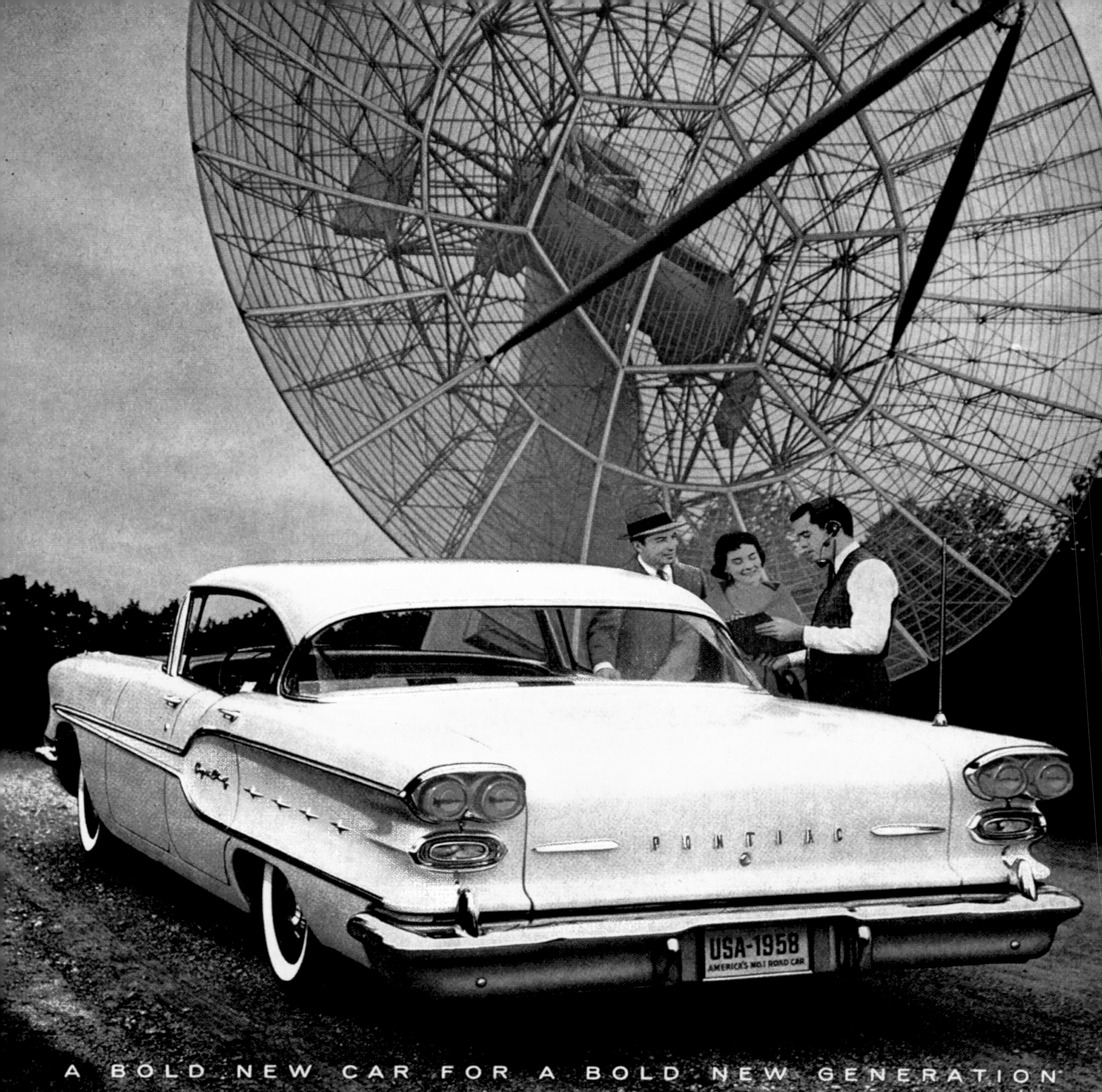
PONTIAC
USA-1958
AMERICA'S No.1 ROAD CAR
A BOLD NEW CAR FOR A BOLD NEW GENERATION

PONTIAC

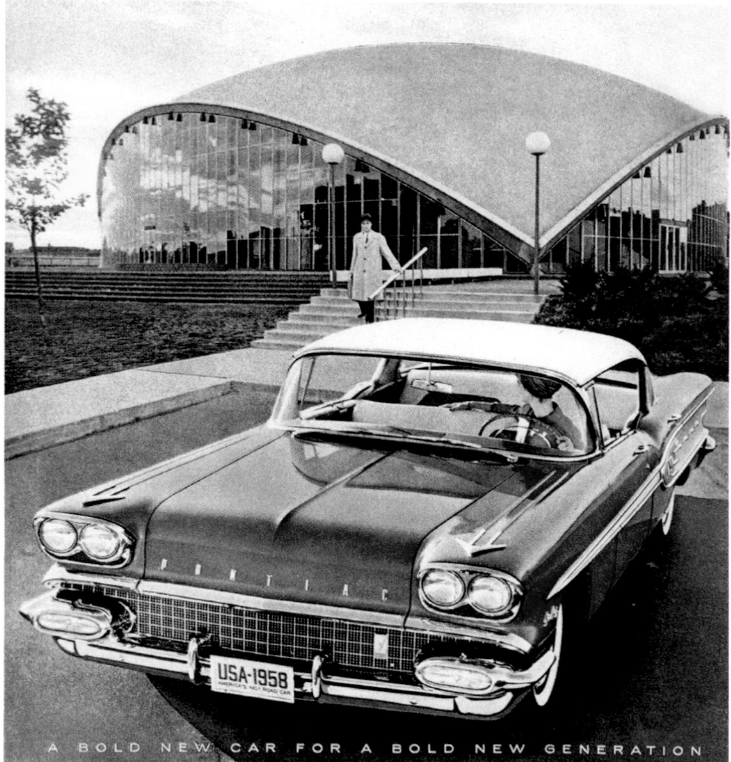

Pontiac Chieftain, 1958

Pontiac Star Chief Catalina, 1958

Pontiac Bonneville Custom Sport Coupe, 1958 ◂

How GM engineers explore new horizons

HERE you see the XP-300 and Le Sabre. The press likes to call them "cars of the future."

Thousands of people have flocked to see them, and the question most often asked is, "When will you build cars like these for the public?"

Well, the answer is—these aren't intended to show exactly what future cars will be like. They were built and rebuilt over a period of several years, to give our engineers and designers the chance to test out fresh ideas, and get these ideas beyond the blueprint and laboratory stage.

You never know, till you get far-in-advance ideas to the point where you can road-test them and let folks look at them, how practical they'll be—and how the public will take them.

We can promise you that, as time goes on, some of these features will begin to appear on cars in regular production.

We say that because it has happened before. Many of today's commonplace features on General Motors cars came right out of "tries" like these in early years.

So Le Sabre and XP-300 are the latest examples of how far we go to make the key to a GM car your key to greater value.

The Top that's Worked by a Raindrop—First drop of rain falling on a sensitized spot between Le Sabre seats starts mechanism which raises and locks top, rolls up side windows. XP-300 has steering post adjustable to driver's height—and seats which are adjustable up and down, forward and backward, and whose contour backs can be moved forward at belt line to ease back strain during long drive. Both have built-in jacks for easy tire changing. Typical of the many GM engineering experiments in these cars—to advance even further passenger comfort and driving ease.

Your Key to Better Engineering —the Key to a General Motors Car

From just such continuous GM engineering experiments as are now being tested in XP-300 and Le Sabre come the superior performance, handling ease and beauty of the 1952 Chevrolets, Pontiacs, Oldsmobiles, Buicks and Cadillacs. Further proof that a key to a GM car is your key to better engineering—and thus to greater value.

GENERAL MOTORS

"MORE AND BETTER THINGS FOR MORE PEOPLE"

CHEVROLET · PONTIAC
OLDSMOBILE · BUICK · CADILLAC
All with Body by Fisher
GMC TRUCK & COACH

Hear HENRY J. TAYLOR on the air every Monday evening over the ABC Network, coast to coast

► Edsel, 1958

It was the wrong car at the wrong time: Ford tried to launch a whole new brand, named for Henry Ford's son. But as the Eisenhower boom was fizzling into a recession, even the Edsel's "horse collar grille" couldn't save it, and the car went down as a $350 million blunder.

Es war der falsche Wagen zur falschen Zeit: Ford versuchte eine ganz neue Marke zu etablieren, benannt nach Henry Fords Sohn. Doch als der Eisenhower-Boom in eine Rezession abdriftete, konnte auch der „Kummet-Grill" den Edsel nicht mehr retten – ein 350 Millionen Dollar teurer Missgriff.

La mauvaise voiture au mauvais moment : Ford tente de lancer une toute nouvelle marque portant le nom du fils du fondateur. Mais l'essor de la période Eisenhower cède alors la place à la récession, et même sa grille de radiateur en forme de collier de cheval ne sauvera pas ce modèle.
Il causera 350 millions de dollars de pertes à son constructeur.

General Motors Dream Cars/Le Sabre and XP-300, 1952

They'll know you've *arrived* when you drive up in an Edsel

tep into an Edsel and you'll learn here the excitement is this year.

ther drivers spot that classic ver- cal grille a block away—and never ail to take a long look at this year's nost exciting car.

n the open road, your Edsel is atched eagerly for its already- amous performance.

nd parked in front of your home, our Edsel always gets even more ttention—because it always says a ot about you. It says you chose elegant styling, luxurious comfort and such exclusive features as Edsel's famous Teletouch Drive—only shift that puts the buttons where they belong, on the steering-wheel hub.

Your Edsel also means you made a wonderful buy. For of all medium-priced cars, this one really new car is actually priced the lowest.* See your Edsel Dealer this week.

**Based on comparison of suggested retail delivered prices of the Edsel Ranger and similarly equipped cars in the medium-price field.*

Above: Edsel Citation 2-door Hardtop. Engine: the E-475, with 10.5 to one compression ratio, 345 hp, 475 ft.-lb. torque. Transmission: Automatic with Teletouch Drive. Suspension: Ball-joint with optional air suspension. Brakes: self-adjusting.

EDSEL DIVISION · FORD MOTOR COMPANY

1958 EDSEL

Of all medium-priced cars, the one that's really new is the lowest-priced, too!

Behold the Incomparable

PACKARD

America's only fine car with...

Torsion-Level Ride — the new suspension principle that outmodes coil and leaf springs

Up to 310 Horsepower — giving you mightier wheel-driving force than any other car

Electronic Touch-Button Drive — the only electronically operated finger-touch control

Twin-Traction Safety Differential — for dramatically safer road-grip the year round

The fastest increase in resale value of any car — up as much as 9.6% in the past year

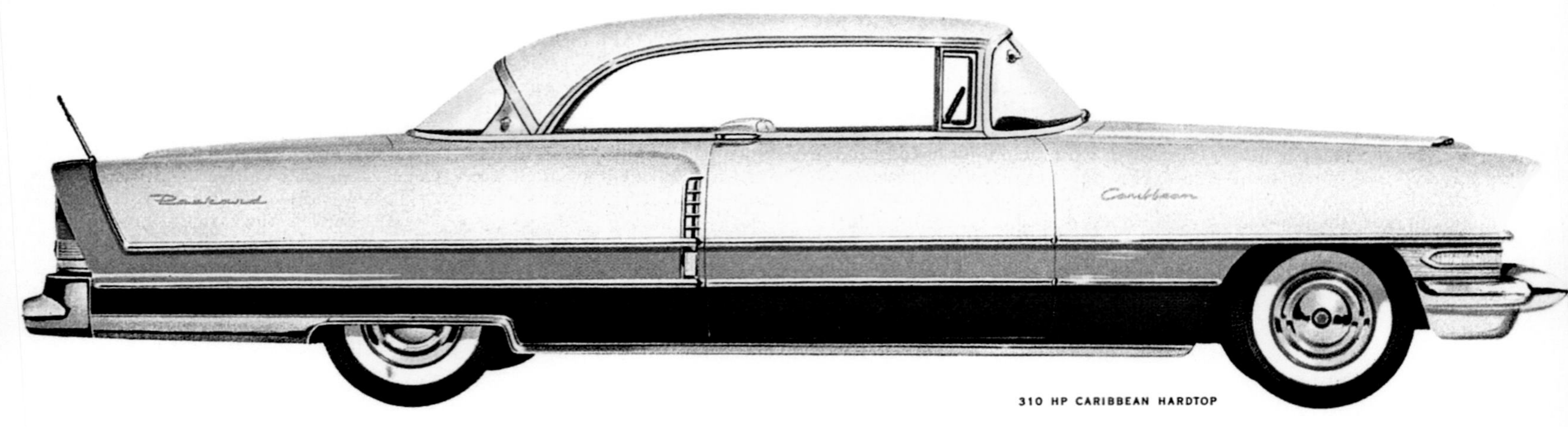

310 HP CARIBBEAN HARDTOP

ASK THE MAN WHO OWNS *the New* ONE

It's New! Only Hudson has...

Miracle H-Power

Sensational new H-145 engine in the fabulous

NEW HUDSON HORNET

There's never been anything like it! And the beauty is, you needn't take our word for it!

All you need do is drive the fabulous new Hudson Hornet—experience the thrilling get-up-and-go of Miracle H-Power—found only in Hudson.

Then notice that the sensational new high-compression H-145 engine that supplies this *performance unlimited* is as quiet and smooth as a sea gull in a glide!

Remember that this amazing H-145 engine is simple in design for low upkeep cost and trouble-free operation. And—it is built to outlast any other engine on the market!

The spectacular new Hudson Hornet itself is breath-takingly beautiful—gracefully streamlined, with a new high note in luxury inside!

And—it is "step-down" designed—lowest built for the world's best and safest ride!

See your Hudson dealer—see for yourself that there's never been anything like Miracle H-Power and the fabulous new Hudson Hornet!

Important today—
perhaps VITAL tomorrow
All Hudsons give high-compression performance on REGULAR GAS!

Hudson... most DURABLE car your money can buy!

Hudson Hornet, 1951 Willys Aero, 1952

Ford Victoria, 1951 Mercury, 1950

Packard Caribbean, 1956 ◂

.......Today the
proudest cars
on the road
glisten with
Olin Aluminum
The exciting Ford Thunderbird is an example. Quality Olin Aluminum is going into the manufacture of most of the fine new cars. Bright, light aluminum resists corrosion, won't rust. No other metal gives car owners such lasting satisfaction. Olin Aluminum, in its first year as a major producer, is already a basic source of supply for the great names in the automotive industry.
OLIN
ALUMINUM
OLIN MATHIESON • METALS DIVISION • 400 PARK AVE. • NEW YORK 22, N. Y.

Olin Aluminum/Ford Thunderbird, 1959

▸ Continental Mark II, 1956

Now, in America, a refreshing new concept in fine motor cars

The excitement it stirs in your heart when you see the Continental *Mark II* lies in the way it has dared to depart from the conventional, the obvious.

And that's as we intended it. For in designing and building this distinguished motor car, we were thinking, especially, of those who admire the beauty of honest, simple lines . . . and of those who most appreciate a car which has been so conscientiously crafted.

The man who owns a Continental *Mark II* will possess a motor car that is truly distinctive and will *keep* its distinction for years to come.

Continental

Mark II

Continental Division · Ford Motor Company

ENJOY GREAT TV ENTERTAINMENT FROM PLYMOUTH! The laugh and love hit of the year, "DATE WITH THE ANGELS," with Betty White, and Lawrence Welk's "TOP TUNES AND NEW TALEN

His love of sports cars . . .

Her love of beauty and comfort . . .

are "married" in the years-ahead *Plymouth*

Hard top, soft top or open—the Thunderbird is the star in *any* setting!

And now: the latest version of America's most exciting car:

Ford THUNDERBIRD for '56

Ready to give you a new lease on driving fun, this newest version of America's favorite dream car is more stunning in style . . . more thrilling in power . . . more luxurious in comfort.

Here, poised for flight you see what many people hardly dreamed possible: a more beautiful, more powerful, more distinctive Thunderbird.

The graceful contours of its long, low lines . . . the unique flair of its new spare-tire mounting . . . the dazzling sheen of its new two-tone colors are but a hint of its newness.

It is when you put the selector in drive position and nudge the gas pedal of a Fordomatic model that the new Thunderbird will really take you by the heart. Nestled beneath that sleek hood lies a new 225-h.p. Thunderbird Y-8, ready to revise all your ideas of how a car should respond.

Now, you may choose hard top, soft top or both. There's a glass-fibre hard top and a foldaway fabric top. Now, the interiors are richer—more beautiful than ever. Now, you get the added protection of Ford's exclusive Lifeguard design. Now, the ride is smoother—the cornering is flatter than ever. And, as always, you may have optional power steering, brakes, windows and seat. Ask your Ford Dealer just how soon *you* can start enjoying the better things of driving.

The 1956 Thunderbird's brand-new rear spare-tire mounting folds back handily, as quick as a wink. It adds as greatly to your luggage space as it does to the over-all beauty of the car.

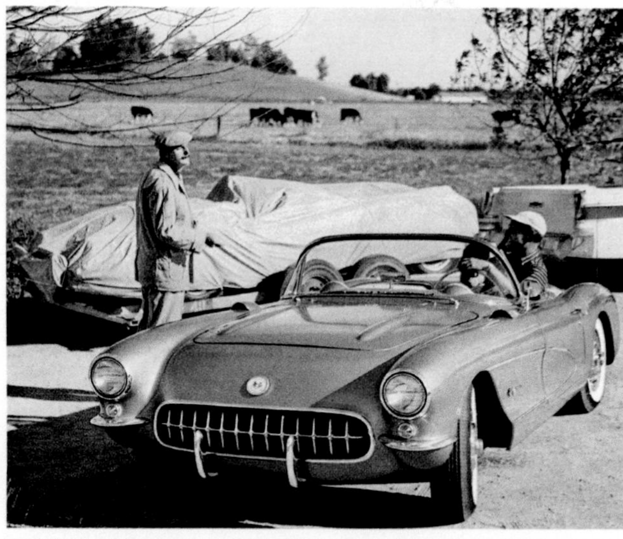

"REALLY, OLD BOY, YOU AREN'T SUPPOSED TO BUILD THAT SORT OF THING IN AMERICA, Y'KNOW."

The unforgivable thing, of course, is this: The new Corvette not only looks delightful and rides like the Blue Train—but it also is quite capable of macerating the competition out on the road circuits.

This dual nature is the classic requirement before you can call a pretty two-seater a *sports car*. And properly so, for this is an honorable name, and only a vehicle with race-bred precision of handling, cornering and control can make a mortal driver feel quite so akin to the gods.

Unlike the gentleman above, who has been a little slow in catching up with current events, most sports car people are becoming aware that the Corvette is truly one of the world's most remarkable cars. Because it does two disparate things outstandingly well: It provides superbly practical motoring, with every luxury and convenience your heart might covet, and accompanies this with a soul-satisfying ferocity of performance.

We could recite the full specifications. But if you are the kind of driver who is meant for a Corvette, you'll want to find out firsthand—and that, sir, would be our pleasure! . . . *Chevrolet Division of General Motors, Detroit 2, Michigan.*

SPECIFICATIONS: 283-cubic-inch V8 engine with single four-barrel carburetor, 220 h.p. (four other engines range to 283 h.p. with fuel injection). Close-ratio three-speed manual transmission standard, with special Powerglide automatic drive* available on all but maximum-performance engines. Choice of removable hard top or power-operated fabric top, Power-Lift windows.* Instruments include 6000 r.p.m. tachometer, oil pressure gauge and ammeter. *Optional at extra cost.*

Ford Thunderbird, 1956

Between a tiny European sports car and a full-size American coupe, the Chevrolet Corvette and Ford Thunderbird aimed to create a separate niche. The Corvette grew longer and more powerful, while the Thunderbird aimed for more refinement. It would show up on the screen in *La Dolce Vita* – but also in *Thelma and Louise*.

Chevrolet Corvette und Ford Thunderbird zielten auf die Nische zwischen einem winzigen europäischen Sportwagen und einem ausgewachsenen US-Coupé. Die Corvette wurde länger und stärker, während der Thunderbird auf mehr Raffinement abzielte. Auf die Leinwand gelangte er in *La Dolce Vita*, aber auch in *Thelma and Louise*.

Entre la minuscule voiture de sport européenne et le gros coupé américain, la Chevrolet Corvette et la Ford Thunderbird visent à créer une nouvelle niche. La Corvette s'allongera et gagnera en puissance, tandis que la Thunderbird optera pour un plus grand raffinement. On la verra à l'écran dans *La Dolce Vita*, mais aussi dans *Thelma et Louise*.

Chevrolet Corvette, 1956

Plymouth, 1957 ◂

Turns on a dime... parks on a dime... runs on pennies

In but a matter of months, businessmen have found the Volkswagen Truck so sound an investment that, today, it has become the fastest growing seller in the U.S.A. Ask your dealer to show you comparative operating costs. He can prove that Volkswagen trucks deliver the goods . . . for less.

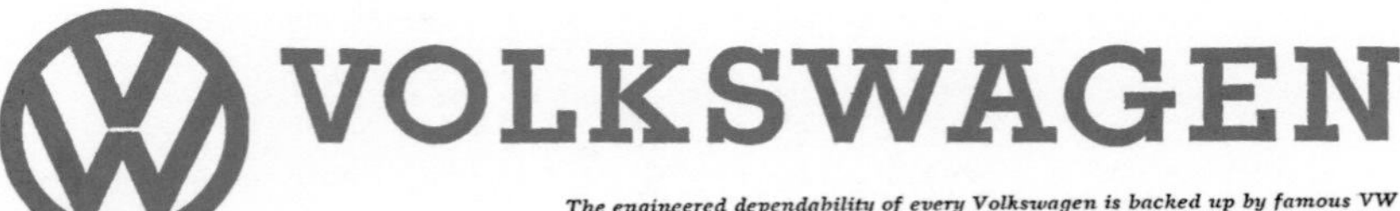

The engineered dependability of every Volkswagen is backed up by famous VW Service and Genuine VW Spare Parts in all 49 states. For free full-color brochure, "Go Places with Volkswagen Trucks," write P. O. Box 2506, N. Y. 17, N. Y.

TIME, OCTOBER 13, 1958

262

Volkswagen Pickup and Panel Delivery, 1958

The German import adopted as an American icon, especially in California, became generic transportation favored by the counterculture – the station wagon of the Woodstock generation.

Das Importmodell, vor allem in Kalifornien zur US-Ikone erkoren, wurde zum beliebtesten Transportmittel der Gegenkultur, mithin zum fahrbaren Untersatz der Woodstock-Generation.

Devenue une icône en Amérique, tout particulièrement en Californie, la petite Allemande représente le moyen de locomotion préféré de la contre-culture – c'est la naissance de la génération Woodstock.

► Chevrolet Fleetline, 1950

►► General Motors Dream Cars/Buick Wildcat, Chevrolet Corvette, Pontiac Parisienne, Oldsmobile Starfire, Cadillac Le Mans, 1953

The Fleetline De Luxe 2-Door Sedan

first

in No-Shift Driving at lowest prices

Drive a Chevrolet with Powerglide Automatic Transmission* and you'll agree it's first and finest for *no-shift driving* at lowest cost. All you have to do is steer, accelerate and stop. There's no clutch pedal—no gears to shift in normal driving. And you glide through all speed ranges with a smooth, unbroken flow of power.

CHEVROLET

and finest

in Valve-in-Head road action with economy

Your own tests will tell you the only way to equal Chevrolet's brand of thrills and thrift is to *buy a Chevrolet!* For here's a combination of acceleration, hill-climbing ability, dependability and economy exclusive to this one low-priced car. That's true whether you choose a Chevrolet with the 105-h.p. Valve-in-Head Engine and Powerglide Automatic Transmission,* or a Chevrolet with the highly improved standard Valve-in-Head Engine and Synchro-Mesh Transmission.

CHEVROLET

**Combination of Powerglide Automatic Transmission and 105-h.p. Engine optional on De Luxe models at extra cost.*

263

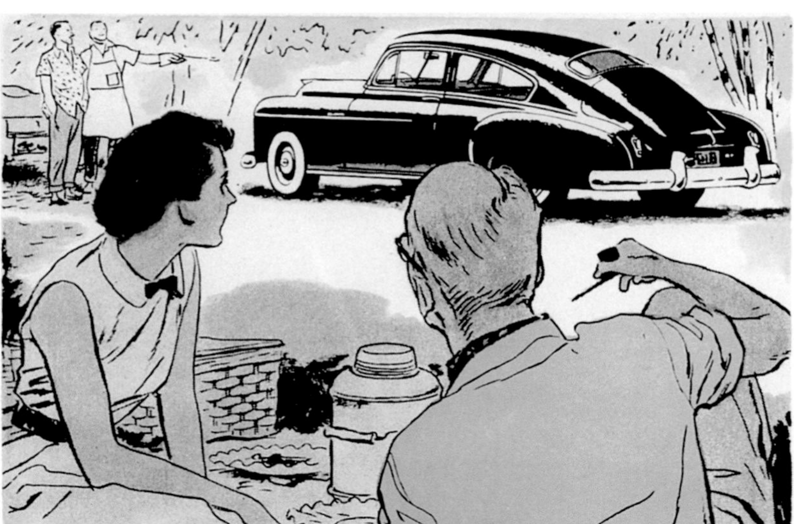

only low-priced car with all these fine car features

Most pleasing of all, Chevrolet brings you feature after feature of the highest-priced cars at lowest prices. For example, Body by Fisher for the finest beauty, comfort and safety. Center-Point Steering and the Unitized Knee-Action Ride for outstanding steering-ease and riding-ease. Curved Windshield with Panoramic Visibility and Proved Certi-Safe Hydraulic Brakes for maximum safety-protection. Buy Chevrolet and you buy the car that's *first and finest at lowest cost!*

AMERICA'S BEST SELLER . . . AMERICA'S BEST BUY

CHEVROLET MOTOR DIVISION, *General Motors Corporation,* DETROIT 2, MICHIGAN

WILDCAT by Buick
Dreams
OUR General Motors engineers are practical men.
they have dreams, too — dreams of exciting new
that some day might be built with new processes, new ma
rials and new techniques now being developed. And, beca
you can't tell about pet ideas until you try them, we gave
staff the go-ahead.
Here are the results — five glamorous hand-built "runnir
models, fabricated of steel and Fiberglas and plastic. All co
bine many never-seen-before advances, all are different. M
GENERA
CORVETTE by Chevrolet

LE MANS by Cadillac
on wheels
an a million people have already acclaimed them at our
cent Motorama Shows from coast to coast.
'e feel these dream cars serve a useful purpose. By finding
ıt which features you, the public, like best in these far-in-
vance models, we can set our sights on the long task of
cluding them on production cars.
'e show them here as another example of the forward-
oking engineering that has long made the key to a General
otors car, your key to greater value.
MOTORS
"More and better things
for more people"
STARFIRE by Oldsmobile
PARISIENNE by Pontiac
GM ENGINEERING
.. PERFECTS TODAY'S PROGRESS
.. PATTERNS TOMORROW'S
PROMISE

With Flying Colors..
OLDSMOBILE
1955 Oldsmobile Super "88" Holiday Coupé. A General Motors Value.

OLDSMOBILE 88

ROCKETS INTO 1955!

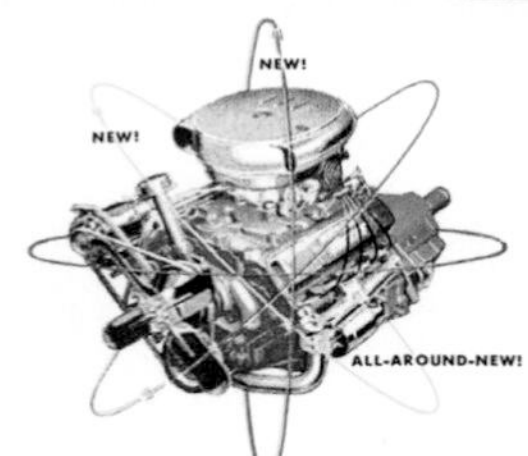

NEW!
NEW!
ALL-AROUND-NEW!

Flashing into the future with flying colors . . . *Oldsmobile for '55!* . . . *more spectacular, more colorful, more powerful* than ever! In three exciting series (Ninety-Eight, Super "88", "88"), every one of them new, all-around-new, *all the way through!* And Oldsmobile's owner-proved "Rocket"—the engine that blazed the way into the Power Era—is all-new, too! New 202 horsepower, new higher torque, new higher compression ratio—new combustion chambers! Every new Oldsmobile has that commanding new "Go-Ahead" look—bold, sweeping front-end design—dramatic new "flying color" patterns—dazzling new styling from front to rear—the newest *new ideas on wheels!* More than ever, Oldsmobile is out ahead to *stay ahead!* See your dealer now . . . see these magnificent new "Rocket" Oldsmobiles for 1955!

▸ Oldsmobile 88, 1952

The car that lent its name to the first rock 'n' roll song – Ike Turner's "Rocket 88" – continued to flaunt chrome details shaped like V-2 rockets and extended taillights that hinted at rocket exhaust frozen in place.

Das Auto, das dem ersten Rock 'n' Roll-Song seinen Namen gab (Ike Turners „Rocket 88") prunkte weiterhin mit Chromteilen ähnlich einer V-2-Rakete und mit verlängerten Heckleuchten, die an erstarrte Raketengase erinnern.

La voiture qui doit son nom à la première chanson de rock'n'roll – « Rocket 88 » d'Ike Turner – arbore encore des éléments chromés en forme de missiles V2 et de grands phares arrière pareils à des échappements gelés de fusée.

Oldsmobile 88, 1952

Johnny and Lucille, Oldsmobile's singing sweethearts, invite you to ride the "Rocket" . . . to drive Oldsmobile's sensational new Super "88"!
TRY 160 H.P.
"ROCKET" ACTION
...in the New Super "88"
You've got to drive it to believe it! Never before has Oldsmobile had such an exciting performance story to tell! For here is a *new* kind of "Rocket" Engine car—*dramatically new* with the flashing 160-h.p. "Rocket" . . . now paired with smooth new Hydra-Matic Super Drive*! The result is performance that truly *stands out* even in this era of high-powered motor cars! GM Hydraulic Steering*, the Autronic-Eye*, and many other new features add to your motoring comfort and safety. Drive Oldsmobile's Super "88" . . . you'll never settle for anything else!
**Hydra-Matic Super Drive, GM Hydraulic Steering, Autronic-Eye—and white sidewall tires (when available) optional at extra cost. Equipment, accessories and trim, subject to change without notice.*
A General Motors Value
"ROCKET" POWERED OLDSMOBILE

It's like money in the bank! Even when you're not using it, nice to know it's there . . . this surge of

extra

CORONET V-EIGHT CLUB COUPE

In the new 140-h.p. Red Ram V-Eight engine, Dodge engineers have provided you with a magnificent reserve of acceleration and performance. You take to the highway with greater confidence, greater safety.

And with this surging Red Ram power, you enjoy nimble change-of-pace of new Gyro-Torque Drive. A new road-hugging, curve-holding ride. A new sense of driving mastery.

If your active life demands an Action Car . . . this sleek, trim Dodge is for you. "Road Test" it . . . soon.

New-All New '53 Dodge

Specifications and equipment subject to change without notice.

The Action Car For Active Americans

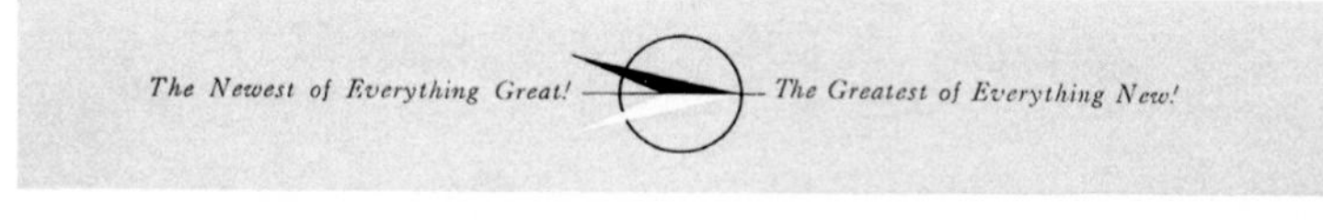

The Newest of Everything Great!
The Greatest of Everything New!

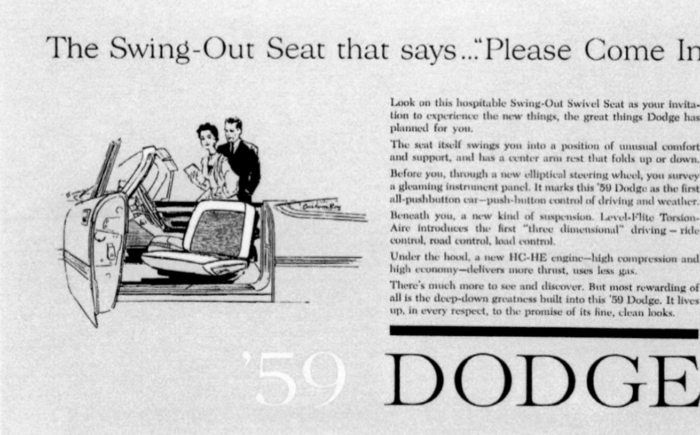

The Swing-Out Seat that says..."Please Come In"
Look on this hospitable Swing-Out Swivel Seat as your invitation to experience the new things, the great things Dodge has planned for you.
The seat itself swings you into a position of unusual comfort and support, and has a center arm rest that folds up or down.
Before you, through a new elliptical steering wheel, you survey a gleaming instrument panel. It marks this '59 Dodge as the first all-pushbutton car—push-button control of driving and weather.
Beneath you, a new kind of suspension. Level-Flite Torsion-Aire introduces the first "three dimensional" driving – ride control, road control, load control.
Under the hood, a new HC-HE engine—high compression and high economy—delivers more thrust, uses less gas.
There's much more to see and discover. But most rewarding of all is the deep-down greatness built into this '59 Dodge. It lives up, in every respect, to the promise of its fine, clean looks.
'59 DODGE

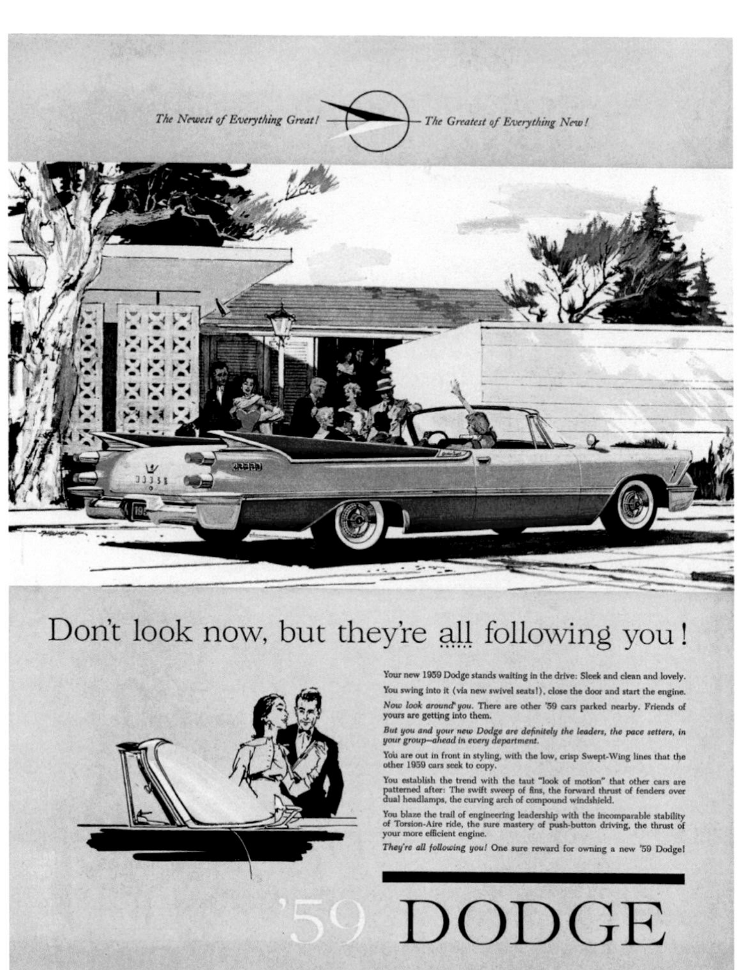

The Newest of Everything Great!
The Greatest of Everything New!
Don't look now, but they're all following you!
Your new 1959 Dodge stands waiting in the drive: Sleek and clean and lovely.
You swing into it (via new swivel seats!), close the door and start the engine.
Now look around you. There are other '59 cars parked nearby. Friends of yours are getting into them.
But you and your new Dodge are definitely the leaders, the pace setters, in your group—ahead in every department.
You are out in front in styling, with the low, crisp Swept-Wing lines that the other 1959 cars seek to copy.
You establish the trend with the taut "look of motion" that other cars are patterned after: The swift sweep of fins, the forward thrust of fenders over dual headlamps, the curving arch of compound windshield.
You blaze the trail of engineering leadership with the incomparable stability of Torsion-Aire ride, the sure mastery of push-button driving, the thrust of your more efficient engine.
They're all following you! One sure reward for owning a new '59 Dodge!
'59 DODGE

Dodge Coronet, 1953 ◂

The quintessential American family car in the age of Ike: the '53 Dodge featured V8 power and plenty of room. The fins would grow.

Die US-Familienkutsche der Eisenhower-Ära war der 53er Dodge mit V8-Motor und reichlich Platz. Die Heckflossen sollten noch größer werden.

La quintessence de la voiture familiale américaine, à l'ére d'Ike Turner : puissance du V-8 et habitacle spacieux. Les ailettes pousseront bientôt.

Dodge Custom Royal Lancer, 1959

Dodge Custom Royal Lancer, 1959

Mercedes-Benz 300d, 1958

One company on the way down and one on the way up met in 1958. Studebaker-Packard agreed to sell Mercedes-Benz cars in its dealerships. But Studebaker lasted only until 1963 – not even Raymond Loewy's exciting Avanti could save it.

1958 begegneten sich zwei Firmen, mit der einen ging es bergab, mit der anderen indes bergauf: Studebaker-Packard war bereit, Autos von Mercedes-Benz in seinen Filialen zu vertreiben. Studebaker war jedoch schon 1963 am Ende – nicht einmal Raymond Loewys aufregender Avanti konnte daran etwas ändern.

En 1958, un constructeur sur le déclin rencontre un constructeur en pleine ascension : Studebaker-Packard accepte de vendre les voitures de Mercedes-Benz. Cela n'empêchera pas Studebaker de fermer ses portes en 1963 : même la fascinante Avanti de Raymond Loewy ne parviendra pas à sauver la firme.

Mercedes-Benz 220S Sedan, 1958

▸ Mercedes-Benz 220SE Coupe, 1963

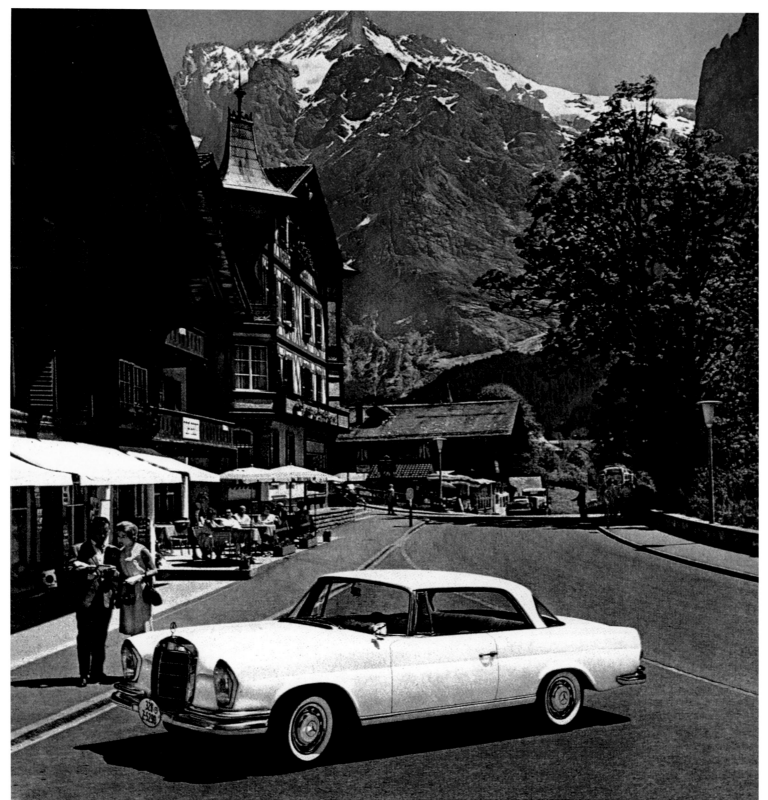

The new Mercedes-Benz 220SE Coupe . . . and why aren't you in the picture?

This Mercedes-Benz Invites You to Europe as its Guest

More than 60,000 owners of Mercedes-Benz motorcars in this country can tell you about substantial savings in fuel, in routine maintenance, in repairs. They will happily confide that, instead of trading in every two or three years, they prefer to keep on enjoying their Mercedes-Benz and keep their money in the bank.

But you can enjoy still another advantage in Mercedes-Benz. Arrange with your dealer to take delivery in Europe . . . the dollar savings can pay for a glorious vacation.

We suggest you visit him, and ask for the figures. And while you are there, take a drive behind the three-pointed silver star!

Mercedes-Benz Sales, Inc.
(A Subsidiary of Studebaker Corporation)
South Bend, Indiana

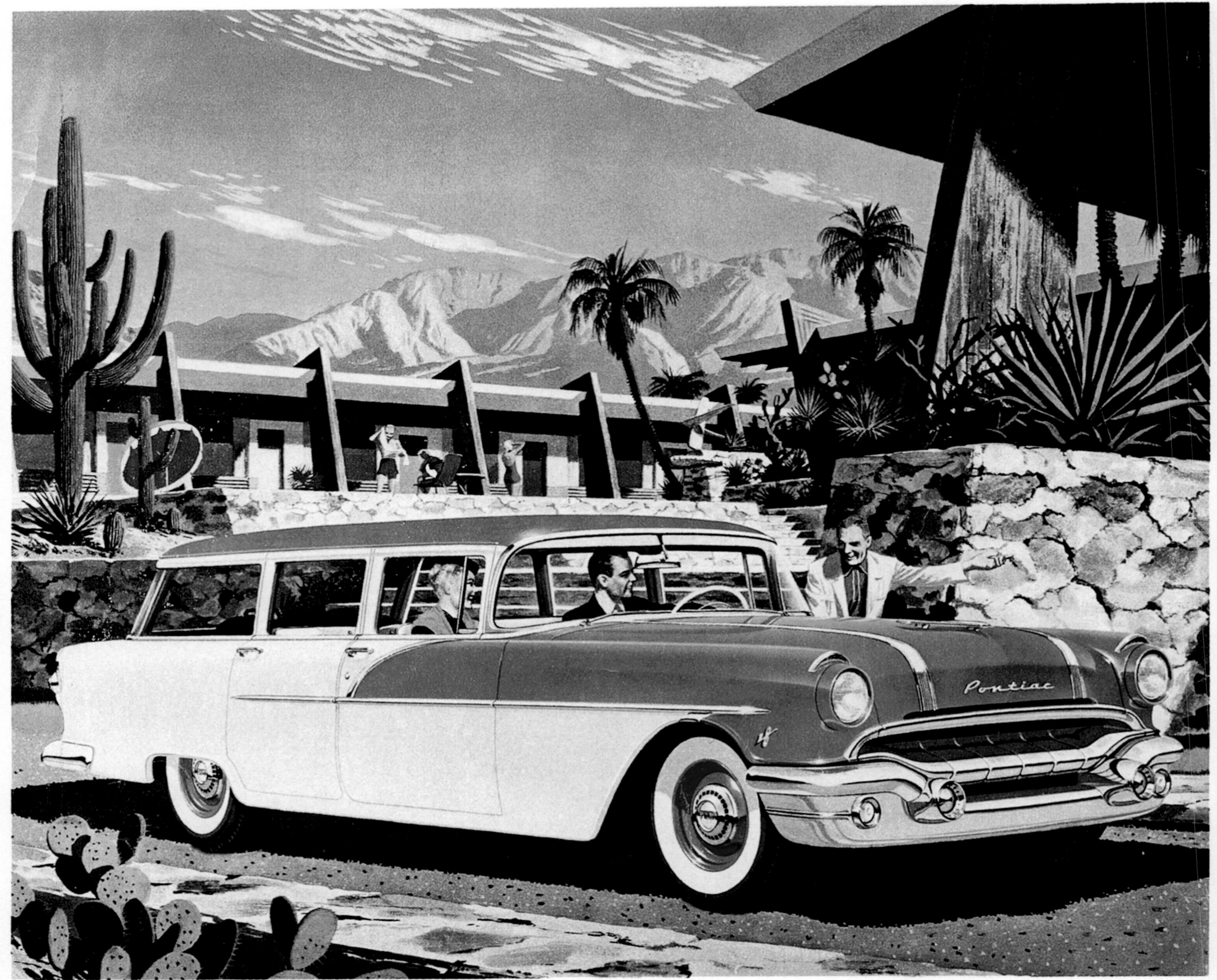

They're Driving the Biggest Thrill of the Trip

Hitting the vacation trail? Pamper yourself—in a '56 Pontiac wonder wagon! From the spacious cockpit of today's station-wagon standout, pick a spot anywhere on the map: As easy as wishing . . . you're there!

And every fleeting mile is a vivid experience in the excitement of *command.* For here is a wagon with a brilliance entirely new to its husky breed! In its every response you will feel the presence of its eager power team, the liveliest on any car *of any body style.*

Pontiac's Strato-Streak V-8 is literally the most modern power plant on the go today. Its surging 227* horses perform with such authority that even long-time Pontiac owners are thrilled as they've never been thrilled before!

And another great engineering triumph, Strato-Flight Hydra-Matic†, turns all this power to flashing action with an all-new, sparkling-smooth alertness *exclusive* with today's Pontiacs!

Remember, too, that along with this go comes glamorous *bigness*—the kind of bigness that gives your Pontiac wagon its "limousine" riding qualities—safeness, steadiness, solid stability.

And you've four to choose from! And, for all their massiveness and power, any of these sleek Pontiac station wagons is astonishingly easy to own. A Pontiac wagon can be yours for less than many lower-powered, "small-car" wagons!

Test pilot a Pontiac station wagon before you complete your vacation plans. You'll reset your sight-seeing sights!

**227 h.p. standard on Star Chief Series. †An extra-cost option.*

PONTIAC MOTOR DIVISION OF GENERAL MOTORS CORPORATION

The '56 Strato-Streak PONTIAC

WITH STRATO-FLIGHT HYDRA-MATIC

Liveliest engines in town . . .

Yessir, when it comes to V-8's, there's just no catching up with Ford. Ford has built more than anybody else . . . *by millions.* Take the 9-passenger Country Squire above. Here's cat-scalding V-8 dash. Thunderbird V-8 dash. Whisks a full load smartly along with a powerful margin of safety. And does it on *regular* gas, for regular savings. Four new "hurry up" Ford engines now await your orders. Take your pick . . . and feel a real blaze start in your heart. (P.S. The Fire Engine, too, is a Ford V-8.)

NEW FORD GALAXIE CLUB VICTORIA—THUNDERBIRD STYLING IN A 6-PASSENGER, 2-DOOR HARDTOP

Beautiful new award-winning proportions · Exclusive luxury lounge interiors with full living-room comfort for all six people · New Diamond Lustre finish never needs waxing · Safety Glass all around · Standard aluminized mufflers for twice the life · 4000 miles between oil changes

59
FORDS
WORLD'S MOST BEAUTIFULLY PROPORTIONED CARS

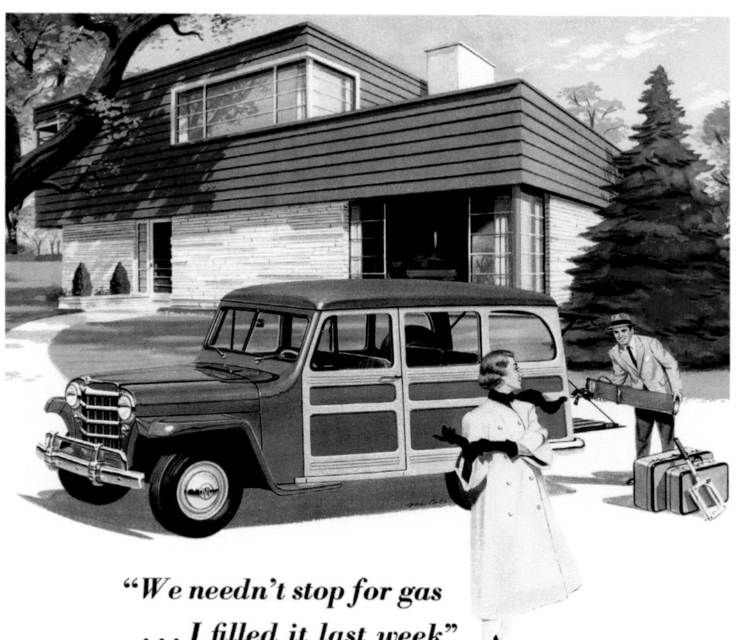
"We needn't stop for gas
. . . I filled it last week"

WILLYS makes sense

—IN ECONOMY —IN EASE OF DRIVING —IN COMFORT

Pontiac Star Chief Safari Station Wagon, 1956 ◂

An ideal vacation cruiser, the Pontiac alluded to up-to-date modernism by posing in front of a resort resembling Frank Lloyd Wright's Taliesin West studio near Phoenix.

Als ideales Urlaubsgefährt gab sich der Pontiac zugleich höchst modern, indem er vor einem Feriendomizil posierte, das Frank Lloyd Wrights Taliesin West Studio unweit von Phoenix, Arizona ähnelt.

Ce modèle, idéal pour partir en vacances, est présenté devant une résidence secondaire qui rappelle l'atelier de Frank Lloyd Wright à Taliesin West (près de Phoenix) ; clin d'œil au modernisme tant prisé ces années-là.

Ford Country Squire and Galaxie, 1959

Willys Station Wagon, 1951

▸▸ Hertz Rent A Car/Chevrolet Impala, 1959

HOTEL
AMBASSADOR
EAST

22724

gowns by Marusia

OUT OF A BRILLIANT PAST . . . *A SUPREME TRIUMPH !*

Only from the great traditions of Cadillac could there come a motor car as surpassingly fine as the creation you see here. It's the Cadillac car for 1958—a brilliant achievement in all the qualities that make it the Standard of the World. And paramount among these is the *practical* satisfaction it renders. From every standpoint, the Cadillac car has become an even wiser purchase for an even wider group of motorists. Whether your favorite is the Sixty-Two Coupe or the Eldorado Brougham, we invite you to inspect its Fleetwood coachcrafting and to spend an hour at the wheel.

GM FORWARD FROM FIFTY

CADILLAC MOTOR CAR DIVISION • GENERAL MOTORS CORPORATION

Light the Way to Safety—Aim Your Headlights • Every Window of Every Cadillac is Safety Plate Glass

Cadillac

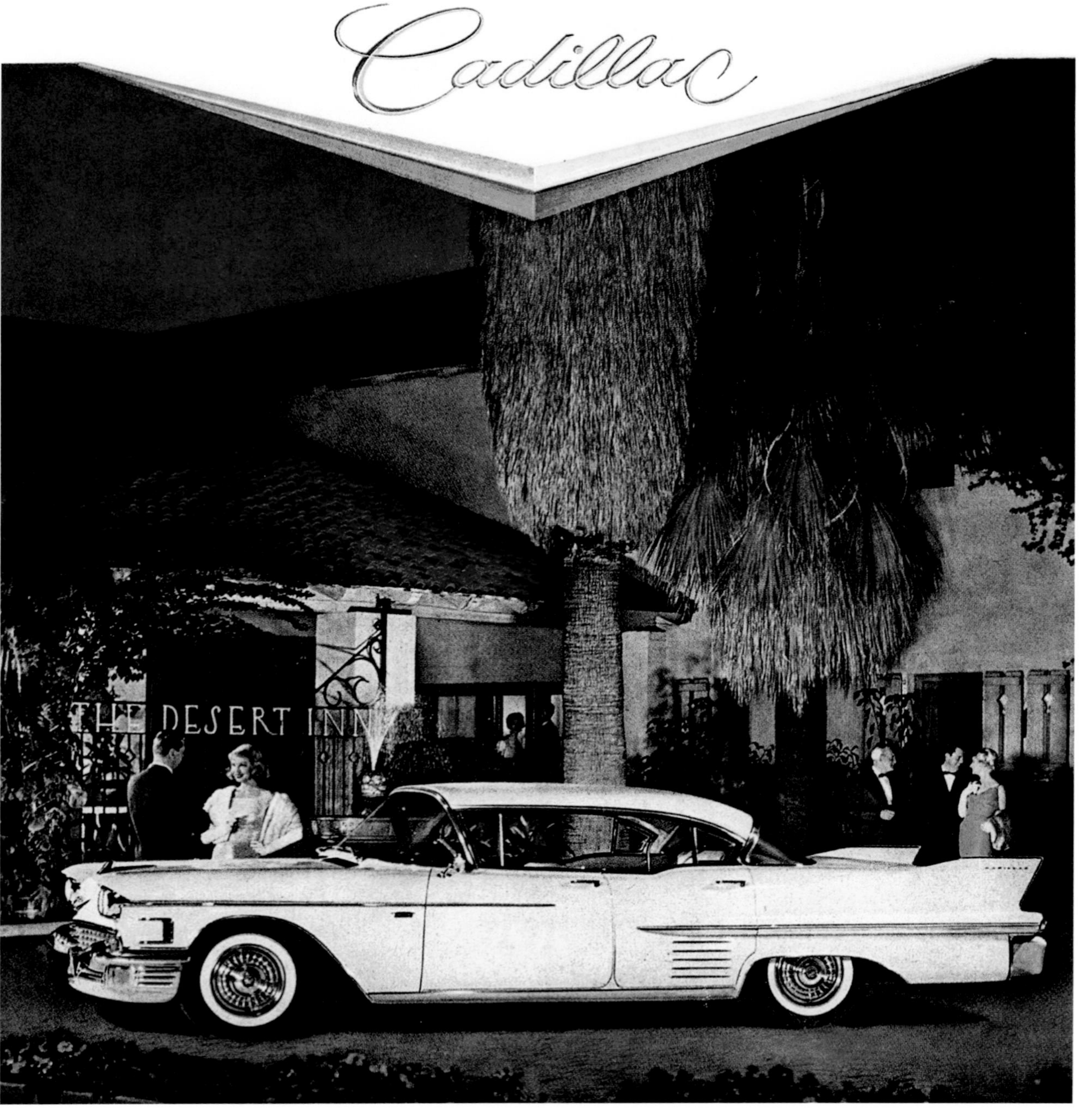

Cadillac Series 62 Park Avenue, 1958

▸ Cadillac Series 62 Coupe DeVille, 1951

Its grace and beauty have captured the hearts of women everywhere—but only the woman who has *driven* it can know how satisfying this great Cadillac is to her *practical* side. Those miles and miles of confident, trouble-free motoring have taught her how wonderfully dependable and free from maintenance expense it is . . . and she's reminded of its remarkable gasoline economy every time she glances at the fuel gauge. And if she looks a little smug now and then—well, she actually paid *less* for her *Cadillac* than many of her friends paid for *other* makes of cars!

Cadillac

CADILLAC MOTOR CAR DIVISION • GENERAL MOTORS CORPORATION

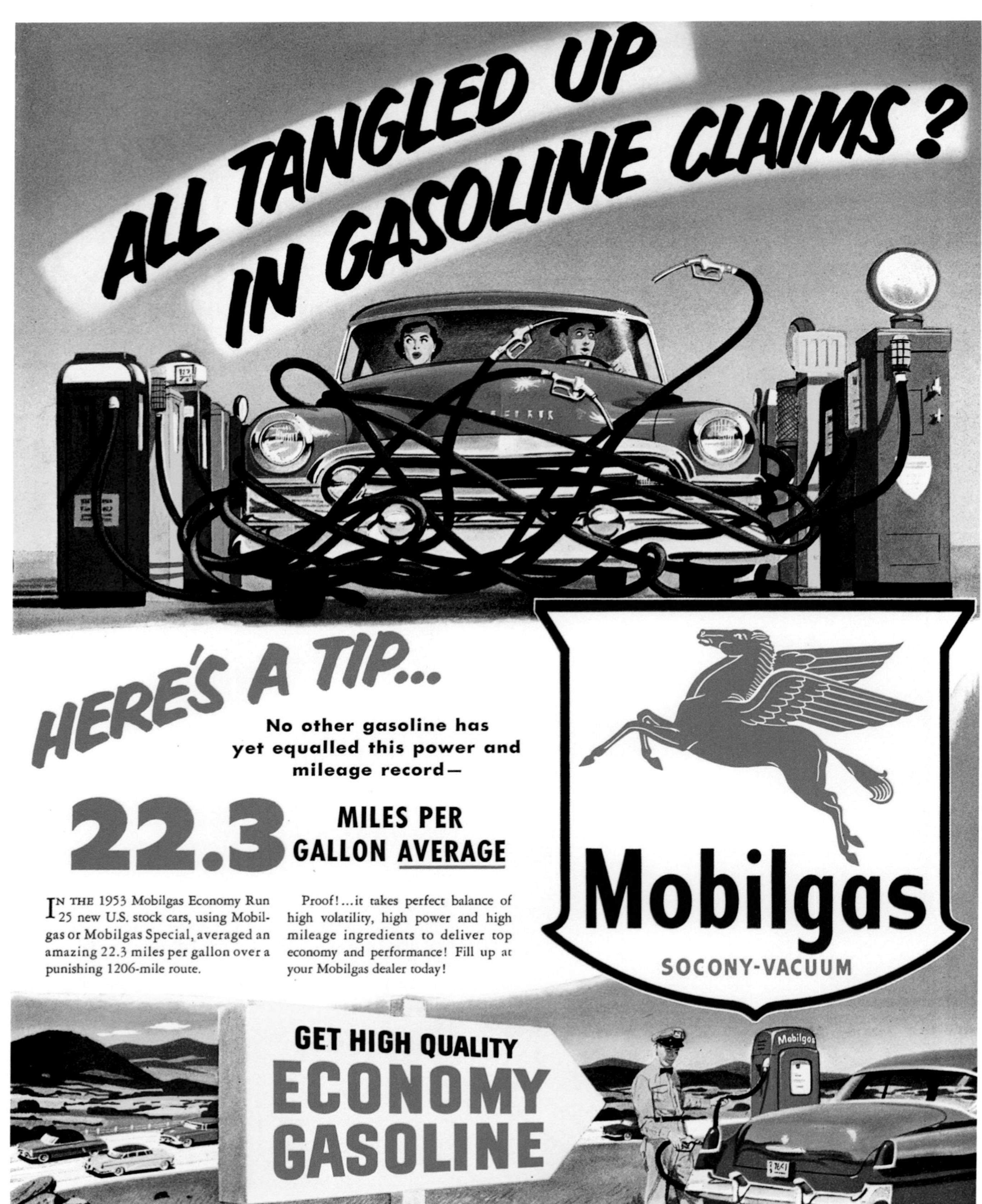

Mobilgas, 1953

Shell Oil, 1952

►► Fisher Body, 1959

Your engine makes
this much Acid every day
...And it's Acid Action—not friction—
that causes 90% of engine wear
ARTZYBASHEFF

New Alkaline Shell X-100 Motor Oil counteracts Acid Action

If you are a typical motorist, in a normal day's driving:—a pint or more of acid is formed and passes through your car's engine, and it's acid action, not friction, that causes 90% of your engine wear. To neutralize the harmful effect of this acid, Shell Research has produced an alkaline motor oil—Shell X-100. Fortified with alkaline "X" safety factors, it neutralizes the acid action, prolonging the life of your engine.

The new Shell X-100 is a Premium Motor Oil. It is a Heavy Duty Motor Oil. In addition, it contains positive cleansing factors that help protect hydraulic valve lifters and other vital parts from fouling deposits.

Shell X-100 is the finest motor oil money can buy. Let your Shell dealer give your engine the protection of this new alkaline Shell X-100 Motor Oil today.

SHELL
X-100
MOTOR OIL
PREMIUM-HEAVY DUTY
SHELL

It's Incomparable!

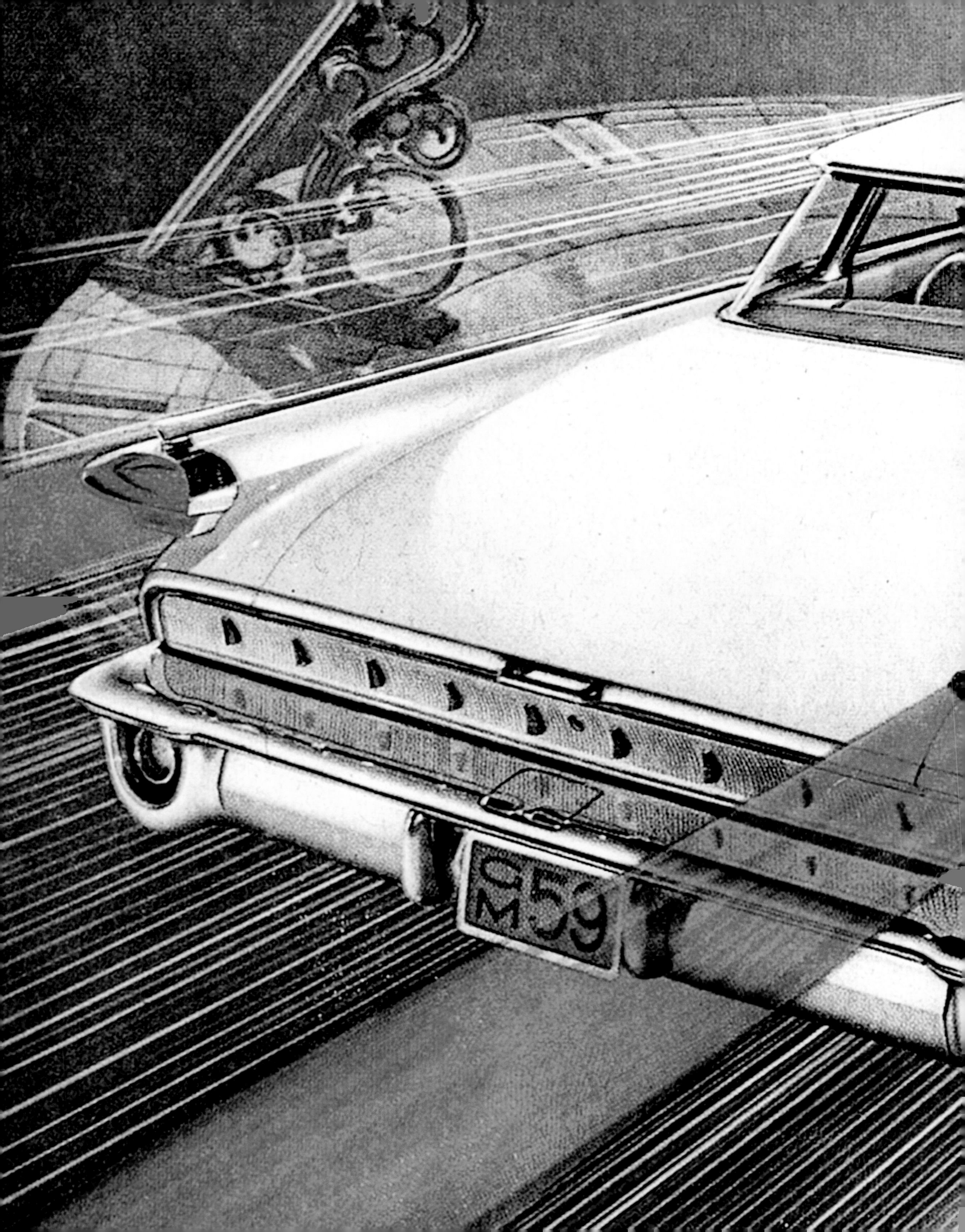

THE ADVERTISING OF THE DECADE WOULD EMPHASIZE CLEAN PHOTOGRAPHY – AS OPPOSED TO THE PREVIOUSLY DOMINANT MEDIUM OF ILLUSTRATION–AND YOUTHFULNESS, AS THE COUNTERCULTURE GREW IN FORCE. THERE WAS A SENSE THAT THE BIG CARS AND OVERLY DRAMATIC STYLING WERE GROWING TIRED.

BEI DEN WERBEANZEIGEN IN DIESEM JAHRZEHNT STANDEN DAS REINE FOTO (IM GEGENSATZ ZUR BISLANG DOMINIERENDEN ILLUSTRATION) UND – MIT BLICK AUF DIE ERSTARKENDE GEGENKULTUR – DIE JUGENDLICHKEIT IM MITTELPUNKT. ES MACHTE SICH DER EINDRUCK BREIT, DASS DIE ZEIT DER GROSSEN SCHLITTEN UND BOMBASTISCHEN DESIGNS ZU ENDE GING.

DURANT CETTE DÉCENNIE, LA PUBLICITÉ S'APPUIE DAVANTAGE SUR LA PHOTOGRAPHIE QUE SUR L'ILLUSTRATION, ANCIEN MÉDIUM DOMINANT, ET S'ADRESSE PARTICULIÈREMENT À LA JEUNESSE, SOUS LA PRESSION DE LA CONTRE-CULTURE. LES GROSSES VOITURES ET LE STYLE TROP IMPOSANT SEMBLENT PASSER DE MODE.

THE PEOPLE'S CAR AND PERSONAL CARS

VOLKS-WAGEN UND PERSONAL-CARS

VOITURE POPULAIRE ET VOITURES PERSONNALISÉES

ONE

Kelly Tires, ca. 1960 ◂◂

Lincoln Continental, 1964 ◂

Ford, 1963

THE '60S REALLY BEGAN IN 1959, WHEN DETROIT BEGAN TO OFFER ITS OWN CROP OF "COMPACTS," small cars to compete with Volkswagen, Renault, and other European imports, and Volkswagen began to advertise its Beetle. New York ad agency Doyle Dane Bernbach got the Volkswagen account and launched what would become known as the "Think Small" campaign — a wry commentary, in word and image, on the heated claims of earlier automobile advertising. By 1969, the year of Woodstock and the first moon landing, American sales of the Volkswagen Beetle reached their highest level ever, and a Disney film called *The Love Bug*, starring a Beetle, was the number-one box-office hit.

The advertising of the decade would emphasize clean photography — as opposed to the previously dominant medium of illustration — and youthfulness, as the counterculture grew in force. There was a sense that the big cars and overly dramatic styling were growing tired. Social critics such as Vance Packard and John Keats, author of the book *The Insolent Chariots* (which included cartoons of Buicks with chrome teeth and Cadillacs with fins like sharks) made fun of auto advertising, the superficialities of the annual model change, the growth in chrome ornament, and the cars' unnecessary length.

Recalling the auto-collision deaths of James Dean, Jayne Mansfield, and other celebrities, and spending more and more time in their cars commuting from the suburbs to urban centers, Americans were becoming more concerned about safety. One car stood out: the Chevrolet Corvair. It arrived in 1960 as General Motors' entry in the compact category. But its independent rear suspension and rear engine placement made the car's tail heavy and dangerous: Drivers could easily lose control, as famed comedian Ernie Kovacs did in his fatal crash. Ralph Nader's attacks on the Corvair (and the Volkswagen Beetle) helped lead to new regulations in impact engineering.

Compacts like the Corvair, Ford Falcon, and Dodge Dart gave way to small personal cars, like the Chevrolet Camaro and the Mustang. In the era of "do your own thing," advertising showed cars as means of self-expression and self-fulfillment. There were new "personal coupes," like the Buick Riviera and Cadillac Eldorado. By the end of the 1960s, the family scenes that dominated '50s advertising were largely replaced by images of young people — often women by themselves — and women at the wheel. Pitches of "fun and sun" for convertibles grew common. Jeep offered a model in blue denim upholstery.

Whether for style or speed, automobiles could be ordered with different engines, different features, and different colors to personalize them. By one calculation, the number of possible theoretical permutations offered by General Motors cars alone was greater than the number of molecules in the galaxy.

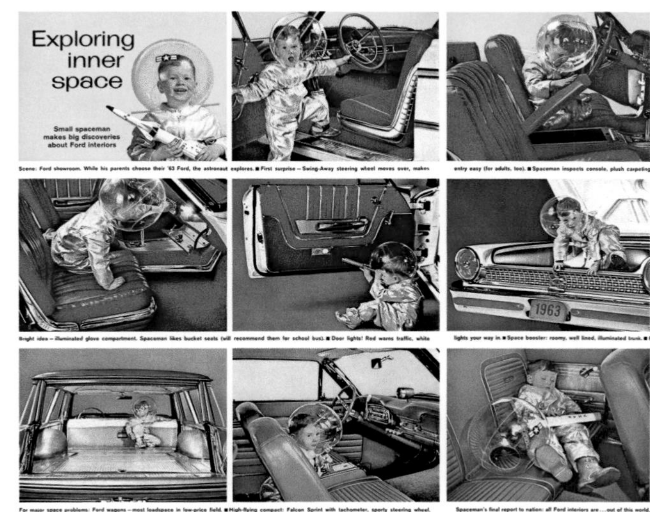

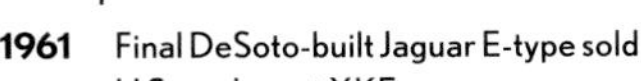

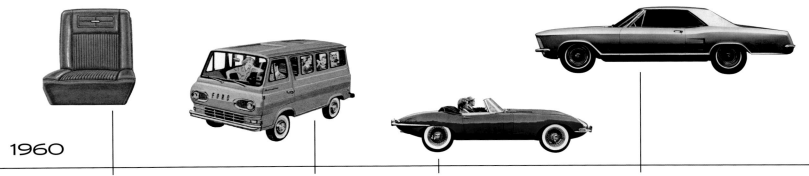

1960

1960 Bucket seats become more common in American cars

Einzelsitze in US-Autos zunehmend verbreitet

Le siège baquet est de plus en plus répandu parmi les Américaines

1961 Ford introduces Econoline van

Ford präsentiert den Van Econoline

Ford lance la camionnette Econoline

1961 Final DeSoto-built Jaguar E-type sold in U.S. as elegant XKE

Letzter Jaguar E von DeSoto in den USA als eleganter XKE vertrieben

Vente de la dernière XKE, élégante Jaguar type E construite par DeSoto aux États-Unis

1963 Bill Mitchell-designed Buick Rivera debuts

Debüt des von Bill Mitchell entworfenen Buick Rivera

Débuts de la Buick Rivera dessinée par Bill Mitchell

DIE SECHZIGER BEGANNEN EIGENTLICH BEREITS 1959, ALS DETROIT SEINE EIGENEN „KOMPAKTEN" PRÄSENTIERTE – kleine Autos, die sich gegen VW, Renault und weitere Importmarken behaupten sollten – und als VW begann, für den Käfer zu werben. Die New Yorker Werbeagentur Doyle Dane Bernbach hatte die Ausschreibung gewonnen und lancierte die später so genannte „Think Small"-Kampagne, ein ironischer Kommentar – in Wort und Bild – zu den großspurigen Behauptungen der bisherigen Autowerbung. 1969, im Jahr von Woodstock und der ersten Mondlandung, verkaufte sich der Käfer in den USA so gut wie nie und der Disney-Film *Ein toller Käfer* wurde zum Kassenschlager.

Bei den Werbeanzeigen in diesem Jahrzehnt standen das reine Foto (im Gegensatz zur bislang dominierenden Illustration) und – mit Blick auf die erstarkende Gegenkultur – die Jugendlichkeit im Mittelpunkt. Es machte sich der Eindruck breit, dass die Zeit der großen Schlitten und bombastischen Designs zu Ende ging. Gesellschaftskritiker wie Vance Packard und John Keats – Autor des Buchs *The Insolent Chariots*, dessen Cartoons Buicks mit Zähnen aus Chrom und Cadillacs mit haifischartigen Heckflossen präsentierten – mokierten sich über die Autowerbung, die Oberflächlichkeit des alljährlichen Modellwechsels, den wuchernden Zierrat aus Chrom und die übertriebene Länge der Karossen.

James Dean, Jayne Mansfield und weitere Berühmtheiten waren mit dem Auto tödlich verunglückt. Und der Durchschnittsamerikaner verbrachte als Pendler immer mehr Zeit in seinem Wagen. Daher machte man sich zunehmend Sorgen um die Sicherheit. Traurige Berühmtheit erlangte der Chevrolet Corvair, ein 1960 von General Motors eingeführter Kompaktwagen. Pendelachse und Heckmotor machten diesen Wagen hecklastig und schwer beherrschbar, wie der Unfalltod des berühmten Komikers Ernie Kovacs zeigte. Ralph Naders Angriffe gegen den Corvair (und den VW Käfer) trugen zur Erarbeitung neuer Vorschriften für die Sicherheit bei.

Auf Kompakte wie den Corvair, Ford Falcon und Dodge Dart folgten kleine Personal-Cars wie der Chevrolet Camaro und der Ford Mustang. In der Ära der Selbstverwirklichung präsentierte man das Auto als persönliches Ausdrucksmittel. Personal-Coupés wie der Buick Riviera und der Cadillac Eldorado betraten die Bühne. Die Familienszenen, die in der Werbung der 1950er-Jahre dominiert hatten, wurden Ende der Sechziger weitgehend durch Bilder von jungen Leuten ersetzt, oftmals Frauen unter sich und Frauen am Steuer. Bei der Werbung für Cabrios reimten sich „fun" und „sun". Und Jeep lancierte ein Modell mit Sitzen aus blauem Jeansstoff.

Autos konnte man nun mit verschiedenen Motoren, Ausstattungen und Farben ordern, jeder nach seinem Geschmack. Man hat einmal ausgerechnet, dass die Zahl der allein von General Motors gebotenen Kombinationsmöglichkeiten größer war als die Anzahl der Moleküle in der Milchstraße.

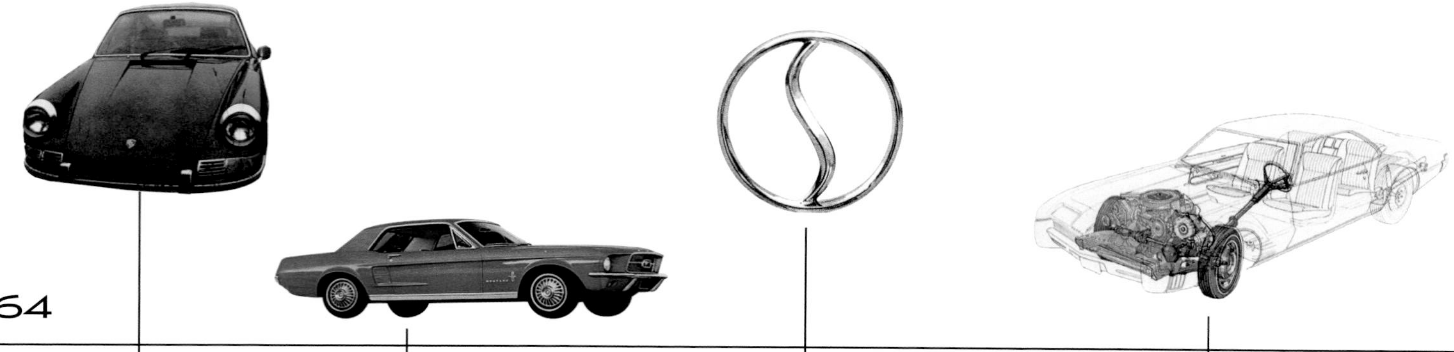

1964 First model year for Porsche's long-running 911 model

Erstes Modelljahr des späteren Dauerbrenners Porsche 911

Commercialisée de longue date, la Porsche 911 est enfin nommée modèle de l'année

1965 Just 18 months after being introduced, one million Ford Mustangs have sold

Nach nur 18 Monaten wurden bereits eine Million Ford Mustang verkauft

18 mois après son lancement, la Ford Mustang s'est déjà vendue à un million d'exemplaires

1966 Studebaker, begun as wagon maker, ceases operations

Der ursprüngliche Wagenbauer Studebaker stellt seine Aktivitäten ein

L'ancien constructeur de chariots Studebaker cesse toute activité

1966 Front-wheel drive Oldsmobile Toronado foreshadows future technology

Frontantrieb des Oldsmobile Toronado als Vorbote künftiger Techologien

La traction avant Oldsmobile Toronado annonce la technologie du futur

Bonneville
VK AF

Pontiac Bonneville, 1967 ◂◂

Pontiac Bonneville, 1960 ◂

▸▸ Chevrolet Impala, 1962

LES ANNÉES 1960 COMMENCENT RÉELLEMENT EN 1959, QUAND DETROIT LANCE SA PROPRE GAMME DE « COMPACTES », des petites voitures destinées à concurrencer les Volkswagen, Renault et autres importations européennes. Volkswagen commence alors sa campagne de publicité pour la Coccinelle. L'agence publicitaire new-yorkaise Doyle, Dane et Bernbach, chargée du compte, lance son fameux slogan « Penser petit »; une campagne qui se moque, texte et image à l'appui, des hyperboles jusqu'alors prisées par la publicité automobile. En 1969, l'année de Woodstock et du premier pas sur la lune, les ventes américaines de la Coccinelle atteignent leur zénith, tandis que le film de Disney *Un Amour de coccinelle* remplit les salles.

Durant cette décennie, la publicité s'appuie davantage sur la photographie que sur l'illustration, ancien médium dominant, et s'adresse particulièrement à la jeunesse, sous la pression de la contre-culture. Les grosses voitures et le style trop imposant semblent passer de mode. Certains auteurs de critiques sociales, dont Vance Packard et John Keats – auteur d'un livre illustré par des Buick dotées de dents en chrome et des Cadillac aux ailerons de requins (*The Insolent Chariots*, 1958) – se moquent de la publicité automobile, de la superficialité de la valse annuelle des nouveaux modèles, des ornementations chromées trop ostentatoires et de la longueur superflue des voitures.

Après les accidents mortels de James Dean, de Jayne Mansfield et d'autres célébrités, et parce qu'ils passent de plus en plus de temps dans leur voiture à aller et venir entre la banlieue et le centre-ville, les Américains se soucient toujours plus de leur sécurité. Un modèle incarne ce problème : la Chevrolet Corvair. Arrivée en 1960 dans la gamme « compacte » de General Motors, elle est lourde et dangereuse en raison de sa suspension arrière indépendante et de son moteur placé à l'arrière : le contrôle du véhicule échappe facilement au conducteur, à l'instar du célèbre comédien Ernie Kovacs, mort au volant. Les attaques de Ralph Nader contre la Corvair (et la Coccinelle Volkswagen) provoquent la mise en place d'une nouvelle réglementation en matière de protection anti-chocs.

Les compactes comme les Corvair, Ford Falcon et Dodge Dart cèdent la place à de petites voitures personnalisées comme la Camaro et la Mustang. À l'époque du « fais comme tu le sens », la publicité présente la voiture comme un moyen d'expression et d'épanouissement personnels. On voit apparaître de nouveaux « coupés personnalisés », notamment le Buick Riviera et le Cadillac Eldorado. Dès la fin des années 1960, les scènes familiales qui prédominaient dans la publicité des années 1950 sont en grande partie remplacées par des images de jeunes, souvent de femmes seules – et de femmes au volant. On vante de plus en plus les avantages de la décapotable, qui permet de jouir du soleil, et que l'on associe à l'idée de plaisir. La Jeep se décline avec des sièges couleur jean.

Qu'il s'agisse de style ou de vitesse, il existe une grande variété de motorisation, d'équipements et de coloris pour chaque modèle, ce qui permet de personnaliser sa voiture. De fait, mathématiquement, le nombre de permutations potentielles offertes par General Motors dépasse à lui seul le nombre de molécules dans la galaxie.

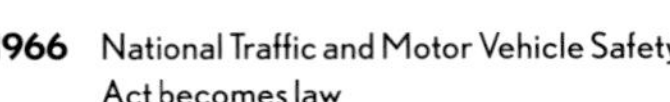

1966

1966 National Traffic and Motor Vehicle Safety Act becomes law

National Traffic and Motor Vehicle Safety Act verabschiedet

Adoption de la loi sur la sécurité du trafic et des véhicules automobiles aux États-Unis

1967 Chevrolet's Camaro released to compete with Ford Mustang

Chevrolet Camaro als Konkurrent des Ford Mustang präsentiert

Lancement de la Chevrolet Camaro, pour concurrencer la Ford Mustang

1969 Seat belts required on all new cars in U.S. with shoulder restraints in front

Sicherheitsgurte (Dreipunktgurt vorn) bei allen Neuwagen in den USA vorgeschrieben

Ceintures de sécurité obligatoires, avec passants aux épaules à l'avant, sur toutes les voitures neuves aux États-Unis

1969 Honda's 600 sedan becomes first production car for motorcycle manufacturer

Honda 600 erstes Serienauto des Motorradherstellers

La Honda S 600 est la première voiture produite par le fabricant de motos

INTERNATIONAL
TERMINAL

PAN AM
PAN AM
PAN AM
4
CHEVROLET
AG-1400

THE DEPENDABLES ARE HERE!

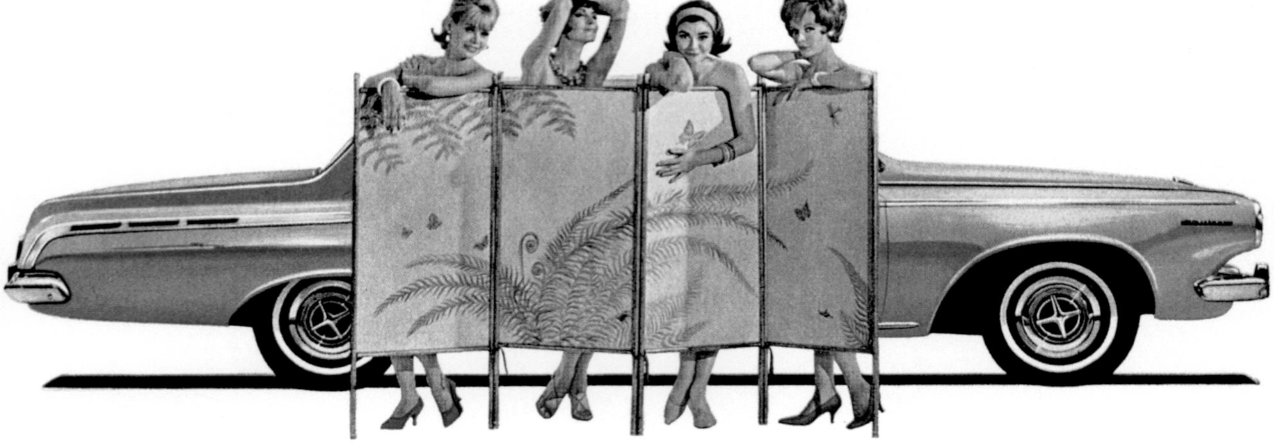

PARDON US WHILE WE SLIP INTO

SOMETHING COMFORTABLE!

INTRODUCING THE 1963 DODGE

The something comfortable in this case is a 1963 Dodge Polara 4-door hardtop. It's not the clinging sort of comfortable, either; you might say that it's more like housecoat comfortable. Lots of room to move around in. Note the roofline. It sweeps straight back instead of sloping off. It means plenty of headroom for front and rear seat passengers. And everyone rides in more comfort, because Dodge seats are chair-high. All 24 Dodge models (in three series) offer you this kind of comfort at a variety of prices, all low. Sedans, hardtops, wagons, convertibles—Dependables all. We've got lots for the male side, too. For economy, a going 225 cu. in. 6. For action, a stable full of V8's ranging from the standard 318 cu. in. V8 to an all-out 426 cu. in. high-performance job. There's more: like self-adjusting brakes, 32,000 miles between grease jobs, and a unitized, rust-protected body. The good looks should already be obvious to you. The rest? See your Dodge Dealer.

PICK A SIZE...PICK A PRICE...PICK A DODGE

Dodge Division of Chrysler Corporation

A FULL LINE OF CARS IN THE LOW-PRICE FIELD!

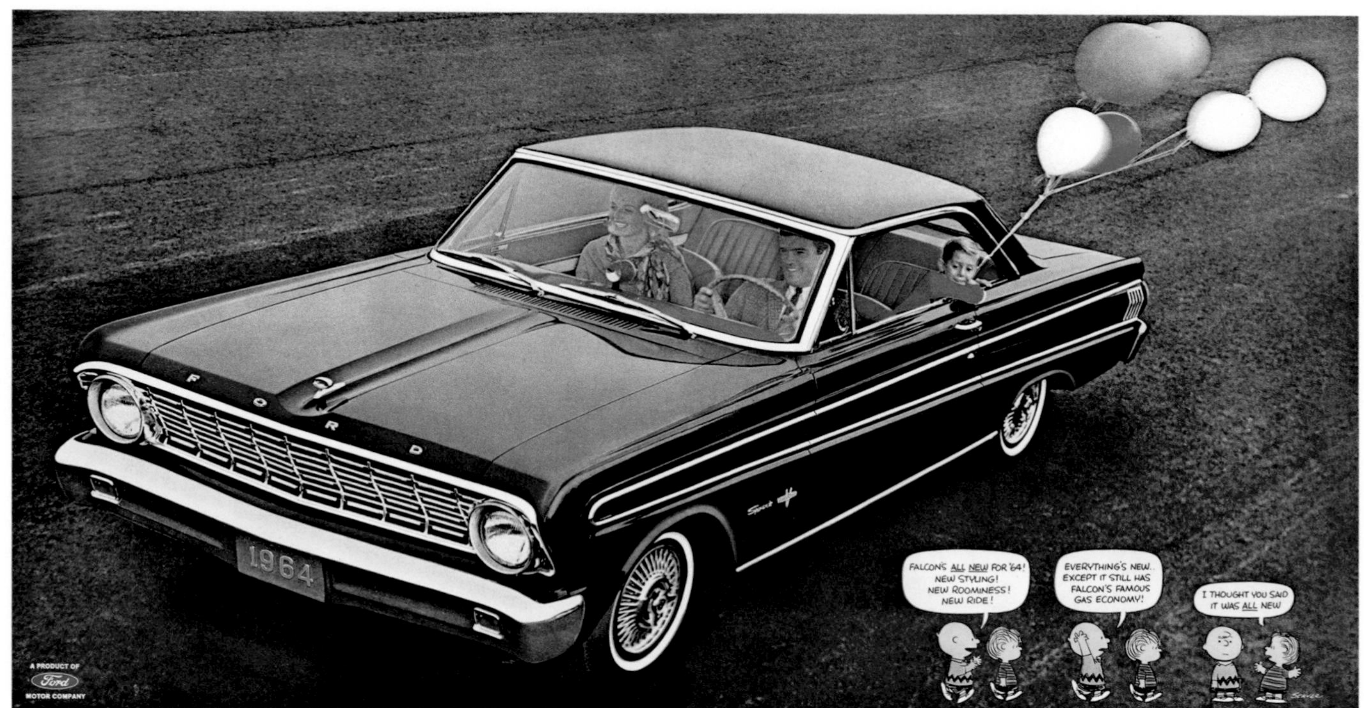

This is the 1964 Falcon–we've kept the economy that made Falcon famous–added new style, new comfort, and the plushest ride ever built into a compact car.

We kept the Six that still holds the all-time Mobilgas Economy Run Record for sixes or eights because we couldn't figure out a way to beat it.

We changed everything else. The new styling needs no explanation – it speaks for itself. The comfort comes from new interior design; we've repositioned front seats, steering wheel and controls for greater convenience and a roomier feeling. The smoothness of Falcon's new ride is something you have to experience to understand; it's due to improved suspensions and wider rear tread.

There's a new, wider choice of features in the Falcon line this year–including a V-8 that won its reputation for toughness in rugged competition on the international rally circuit. Price? Still pure Falcon. How about *that*, Charlie Brown?

TRY TOTAL PERFORMANCE FOR A CHANGE!

Falcon · Fairlane · Ford · Thunderbird

295

Ford Falcon, 1961

The Falcon was Ford's contribution to the compact car market in 1960. According to legend, it was invented by Ford's then-president Robert McNamara, who scribbled the specs on the back of a hymn list one Sunday during church services. Salesmen hated it, but it sold in the millions through the '60s, providing the underpinnings for the future Mustang.

Der Falcon war Fords Beitrag im Segment der Kompaktwagen des Jahres 1960. Ausgedacht hatte ihn sich Fords damaliger Präsident Robert McNamara, angeblich indem er eines Sonntags während der Messe die technischen Grunddaten auf die Rückseite eines Liederzettels kritzelte. Die Verkäufer hassten den Wagen, der sich während der gesamten Sechziger jedoch millionenfach verkaufte und die Basis für den künftigen Mustang lieferte.

La Ford Falcon est le modèle proposé par Ford pour le marché de la compacte en 1960. D'après la légende, elle incarnerait le rêve du président d'alors, Robert McNamara, qui en aurait griffonné les caractéristiques au dos de sa liste de cantiques un dimanche à la messe. Détestée des vendeurs, elle se vendra par millions tout au long des années 1960 et servira de base à la future Mustang.

Dodge Polara, 1963 ◂

Jaguar elegance: The beauty that's more than skin-deep

Inspect each sweep, each curve, each fluid line of any Jaguar, and you bear witness to Jaguar elegance—a grace of styling that has been engineered from within the heart of the automobile itself. Jaguar elegance is reflected here in two exciting motor cars. One, the new Jaguar XK-E, is available either as an open sports roadster with interchangeable soft or hard top or a completely enclosed *Gran Turismo* coupe. For the family man who requires a roomier vehicle, there is the versatile Jaguar 3.8 Sedan. Pure Jaguar from the word go, this car has been titled "the sedan that behaves like a sports car." Discover Jaguar elegance yourself. See and drive either of these fine Jaguars soon at your local dealer's. JAGUAR CARS INC., 32 East 57th Street, New York 22, N. Y.

Technical Service and Parts Headquarters, 42-50 Twenty-First St., Long Island City 1, N. Y.

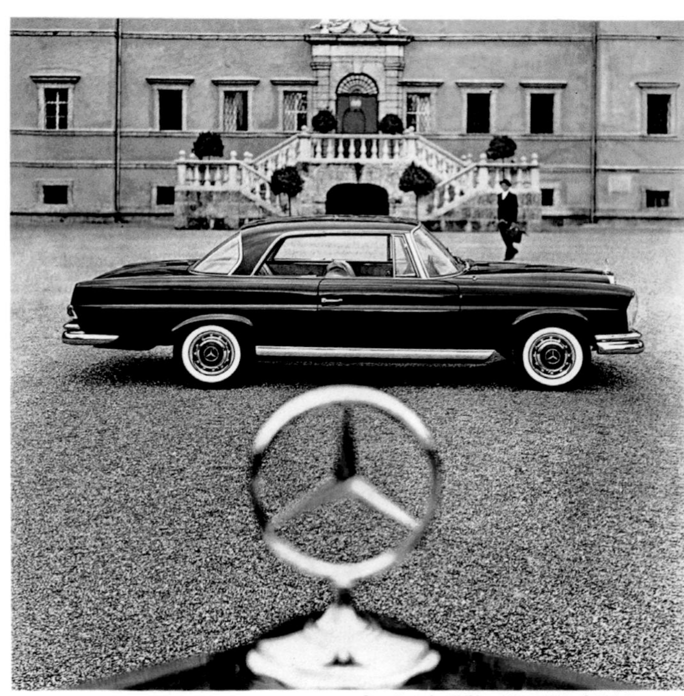

The new Mercedes-Benz 220 SE Coupe photographed at Helbrun Castle in Austria

Coupe d'Etat

For over half a century, it has been the pleasure of men of state to drive or be driven in a Mercedes-Benz. Mercedes-Benz now offers its newest car, a veritable coupe of state, to the discriminating few who can afford to be seen in this, the finest of machines. It is the new 220 SE coupe with a fuel injection engine, optional power steering and a choice of automatic or four-speed transmission. Its interior is completely hand-fitted with elegant leather and wood embellishments and represents the best of the coachmaker's art. There is no similar car in the world. It combines sports-like performance with the dignity of diplomacy. Further, it carries its silver three-pointed star in the restful silence of complete discretion. That, of course, is entirely in keeping with the seventy-five-year-old tradition of Mercedes-Benz.

Mercedes-Benz Sales, Inc., South Bend, Indiana *(A Subsidiary of Studebaker-Packard Corporation)*

HOLIDAY/APRIL

The new Mercedes-Benz 190 Sedan, available with gasoline or diesel power

The Human Reasons for Owning a Mercedes-Benz

The excellence of this 190 Sedan itself would be reason enough. It is a full-size car of modest price (about $3,900)—impeccably styled, comfortable, masterfully built.

You may have a gasoline engine, or the only passenger diesel proved over 26 years.

But the human reasons are even more important. The fine people shown here are fathers, sons, daughters from the hundreds of families who have, for generations, built a special quality into Mercedes-Benz.

The hand-stitched upholstery, the hand-smoothed coachwork, the fact that every major moving part is bench-tested before assembly—these are the hallmarks of honest work, proud work, built to endure.

Your Mercedes-Benz will endure. It will stir your own pride years after it has paid for itself. And it will still bring you this unique thrill of ownership: the zest of motoring behind the silver three-pointed star.

Mercedes-Benz Sales, Inc. *(A Subsidiary of Studebaker Corporation)* South Bend, Indiana

HOLIDAY/APRIL

Mercedes-Benz 220SE Coupe, 1962

Mercedes-Benz 190 Sedan, 1962

Jaguar XK-E and 3.8, 1962 ◂

2 shapes known

Nobody really notices Coke bottles or Volkswagens any more.

They're so well known, they blend in with the scenery.

It doesn't matter what the scenery is, either. You can walk in and buy a VW in any one of 136 countries.

And that takes in lots of scenery.

Deserts. Mountains. Hot places. Cold places.

Volkswagens thrive.

Hot and cold don't matter; the VW engine is air-cooled. It doesn't use water, so it can't freeze up or boil over.

And having the engine in the back makes all the difference when it comes to mud and sand and snow.

the world over.

The weight is over the power wheels and so the traction is terrific.

VWs also get along so well wherever they are because our service is as good in Tasmania as it is in Toledo.

(The only reason you can't buy a Volkswagen at the North Pole is that we won't sell you one. There's no VW service around the corner.)

We hear that it's possible to buy yourself a Coke at the North Pole, though.

Which makes us suspect there's only one thing that can get through ahead of a Volkswagen.

A Coke truck.

How to buy a new Buick.
(An easier lesson than you might expect.)

Not only is owning a new Buick pleasant, it's entirely possible. What you do is this—first, you just look. Long and hard. At the styling. At the way things fit. At the interiors, with their rich fabrics and vinyls. Next, you drive. A LeSabre 400, say, like the one in our picture. Choose this one and you get a 250-hp Wildcat V-8 and that feather-smooth, Super Turbine automatic of ours. (Plot your test route past your house and watch the neighbors eat their hearts out.) And finally, you price. That should be the start of a long and beautiful friendship. Visit your Buick dealer soon. Your friendly Buick dealer.

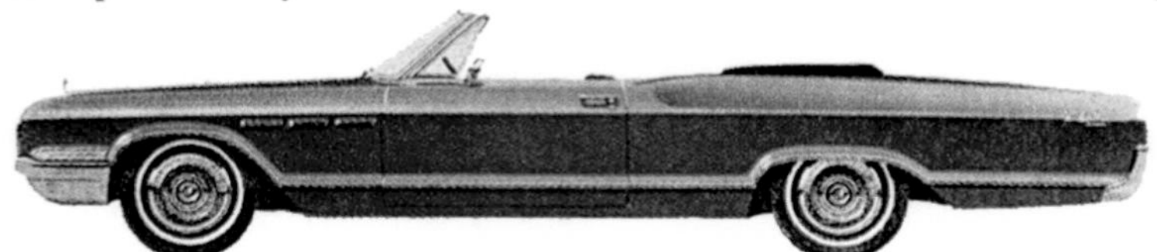

Wouldn't you really rather have a Buick?

BUICK MOTOR DIVISION

Your eyes light up when you first see the '65 Buick?
You should see what the '65 Buick
does when it sees you.
Buick '65 Buick
It glows, if it's a new Skylark.
Skylark is one car you get with Wall to Wall
taillights. And a lively V-6 engine.
And what you get in every Buick:
A little more care in fitting things
together. A little more money spent
in places you may never see: Tuned
suspensions. Drivelines that are
smoother. Finned brake drums. More
carefully placed insulation. (Hush.)
And a little more effort in places you
do notice: In Body by Fisher. Switch-
the-pitch, if you go for Super Turbine auto-
matic. Brakes that stay with you. Fresh styling.
In the intermediate size Skylark in the picture
and in every size '65 Buick. Wildcat, Le Sabre,
Special, Electra 225, Riviera—every new Buick.
People who know Buick know this: you get more
out of a Buick, because we put more in it.
And people who don't know Buick, should.
Wall to Wall taillights—bright-night look for the new Skylark.
Skylark
Wouldn't you really rather have a Buick?
Buick Motor Division • General Motors Corporation

301

Volkswagen Beetle, 1962 ◂◂

The shapes of the Beetle and the Coca-Cola bottle became icons, instantly recognized around the globe. New York ad agency Doyle Dane Bernbach handled the VW account through the mid-'70s, creating one of the most lauded print campaigns in advertising history.

Käfer wie Cola-Flasche wurden zu Ikonen, die man weltweit sofort wiedererkannte. Mitte der 1970er-Jahre für die VW-Werbung in den USA zuständig, kreierte die New Yorker Werbeagentur Doyle Dane Bernbach eine der meistgepriesenen Anzeigenkampagnen überhaupt.

Les formes de la Coccinelle et de la bouteille de Coca-Cola deviennent des icônes immédiatement reconnaissables dans le monde entier. L'agence de publicité new-yorkaise Doyle, Dane Bernbach s'occupera du compte VW tout au long des années 1970, créant une des campagnes de presse les plus applaudies dans l'histoire de la publicité.

Buick Skylark, 1965

Buick LeSabre, 1965 ◂

CORVETTE
Corvette Sting Ray Sport Coupe
'66 CORVETTE BY CHEVROLET
Now you hear the big news about Corvette by Chevrolet. For 1966, it's horsepower! Standard V8 is 327 cu. in., 300 hp. There's a 350-hp edition you can order, too. You swashbucklers just ask, and we'll drop in our new Turbo-Jet 427 under its own high-domed hood. "Street" version is 390 hp with four-barrel carburetor and hydraulic lifters. The performance engine (special cam, solid lifters and more) cranks out 425 hp!
And Corvette knows how to handle all this: full independent suspension, sports-car steering, four-wheel disc brakes. If a package like this doesn't tempt you into the '66 Corvette, just look how it's wrapped.
Chevrolet Division of General Motors, Detroit, Michigan
CHEVROLET
Corvair Corsa Sport Coupe

You speak independent suspension, four-on-the-floor, bucket seats and like that? We hear you.

Now you can sample America's sportiest looking, sportiest acting low-priced car for 1966: Corvair by Chevrolet. A lot's new. Trim touches here and there. Adjustable headrests you can add. A new fully synchronized 3-speed for creamy smooth shifting.

A lot's *not* new. You still get bucket seats in Corsas and Monzas. Corvair's engine still rides in back so you go when other cars won't. It's still air-cooled—away with water and hoses and antifreeze! You still get a big choice in Sixes, from our 95-hp miser to the 180-hp Turbo-Charged version you can order in Corsas. The '66 Corvair: for people who *like* to drive.

Chevrolet Corvette and Corvair, 1966

The first Chevrolet Corvair, introduced in 1960, had major safety problems that earned it the scorn of consumer advocate Ralph Nader. But in its second manifestation, the performance problems were corrected, and the body lines were among the most elegant on the market, appealing even to Elvis Presley. This was not enough to save the car, whose production ended with the 1969 model year.

Der 1960 eingeführte Chevrolet Corvair hatte zunächst massive Sicherheitsprobleme und wurde so zur Zielscheibe des Verbraucherschutzanwalts Ralph Nader. Bei dem überarbeiteten Modell gab es diese Probleme nicht mehr; zudem konnte es mit einer überaus eleganten Linienführung aufwarten, die sogar Elvis Presley zusagte. Dies konnte jedoch nicht verhindern, dass die Produktion mit dem Modelljahr 1969 auslief.

La première Chevrolet Corvair, lancée en 1960, pose d'importants problèmes de sécurité qui lui valent le mépris du défenseur des consommateurs Ralph Nader. Toutefois, pour sa seconde édition, ses performances sont corrigées et sa carrosserie fait partie des plus élégantes du marché. Elle séduit même Elvis Presley. Cela ne suffira néanmoins pas à sauver le modèle, dont la production s'arrêtera en 1969.

► Chevrolet Corvair, 1964

About the only thing that can come between a Corvair owner and his Corvair is

his wife

'64 Corvair Monza Club Coupe

Like most men, the fellow riding the bench has pretty definite opinions on what he buys in the way of neckties, fly rods—and cars. But right now he's having some second thoughts on just who talked whom into buying a new Corvair.

Sure, he had his for-men-only reasons. Output in the standard engine is up nearly 19 per cent this year—to 95 hp. (And in the new Monza Spyder models it's a virile 150 hp.)

He also had a knowledgeable appreciation of Corvair's steering, cornering and rear-engine traction. Things his wife really couldn't be expected to be interested in.

Tidy styling and tasteful (she called them "chic") interiors—that's all that concerned her. Or so our bench warmer thought. Until he began counting his commuter tokens one day.

The point is that the same things he liked about the car—its spirit, the ease with which it turns and fits into parking places, the way it grips on ice, mud and snow—his wife liked too. Maybe even more so.

Matter of fact, it's sometimes occurred to us that if we built a car for women only we probably couldn't make it more to their liking than this one. Couple of us married fellows were talking about that at the bus stop just the other day. . . . *Chevrolet Division of General Motors, Detroit, Michigan.*

CORVAIR
MONZA
CHEVROLET
Chevrolet • Chevelle • Chevy II • Corvair • Corvette
THE GREAT HIGHWAY PERFORMERS

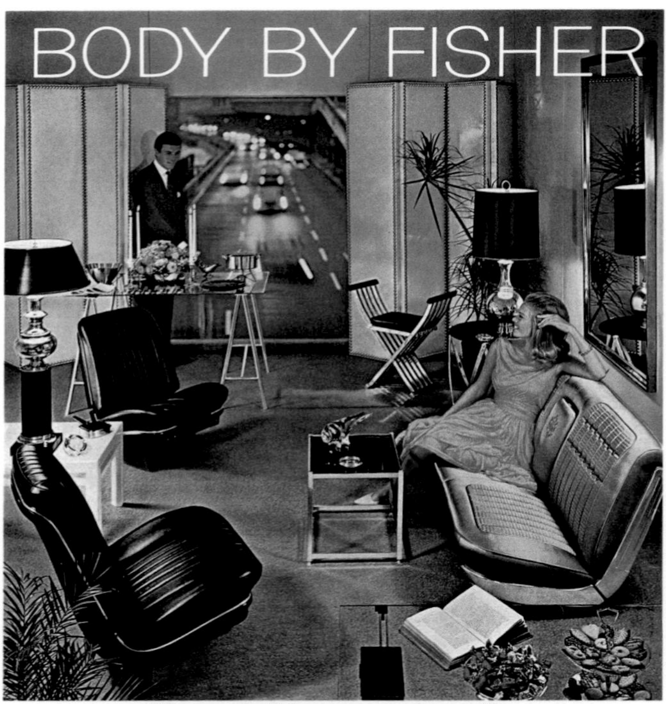

Who put the living room on the road?

This elegant room is "furnished by Fisher." Plush carpeting, luxurious vinyls, bright chrome, deeply cushioned upholstery...even a new reclining bucket seat. And with Sound Barrier Silencing, conversation is as easy and intimate as in your own living room. For the pleasures of home, there's no place like Body by Fisher, the only car body known by name. Remember, so much of the buy is in the body. And Body by Fisher makes a GM car a better buy: Chevrolet, Pontiac, Oldsmobile, Buick, Cadillac.

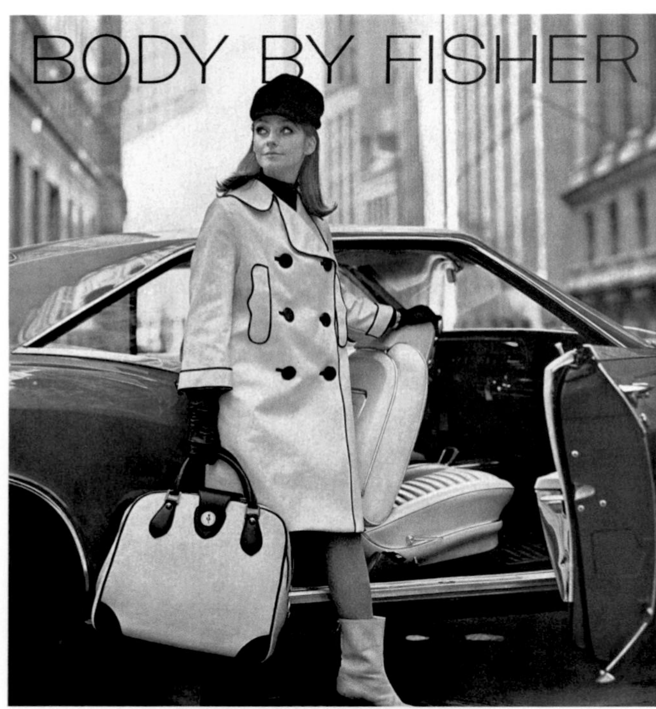

LUGGAGE BY MARK CROSS

Our seat fabrics travel beautifully

This sophisticated travel coat and case are made with the same vinyls we use for seat covers. The best we can find. They're easy-care. They travel tirelessly, beautifully, in a GM car with Body by Fisher. So will you. Remember, every car has a body, but only GM cars have Body by Fisher. And Body by Fisher makes it a better buy: Chevrolet, Pontiac, Oldsmobile, Buick, Cadillac.

Fisher Body, 1966

Fisher Body, 1966

▸ Pontiac Tempest, 1963

You don't really need Wide-Track . . . unless you drive a car.

Oddly enough, most people don't ride on motorcycles too much, except for fun. And what's fun on a 'cycle isn't fun in a car—namely, leaning 'way over to help get around a turn. That's why we put Wide-Track on Tempest this year: to keep you stable and level when you turn. Tempest isn't the only car with Wide-Track, but we don't fret about the competition. We make the other one too. **Wide-Track Pontiac Tempest**

1960 BUICK *with* GUIDE-MATIC

Ease your way through the night behind the wheel of the Turbine Drive Buick "60" and discover the new assurance that comes from driving with Guide-Matic. It's so easy to relax while the Guide-Matic Power Headlight Control selects the right light for passing, for turning, for city or turnpike cruising. And, you'll notice Guide-Matic always remembers, even when you could forget.

Most of all you'll want to try Safety Salute and see how it helps make courtesy contagious. For with Guide-Matic's exclusive Safety Salute, you can urge other nighttime drivers to *dim-down* their brights at the instant you're dimming your own.

Why be without the final touch of safety and convenience when factory-installed Guide-Matic is one of the lower cost options you can buy?

SAFETY SALUTE works like this . . . energized by the lights from an oncoming car, Guide-Matic fades down your bright beams ○○ 1 ○○ to a soft glow, signaling the other driver to dim his brights ●● 2 ●● . An instant later, the inboard beams turn off ●● 3 ●● , restating . . . with greater urgency . . . a safety message that can't be ignored. Once you've passed in perfect safety, all four lamps instantly switch back to ○○ 4 ○○ bright.

Look for Safety Salute tonight, try Guide-Matic tomorrow.

GUIDE-MATIC
POWER HEADLIGHT CONTROL

DEVELOPED BY GUIDE LAMP DIVISION • GENERAL MOTORS CORPORATION • ANDERSON, INDIANA

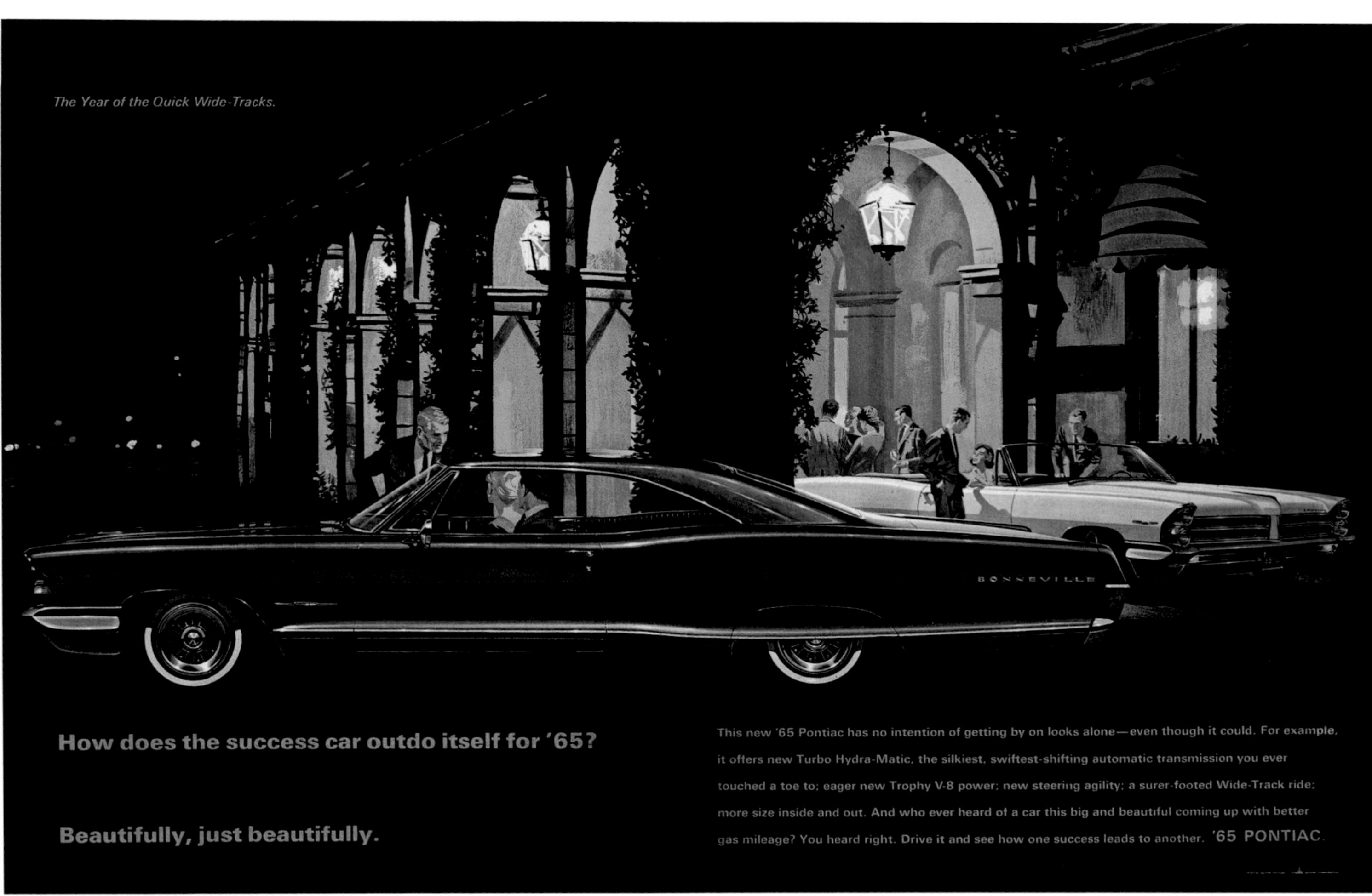

Pontiac Bonneville, 1965

Buick, 1960 ◂

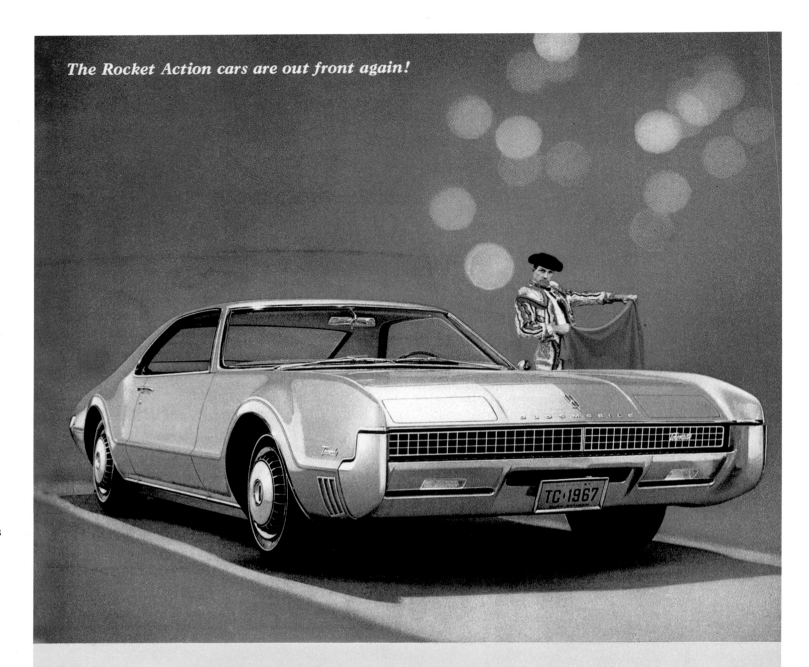

The Rocket Action cars are out front again!

After you've walked off with all the honors, what do you do for an encore?

Meet Olds Toronado—'67 edition.

Awards for this. Awards for that. Awards for just about everything. But rest on its laurels? Not Toronado. Swinging new look outside. Posh new detailing inside. Doors with torsion-bar spring assists that open easier than ever to the flat-floored, room-for-six interior. Even that fabulous front-wheel-drive ride is smoother and quieter for '67. And front disc brakes and radial ply tires are available. Trend-setting Toronado: Proved and applauded by tens of thousands of satisfied owners. Greater than ever the second time around!

▸ *See next four pages for more exciting news from Olds!*

OBEY
LAWS
DRIVE
SAFELY

Olds thinks of your safety, too, with the GM-developed energy-absorbing steering column that can compress on severe impact up to 8¼ inches; with four-way hazard warning flasher; outside rearview mirror; dual master cylinder brake system, plus many other safety features—all standard for '67.

Engineered for excitement . . . Toronado-style!

Oldsmobile Toronado, 1967 ▸ Oldsmobile Jetstar 88, 1966

STEP
OUT FRONT
IN '66 ... *in a Rocket Action Olds!*

Just what did Oldsmobile have in mind building all those extras in a car as low-priced as Jetstar 88? You.

HE
OR
SHE
?

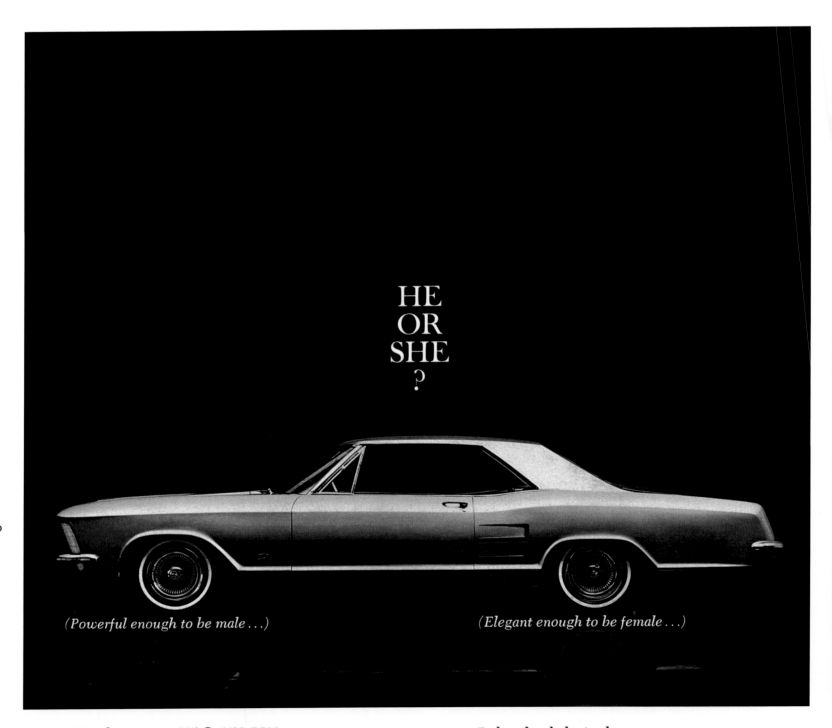

(Powerful enough to be male . . .)

(Elegant enough to be female . . .)

Max. horsepower: 325 @ 4400 RPM.
Max. torque: 445 ft.-lbs. @ 2800 RPM.
Automatic Turbine Drive transmission.
Compression ratio — 10:25 to 1.
Power brakes, finned aluminum front drums.
Four-barrel carburetor, dual exhausts.
Specially tuned suspension system.
Extremely low center of gravity.
Rear axle ratio — 3.23 to 1.

Body-tailored classic elegance.
Four passenger; individual bucket seats.
Four-way adjustable driver's seat.*
Minimum use of chrome.
Sheer side windows without usual frames.
Seven position steering wheel.*
Front and rear door releases on each door.*
Brushed aluminum center sports console.
Magnificent door-to-door carpeting.
**Opt. at extra cost*

THE RIVIERA BY BUICK
America's bid for a great new international classic car

GM
Corvette This is pure essence of sports car: long hood, short rear deck, an eager look, responsive engine, big wheelwells to make room for road-grabbing wide oval tires. Touches of tomorrow include a futuristic cockpit, gauges aplenty and a sleek fiberglass body that hides away windshield wipers and headlights until you need them. The '68 Corvette—America's only true sports car, reborn.
Camaro If Corvette ever turned into a family car, it'd be a Camaro. There's Corvette styling in its long hoo and bucket-seated interior; Corvette-like handling in the way it hugs the road. And Corvette response with V8 engines you can order up to the Turbo-Jet 396 with 325 hp. Now, you can equip any Camaro with new customizing sports trim: a bol stripe design, sporty wheel covers, a rear deck "spoiler," colors borrowed from Corvette (Bronze, British Green, LeMans Blue) or new Rallye Green, exclusively Camaro's. See them at your Chevrolet dealer's Sports Department.
Foreground: Camaro SS Sport Coupe; background: Corvette Sting Ray Coupe
The resemblance is more than coincidental.
CHEVROLET

Buick Riviera, 1963 ◂

Designer Bill Mitchell, who had created the classic Cadillac Sixty Special in 1938, created a masterpiece of the Detroit genre with the crisp-edged Buick Riviera, inspired, he said, by "English tailoring." The car was advertised like a fine suit.

Bill Mitchell, der bereits 1938 den klassischen Cadillac Sixty Special entworfen hatte, schuf mit dem kantigen Buick Riviera ein Meisterwerk à la Detroit, nach eigenem Bekunden inspiriert durch das „englische Schneiderhandwerk". Entsprechend wurde der Wagen wie ein feiner Anzug angepriesen.

Le designer Bill Mitchell, créateur en 1938 de la classique Cadillac Sixty Special, conçoit un chef-d'œuvre du genre avec la Buick Riviera, dont le style dépouillé s'inspire, selon ses dires, des « tailleurs anglais ». La publicité la compare d'ailleurs à un beau costume.

Chevrolet Camaro SS, Corvette, 1968

► Rambler Marlin, 1965

Under design chief Richard Teague, American Motors experimented with novel designs to compete. The Marlin's sweeping roof and curves suggested an acquaintance with Eero Saarinen's furniture and architectural designs, from his Tulip collection of tables and chairs to the TWA terminal at New York's John F. Kennedy Airport.

Unter Chefdesigner Richard Teague experimentierte American Motors mit neuartigen Designs. Das geschwungene Dach und die Kurven des Marlin lassen eine Vertrautheit mit dem Werk von Eero Saarinen vermuten – seien es die Tische und Stühle der Tulip-Kollektion oder der TWA-Terminal auf dem John F. Kennedy Airport in New York.

Sous la houlette de son designer en chef, Richard Teague, American Motors expérimente des styles novateurs pour rester dans la course. Le toit et les courbes de la Marlin ne sont pas sans évoquer le mobilier et l'architecture d'Eero Saarinen, célèbre pour sa collection de tables et de chaises tulipes et le terminal de la TWA à l'aéroport John F. Kennedy de New York.

Honda 600, 1969

Rambler takes off—the Marlin comes on. Meet America's first man-size sports-fastback!

You're looking at the most exciting Rambler ever built—Marlin! A car unlike anything else on the scene today. Here's too much automobile to be just another fastback—too much luxury to be just another sport car—too much solid value to be anything but a Rambler. You get dazzling performance, including the might of a 327 cu.-in. V-8 option. You get Power Disc Brakes and individually adjustable reclining front seats, *standard*. You get a choice of practically any sports option you can name, like floor shifts, console, bucket seats, wire-wheel covers—plus *all* the solid extra-value features Rambler provides at no extra cost, such as Deep-Dip rustproofing, Double-Safety Brakes (separate systems, front and rear)—and more. Catch the Marlin in all its excitement—at your Rambler dealer *now*. In limited production, but stepping up fast. American Motors—Dedicated to Excellence

Marlin By Rambler

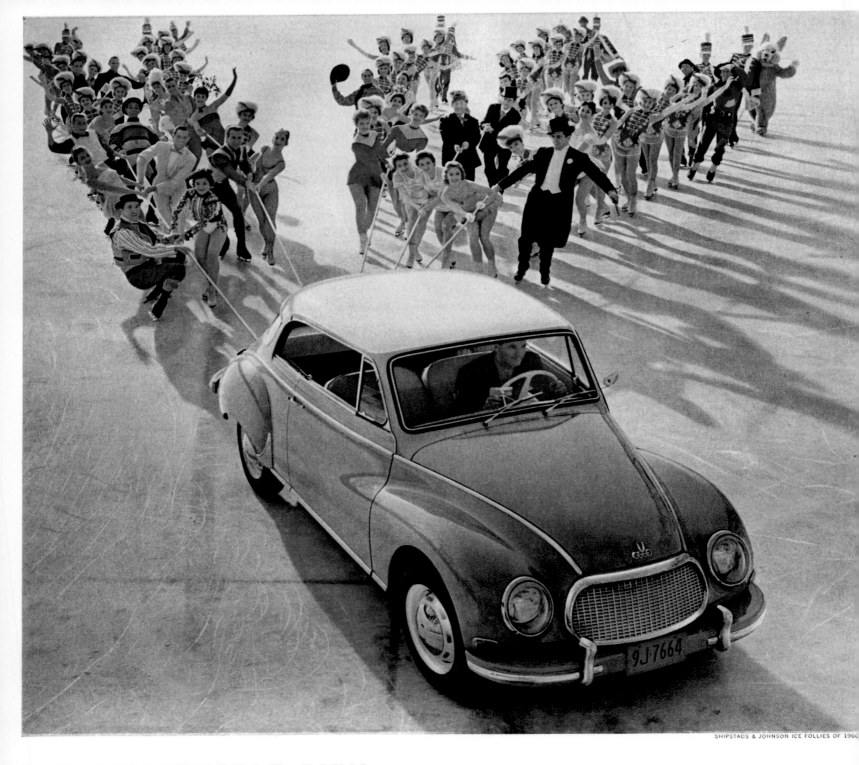

SHIPSTADS & JOHNSON ICE FOLLIES OF 1960

THE REMARKABLE DKW

SURFEOOTED AS THE CAST OF THE ICE FOLLIES...

DESIGNED TO GO WHERE OTHER CARS LOSE TRACTION!

(AND IT DOES IT ON THREE CYLINDERS AND SEVEN BASIC MOVING ENGINE PARTS)

WHY IS THE DKW A STAR PERFORMER ON ICE... OR SNOW, SAND OR MUD? Front wheel drive is the reason why. The DKW engine powers the front wheels and *pulls* the car over ice, snow, mud or sand. Other cars are pushed as the engine drives the rear wheels. The DKW traction is extraordinary. The rear end won't slide or slither on slippery surfaces.

WHAT ABOUT THE SEVEN BASIC MOVING ENGINE PARTS? The DKW has no camshafts, no timing gear, no valves. Consequently, maintenance and repairs are minimized. *Costs are decidedly lower!* The seven parts? Three pistons, three connecting rods, one crankshaft. Simple!

WINTER WON'T WORRY YOU IN A DKW! It starts in seconds at temperatures below zero. Why? DKW lubrication is by oily vapor. Oil is mixed with the gas and cannot gum up the pistons in cold weather. Plenty of comfort, too. Bountiful space, flat floors (no drive shaft), large trunk. Heater and defroster are standard equipment.

MORE TO THE STORY! The DKW is elegantly crafted in West Germany to exceptionally high quality standards. Your dealer can show you the details. See him. Drive it and learn why DKW means *Das Kleine Wunder*. Don't wait.

DKW cars are manufactured by Auto Union in West Germany, which also manufactures Auto Union cars. The line ranges from two-door coupes to station wagons and commercial vehicles. DKW's and Auto Unions are distributed in the U.S.A. by Mercedes-Benz Sales, Inc. (Subsidiary of Studebaker-Packard). For the name of your DKW-Auto Union Dealer write to: Mercedes-Benz Sales, Inc., South Bend 27, Ind.

Join the "Personal Car" Set

IMPORTED

Metropolitan *"1500"*

World's Smartest Smaller Car

Here's ideal transportation for two people *plus*—with almost 50-inch front seat hip room. And the rear occasional seat is handy for smaller children, pets or packages. Comes in smart convertible and hardtop models.

Conceived and engineered in the U.S. to provide comfort you're used to, the Metropolitan "1500" is built in England to European standards of craftsmanship. The peppy 55 H.P. engine provides thrilling responsiveness with top economy—*perfect* for around-town driving or turnpike cruising.

Join the Personal Car Set soon. You'll enjoy owning and driving a car so appropriate for your *personal* motoring needs. Parts and service available coast to coast.

TEST-DRIVE THE "MET" AT YOUR RAMBLER-METROPOLITAN DEALER

Rambler Metropolitan, 1960

Like a quirky mascot, the lovable and toylike Metropolitan enjoyed a niche market. The Metropolitan name, however, outlasted that of Nash.

Gleich einem skurrilen Maskottchen besetzte der liebenswerte, spielzeugartige Nash Metropolitan eine Marktnische. Die Marke Nash sollte indes vom Namen Metropolitan überdauert werden.

Sorte de mascotte originale, la charmante et ludique Nash Metropolitan bénéficie d'une niche sur le marché. Le nom du modèle vivra toutefois plus longtemps que celui du constructeur.

DKW, 1960 ◂

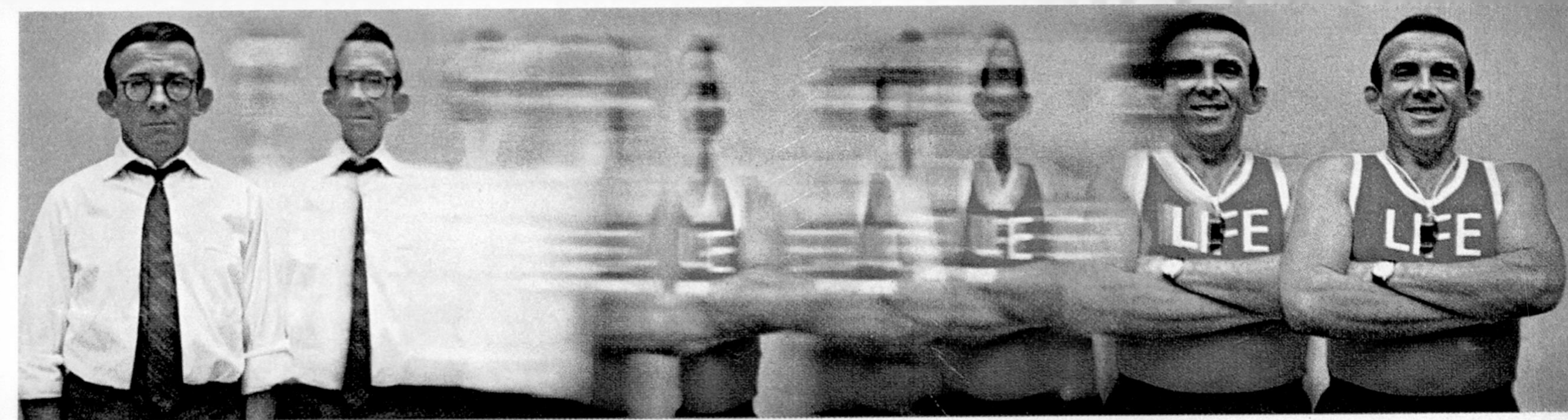

Sidney spent Sundays seashelling at the seashore. Then Sidney started digging the '68 Mustang—the great original. Dug the models: hardtop, fastback and convertible. Liked the low price, too, which left Sidney lots of clams to design his own Mustang, Sidney style. Now Sidney's making waves all over. Last week he saved 3 bathing beauties. (And they all could swim better than Sidney!)

Only Mustang makes it happen!

MUSTANG

Mustang Fastback GT

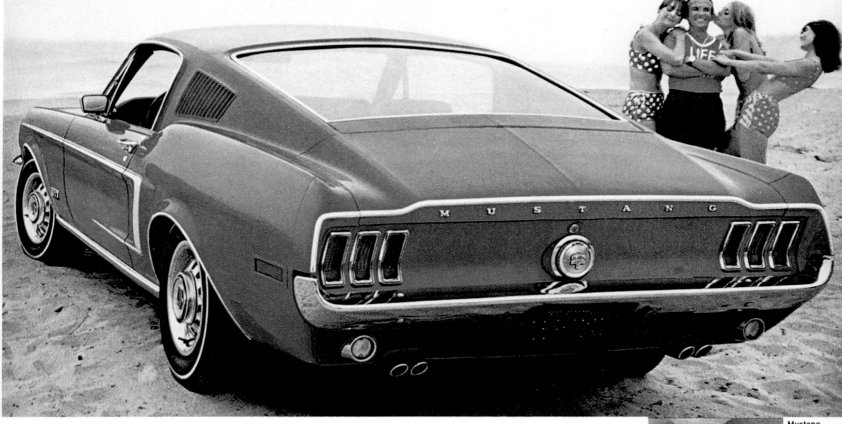

FACTS ABOUT THE 1968 MUSTANG: Mustang's list of standard equipment can't be matched by any other sporty car in its price range. Includes floor-mounted stick shift with fully synchronized 3-speed transmission, bucket seats, door-to-door carpeting, all-vinyl trim, 5-pod instrument cluster. And Mustang gives you a range of options no competitor offers. Like SelectShift with 3 forward speeds—can be used as a manual or an automatic; available with any model, any engine. Or an all-pushbutton AM Radio/Stereosonic Tape System. V-8's up to 390 cu. in. And the broadest choice of performance options around: including a special heavy-duty suspension, front power disc brakes on all models, wide-oval tires, and more.

FORD

Ford ...has a better idea.

Ford Mustang, 1966

Although built on the mechanical underpinnings of the humble Ford Falcon, the Mustang was sold as the car you design yourself. A highly personalized vehicle with many options, it was unveiled at the New York World's Fair in 1964, to great success.

Obwohl er mechanisch auf dem bescheidenen Ford Falcon basierte, wurde der Mustang als Wagen verkauft, den man selbst entwirft. Das dank zahlreicher Optionen stark personalisierbare Auto wurde 1964 auf der Weltausstellung in New York enthüllt und begeisterte.

Bien que reprenant les bases mécaniques de l'humble Ford Falcon, la Mustang est vendue comme une voiture à concevoir soi-même. Ce véhicule hautement personnalisé, avec quantité d'options, lancé à la Foire internationale de New York en 1964, connaîtra un immense succès.

Ford Mustang, 1968 ◂

▸▸ Plymouth, 1961

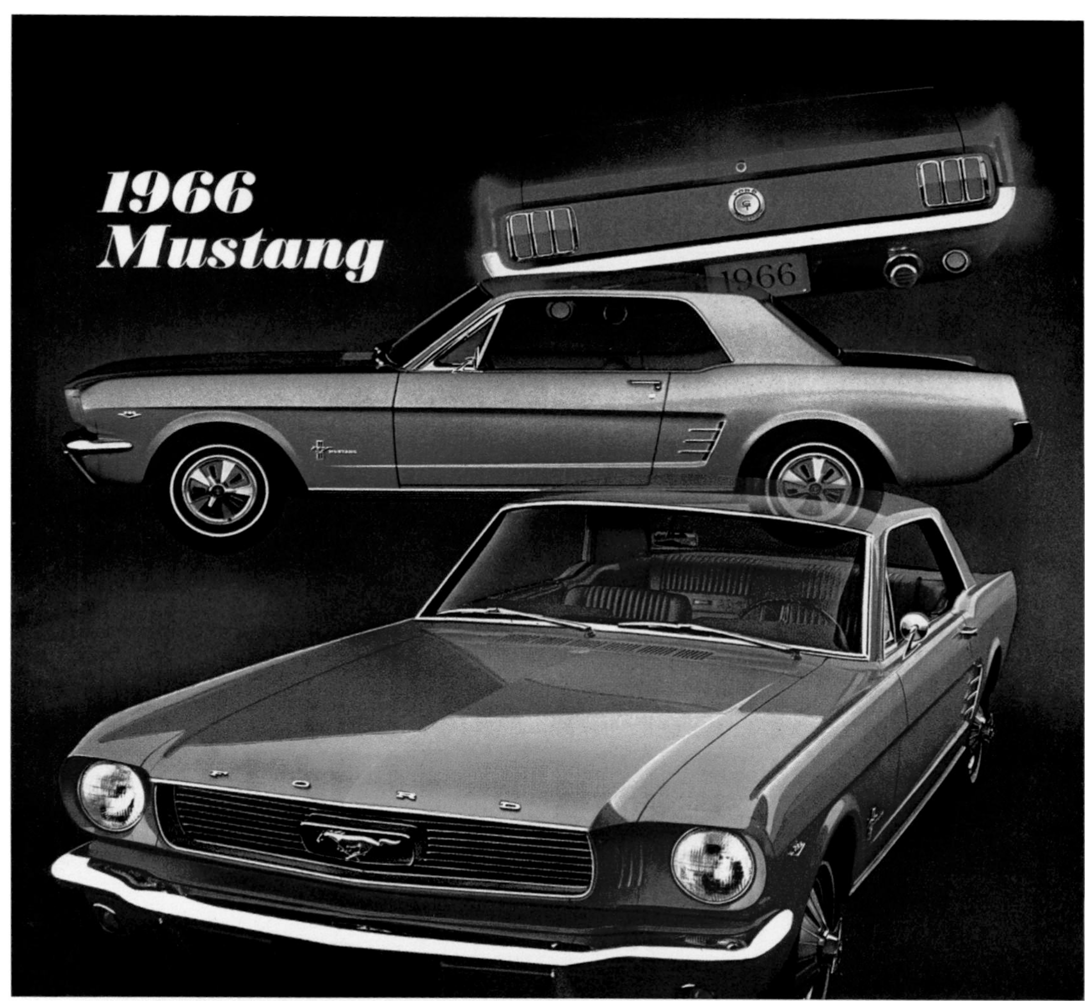

1966 Mustang Hardtop

If you thought we couldn't improve on a winner
—try Mustang '66!

The changes are subtle but significant. A new grille for a bright, fresh front-end look. New options like the Stereo-sonic tape system. (It gives you over 70 minutes of music on an easy-loading tape cartridge.) All the wonderful features that made Mustang a success are still standard. After all, why change Mustangs in mid-stream?

The '66 Mustang comes with bucket seats, all-vinyl interiors, floor-mounted shift, full carpeting and many other luxuries at no extra cost. It is an exceptionally practical car with its lively 200-cubic-inch Six. It handles like a candidate for the Monte Carlo Rallye and is so handsome it tends to make anything near its price look tired. This is the basic Mustang.

But if you want more action, greater luxury, Mustang offers you an exceptional range of options. You can design your own sports-Mustang with GT options like front disc brakes; 289-cubic-inch Cobra V-8 with four-barrel carburetor and solid lifters; four-speed, fully-synchronized manual transmission or 3-speed Cruise-O-Matic—and more. Luxury-lovers can have air-conditioning, power brakes and steering, vinyl-covered top, or a specially elegant interior décor package... just to name a few.

If you haven't driven a Mustang yet ... do it soon. It's bound to improve your outlook on driving.

317

Announcing the most beautiful turn of th

61 PLYMOU

ntury! Plymouth for '61!

TH...SOLID BEAUTY

merica's No. 1 low-price economy car...a Chrysler-engineered product

*The XP-755 Chevrolet Corvette Shark: 102.1" wheelbase, 192.2" overall, 327-cubic-inch displacement, V-8 engine featuring Roots-type supercharger, 4 side-draft carburetors developing over 400 horsepower.

Shark by Chevrolet—ACtion sparked by AC

The same AC Spark Plugs that add power to this car of tomorrow are available for your car today! Engineers specify ACs for experimental cars like the Corvette Shark because of AC's self-cleaning Hot Tip. It heats faster to burn away fouling carbon deposits — delivers longer peak power — greater economy for every car! Don't experiment with your spark plugs, ask for ACtion . . . ask for AC.

AC SPARK PLUG — THE ELECTRONICS DIVISION OF GENERAL MOTORS

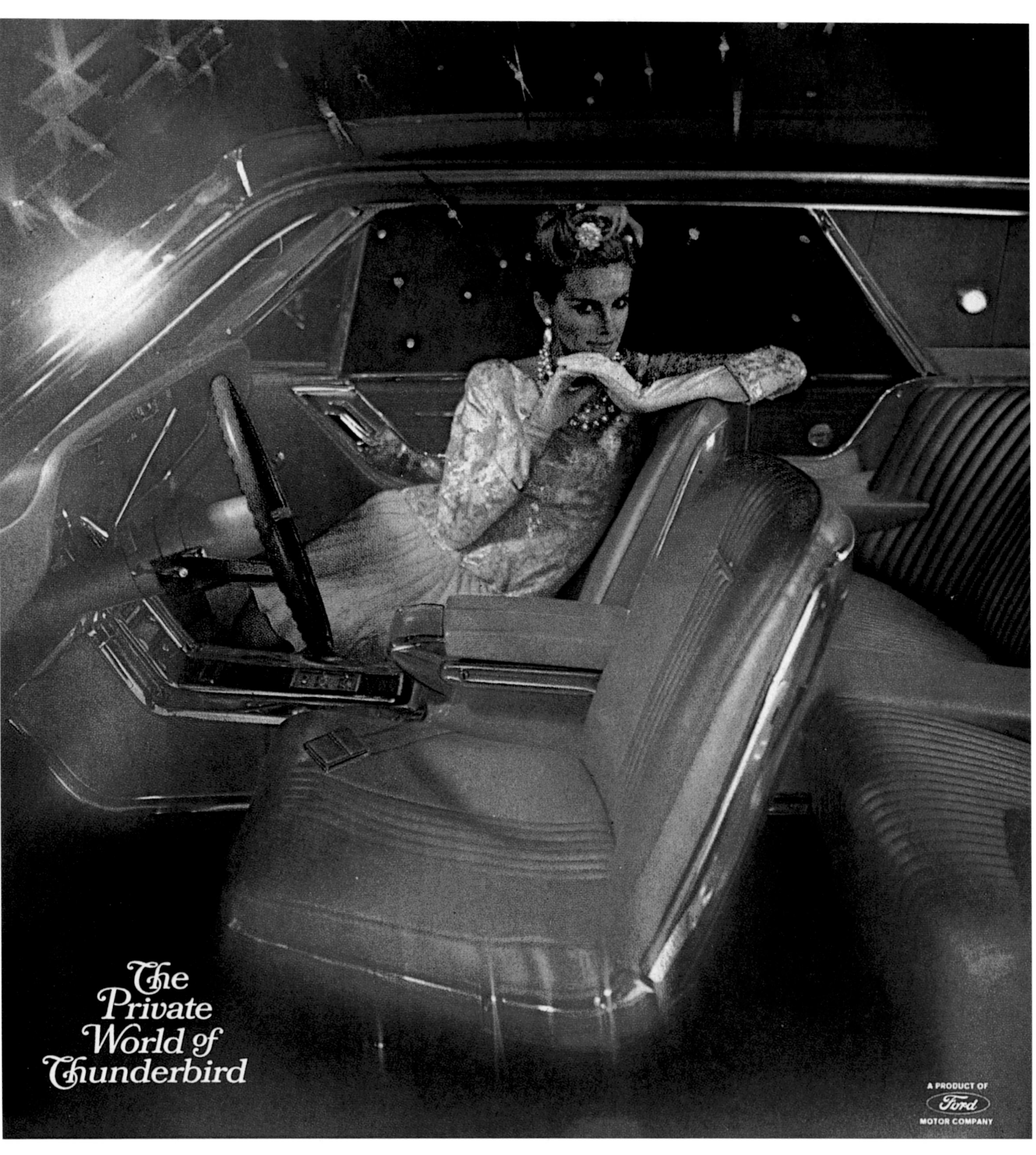

Ford Thunderbird, 1965

AC Spark Plugs/Chevrolet Corvette, 1963 ◂

THE SATURDAY EVENING POST

Snow piles up, up, up. Who cares? Let it snow—on we go, on and on and on and on and on and

For six winters, Americans have watched the Dauphine meet every type of snow situation and conquer it as no other car in the history of cars. The Winter Wonder-Car has not been fazed by snow-clogged drive-ways, nor by sloshy, slippery slopes./ Other cars stop; the Dauphine goes./ Why? Better weight distribution and time-tested rear-engine traction are the technical reasons for this superior performance./ A few of the other winter-time superiorities of the Dauphine: an extra-hot heater at no extra cost (defroster, too), the well-kept promise of 40 miles to the gallon. (Incidentally, all the "free extras" included in the price actually add close to $150 worth of value to your buy!) Check out the facts for yourself. Stop in at one of the thousand and one authorized Renault Dealers in North America soon. Plan to test-drive the Winter Wonder-Car with the all-time Wonder Price: $1385*

RENAULT
Dauphine

You get just a little bit more

*suggested retail price, POE, East Coast. Renault Inc., 750 Third Ave., N.Y. 17, N.Y.

► Renault Dauphine, 1960

Americans were increasingly interested in things European. But most French and Italian manufacturers were not able to sell as much as they'd hoped to in the United States, due to limited dealer networks and the power of Detroit. For most Americans in the '60s, big was still beautiful.

In den USA interessierte man sich zunehmend für alles Europäische. Die meisten französischen und italienischen Hersteller verkauften dort jedoch nicht so viele Autos wie erhofft, denn das Händlernetz war einfach zu klein und der Einfluss von Detroit zu groß. Und für die meisten Amerikaner galt in den Sechzigern weiterhin: big is beautiful.

Les Américains s'intéressent de plus en en plus à l'Europe, mais les constructeurs français et italiens vendent peu aux États-Unis en raison d'un réseau de distribution limité et du pouvoir de Detroit. Pour la plupart des Américains, la devise reste « plus c'est grand, plus c'est beau ».

Fiat 1200 Spider and 600, 1961

Renault Dauphine, 1961

L'ANATOMIE FRANÇAISE DE L'AUTOMOBILE OR, HOW TO MAKE YOUR DRIVING FUN AGAIN

La Silhouette: Probably one of the handsomest body styles around today. Paris-designed, French-built. ⋆ Quiet, ⋆ authoritative, elegant.

Les Portes: 4 doors for easy-in, easy-out. New safety-locks for back doors.

Les Dimensions: Outside: 155 inches total length! Parks, maneuvers accordingly./ Inside: Roomier than you imagine. No hump in floor means better leg-and-foot room.

La location du moteur: *The water-cooled (quieter) engine is in the rear. Time-tested, road-tested, user-tested, and proven. It provides superior traction and road-holding qualities. Easily accessible: simple to service.*

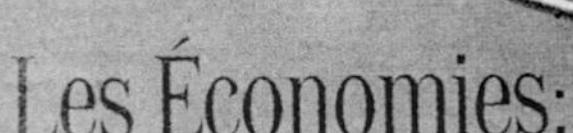

Les Économies: Purchase price is $1645*/ You get up to 40 mpg/ Optional extras: sun-roof, dual heater, windshield washers./ More than 1000 authorized dealers in the U.S. & Canada with factory-trained men, service & parts./ Drop in at the nearest for a lesson on car anatomy. You will profit. Bien sûr.

La Garantie Unique

A 6-month service & parts warranty (with no mileage limitations!) at any Renault Dealership everywhere in the world.

La Nouvelle Suspension: News! Renault-Exclusive! Patented new suspension system assures smoother, bounce-free ride on all kinds of roads and terrain. Enhances driver and passenger comfort. Try it & see!

Le Car Hot: RENAULT Dauphine

TUNE IN "MARKHAM" STARRING RAY MILLAND: CBS-TV, THURSDAYS, 9:30-10 P.M., EASTERN TIME

*SUGGESTED RETAIL PRICE, POE, EAST COAST. STATE & LOCAL TAXES EXTRA. FREE BROCHURE AT DEALER OR RENAULT, INC., 750 3RD AVE., N.Y. 17, N.Y. OVERSEAS DELIVERY FOR EUROPEAN TRAVELERS. SEE LOCAL DEALER OR WRITE RENAULT, BOX 158, L.I. CITY 4, N.Y.

Meet the *Scout*®!

A whole new idea in low-cost transportation...

Here's America's new quick-change artist. In minutes you can make your INTERNATIONAL Scout whatever kind of vehicle you want. The cab top, doors and windows are readily removable; the windshield folds down. No other vehicle is so changeable and so storm-snug. Then there's the full-length Travel-Top. Now the Scout can become a multi-purpose delivery unit or convertible, a light-duty pickup or runabout.

It's a working partner, a pleasure companion. You can buy the new Scout with two-wheel-drive or four-wheel-drive, depending on the roads you travel or the jobs you want done. Take your friends hunting in rough country, take the family on a picnic, haul loads. And the Scout is compact: less than 13 feet overall, 100-inch wheelbase, 68 inches wide, 67 inches high. New INTERNATIONAL Comanche 4-cyl. 90 hp. engine goes easy on gas, oil, and upkeep.

Let your imagination roam—isn't the Scout the only one that spans all your needs? Your INTERNATIONAL Scout Dealer or Branch is the place to go to find out everything you can do with the Scout.

This is the Scout, a neat, nimble pickup with 5-ft. long loadspace.

Same Scout with cab top off. Takes you only minutes to remove.

Same Scout stripped, with doors and windows off, windshield down.

Same Scout for delivery work with optional full-length Travel-Top.

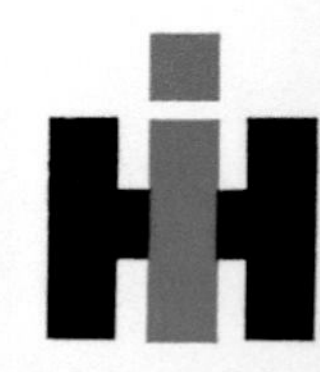

International Harvester Company, Chicago

International Travelall, 1960

International Scout, 1961 ◄

WHEN YOU FIRST DRIVE UP IN A CADILLAC, *even old friends see you in a new light. This is going to be especially true when you make your initial entrance in a 1963 Cadillac. A newly refined engine moves the big car so silently you must announce your arrival with a tap of the horn. And when the inevitable inspection comes be prepared for "Ohs" and "Ahs" at the craftsmanship, luxury and elegance of the widest choice of personal options in Cadillac history. Isn't there someone you'd like to surprise? Go ahead and do it. Your Cadillac dealer will help you to stage the scene.*

Cadillac Motor Car Division • General Motors Corporation

Cadillac Coupe de Ville, 1962

Cadillac Series 62, 1963 ◄

The Coupe de Ville · Jeweled "V" and Crest created by Cartier

Cadillac splendor

Even the most brilliant occasions seldom surpass in splendor
the Cadillac journey that takes you there.

Cadillac Motor Car Division · General Motors Corporation

Skyrocket!
A fiery new class of cars is here . . . Oldsmobile for '61! Sparked by the spirit of an exciting
new SKYROCKET Engine—blazing a bright new trail in automotive performance
Oldsmobile . . . with a completely new and smoother-than-ever
Hydra-Matic Drive* featuring Accel-A-Rotor action for quick, silken getaway!
Oldsmobile . . . with crisp, sleek style that reflects its flashing performance . . .
and the roomiest, most glamorous, easiest-to-get-into interiors you ever saw!
All this is exclusively yours in the spirited new Olds for 1961
. . . featuring Fashion-Line design and SKYROCKET performance!
Join the style leaders in a new '61 Olds . . . at your dealer's now!
OLDSMOBILE DIVISION OF GENERAL MOTORS CORPORATION
*Optional at extra cost.
OLDSMOBILE
Super 88
More spirited than ever for '61!
OLDSMOBILE
S-88-61

Wonderful outdoor fun is found on Isle Royale National Park in Lake Superior. It's about 70 miles by ferry from Michigan's Upper Peninsula—plus, for this family, an exciting drive from home in a new 1960 Pontiac.

What a thrilling trip—in a new 1960 Pontiac Bonneville Custom Safari.

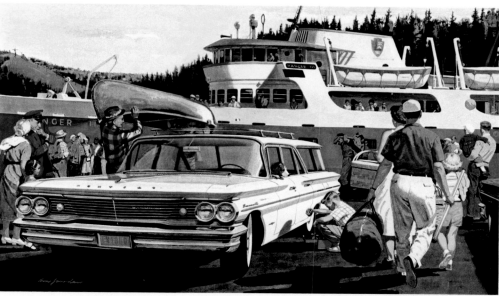

THERE'S NOTHING LIKE A NEW CAR TO PUT NEW ZEST IN THE LIFE YOU LEAD

A new car is sheer excitement on wheels—a nice new break from the old routine—even sitting in the driveway it does something for you. All the '60 models will liven your life—though, frankly, we feel our own GM cars for '60 offer more zest than the rest.

About this word "zest"—the dictionary says . . . keen enjoyment . . . exciting quality. In terms of a family with a new car, it means, "What are we waiting for? Let's see all those places we've read about, heard about, talked about!"

Now is the time to include a new car in your vacation planning. There are so many outstanding features in the GM line of fine cars that will add zest to your summer vacation—and for a long time to come. The comfort of roomy Bodies by Fisher, the security of Safety *Plate* Glass in every window, the safety of advanced new suspension systems—they're all ready to help make this the greatest summer you've ever seen for family fun and easy traveling!

Best of all, you're sure to find the car that meets your family's requirements. Spacious station wagons, high-styled sedans, eye-catching convertibles—and your selection of sizes. Nothing you can buy for the money will return so much over so long a time as a new car—and your friendly General Motors dealer can quickly show you just how easy it is to own one. See him soon. Like today.

GO GM FOR '60
CHEVROLET · PONTIAC · OLDSMOBILE · BUICK · CADILLAC · ALL WITH BODY BY FISHER

GENERAL MOTORS

329

Rare treat—an Indian rodeo at Chinle, Arizona, and a trip in a sleek new Buick Invicta Three-Seat Estate Wagon!

Rare sight—sandstone buttes in the Navajo's Monument Valley.

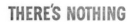

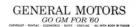

THERE'S NOTHING LIKE A NEW CAR FOR HONEST-TO-GOODNESS FAMILY FUN

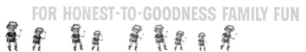

Nothing else for the money pays off more handsomely in pleasure, safety and dependable service for your family than a new car. Although all makes have marked improvements this year, we naturally prefer our new General Motors cars—and hope you do, too.

We're sure you'll agree that few things create so much excitement around the house as the arrival of a sparkling new car. The whole family swarms through it, "Oh-ing" and "Ah-ing" at all the fine new features . . . eager to get going for that first wonderful ride.

And when you take to the road—either cross-town or cross-country—you really begin to appreciate the comfort, convenience and safety that only a new car can provide. You go more places, more often, and with more fun for your family.

Nothing for the money serves you so well in so many different ways as a new car. Any new car, that is—though we feel the General Motors line offers more of everything you want in a new car. Look over our wide-as-the-world selection for '60—everything from "dreamboat" sedans to smartly styled wagons to snappy convertibles. You're sure to find one that's just right for your family. And with GM cars, you get the craftsmanship, the solid construction and engineering advancements that add up to many years of motoring pleasure. Why not visit your General Motors dealer now to get the complete story? The fun starts when you bring that brand-new beauty home.

GENERAL MOTORS
GO GM FOR '60
CHEVROLET · PONTIAC · OLDSMOBILE · BUICK · CADILLAC · ALL WITH BODY BY FISHER

Pontiac Bonneville Custom Safari, 1960

Buick Invicta, 1960

Oldsmobile Super 88, 1961 ◂

You can put yourself in this picture for less money, with more comfort, better performance, and get more back when you trade. Doubt it? Any Studebaker Dealer will prove it to you in ten minutes.

The Beautiful **LARK** *by* STUDEBAKER

Three lovely Larks to follow the sun:
The luxurious Daytona Hardtop with exclusive sunroof.
The powerful, spacious Lark Wagon.
The sweetheart of the line, the lively Daytona Convertible.

Important Announcement

Today we introduce the beautiful new 1964 Studebaker.

You will find it different from any other car. We are an independent company, with independent ideas.

We think the small cars are too cramped and flimsy, the big cars are too expensive and hard to maneuver.

We have built this thinking into the new Studebaker. We set new standards in interior room. The car is longer than last year but has lost none of its maneuverability.

It is built like a fort. It makes no compromises. I'm proud of this.

As a family man, I want my car to be the safest on the road. Studebaker is exactly that. For example, completely padded instrument panels are standard on all models. And Studebaker surrounds you with a "girder of safety"—the "bridge-constructed" Armor Guard frame. You can have caliper disc brakes, the safest kind in the world.

As a car enthusiast, I like a "hot" car—and Studebaker can match performance with cars costing $3,000 to $4,000 more.

As a business man, I prefer the "long value" dollar to the "low" dollar. Studebaker does not "skimp" down to a price, but builds up to high standards of comfort and economy and plain honest money's worth.

If this kind of car appeals to you, I invite you to turn the page and see the beautiful '64 Studebaker—the one new car that's Different...by Design.

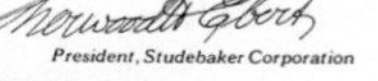

President, Studebaker Corporation

Studebaker Lark, Avanti, and Wagonaire, 1964

Studebaker Lark, 1962 ◂

MERCURY announces its newest sizzler, the.
Marauder

FLEET!

METEOR MAKES DRIVING COME ALIVE WITH NEW LIGHTNING 260 V-8

For 1963, Meteor is the hot brand. Meteor is the sparkling new arrival in the low-price field. Meteor is the line where every model is a beauty. Each is available with a spirited new Lightning 260 V-8 engine. Each is low in price . . . surprisingly low for a car with so much room, quality and power. Low on upkeep, too. For Meteor has every service-saver found in cars costing hundreds of dollars more. They greatly reduce ownership costs for oil, brake adjustments, anti-freeze, lubrication, and other routine maintenance. There are four frisky new sedans to choose from. Three new wagons. Two new hardtops, including the sporty S-33 bucket-seater shown. Try the breezy feeling that's swept into the low-priced field. Try the '63 Mercury Meteor.

'63 MERCURY METEOR

COMET · METEOR · MONTEREY: PRODUCTS OF  MOTOR COMPANY · LINCOLN-MERCURY DIVISION

Mercury Meteor, 1963

Mercury Marauder, 1963 ◂

The window that came in out of the rain

Monterey's new rear window stays clear in rain or snow. Notice how it's recessed, slants inward. On hot days, it opens for breezeway ventilation. Also, the overhanging roof keeps the rear seat shady, increases rear-seat headroom, keeps glare off the rear window for better rearview visibility. Other news: a Marauder 390 V-8 is now standard; a single-unit AM-FM radio is optional.

COMET · METEOR · MONTEREY PRODUCTS OF Ford MOTOR COMPANY · LINCOLN-MERCURY DIVISION

Classic beauty in a smart new size

Lincoln Continental for 1961...ideal in size...styled in the Continental tradition ...engineered for unprecedented reliability

Today, Lincoln Continental presents a new concept in fine cars...a full six-passenger luxury automobile with the fundamental convenience of rational size...a car that is designed to handle, turn and park with superb ease.

The 1961 Lincoln Continental is built to unprecedented standards of quality and reliability—standards shared with no other car in America. In fact, tolerances on many parts are so demanding that special machine tools had to be designed and built before the parts could be manufactured.

Extraordinary reliability

A trouble-free car is the essential foundation of true motoring satisfaction. That is why every single car is given a 12-mile road test (and the inspection list has 189 check points!). Why parking brake conduits are lined with nylon so cables cannot rust and stick. Why the electric motors that operate the power windows are dipped in latex rubber to seal out moisture. Why front suspension points that formerly required lubrication every 2,000 miles now have a sealed lubrication system that needs attention only at 30,000-mile intervals. Why, in fact, we insist on several thousand extra operations that we could eliminate without any visible change in the car. All these extra operations are performed on every 1961 Lincoln Continental to make it as trouble-free as possible.

Other specific features contribute to the comfort and convenience of the 1961 Lincoln Continental: The only center-opening doors on any American automobile—counterbalanced for a wonderful new ease of entrance, and all safety-locked at a flick of the driver's finger. Seats cushioned in nearly three times the amount of foam rubber used on other luxury automobiles. And the 1961 Lincoln Continental has been so thoughtfully engineered and so carefully built that maintenance servicing, including oil changes, is necessary only at 6,000-mile intervals—just twice a year under normal driving conditions.

The merit of ideal size

Interior space is astonishing in so sleek a vehicle (front seat hip room is *virtually the same*, even though the car is narrower; the driver's leg room is increased, though the car is 14 inches shorter over-all). Equipment is so complete that power brakes, power steering, even power window lifts are *standard*. And, particularly noteworthy, the line includes America's only four-door convertible.

Enduring Continental styling

Here is the modern convenience of sensible size brilliantly set forth in the enduring beauty of a new concept of Continental styling. This classic design makes possible an authentic luxury car that is not one inch longer than it absolutely must be to convey six passengers in deep-cushioned ease and superlative smoothness.

Frankly, if you love beautiful machinery, you owe yourself an hour at the wheel of the new Lincoln Continental. For only those who have driven it can begin to know how completely it outmodes everything that has gone before it. Lincoln-Mercury Division Ford Motor Company

LINCOLN CONTINENTAL

America's first ideally sized fine car

Lincoln Continental, 1961

With its low fenders and double or "suicide" doors, the elegant 1961 Lincoln Continental became an icon. It showed up in the James Bond film *Goldfinger* and was dubbed President Kennedy's limousine. As classy as Sinatra in a tux, the Continental suggested the high life and was considered to be the honorary car of the Rat Pack.

Mit seinem tief heruntergelassenen Blechkleid und den Portal- oder „Selbstmördertüren" wurde der elegante 1961er Lincoln Continental zur Ikone. Er hatte einen Auftritt im Bond-Film *Goldfinger* und firmierte als Staatskarosse von Präsident Kennedy. So nobel wie Frank Sinatra im Smoking, verströmte der Continental puren Luxus und galt als eine Art „Dienstwagen" des „Rat Pack".

Avec ses pare-chocs bas et ses doubles portes dites « suicide », l'élégante Lincoln Continental 1961 deviendra la limousine du président Kennedy et fera une apparition au cinéma avec James Bond dans *Goldfinger*. Aussi appréciée de la jet-set, la Continental sera considérée comme la voiture officielle du Rat Pack (la bande d'amis de Sinatra).

Mercury Monterey, 1963 ◂

▸▸ Ford Galaxie, 1960

1960
The long, elegant silver curve now moving over the American Road on hundreds of thousands of 1960 Fords has become the hallmark of success. To its last beautifully proportioned inch, this is the decisive style of the decade, a direction-pointer as certain as a compass needle.
The Galaxie is a clear-cut expression of the newest Ford styling trend—the uniquely formal roof balancing beautifully on the graceful sweep of its long, sophisticated body. Here, in Ford, you find distinctive automotive luxury at its finest . . . the first fashion of the sixties in America's best-selling car—the car with the *silver curve of success.*
FORD DIVISION, Ford Motor Company,
See "FORD STARTIME" in living color Tuesdays on NBC-TV

the long, sophisticated line
that flows
through Ford
styling
has become
the
silver
curve of
success
Galaxie
Galaxie
by Ford
FORD—The Finest Fords of a Lifetime
FALCON—The New-Size Ford
THUNDERBIRD—The World's Most Wanted Car

SEE JOHN WAYNE IN "THE SPIRIT OF THE ALAMO" NOV. 14, ABC-TV

THE BONNEVILLE SPORTS COUPE FOR 1961

The well-ordered Pontiac for '61 trims width outside the wheels for better balance

Balance is the big factor in pleasant, comfortable travel!

It's achieved by distributing as much weight as possible directly between the wheels. Pontiac '61 has more of its weight between the wheels than any other car. You have the feeling of sitting erect even when swinging around curves and corners.

If you travel a lot . . . or just want to enjoy your travel a lot more . . . try new Wide-Track at any of our fine Pontiac dealers. PONTIAC MOTOR DIVISION · GENERAL MOTORS CORPORATION

THE ONLY WIDE-TRACK CAR

PONTIAC '61—It's all Pontiac! on a new Wide-Track!

Pontiac Bonneville, 1960

Paintings emphasized the low and wide stance of Pontiac's famed "Wide Track" bodies, the look that differentiated it from GM's other brands.

Das Tiefe und Gedrungene von Pontiacs „Breitspur"-Karosserien – ein Look, der sich von den übrigen GM-Marken abhob – wurde zeichnerisch noch stärker hervorgehoben.

Les illustrations soulignent la largeur et l'abaissement des fameux châssis à voie large, un style qui distingue les Pontiac des Buick, Chevrolet et autres marques de GM.

Pontiac Bonneville, 1961 ◂

The 1960 Bonneville Convertible

Why ladies like the security of Wide-Track driving

A wider track is a wider stance. A wider stance is stability, safety, balance, less lean and sway, easier maneuvering, better control, more confidence and security at the wheel. Pontiac has a wider stance than any other car. A very pleasant demonstration of Wide-Track driving is yours for the asking. See or call one of our fine dealers this week.

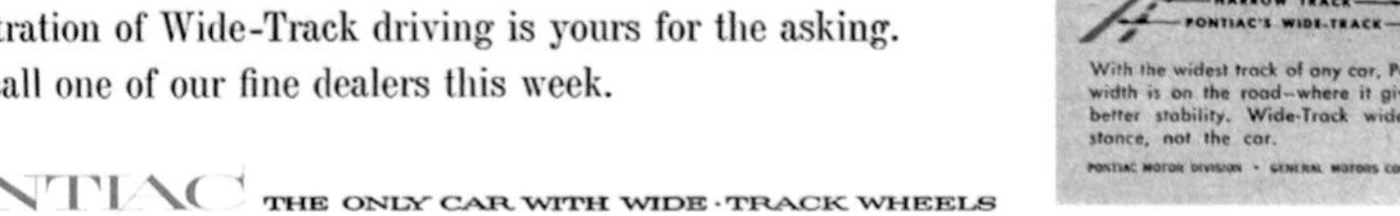

PONTIAC THE ONLY CAR WITH WIDE-TRACK WHEELS

NARROW TRACK

PONTIAC'S WIDE-TRACK

With the widest track of any car, Pontiac's width is on the road—where it gives you better stability. Wide-Track widens the stance, not the car.

PONTIAC MOTOR DIVISION • GENERAL MOTORS CORPORATION

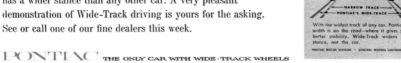

Think small.

Our little car isn't so much of a novelty any more.

A couple of dozen college kids don't try to squeeze inside it.

The guy at the gas station doesn't ask where the gas goes.

Nobody even stares at our shape.

In fact, some people who drive our little flivver don't even think 32 miles to the gallon is going any great guns.

Or using five pints of oil instead of five quarts.

Or never needing anti-freeze.

Or racking up 40,000 miles on a set of tires.

That's because once you get used to some of our economies, you don't even think about them any more.

Except when you squeeze into a small parking spot. Or renew your small insurance. Or pay a small repair bill. Or trade in your old VW for a new one.

Think it over.

Volkswagen Beetle, 1962 ◄

In a burst of advertising genius, VW's "Think Small" ad campaign, with its tiny photo, undercut the big-car, big-fin, big-advertising claims. The Beetle led sales of European cars in the United States in the 1950s. It was an unlikely success: A car developed in Germany during World War II and quite small compared to American entries, its appeal was its dependability, economy, and high quality of construction.

In einem Werbe-Geniestreich konterkarierte VWs Anzeigenkampagne „Think Small" mit ihrem winzigen Foto das gewohnte Werbetamtam. Der Käfer war in den USA der Fünfziger das meistverkaufte europäische Auto – ein unerwarteter Erfolg: Der während des Zweiten Weltkriegs in Deutschland entwickelte Wagen war für US-Verhältnisse ziemlich klein, doch er gefiel dank seiner Zuverlässigkeit, Wirtschaftlichkeit und hohen Qualität.

Dans un éclat de génie, la campagne « Penser petit » de VW, avec sa photo minuscule, casse l'idée de la grosse voiture pleine d'ailerons qui s'affiche en grand dans les autres publicités. La Coccinelle réalise les meilleures ventes de voitures européennes aux États-Unis dans les années 1950, un succès inattendu pour cette voiture, toute petite par rapport à ses rivales américaines, conçue en Allemagne pendant la Seconde Guerre mondiale. Elle séduit cependant par sa fiabilité, son prix et sa grande qualité de construction.

Volkswagen Beetle, 1966

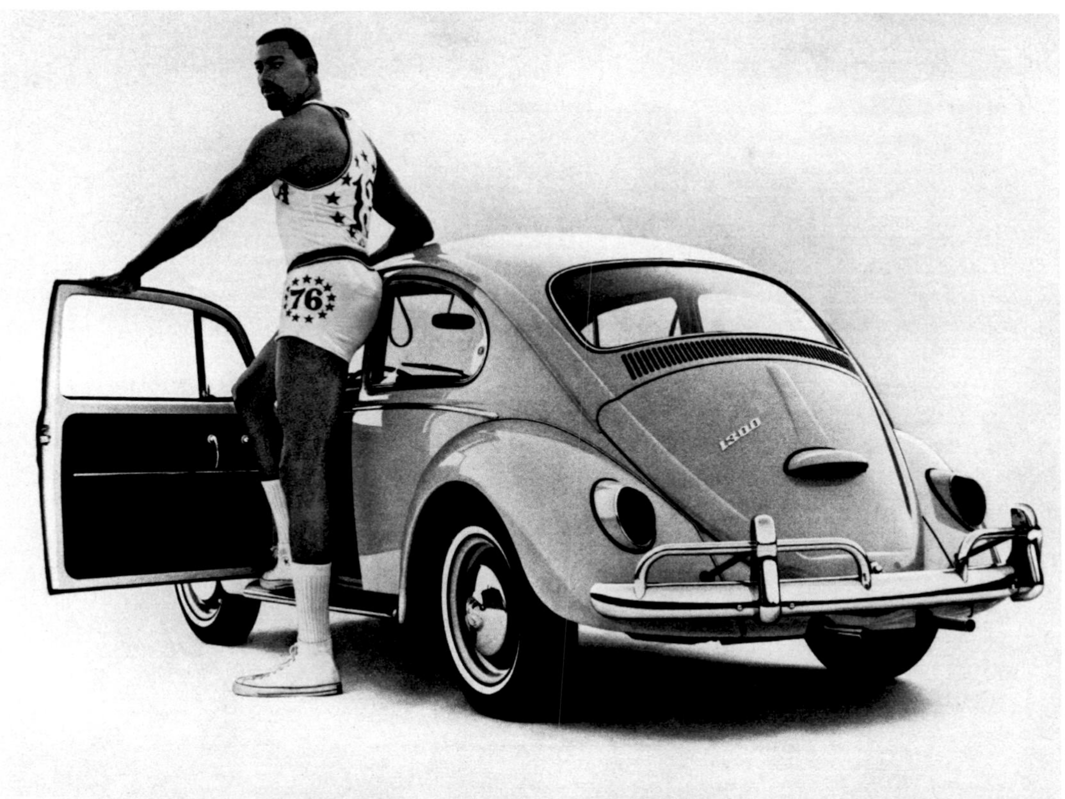

©VOLKSWAGEN OF AMERICA, INC.

They said it couldn't be done.
It couldn't.

We tried. Lord knows we tried. But no amount of pivoting or faking could squeeze the Philadelphia 76ers' Wilt Chamberlain into the front seat of a Volkswagen.

So if you're 7'1" tall like Wilt, our car is not for you.

But maybe you're a mere 6'7".

In that case, you'd be small enough to appreciate what a big thing we've made of the Volkswagen.

There's more headroom than you'd expect. (Over 37½" from seat to roof.)

And there's more legroom in front than you'd get in a limousine.

Because the engine's tucked over the rear wheels where it's out of the way (and where it can give the most traction).

You can put 2 medium-sized suitcases up front (where the engine isn't), and 3 fair-sized kids in the back seat. And you can sleep an enormous infant in back of the back seat.

Actually, there's only one part of a VW that you can't put much into:

The gas tank.

But you can get about 29 miles per gallon out of it.

Introducing the first competition for our luxury 4-door Plymouth VIP.
The new 2-door hardtop VIP.
PLYMOUTH
Door assist grips, safety release handles and fine ornamentation.
Foam-padded, pull-down center armrest.
Padded instrument panel with inset courtesy lights.
Except for its dashing 2-door hardtop styling, the new VIP has the same luxurious details of the 4-door model. And that's saying a lot. Beautiful finishing throughout.
Outside, an optional vinyl roof covering for true limousine look. Inside, fine furniture. Elegant fold-down center armrest. And luxury touches like extra-thick foam-padded seats covered in plush cloth-and-vinyl upholstery fabrics and finished with biscuit pleating, wall-to-wall carpeting, vinyl ornamentation with the look of fine wood. And a beautifully detailed door assist grip.
With VIP, you can choose a number of convenience and performance options never available from Plymouth before. Among these are a Tilt-a-Scope steering wheel that adjusts up and down—in and out—for your convenience.
And with VIP you get a host of standard equipment features.
Like deluxe wheel covers and rear fender skirts. And back-up lights, outside rear-view mirror, padded dash, variable-speed windshield wipers and electric washer, fender-mounted turn signal indicators and even courtesy lights inset in the instrument panel.
The 318-cubic-inch V-8 is standard but the optional engines include a two-barrel-equipped 383-cubic-inch engine, a four-barrel 383 and a mighty 440-cubic-inch V-8.
One final note. Both models of Plymouth VIP introduce a revolutionary concept in luxury cars. You can afford them.
Take a look at the newest VIP. Then take one for a test ride. And then take one home. Your Plymouth Dealer is the man that can arrange all of this. See him now.
See Plymouth in action on the Bob Hope Show, NBC-TV.
PLYMOUTH DIVISION CHRYSLER MOTORS CORPORATION
Let yourself go... Plymouth
VIP FURY BELVEDERE VALIANT BARRACUDA

▸ Valiant, 1960

The Plymouth Valiant and Dodge Dart were rugged, economical entries in the compact car race, with the durable "slant six" engine.

Mit ihrem haltbaren Slant-6-Motor waren Plymouth Valiant und Dodge Dart ebenso robuste wie sparsame Wettbewerber im Segment der Kompaktwagen.

La Plymouth Valiant et la Dodge Dart sont de solides modèles d'entrée de gamme qui vont participer à la course à la voiture compacte, plus économique, avec un moteur durable baptisé « slant six ».

Plymouth Fury VIP, 1966

▸▸ Chevrolet Impala, 1963

BY THE SEAT OF YOUR PANTS

Behind the wheel, that's the place to buy Valiant. You'll feel real skedaddle (101 horses worth) from an *inclined* engine that stretches regular gas like rubber bands. You'll feel a ride like nothing ever, mill-pond smooth, quiet as a clam. It's called Torsion-Aire, and it's teamed up with a fully unitized body—rust, rattle and squeak proofed. You'll have an alternator electrical system that makes your battery last longer, a trunk as big as a cave (25 cubic feet of it), and plenty of traveling room for a family of six. Like what you read? You'll like driving Valiant better. Go see the man who sells 'em. You'll like him too. Valiant, the car you'd want at *any* price

Valiant

NEW FROM CHRYSLER CORPORATION

CHEVROLET
CHEVROLET

THE '70S HAD BEGUN WITH A BOOM IN MUSCLE CARS SUCH AS THE DODGE CHALLENGER, PLYMOUTH BARRACUDA, FORD TORINO, CHEVROLET CAMARO, AND PONTIAC GTO, BUT GAS-THRIFTY SMALL CARS PREVAILED IN THE FACE OF THE ENERGY CRISES, GASOLINE LINES, AND NATIONAL MALAISE.

BEGONNEN HATTEN DIE 1970ER-JAHRE NOCH MIT EINEM BOOM VON MUSCLE-CARS WIE DEM DODGE CHALLENGER, PLYMOUTH BARRACUDA, FORD TORINO, CHEVROLET CAMARO UND PONTIAC GTO. DOCH ANGESICHTS DER ENERGIEKRISEN, SCHLANGEN AN DEN TANKSTELLEN UND DES LANDESWEITEN KATERS TRUGEN SPRIT SPARENDE KLEINWAGEN DEN SIEG DAVON.

SI LE DÉBUT DES ANNÉES 1970 VOIT L'ESSOR DES GROSSES CYLINDRÉES TELLES QUE LES DODGE CHALLENGER, PLYMOUTH BARRACUDA, FORD TORINO, CHEVROLET CAMARO ET PONTIAC GTO, LES PETITES VOITURES MOINS GOURMANDES EN CARBURANT S'AFFIRMENT TRÈS VITE DANS LE CONTEXTE DU « MALAISE NATIONAL » SUSCITÉ PAR LA CRISE DE L'ÉNERGIE ET LES FILES D'ATTENTE À LA POMPE.

1970-

RUNNING ON EMPTY
FAHREN AUF RESERVE
PRATIQUEMENT À SEC

-1979

Jaguar XK-E, 1970 ◂◂

Pontiac LeMans, 1971 ◂

Plymouth Sapporo, 1978

A REVOLUTION IN THE WORLD OF AUTOMOBILITY BEGAN ON THE VERY EARLY MORNING OF OCTOBER 6, 1973. The comfortable enjoyment of inexpensive travel many in the West had gotten used to began to change the moment that 1,400 Syrian tanks approached Israeli outposts in the Golan Heights, triggering the Yom Kippur War and the resultant Arab oil embargo. Within a few weeks, gasoline prices soared. In the United States, gas stations posted hastily drawn signs declaring "No Gas." Local governments instituted rationing systems based on odd- and even-number license plates.

The '70s had begun with a boom in muscle cars such as the Dodge Challenger, Plymouth Barracuda, Ford Torino, Chevrolet Camaro, and Pontiac GTO, but gas-thrifty small cars prevailed in the face of the energy crises, gasoline lines, and national malaise. The era saw the arrival in force of Japanese imports in the United States and of "world cars" like Ford's Fiesta and GM's Opel, and a sense of limits and frugality was reflected in advertising. Sales of small cars increased within months of the first "oil shock," in 1973. The second shock, occasioned by the overthrow of the Shah of Iran, in 1979, confirmed that things had changed forever.

Detroit began to downsize its cars, producing such controversial designs as the "bustleback" Cadillac Seville (so named for its sloped trunk) and the Chevrolet Citation. New "econoboxes" were still much larger than Renaults or Opels, but Americans felt constrained by them. Although Ford advertising attempted to compare the Pinto to the Model T — as economical, dependable transportation — the car was criticized. Similarly, General Motors' big buildup for its Chevrolet Vega fell flat. Both economy cars soon gained bad reputations and became the butts of jokes. Even more derided, though later seen as lovable "geek" cars, were AMC's Gremlin and Pacer.

The old methods of advertising, like the old formulas of designing and building cars, seemed to have failed. Detroit was in crisis. In the past, advertising pitched particular technical innovations, but this era carried much more

emotional freight. Print advertising was heavily influenced by television advertising, with its atmospherics.

Still, some advertising stuck with familiar formulas. Cadillac continued to show jewelry and furs, and used a typeface that suggested an invitation to a dress ball or a wedding. Style and design coming from Detroit grew to rococo parodies of their '50s incarnations. Long, chromed Lincolns and Cadillacs were available in Bill Blass and Givenchy editions. Chrysler advertisements starring actor Ricardo Montalbán praising Corinthian leather became the basis of stand-up comedy routines and vernacular humor.

But the Japanese carmakers, Honda, Toyota, and Nissan, expanded their sales. Honda touted its CVCC engine, used in the small Civic, as the first to meet new U.S. standards of cleanliness and efficiency. A new generation of ads touted their low price and fuel mileage. Offering what came to be called "surprise and delight" features — small items like coin holders — they also began to boast of safety features, a factor rarely seen in the past.

1970

1970 Jeep releases popular Renegade

Jeep präsentiert den beliebten Renegade

Jeep lance la populaire Renegade

1971 Surpassing European models, Japanese brands become best-selling imports in U.S.

Die Japaner setzen sich gegen die Europäer als meistverkaufte US-Importwagen durch

Dépassant les modèles européens, les Japonaises caracolent en tête des importations américaines.

1973 American Motors Gremlin issued in denim edition: "The car that wears the pants"

Jeans-Edition des Gremlin von American Motors („Das Auto, das die Hosen anhat")

La Gremlin d'American Motors sort en édition denim : c'est « la voiture qui porte le pantalon »

1973 Volkswagen Beetle number 15,007,034 produced, breaking Model T's record

Der 15 007 034. VW Käfer läuft vom Band und bricht damit den Rekord des Ford Model T

Production de la 15 007 034e Coccinelle Volkswagen ; le record du modèle T est battu

MIT DEM MORGENGRAUEN DES 6. OKTOBER 1973 SOLLTE SICH DIE WELT DER AUTOMOBILITÄT NACHHALTIG VERÄNDERN. Die Freude am preiswerten Reisen, an die sich viele im Westen gewöhnt hatten, trübte sich in jenem Moment, als 1400 syrische Panzer sich den israelischen Vorposten auf den Golanhöhen näherten – gefolgt vom Jom-Kippur-Krieg und einem Ölembargo der arabischen Länder. Die Kraftstoffpreise schnellten innerhalb weniger Wochen in die Höhe. Eilig dahingekritzelte Schilder mit der Aufschrift „kein Benzin" zierten die Tankstellen. Kraftstoff wurde rationiert, nach Maßgabe gerader und ungerader Endziffern auf den Nummernschildern.

Begonnen hatten die 1970er-Jahre noch mit einem Boom von Muscle-Cars wie dem Dodge Challenger, Plymouth Barracuda, Ford Torino, Chevrolet Camaro und Pontiac GTO. Doch angesichts der Energiekrisen, Schlangen an den Tankstellen und des landesweiten Katers trugen Sprit sparende Kleinwagen den Sieg davon. Stark zulegen konnten japanische US-Importe und „Weltautos" wie der Ford Fiesta und die Marke Opel. Dass es Grenzen gab und Sparsamkeit angesagt war, spiegelte sich auch in der Werbung wider. Innerhalb weniger Monate nach dem ersten Ölpreisschock von 1973 ging der Absatz von Kleinwagen in die Höhe. Nach dem Sturz des Schahs von Persien 1979 untermauerte die zweite Energiekrise, dass eine neue Zeit herangebrochen war.

Detroit begann seine Autos zu verkleinern und produzierte solch umstrittene Modelle wie den Cadillac Seville (mit seinem kurzen, stark abfallenden Kofferraum) und den Chevrolet Citation. Die neuen „Sparmodelle" waren immer noch viel größer als ein Renault oder Opel, doch die Amerikaner fühlten sich eingezwängt. Die Ford-Werbung versuchte den Pinto als wirtschaftliches und zuverlässiges Transportmittel mit dem Model T zu vergleichen, doch es hagelte Kritik. Ohne Wirkung blieb auch das von General Motors um den Chevrolet Vega veranstaltete Werbetamtam. Beide Sparmodelle ernteten schon bald einen schlechten Ruf und wurden zum Witzthema. Noch übler verspottet wurden AMCs Gremlin und Pacer, wenngleich man sie später als liebenswerte Extravaganzen betrachtete.

Die althergebrachten Methoden der Werbung waren offenbar ebenso gescheitert wie die alten Formeln des Autobaus. Detroit steckte in der Krise. Bisher hatte sich die Werbung stets auf technische Innovationen konzentriert, doch nun war eine weitaus emotionsgeladenere Zeit angebrochen. Und die Anzeigenwerbung sah sich durch die stimmungsvollen TV-Spots stark beeinflusst.

Dennoch hielt die Werbung bisweilen an den vertrauten Formeln fest. Cadillac präsentierte weiterhin Schmuck und Pelze und eine Schrift, die an eine Einladung zu einem Kostümball oder einer Hochzeit erinnerte. Die aus Detroit offerierten Kreationen wurden zu rokokoartigen Parodien der Schöpfungen der 1950er-Jahre. Lange, verchromte Lincolns und Cadillacs waren als Edition Bill Blass oder Givenchy erhältlich. Die Chrysler-Werbung mit dem Schauspieler Ricardo Montalbán und seinem Lob des fiktiven „korinthischen Leders" wurde von Stand-up-Comedians und in deftigen Witzen aufgegriffen.

Honda, Toyota und Nissan indes konnten zulegen. Honda verwies stolz darauf, dass der im Civic verwendete CVCC-Motor als erster die neuen US-Schadstoff- und Verbrauchsnormen erfüllte. Neben dem niedrigen Preis stand plötzlich auch die Reichweite pro Tankfüllung im Zentrum der Anzeigenwerbung. Man warb mit netten Extras wie dem Münzhalter, zugleich begann man jedoch auch, die gebotenen Sicherheitsmerkmale herauszustellen – was früher nur selten vorgekommen war.

1973

1973 Energy shortages lead to gasoline lines; will last for two years

Benzinrationierung führt zwei Jahre lang zu Schlangen an den Tankstellen

Pendant deux ans, la pénurie d'énergie génère des files d'attente à la pompe

1975 U.S. traffic safety administration names Volvo 240 standard-bearer for safety

US-Verkehrssicherheitsbehörde zeichnet den Volvo 240 als sicherstes Auto aus

Le gouvernement américain cite la Volvo 240 en exemple pour son respect des normes de sécurité

1975 BMW establishes North American division in Montvale, New Jersey

BMW gründet in Montvale (New Jersey) BMW of North America

BMW s'installe en Amérique du Nord à Montvale, dans le New Jersey

1976 Actor Ricardo Montalban endorses "soft Corinthian leather" of Chrysler Cordoba

Der Schauspieler Ricardo Montalbán rühmt das „weiche korinthische Leder" des Chrysler Cordoba

L'acteur Ricardo Montalbán vante le « cuir corinthien » de la Chrysler Cordoba

PAN AM

Dodge Charger, 1970 ◂◂

Ford Thunderbird, 1970 ◂

▸▸ Chevrolet Impala, 1972

AU MATIN DU 6 OCTOBRE 1973, LE MONDE DE L'AUTOMOBILE CONNAÎT UN BOULEVERSEMENT RADICAL. L'agrément et le confort des déplacements bon marché auxquels nombre d'Occidentaux se sont habitués sont remis en cause par l'avancée de 1400 tanks syriens dans les territoires occupés par Israël sur les hauteurs du Golan ; c'est le début de la guerre du Kippour, qui va entraîner l'embargo pétrolier des pays arabes. En quelques semaines, le prix de l'essence s'envole. Aux États-Unis, les stations-service affichent très vite des panneaux « pompes vides ». Les autorités locales instaurent un système de rationnement fondé sur les numéros pairs et impairs des plaques minéralogiques.

Si le début des années 1970 voit l'essor des grosses cylindrées telles que les Dodge Challenger, Plymouth Barracuda, Ford Torino, Chevrolet Camaro et Pontiac GTO, les petites voitures moins gourmandes en carburant s'affirment très vite dans le contexte du « malaise national » suscité par la crise de l'énergie et les files d'attente à la pompe. L'époque sera marquée par l'arrivée en force aux États-Unis des modèles d'importation japonais, des voitures de marque fabriquées à l'étranger, comme la Ford Fiesta ou l'Opel de GM et un sentiment d'austérité que reflétera la publicité. Les ventes de petites voitures augmentent en quelques mois après le premier « choc pétrolier » de 1973. Le second choc, occasionné par le renversement du Shah d'Iran en 1979, scelle le changement irréversible intervenu dans le secteur automobile.

Detroit se met à produire des voitures plus modestes, mais controversées, comme la Cadillac Séville « bustleback » (qui tire son nom de son coffre plus court) et la Chevrolet Citation de la fin des années 1970. Ces nouveaux modèles consomment certes moins d'essence, mais les Américains s'y sentent à l'étroit, bien que ces « petites boîtes économiques » soient plus spacieuses que les Renault ou les Opel. Malgré les tentatives de Ford pour comparer la Pinto au modèle T dans ses publicités, cette voiture économique et fiable suscite les critiques. De même, le battage médiatique de General Motors autour de sa Chevrolet Vega tombe à plat. Ces deux modèles s'attirent très vite une mauvaise réputation qui donne prise à toutes sortes de moqueries. Bien qu'appréciées par la suite par une poignée de passionnés, la Gremlin et la Pacer d'AMC sont tout aussi décriées.

Les vieilles recettes publicitaires ne semblent pas mieux réussir que les anciennes méthodes de production. Detroit est en crise. Par le passé, la publicité soulignait les innovations techniques mais l'époque est davantage à la charge émotionnelle. La publicité imprimée est fortement influencée par la publicité télévisée et son pouvoir d'évocation.

Quoi qu'il en soit, certaines campagnes s'en tiennent aux formules habituelles. Cadillac continue de miser sur la joaillerie, la fourrure et une typographie digne d'un carton d'invitation à un bal ou un mariage. Le style et le design de Detroit virent à la parodie rococo de ses productions des années 1950. Longues Lincoln et Cadillac chromées sont proposées en édition « Bill Blass » et « Givenchy ». Le « cuir corinthien » vanté par l'acteur Ricardo Montalbán dans les publicités pour Chrysler devient lui aussi une source de plaisanterie.

Les constructeurs japonais (Honda, Toyota et Nissan), en revanche, accroissent leurs ventes. Honda fait valoir que son moteur CVCC, qui équipe la petite Civic, est le premier à satisfaire les nouveaux critères américains de propreté et d'efficacité. Une nouvelle génération de publicités vante leur prix et leur taux de consommation au kilomètre. Réservant d'« agréables surprises » sous formes de petits accessoires, comme un porte-monnaie, ces modèles commencent à s'équiper également sur le plan de la sécurité, aspect trop rarement abordé par le passé.

1976

1976 New generation of downsized cars appears from Detroit

Detroit präsentiert eine neue Generation von kleiner dimensionierten Modellen

Apparition d'une nouvelle génération de petites voitures à Detroit

1977 Saab develops turbocharged engine later popularized in 900 Turbo

Saab entwickelt den Turbomotor, der später beim 900 Turbo Anklang finden wird

Saab élabore le moteur turbo, popularisé par la 900 Turbo

1977 Smokey and the Bandit film stars Burt Reynolds and his Pontiac Firebird

Burt Reynolds und sein Pontiac Firebird sind die Helden in dem Film *Ein ausgekochtes Schlitzohr*

Burt Reynolds tient la vedette du film *Cours après moi Shérif* avec sa Pontiac Firebird

1979 Lee Iacocca saves sinking Chrysler with $1.2 billion promise from U.S. Congress

Lee Iacocca rettet die stark angeschlagene Chrysler Corporation mit einer vom US-Kongress verabschiedeten Bürgschaft von 1,2 Mrd. US-Dollar

Lee Iacocca évite la faillite à Chrysler en obtenant 1,2 milliard de dollars du Congrès américain

CHEVROLET

BEAT THE SYSTEM. BUY A VOLVO.

JAGUAR

Defy comparison.

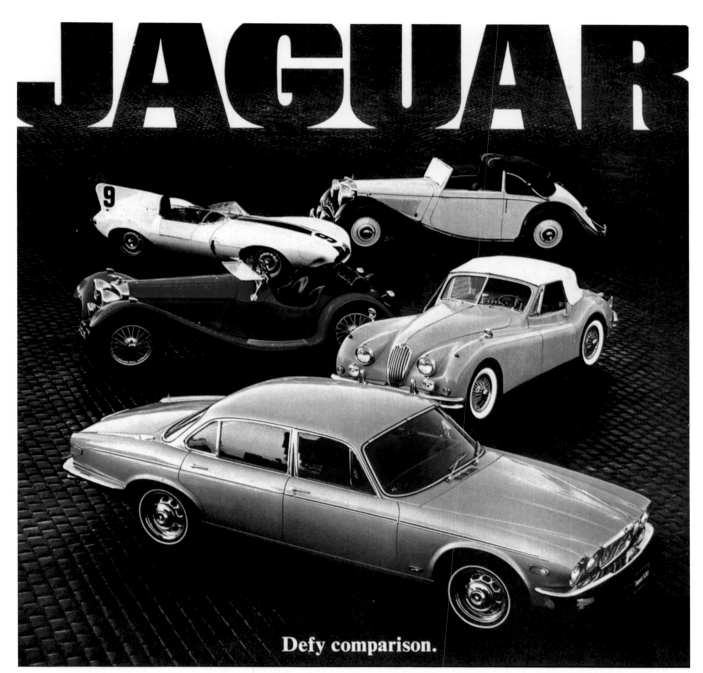

Jaguars have always been defiantly individual cars. Consider the XJ12; it is literally a class of one, the only production four-door V-12 sedan in the world. And this uncompromising machine is unique in ways that extend far beyond its source of power.

The XJ12 handles with the agility and precision of all-independent suspension, rack and pinion steering and power disc brakes on all four wheels. The great smoothness and response of the electronically fuel-injected V-12 only enhance the car's remarkable all-round performance characteristics.

The inner world of this uncommon sedan is a harmony of thoughtful luxuries: hand-matched walnut veneers enrich the dashboard. Topgrain hides cover the seats. The car is totally considerate of its occupant's every wish: there are no factory options whatever. Even the thermostatically-controlled heat and air conditioning and the AM/FM stereo radio and tape deck are standard.

Still another Jaguar amenity is a remarkably thoughtful warranty: for 12 months, regardless of mileage, Jaguar will replace or repair any part of the car that is defective or that simply wears out, provided only that the car is properly maintained. The only exceptions are the tires, which are warranted by the tire manufacturer, and spark plugs and filters, which are routine replacement items. Even then, if the plugs or filters are defective, Jaguar will pay to replace them.

In a world filled with common denominators, it is refreshing to know that Jaguar remains defiantly incomparable. For the name of the Jaguar dealer nearest you, call these numbers toll-free: (800) 447-4700, or, in Illinois, (800) 322-4400. British Leyland Motors Inc., Leonia, New Jersey 07605.

Jaguar XJ12, 1978

Volvo, 1971 ◂

▸▸ Volkswagen Beetle, 1970

We do our thing.

The funny thing is, we didn't even know we had a "thing".

We've been perfecting one car for 25 years, steering clear of the idiocy of annual model changes.

Our only worry has been how to make the VW work better, not look different.

And we haven't done badly at all: The 1970 VW is faster and quieter with a longer-lasting engine than any other beetle.

But you still need a scorecard to tell the '70 from other years. Or any year from any other year.

Nobody in the world makes and services a car as well as we do. Because nobody's been doing it as long on one model.

We still use old-fashioned words like "nifty," "peachy" and "swell".

And we stick to old-fashioned ideas like craftsmanship and dedication and skill.

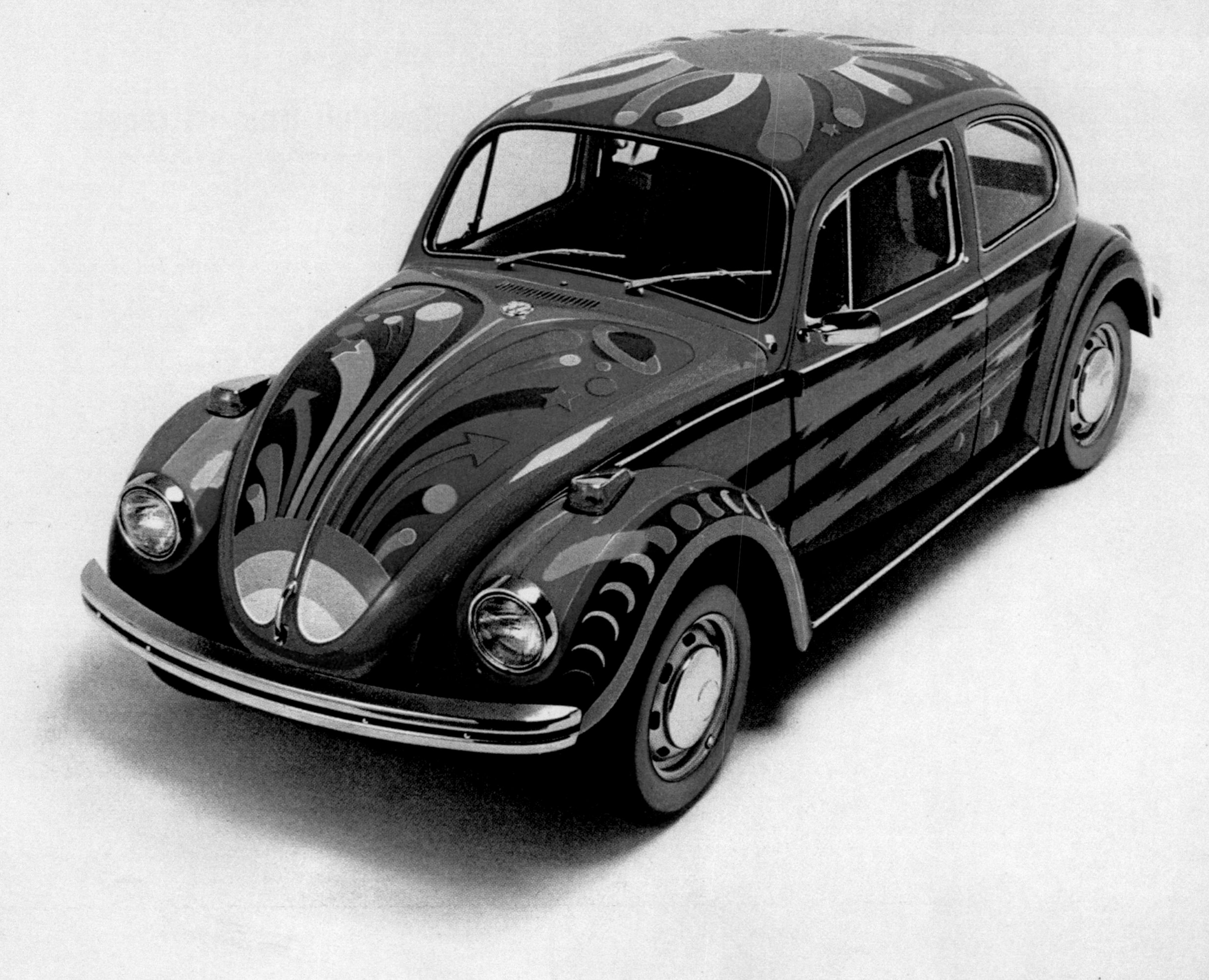

You do yours.

Then, for $1839*, our thing becomes your thing. And what happens is wild.

People treat VWs like something else.

They polish them, scrub them, stripe them and flower them in very far-out ways.

Why? Why mostly on Volkswagens?

We think it's affection, pure and simple.

A VW is a new member of the family who happens to live in the garage.

And when a VW moves in, people flip out.

Driving a VW, we are told, is a groove.

You don't get zapped with freaky running costs. Or zonked with kinky maintenance bills. Or clobbered with crazy depreciation.

We've built the VW durably enough to withstand heat, cold, flood, snow, sand, mud.

Yet it's durable enough to withstand a whole new generation.

Maybe *you* thought we were in a rut. When all the time we were really in the groove.

LEASE A LEGEND. THE PORSCHE 924.

Why lease an ordinary car when you can lease a new 1979 Porsche?

The Porsche 924.

It's designed to carry on the Porsche tradition of winning. A tradition that spans 31 years and includes over 400 major racing victories.

It's also designed for the practicality of today. Its unique rear transaxle provides virtually perfect 50-50 weight distribution between front and rear—for balanced road holding and braking.

Its aerodynamic design is aesthetically pleasing—and practical. In wind tunnel tests, it registers an amazingly low drag co-efficient of only 0.36.

Best of all, even with options, leasing a 924 is surprisingly affordable.

So visit your Porsche + Audi dealer and test drive a living legend.

PORSCHE + AUDI
NOTHING EVEN COMES CLOSE

Triumph TR7, 1977

Porsche 924, 1979 ◂

You may never need all 120 safety features in your Mercedes-Benz. But it's comforting to know they're there.

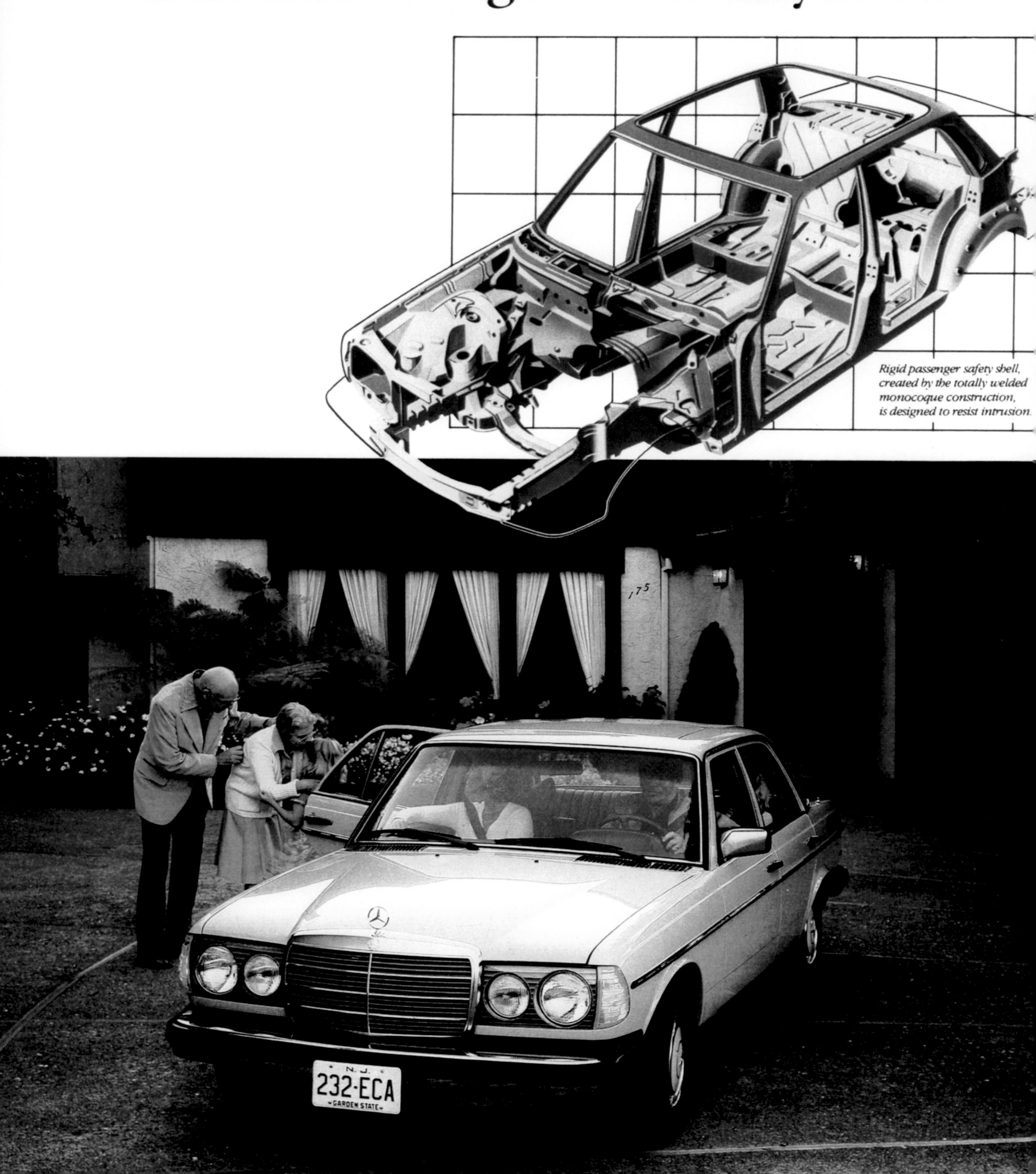

Rigid passenger safety shell, created by the totally welded monocoque construction, is designed to resist intrusion.

Le Car
Le City Car
One of the reasons Le Car has caused so much excitement in this country is because of what it can do in the city. There isn't a car in town that can match Le Car for parking, maneuverability, ease of handling and smooth ride.
Le Car fits in a smaller parking space than any other car in its class.
Even though Le Car has a longer wheelbase than Honda Civic or VW Rabbit, it has a shorter overall length. So Le Car will fit in a space that the others have to pass by. Add to this Le Car's short 32-foot turning circle and you can see why the parking problems of the city are no problem for Le Car.
A highly responsive car that handles with ease.
Parking is not the only difficulty you'll encounter in the city. Driving is another. Le Car is equipped with front-wheel drive, rack and pinion steering, four-wheel independent suspension and Michelin steel-belted radials, all standard. (Honda, Rabbit, Chevette and Fiesta don't offer this combination of standard features.) The result is that Le Car can zip in and out of, around and through traffic.
And Le Car's ride is so remarkably smooth that Car & Driver reported, "The rough-road ride in Le Car is a new standard for small cars. It waltzed across the worst roads we could find – the cratered surfaces of Manhattan – as though it was fresh pavement."
Although Le Car is small on the outside you could never tell from its roomy inside. Le Car is designed to give you the most interior room while using the least exterior space.
A world of satisfied Le Car owners.
In Europe, nearly two million people drive Le Car with a passion. That's more than Fiesta and Rabbit combined. Here in America, Le Car sales more than doubled in 1977. What's more, in an independent study, Le Car owner satisfaction was rated an amazingly high 95%. The price for all this? A very satisfying $3495.*
Obviously, a lot of people are doing a lot more than just driving Le Car in the city. So if you really want to see how much fun Le Car can be, flip open the giant sun roof (optional) and take Le City Car for a drive in the country. For more information call 800-631-1616 for your nearest dealer. In New Jersey call collect 201-461-6000.
*P.O.E. East Coast: Price excludes transportation, dealer preparation and taxes. Stripe, Mag wheels, Sun roof and Rear wiper/washer optional at extra cost. Prices higher in the West. Renault USA, Inc. ©1978.
Le Car by Renault

Le Car
Le Fun Car
Le Car looks like fun.
Right off the bat, Le Car looks like no other small car. The big optional Fun Roof brightens Le Car's insides even on cloudy days. And Le Car's giant rear hatch opens wide right down to the bumper. To swallow even the rewards of a weekend's worth of antique hunting.
Le Car drives like fun.
Le Car's front-wheel drive, four-wheel independent suspension, rack and pinion steering and Michelin steel-belted radials, (a combination of standard features other small cars don't offer as options) make it a ball to drive. As well as a pleasure to ride in. As noted by Car & Driver who said that in terms of interior volume versus exterior space, "there isn't a car on earth that can match Le Car."
Le Car owners are all smiles.
In four independent studies, Le Car owner satisfaction was rated an amazingly high 95%.
No wonder. Given all Le Car has going for it, and the low price it goes for ($3,725*), it's easy to see why Le Car satisfies.
Renault USA, Inc.
Marketing Department
100 Sylvan Ave., Englewood Cliffs, N.J. 07632
Please send me more information about Le Fun Car.
Name
Address
City State Zip
Le Car by Renault

Renault Le Car, 1978

Clever advertising playing on its French origins could not overcome the limited appeal of Renault's tiny hatchback. The company made one final attempt at success in the United States by purchasing AMC. Within a few years most French and Italian makers would be absent from the American scene.

Renaults winziges Schrägheck-Modell stieß kaum auf Resonanz, woran auch clevere Werbung, die mit seiner französischen Herkunft spielte, nichts ändern konnte. Die Übernahme von AMC bedeutete einen letzten Versuch, in den USA Fuß zu fassen, doch innerhalb weniger Jahre waren die meisten französischen und italienischen Hersteller in den USA von der Bühne verschwunden.

Une publicité maligne jouant sur les origines françaises de la voiture qui ne parviendra toutefois pas à surmonter le dédain des Américains pour cette minuscule deux-portes. Dans une dernière tentative de conquête des États-Unis, Renault rachète AMC, mais c'est en vain. Quelques années plus tard, la plupart des constructeurs français et italiens auront complètement disparu de la scène américaine.

Renault Le Car, 1978

Mercedes-Benz E-Class, 1979 ◂

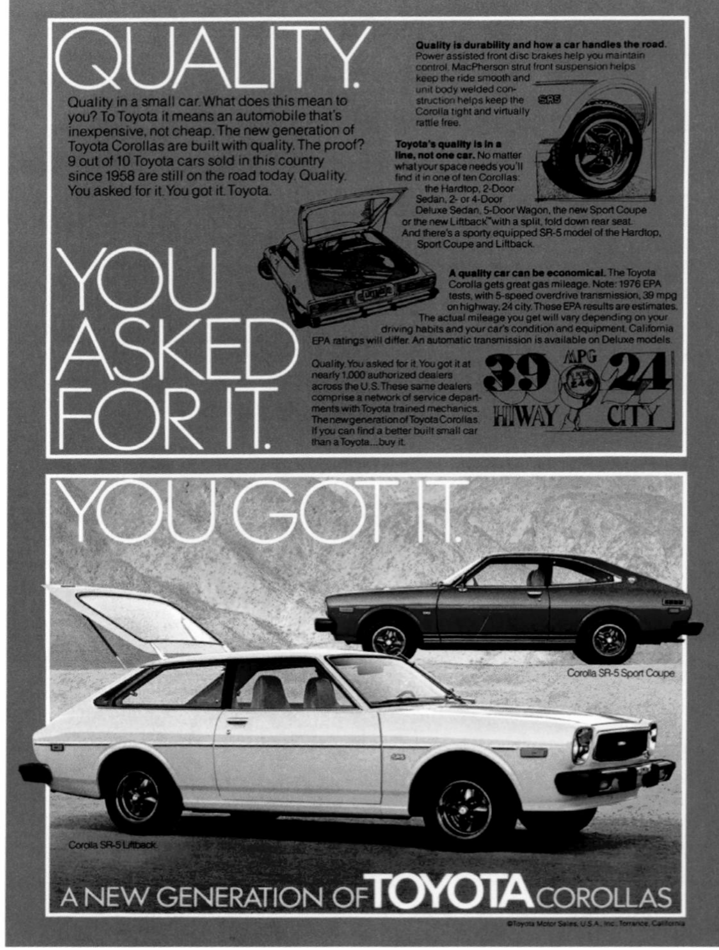

Toyota Corolla, 1976

Toyota Celica, 1980

► Datsun B-210 GX, 1978

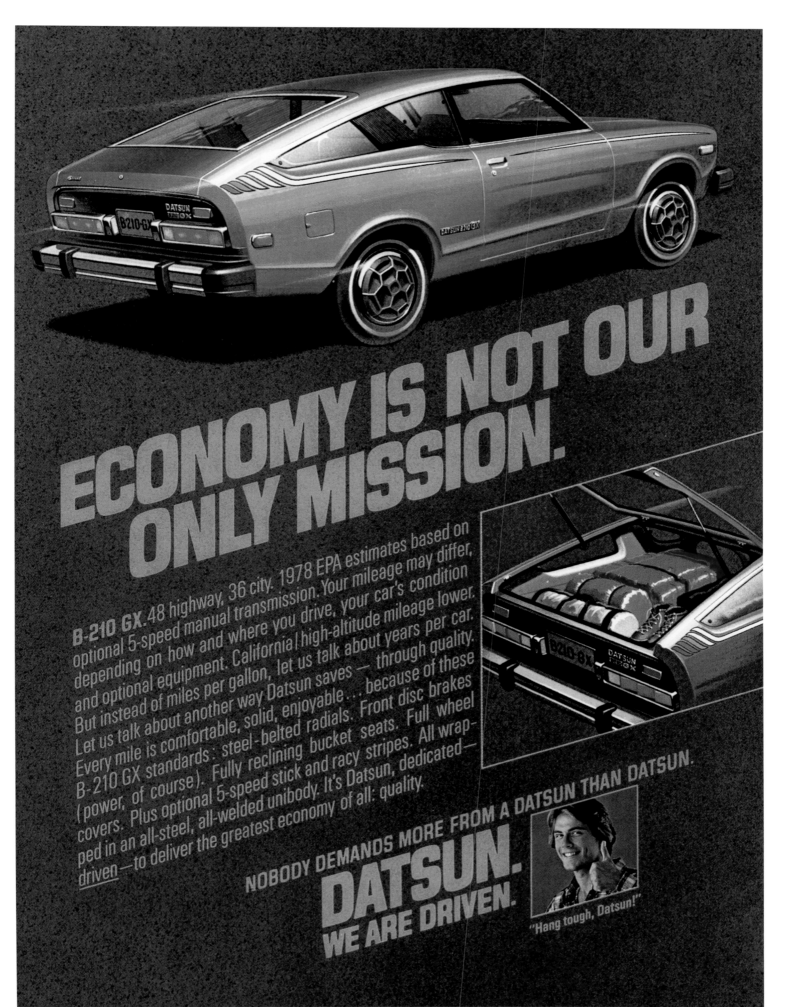

ECONOMY IS NOT OUR ONLY MISSION.

B-210 GX. 48 highway, 36 city. 1978 EPA estimates based on optional 5-speed manual transmission. Your mileage may differ, depending on how and where you drive, your car's condition and optional equipment. California/high-altitude mileage lower. But instead of miles per gallon, let us talk about years per car. Let us talk about another way Datsun saves — through quality. Every mile is comfortable, solid, enjoyable ... because of these B-210 GX standards: steel-belted radials. Front disc brakes (power, of course). Fully reclining bucket seats. Full wheel covers. Plus optional 5-speed stick and racy stripes. All wrapped in an all-steel, all-welded unibody. It's Datsun, dedicated—driven—to deliver the greatest economy of all: quality.

NOBODY DEMANDS MORE FROM A DATSUN THAN DATSUN.

DATSUN.
WE ARE DRIVEN.

"Hang tough, Datsun!"

The new Toyota Corolla. Some people find the left rear window its most beautiful feature.

$1798.* That's the beauty mark you'll find on the sticker of every Corolla Sedan. But the sedan is just one version of a beautiful Corolla price.

Two other Corollas have left rear windows that are just as appealing. The sporty Corolla Fastback at $1918.* The roomy Corolla Wagon at a mere $1958.*

Yet, as inexpensive as it is, the Toyota Corolla doesn't rely on price alone. It has fully reclining bucket seats. It has thick wall-to-wall nylon carpeting. It has an all-vinyl interior. To make it all the more beautiful.

But one of the most beautiful surprises in the Toyota Corolla is the amount of legroom. There's not an economy car around that comes close.

As for being practical, the Toyota Corolla does a beautiful job there, too. With carpets that snap in and out so you can clean them easily. With front disc brakes for safer stopping. With undercoating to prevent rust, corrosion and noise. With unit construction and a lined trunk to prevent rattles and squeaks. And with a very practical sealed lubrication system to end chassis lubes forever.

An economy car that comes loaded. That's the real beauty of the Toyota Corolla.

But with the beautiful price of $1798,* we can't blame you for being attracted to the left rear window.

TOYOTA
We're quality oriented

Toyota Corolla, 1970

Although it appeared in a number of body styles around the world, by the 1970s, Toyota's Corolla model was a true "world car," and a rival to the Volkswagen's Beetle for planetary popularity.

Wenngleich er in den Siebzigern weltweit in unterschiedlichem Gewand erschien, war der Toyota Corolla ein echtes „Weltauto" und konkurrierte mit dem VW Käfer um globale Popularität.

Bien que lancée avec divers styles de carrosseries à travers le monde dans les années 1970, la Toyota Corolla est un véritable « modèle mondial », qui rivalise avec la Coccinelle Volkswagen en termes de popularité planétaire.

► Toyota Celica, 1974

Freestyle Toyota

When we asked George Barris to turn a Celica GT into the ultimate ski car, he went crazy. Of course, we gave him a pretty fancy car to begin with. Our 1975 Celica GT comes standard with an AM/FM stereo radio, 5-speed overdrive transmission, tach, radials, 2.2 liter hemi-head engine, reclining buckets, etc. Well, as you can see, George added a few things. Body work, special paint, aircraft instrumentation, Citizens Band radio and PA system. For starters.

Freestyle Kneissl

Then we asked Franz Kneissl to give us a freestyle ski. Wide at the shovel and tail like the famous Kneissl Short Comp. Narrow at the waist for quick turns. With pre-stressed racing edges, Kneissl clear racing base and Molded Duroplast Core. Perfect for bump skiing.

Freestyle Toyota-Kneissl Ski Team

369

Donovan Phillips, Penelope Street and Chris Thorne. They'll be going up to freestyle competitions in their one-of-a-kind Toyota and challenging the bumps on Kneissl Freestyle Skis.

Small car specialists for over 40 years

TOYOTA

Garmont boots, Geze bindings and clothes by Saska Sports Industries.

See how much car your money can buy.

PHOENIX by PONTIAC

This is the first Pontiac Phoenix. It's our new six-passenger luxury compact. And it typifies the special way we feel about cars.

We think a car's styling should be clean. Strong. Arresting. Like our new Phoenix.

We think a car should be comfortable, but not overbearing. So we gave Phoenix full-width seats with a fold-down center armrest. Really nice fabrics. Cut-pile carpet. Padded door panels. A very functional instrument panel. Even a cushioned steering wheel. They give Phoenix a quiet kind of luxury we think you'll like.

We think a car should move down the road with authority. With its standard V-6 or available V-8, Phoenix does.

We think Phoenix is a pretty special compact. The kind you've been waiting to buy or lease. That's why it's arriving at your Pontiac dealer's now.

PONTIAC THE MARK OF GREAT CARS

GM

Our lowest priced Honda isn't so simple.

The Honda Civic® 1200 Sedan is our lowest priced Honda.* We hope that statement doesn't put you off.

We know that lots of people tend to be suspicious when they see the words "lowest priced." Especially when it's a car. They immediately think of some stripped-down model calculated to snag the unwary buyer by means of a seductive price tag.

That's why we're running this ad. To let you know that, despite its very reasonable price, the Civic 1200 Sedan gives you such traditional Honda engineering refinements as transverse-mounted engine, front-wheel drive, rack and pinion steering, power-assisted dual-diagonal braking system with front discs, and four-wheel independent MacPherson strut suspension.

And that's not all. The Civic 1200 Sedan abounds with standard features that other manufacturers might charge you extra for.

*Not available in Calif. and high altitude areas. Manufacturer's suggested retail price excluding freight, tax, license, title, and options. ©1978 American Honda Motor Co., Inc. Civic 1200 is a Honda trademark.

These include reclining bucket seats, adjustable head rests, wall-to-wall carpeting, opening rear-quarter windows, inside hood release, rear-seat ash tray, plus the instrument cluster shown opposite, a simple layout that nonetheless provides the added convenience of a trip odometer.

Like our other two Honda cars – the Civic CVCC® and the Honda Accord® – the Civic 1200 doesn't need a catalytic converter and runs on unleaded or money-saving regular gasoline.

So there you have it. The Honda Civic 1200 Sedan. Because it's a Honda, it's a simple car. But not so simple as its price would lead you to believe.

HONDA
We make it simple.

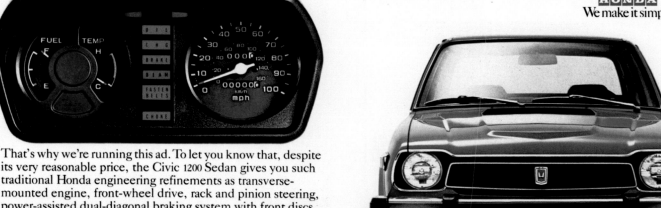

Honda Civic, 1978

Sturdy, reliable, and economical Japanese imports like the Honda Civic outdid gadget-laden American models in the 1970s. Their advertising, however, emphasized their surprising number of amenities.

Robuste, zuverlässige und wirtschaftliche Japan-Importe wie der Honda Civic übertrumpften die mit Schnickschnack überfrachteten US-Modelle der 1970er-Jahre. In der Werbung betonte man dennoch ihre überraschende Fülle von Annehmlichkeiten.

Dans les années 1970, les solides Japonaises, fiables et économiques, dament le pion aux modèles américains qui offrent pourtant pléthore de gadgets, comme en témoignent les publicités vantant leur nombre surprenant d'équipements.

Pontiac Phoenix, 1977 ◄

Playboy thinks a lot of its Bunny of the Year.

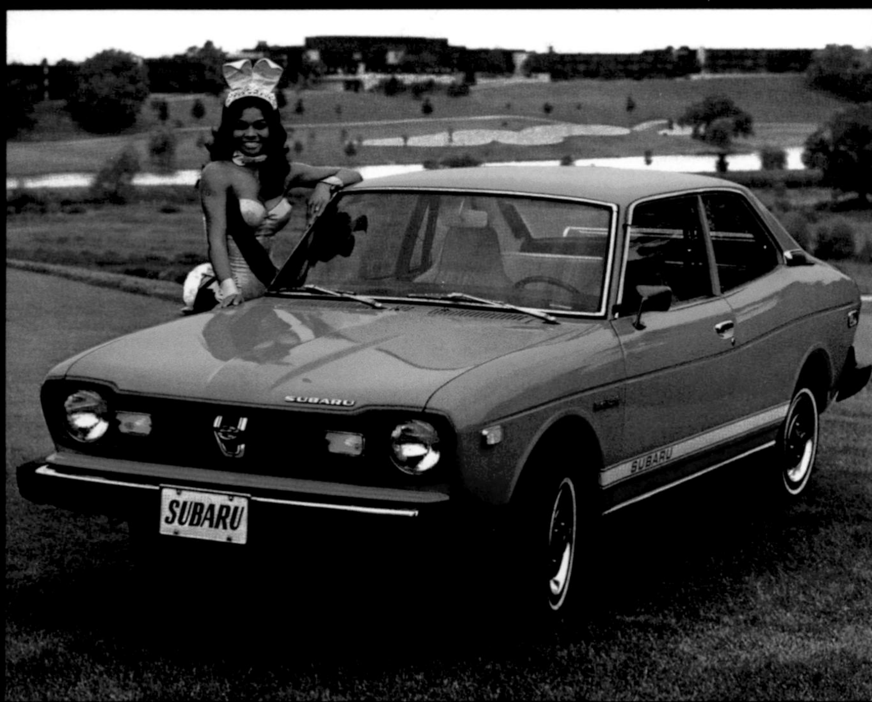

That's why they gave her a Subaru.

Subaru. The front wheel drive performer that averages over 27 miles per gallon.
And, to make it almost too good to be true—it's now backed with a strong 12-month, Unlimited Mileage Warranty.
See it and drive it at your local Subaru dealer.

Subaru Front Drive **You could buy it for gas mileage alone. But there's so much more.**

▸ Honda Civic, 1975

Women did not "only drive automatic transmissions" but many wanted a car to be nothing more than a transportation appliance, albeit with reliability and economy. Capitalizing on the jargon of a vibrant and active women's liberation movement, Honda's strategy sought to tap into a new brand of female customers.

Frauen fuhren nicht „nur Automatik", doch viele wünschten sich lediglich einen fahrbaren Untersatz, der zuverlässig und wirtschaftlich sein musste. Honda bediente sich des Jargons einer dynamischen Emanzipationsbewegung und versuchte so, eine neue Art von Kundinnen zu gewinnen.

Non seulement les femmes préfèrent les automatiques, mais beaucoup ne voient dans la voiture qu'un moyen de locomotion, qu'elles veulent fiable et économique. Capitalisant sur le jargon du mouvement de libération des femmes, la stratégie de Honda vise un nouveau type de consommatrices : la femme active et indépendante.

Subaru, 1974

"Women only drive automatic transmissions."

Some car manufacturers actually believe women buy cars for different reasons than men do.

So they build "a woman's car." Oversized, hopelessly automatic and dull.

At Honda we designed just one thing. A lean, spunky economy car with so much pizzazz it handles like a sports car.

If you're bored with cars designed only to get you from point A to point B, without responding to you the driver, maybe you ought to take the Honda Civic for a spin.

We've got a stick shift with an astonishing amount of zip. Enough to surprise you. We promise.

Or, if you prefer, Hondamatic.™ It's a semi-automatic transmission that gives you convenience, but doesn't rob you of involvement.

Neither one is a woman's car.

Honda Civic.

We don't make "a woman's car."

MG
MIDGET
MG Midget.
High-flying fun.
Low-flying pricetag.
In the wide-open MG Midget, you can fly now, pay little, and even save money on gas while enjoying all the fun of owning a real, live, top-down sports car while you're still young enough to enjoy it.
The Midget is, in fact, the lowest-priced true sports car on the market.
The Midget has rack and pinion steering, short-throw four-speed stick, front disc brakes and an agility in turns and a feel for the road that make it a joy to handle. Not to mention an impressive EPA-rated 34 MPG on the highway and 22 MPG in the city. (Naturally, these are estimates and the actual mileage you get may vary depending on the car's condition and how and where you drive, optional equipment, and may be lower in California.)
If whatever you're driving is getting you down, go fly a Midget. It's fun. It's inexpensive. It's thrifty to run. For the name of the dealer nearest you, call these numbers toll-free: (800) 447-4700, or, in Illinois, (800) 322-4400.
MG
MIDGET
BRITISH
LEYLAND
British Leyland Motors Inc., Leonia, New Jersey 07605.

1979 RABBIT. THE CAR EVERYBODY'S TRYING TO COPY.

No wonder.

How often does a car come along with the Rabbit's combination of engineering, performance, space and handling?

And when you realize that even General Motors named our Rabbit the best of five economy cars tested, including one of their own, it's not surprising that the Rabbit became the best-selling import in Detroit.

So you can't blame people for trying to make their cars look like ours.

But to look like a Rabbit is not to be a Rabbit.

The Rabbit is available with a C.I.S. fuel-injected engine. The copies aren't.

Not all the copies match our Rabbit's room. For example, the Ford Fiesta has only 2/3 as much trunk space as the Rabbit. As a matter of fact, the Rabbit has more trunk space than a $90,000 Rolls. And more passenger space than 35 other cars on the market.

And after testing the 13 most popular '78 economy cars in America, here's what the editors of Car and Driver had to say: "The Rabbit's total design is more astute than that of any other car in this test... And painstaking year-to-year refinement has made the Rabbit good at everything it does."

Of course, this excellence has a price. The Rabbit costs slightly more than its imitators. But as the editors so aptly put it, "...the Rabbit delivers on the investment."

Four years ago, other car manufacturers bought our Rabbits by the dozens. Then took them apart to see how we did it. Now we're beginning to see the fruits of that labor.

One of these days, they may even get it right.

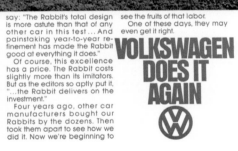

VOLKSWAGEN DOES IT AGAIN

Volkswagen Rabbit, 1979

MG Midget, 1977 ◂

▸▸ Audi Fox and Porsche Turbo Carrera, 1977

COME IN AND DRIV

"Legend." That's a pretty strong word, isn't it?

Though we sincerely doubt anyone would consider it too strong when referring to Porsche. After having become possibly the foremost name in racing. After almost thirty years of major automotive innovations not only on the track but on the road. Culminating in the Porsche Turbo Carrera, a car built with such painstaking pride and to such exacting standards that it takes twelve days to build one.

And Audi's credentials are equally impressive.

You probably didn't know it, but Audi has a history that dates all the way

The 1977 AUDI

Our $5445* Audi Fox Sedan with new aerodynamic front-end design and fuel-injected engine which propels the car from 0 to 50 in 8 seconds yet delivers EPA estimated 36 mpg on the highway and 24 in the city for standard shift model (mileage may vary with driver, car's condition and equipment). *Suggested 1977 retail price, P.O.E. Transportation, local taxes, and dealer delivery charges, additional. Whitewalls optional.

ONE OF OUR LEGENDS.

back to 1904 (that's before the Model T). A history that includes a succession of accomplishments on the track and on the road. (Would you believe back in the 30s we had such advanced features as front-wheel drive and dual braking systems?)

But more important than any specific feature of either car is a dedication to engineering excellence and innovation that has been a hallmark of Porsches and Audis through the years. That has separated them from other cars. That has made them more than just…cars.

PORSCHE
+AUDI

The 1977 PORSCHE

Our $28,000* Porsche Turbo Carrera: Not only the fastest production car Porsche ever built (0 to 60 in less than 6 seconds) but the most luxurious (supple leather seats, deep-cut pile carpeting, automatic temperature control, even 4-speaker stereo). *Suggested 1977 retail price, P.O.E. Transportation, local

The answer to low cost transportation is simplicity itself.

Maverick, the original "simple machine," is answering a lot of questions...

Fewer repair bills? Simple. According to an independent survey, Maverick has the lowest frequency-of-repair record of any American car.

Better gas mileage? Simple. In simulated city/suburban driving, the standard 100-horsepower-six engine delivers an average of 22 miles per gallon. Less servicing? Simple. One-sixth as many lube jobs and one-half as many oil changes as the leading import. Easier parking? Simple. Maverick has the smallest turning circle of any U.S. compact. Longer life? Simple. Unitized body, deep-down rustproofing and four coats of electrostatically applied paint. And with Maverick, you can choose 2-door, 4-door or sporty Grabber model—with any of three sixes or V-8.

Any more questions? See the simple machine at your Ford Dealer's.

MAVERICK
The Simple Machine

MAVERICK 

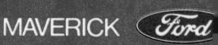

Ford Maverick, 1971 ◂

Ford tried again to reclaim the mantle of value leader, offering economy and durability for the middle of the American market, but its Maverick lacked reliability.

Wirtschaftlichkeit und Langlebigkeit im mittleren Marktsegment bietend, versuchte Ford nochmals, den Pokal für die höchste Wertigkeit zurückzuerlangen, doch dem Maverick mangelte es an Zuverlässigkeit.

Ford tente à nouveau de regagner le titre de meilleur constructeur en termes de rapport qualité/prix en lançant des modèles économiques et durables de milieu de gamme sur le marché américain, mais le manque de fiabilité de la Maverick lui sera fatal.

Ford Mustang, 1971

Control and balance make it a beautiful experience.

You don't sail a boat just to get across the water.

The fun is in the doing.

The pleasure of motion under control.

Mustang drivers understand tha If all they wanted was to get from here to there, they'd be driving something else. Not a Ford Musta

With independent front suspension and an anti-sway bar to give you good control, good road handling.

With bucket seats to position yo comfortably behind the wheel.

With a cockpit design and floor mounted shift that give you a beautiful feeling the instant you'r inside.

There are five sporty Mustang models: Hardtop, SportsRoof, Convertible, Mach 1, Grandé. And a selection of five engines, three transmissions. What it takes to make driving a beautiful experience is what Ford puts into Mustang.

1972 Mustang Mach 1

FORD MUSTAN

FORD DIVISION Ford

INTRODUCING THE NEW BREED
Presenting a whole New Breed of Mustang for '79. Dramatic new sports car styling gives this Mustang one of the most efficient aerodynamic designs of any car now built in America. Mustang's precise handling helps it flatten corners. Choose from four engines: a standard 2.3 litre overhead cam, and options of V-6, V-8 ... even a Turbocharged Mustang. And with all this, Mustang is still sticker priced to help you bring one home, in 2- or 3-door models. Capture one at your Ford Dealer now.
FORD MUSTANG
FORD DIVISION
Ford
FORD MUSTANG '79

Ford Mustang, 1979

Ford Mustang, 1972 ◂

▸▸ Mercedes-Benz 450SEL, 1976

How to tell a Mercedes-Benz 450SEL from all the rest.

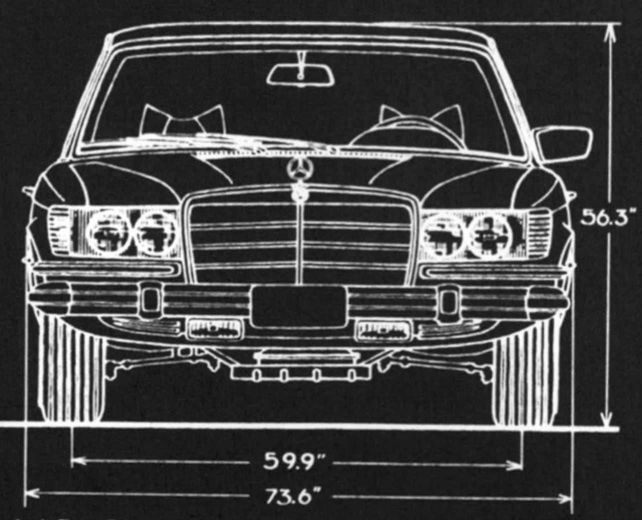

450 SEL

CONTEMPORARY VERSION OF CLASSIC TOURING CAR. TRIM EXTERIOR SIZE, UNUSUALLY GENEROUS INTERIOR ROOM. A LIMITED EDITION AUTOMOBILE.

UNIQUE ENGINE: 8 CYLINDERS, V-TYPE, OVERHEAD CAMSHAFT. BREAKERLESS TRANSISTORIZED IGNITION. C.I.S. MECHANICALLY-OPERATED FUEL INJECTION. ELECTRIC FUEL PUMP. FORGED STEEL CRANKSHAFT. SODIUM FILLED EXHAUST VALVES. LIGHT ALLOY CYLINDER HEAD.

CONTROL PANEL.

- ADJUSTABLE AIR VENTS.
- AUTOMATIC CLIMATE CONTROL.
- AM/FM STEREO RADIO WITH ADJUSTABLE ELECTRIC ANTENNA.
- ELECTRICALLY OPERATED WINDOWS.

- 3-SPEED AUTOMATIC TRANSMISSION WITH TORQUE CONVERTER.
- FULL INSTRUMENTATION PLUS TACHOMETER.
- CRUISE CONTROL.

POWER STEERING: RECIRCULATING BALL-TYPE. TURNING CIRCLE: 39'. TELESCOPIC STEERING COLUMN. ADDITIONAL SHOCK ABSORBER DAMPENS ROAD VIBRATIONS.

STEERING GEAR CASE: LOCATED BEHIND FRONT AXLE FOR SAFETY.

COLLAPSIBLE EXTREMITIES, RIGID PASSENGER SHELL.

GAS TANK: MOUNTED OVER REAR AXLE, 45 INCHES IN FROM REAR BUMPER AND SURROUNDED BY STEEL BULKHEADS

SAFETY BUMPERS: RUBBER PROTECTED WITH HYDRAULIC REGENERATIVE SHOCK ABSORBERS.

34.4" 38.6" 37.1" 19.6" 19.4" 41.7" 38.1"
116.7"
209.4"

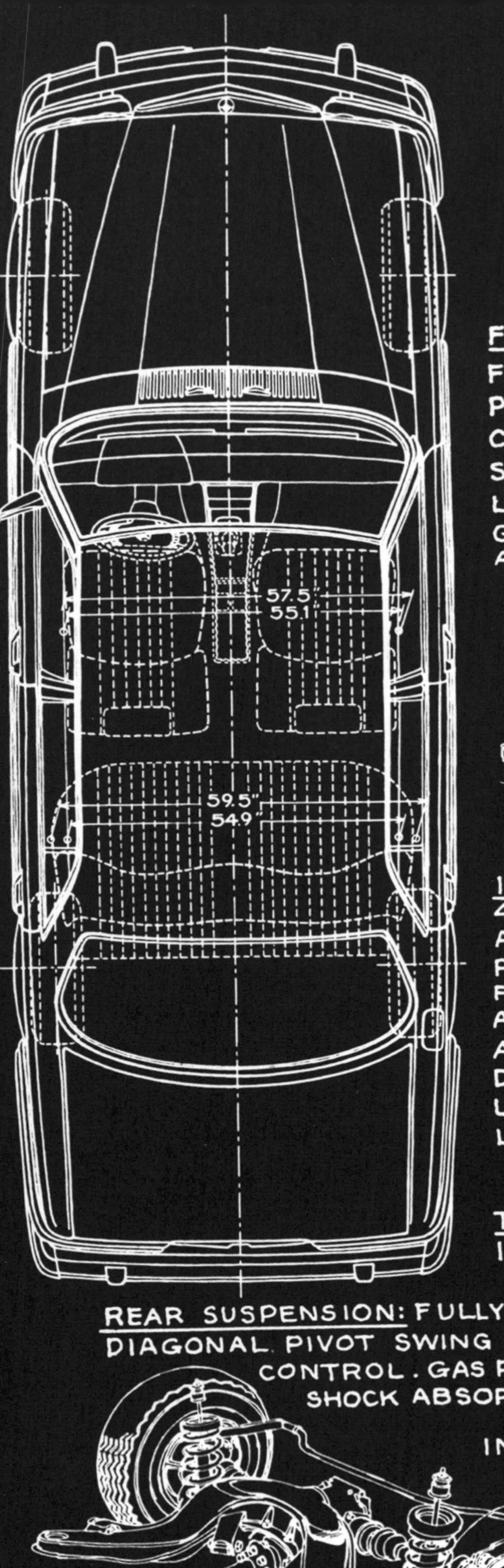

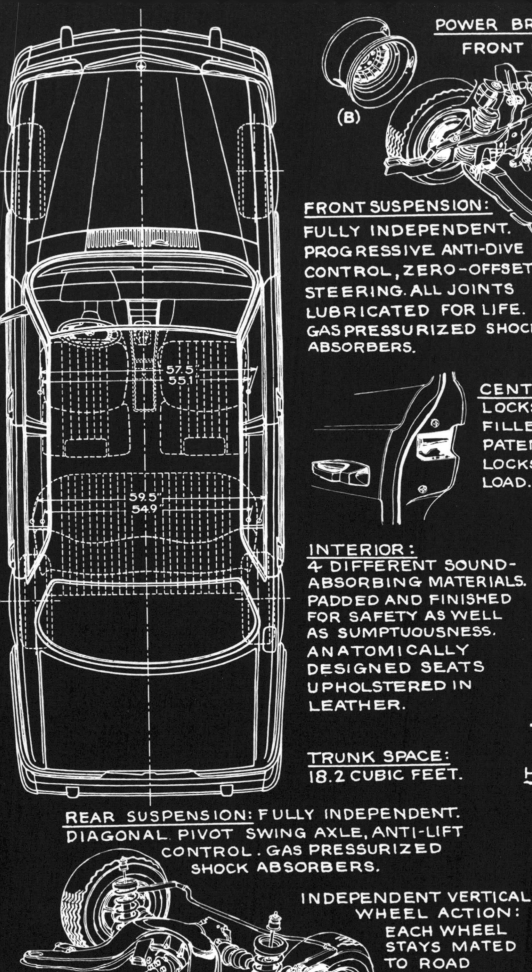

POWER BRAKES: 4-WHEEL DISCS (A). FRONT DISCS VENTILATED. FURTHER COOLED BY TURBOBLADES (B). AUXILIARY DRUM BRAKES ON REAR WHEELS. DUAL HYDRAULIC SYSTEM FOR SAFETY.

(B)

FRONT SUSPENSION:
FULLY INDEPENDENT. PROGRESSIVE ANTI-DIVE CONTROL, ZERO-OFFSET STEERING. ALL JOINTS LUBRICATED FOR LIFE. GAS PRESSURIZED SHOCK ABSORBERS.

CENTRAL LOCKING SYSTEM:
LOCKS ALL DOORS, TRUNK, GAS FILLER PORT IN ONE MOTION. PATENTED TAPERED CONE DOOR LOCKS WITHSTAND OVER 6000 LB. LOAD.

INTERIOR:
4 DIFFERENT SOUND-ABSORBING MATERIALS. PADDED AND FINISHED FOR SAFETY AS WELL AS SUMPTUOUSNESS. ANATOMICALLY DESIGNED SEATS UPHOLSTERED IN LEATHER.

TRUNK SPACE:
18.2 CUBIC FEET.

HOOD ORNAMENT: SINCE 1886, SYMBOL OF AUTOMOBILES ENGINEERED LIKE NO OTHER CARS IN THE WORLD.

REAR SUSPENSION: FULLY INDEPENDENT. DIAGONAL PIVOT SWING AXLE, ANTI-LIFT CONTROL. GAS PRESSURIZED SHOCK ABSORBERS.

INDEPENDENT VERTICAL WHEEL ACTION: EACH WHEEL STAYS MATED TO ROAD SURFACE.

450 SEL TOURING SEDAN	
SEATING: 5	
Nº 1160011299	
© MERCEDES-BENZ OF NORTH AMERICA INC. 1976	

New Ford Ranchero...the pickup car!

If you've an idea Ford's all-new Ranchero is a high-spirited sports car, you're right. If you think Ranchero is a handy, hard-working pickup, right again. For Ranchero is a beautiful blending of both. It offers a ride that's both smoother and quieter with a wheelbase that's four inches longer than last year. New strength and durability with a solid big-car frame. And clean responsive handling with a new link coil rear suspension. Front disc brakes are standard, and you can choose any of six spirited engines up to a 429 V8. Big new loadspace, too, with a new box that's longer at the rail and wider at the floor. 4-foot panels easily slide between wheelhousings. And campers or boaters will welcome a new towing capacity of up to 6,000 pounds. See a Ranchero 500, GT or Squire at your Ford Dealer's soon. With so much that's so right, you can't go wrong.

A better idea for safety: Buckle up.

All-new FORD RANCHERO

Ford

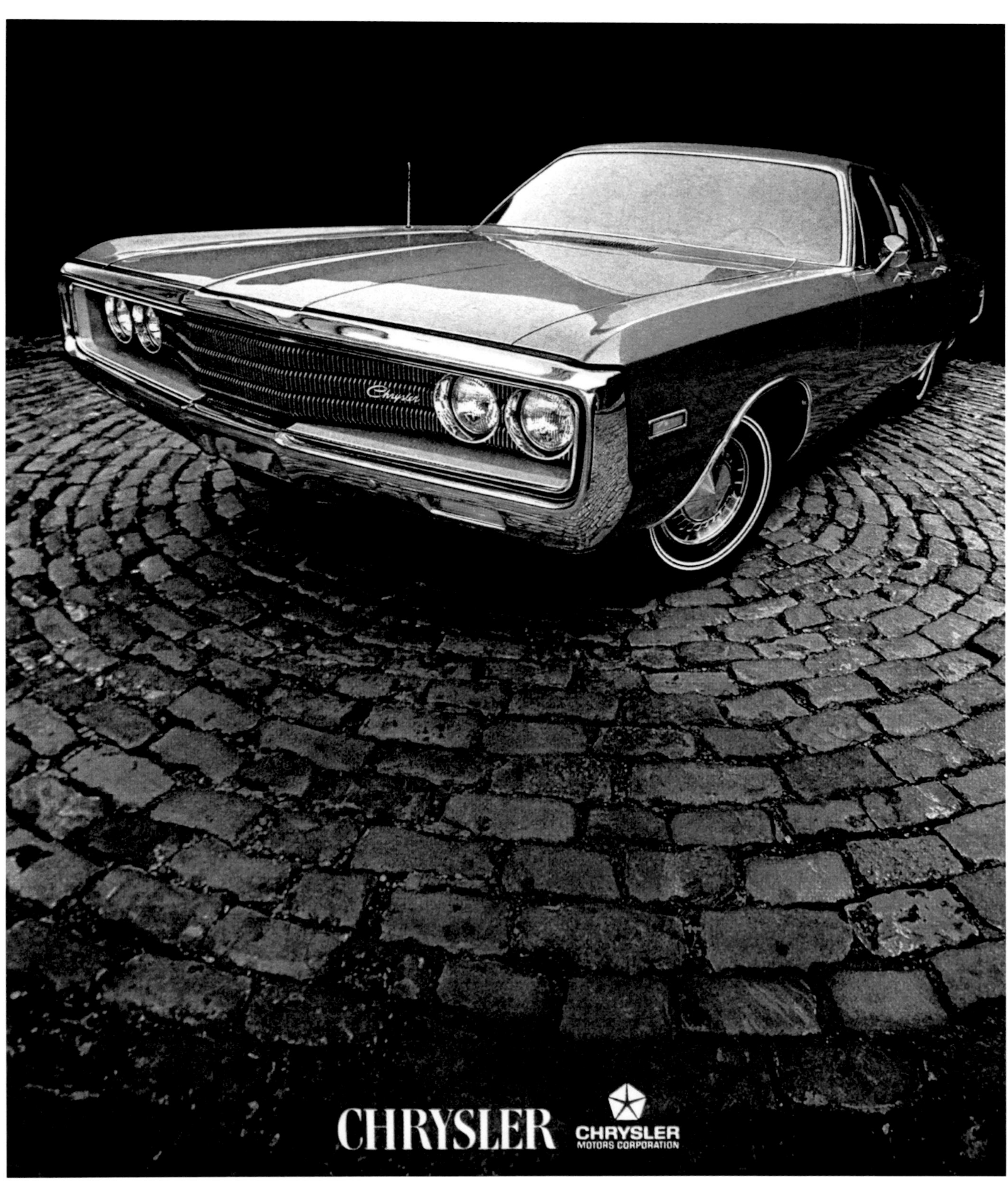

Chrysler, 1970

Ford Ranchero, 1972 ◂

We have a very strong respect for other people's money.

The 1972 mid-size Ford Torino is very strong proof of it.

The new Torino now has a rugged body/frame construction like our quiet Ford LTD.

And a tough new rear suspension.

Torino's even built a little heavier and a little wider this year.

It's so solid on the road, steady on the curves and smooth on the bumps, we've been calling it the "Easy Handler."

Torino's even bigger inside.

With Torino's standard front disc brakes, you *stop*. Really Stop!

And you'll like the reassuringly positive feel of Torino's new integral power steering. (It's optional.)

And Ford did all this to make Torino a better value for you...quite possibly more car than you expected.

And quiet because it's a Ford.

Find out at your local Ford Dealer's.

Gran Torino Hardtop. One of 9 new models. Bucket seat interior, vinyl roof, wheel trim rings and white sidewall tires are optional.

More car than you expected.

FORD TORINO

FORD DIVISION Ford

American Motors Gremlin, 1973

The struggling American Motors Corporation, cobbled together from the wreckage of several defunct brands, tried to get by on novel designs and low prices. AMC design chief Richard A. Teague came up with the highly successful Gremlin, which was promoted as the first subcompact designed and manufactured entirely in the United States.

Aus den traurigen Resten diverser untergegangener Marken zusammengefügt, versuchte die angeschlagene American Motors Corporation sich mit neuen Designs und niedrigen Preisen zu behaupten. AMCs Chefdesigner Richard A. Teague kreierte den sehr erfolgreichen Gremlin – beworben als der erste in den USA entworfene und auch zur Gänze gefertigte Kleinwagen.

Fondée sur les cendres de diverses marques, la firme American Motors tente de surmonter ses difficultés grâce à un design novateur et à des prix bas. La Gremlin dessinée par le designer en chef Richard A. Teague remporte alors un énorme succès. Sa promotion souligne qu'il s'agit de la première subcompacte entièrement conçue et manufacturée aux États-Unis.

Ford Torino, 1972 ◂

Anatomy of a Gremlin

1. Gremlin is the only little economy car with a standard 6-cylinder engine.
2. Reaches turnpike speed easily.
3. Weighs more than other small cars. And its wheels are set wider apart.
4. Has a wider front seat.
5. A wider back seat.
6. And more headroom in the trunk.

And only American Motors makes this promise: The Buyer Protection Plan backs every '73 car we build. And we'll see that our dealers back that promise.

AMERICAN MOTORS BUYER PROTECTION PLAN

1. A simple, strong guarantee, just 101 words! When you buy a new 1973 car from an American Motors dealer, American Motors Corporation guarantees to you that, except for tires, it will pay for the repair or replacement of any part it supplies that is defective in material or workmanship. This guarantee is good for 12 months from the date the car is first used or 12,000 miles, whichever comes first. All we require is that the car be properly maintained and cared for under normal use and service in the fifty United States or Canada, and that guaranteed repairs or replacement be made by an American Motors dealer.
2. A free loaner car from almost every one of our dealers if guaranteed repairs take overnight.
3. Special Trip Interruption Protection.
4. And a toll free hot line to AMC Headquarters.

AMC Gremlin

We back them better because we build them better.

▸ Ford Pinto, 1972

Ford tried to position its Pinto as a successor to the Model T in terms of durability and value. But the public didn't buy it. Gas tanks that exploded in rear-end collisions eventually turned the name Pinto into a grim, television-talk-show punch line.

Ford suchte seinen Pinto als Nachfolger des Model T in Sachen Beständigkeit und Hochwertigkeit zu positionieren – allerdings ohne Erfolg. Tanks, die bei Auffahrunfällen explodierten, machten den Namen Pinto zur Pointe derber Witze in spätabendlichen TV-Shows.

Ford tente de positionner la Pinto comme le successeur du modèle T en termes de durabilité et de rapport qualité/prix, mais le public n'adhère pas. Parce qu'il arrivait que son réservoir explose en cas de collision arrière, ce modèle a suscité nombre de plaisanteries morbides.

Chevrolet Vega, 1971

THE LITTLE CAR THAT GROWS ON YOU.

There are two ways of looking at the Vega Hatchback Coupe.

One, you can look at it as a sporty little 2-seater which, unlike most sporty little 2-seaters, has a back seat you can flip up on those rare occasions when you have three or four people aboard.

Or you can look at it as a sporty little 4-seater which, unlike a lot of sporty little 4-seaters, has a back seat you can flip down when you have a lot of stuff to haul, like on Saturday.

The Vega Hatchback was designed from the outset to be a Hatchback.

It isn't an afterthought.

It is a beautifully balanced, beautifully engineered car with a lot more than just a lot of loadspace to entice you.

There's Vega's surprisingly responsive overhead cam engine, for example. And standard front disc brakes. A double-panel steel roof, side-guard beams in the doors, a 50,000-mile air cleaner, even an electric fuel pump that cuts out to stop the car if the oil pressure ever drops too low.

Vega. It grows on you.

And it's growing on America.

GM
MARK OF EXCELLENCE

Buckle your seat and shoulder belts.
It's an idea you can live with.

We've come a long way from basic black.

1926 Ford Model T Coupe.

1972 Ford Pinto Runabout with Sprint Decor Option.

If you find yourself staring whenever you see a Model "T" go by, we don't blame you. It was some kind of car. (Even if it did come mostly in black.) It was simple. It was tough. And if something went wrong, you could probably fix it with a screwdriver and a pair of pliers.

Pinto has many of those same qualities. Which is good to know if you're the kind of person who likes cars, and likes to work on them. Pinto is the kind of car you can work on, without having to be some kind of master mechanic. It's also a car you can work with. There are lots of things you can add—both from Pinto's list of options and from the specialty equipment people. If you start with the Sprint Option we've shown, you don't even have to start with basic black.

Sprint Decor Group includes the following equipment: Red, White and Blue Exterior Accents. Trim Rings with Color-Keyed Hubcaps. Dual Racing Mirrors. Red, White and Blue Cloth and Vinyl Bucket Seats. Full Carpeting. Deluxe 2-Spoke Steering Wheel. Stars and Stripes Decal. A78 x 13 White Sidewall Tires. Blackout Grille.

When you get back to basics, you get back to Ford.

FORD PINTO

Better idea for safety...buckle up!

FORD DIVISION

Do you hear vibrations? We don't. Horizontally-opposed engine at work. Quiet.

Do you have front-wheel drive? We do. Our front-wheel drive makes safety corners, surefoot curves, holds the road, zips through ice or snow. Power to the front wheels!

Turning circle. Just 31.5 easy little feet. Feet smaller than you-know-whose.

Inboard brakes. We've taken our front brakes out of the wheels which gives you 1: a remarkable stable ride with 2: marvelously light-handed steering.

Hey, racing fans. Rack-and-pinion steering.

2 doors not enough? For about $100 more, we can also give you 4.

What? Your back windows don't open? Ours do.

Oh, the room in the trunk; it boggles the mind. How do you like 6 full sets of golf-clubs plus 3 hefty suitcases? We like 48 soccer balls.

THE WHAT?

Look. No fan, no fan belt. Listen. No fan noise. Learn. It takes a lot of horses to drive the fan. We use ours to drive the car.

How do we keep it cool? With two radiators, not one. And a clever thermostatic device that automatically takes over when the going gets hot.

Where's the spare? With the jack and the engine locked under the hood. Doesn't everybody?

6-footer leg-room up front. And nobody has to ride side-saddle in back.

Oh, my aching back? Not in our Subaru. An orthopedist designed our seats. Anatomical, adjustable, and ahhh, reclining.

You know what's missing? That hump in the floor, thank goodness.

Independent suspension, all 4 wheels. Takes the ump out of bump, even in back.

The price? $1898.40* and not stripped down, but loaded with the options most people buy. *Total suggested retail price. Local taxes, dealer prep, inland freight, etc., extra.

THE SUBARU.

390

The Subaru is not a Japanese Beetle.

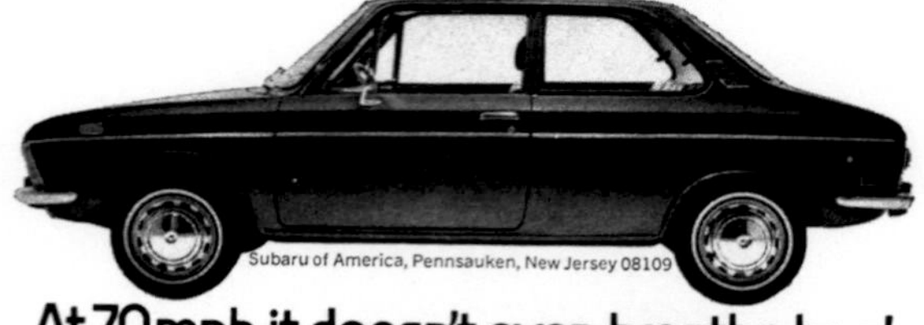

At 70mph it doesn't even breathe hard.

For dealer nearest you, call toll free: 800-631-4299. In New Jersey, 800-962-2803. Subaru. A product of Fuji Heavy Industries Ltd. Japan.

Subaru, 1971

▸ MGB, 1976

▸▸ Ford Econoline Cruising Van and Pinto Cruising Wagon, 1977

MGB presents the world's biggest sunroof.
A super sunroof, a fully-convertible top that opens wide to let the sunshine in: it's standard equipment on every 1976 MGB. Along with the classic look and wide-open performance that have made MG famous for 50 years as one of the world's great sports car bargains.
MGB holds the Class E Championship in the Sports Car Club of America's national competition, as it has for four of the last five years.
Performance like this can't be faked: you can't fool a finish line with a flashy paint job or a fancy name. MGB's authentic sports car performance and crisp handling grow naturally out of standard equipment like radial tires, front disc brakes, short-throw, four-speed stick shift, rack and pinion steering and a race-proven 1798 cc engine.
If what you're driving makes you forget what fun is, take one MGB, fast. For the name of your nearest MG dealer, call these toll-free numbers: (800) 447-4700, or, in Illinois, (800) 322-4400.
MGB the wide-open sports car.
BRITISH LEYLAND MOTORS INC., LEONIA, NEW JERSEY 07605
BRITISH
LEYLAND

TWO MUCH!
New Ford Cruising Wagon.
New Ford Cruising Van.
They come already customized! Forget the time, hassle and hard work of doing it yourself. Ford did it for you. All you add is your personal touch. Whatever size you're looking for, Ford's got it. With outsides as hip as you see them here. The insides—sharp. From new with-it colors to soft shag for comfort—to just about every "trick" in the book. You not only have it made when you go new Ford Cruising Wagon or Van, you have it *custom* made. When America needs a better idea, Ford puts it on wheels.
Wheels shown are optional. Check your local Ford Dealer for availability.
ECONOLINE 150

Cruising Van.
Inside and out—it's ready to roll. Mag-style wheel covers, shag carpeting over entire cargo area, including floor, walls, ceiling, side and rear. Plus! Porthole windows, spare tire and cover, and roof rack. The Industry's first Factory-built completely customized van!
CHATEAU
Firestone
137 PID
Pinto Cruising Wagon.
Part wagon, part van, all fun. Ford's restyled Pinto wagon up front, wide open van room in rear. Has bubbled porthole windows, front spoiler, dual racing mirrors, styled steel wheels with trim rings, and sports rallye package. An Industry exclusive! Choose from many color and tape stripe combinations.
Wild wagon stuff!
A super interior. Stylish and comfortable. A roomy wagon combined with the class and kicks of the hot Van look.
Captain's Chairs for easy livin'.
Great way to ride 'n relax. Swivel to rap, or turn easily to the back. Fold-down arm rests, too.
FORD
FORD DIVISION
Ford

394

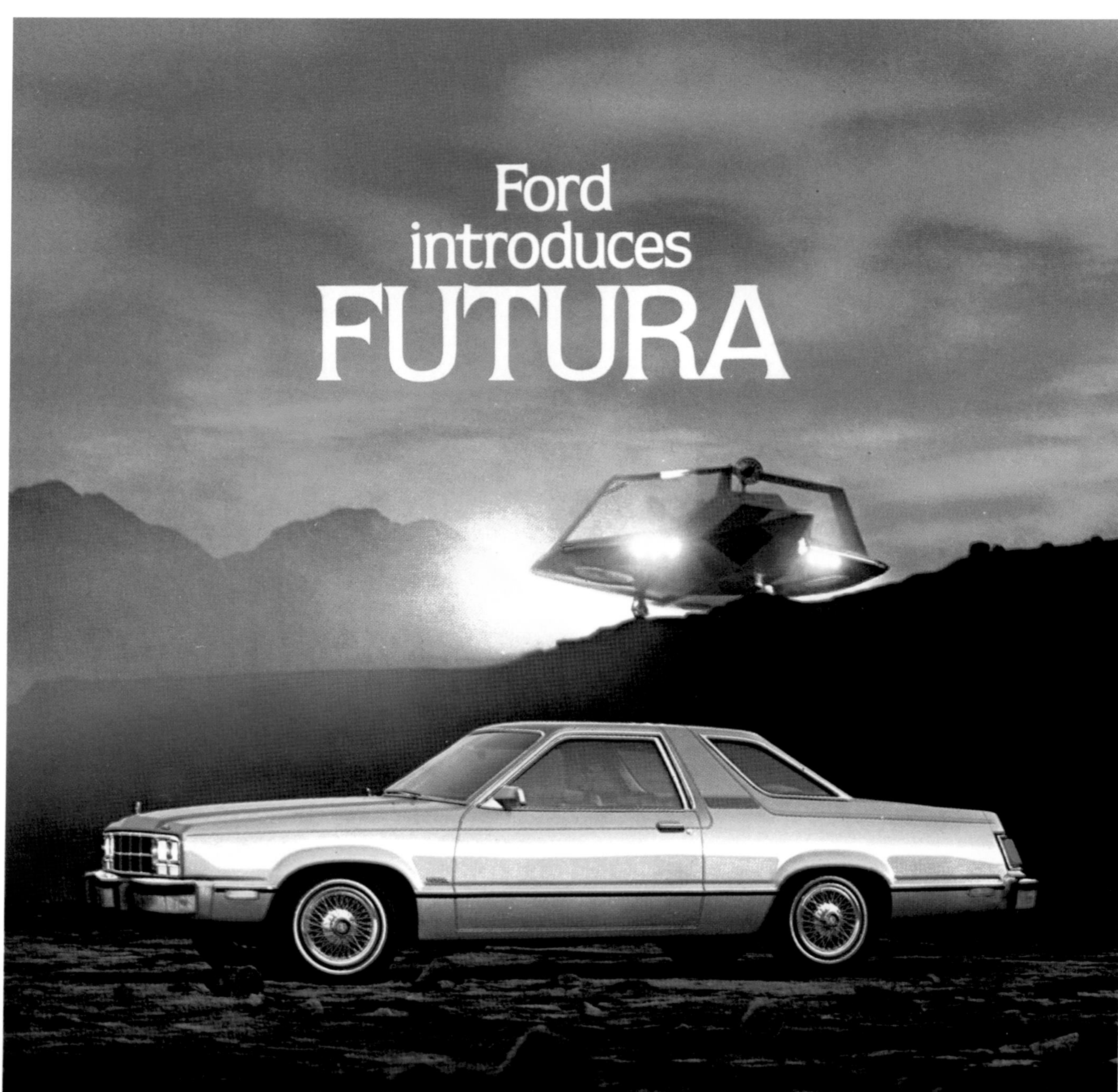

A combination of styling and technology for 1978...and beyond.

Here is a car for the automotive future. With dynamic styling inside and out. Comfort for five passengers, yet fuel and cost efficiency for the years ahead. A car realistically priced for today. The new Futura. Before you consider any other car available today, read on...

Scheduled Maintenance 50,000 miles about $150.*

Futura is a car engineered to hold down the costs of maintenance. Ford estimates that with automatic transmission and Futura's standard engine, 50,000 miles of scheduled maintenance will cost only about $150. (*Based on Ford labor time standards, a $14.50/hour labor rate and Ford's suggested parts prices in effect Aug., 1977.)

33 MPG (hwy) 23 MPG (city)

Futura's EPA mileage estimates—with 2.3 litre engine and manual 4-speed—are the highest of any car in its class. Of course, your actual mileage may vary depending on how you drive, your car's condition and optional equipment. Calif. ratings are lower. Futura is also available with 3.3 litre 6-cylinder and 5.0 litre V-8 engines.

$4,267 as shown

Futura's sticker price excluding taxes, title and destination charges.

Visit your local Ford Dealer for a personal test drive. And find out what's ahead for 1978...and beyond.

The new Futura.

FORD FAIRMONT
FUTURA

FORD DIVISION

Ford
75th ANNIVERSARY

Ford Futura, 1978

► Rolls-Royce Silver Wraith II, 1977

Rolls-Royce brings back a great name. Silver Wraith II.

The last of the Silver Wraiths was built in 1959. Or so it seemed at the time.

But the richest of Rolls-Royce memories have a way of living on in the newest of Rolls-Royce motor cars. And so it is with the Silver Wraith II of 1977.

The Timeless Pleasure

The long, sleek look of the Silver Wraith II reflects a time gone by.

You can sense it in the graceful lines, the contrasting top, the gleaming bright work, the tasteful craftsmanship and the roomy interior.

And, for the most up-to-date reasons, the Silver Wraith II is a new air of comfort, a new sense of quiet and a new feeling of command.

A new rack-and-pinion steering system makes the Silver Wraith II quick to respond and rewarding to drive, no matter how narrow the road or sudden the curve.

A unique automatic air-conditioning system maintains any temperature you desire at two levels of the interior. And, because the system creates a rarefied atmosphere all your own, its built-in sensors alert you to outside temperatures as well as icy roads.

The Silver Wraith II also offers you the sophistication of an advanced electrical system, the performance of a quiet V-8 engine, the security of a dual braking system and the sensitivity of a self-leveling suspension.

And, to name one of the many other subtle details you'll discover, the electronic odometer will contemplate recording the miles from 000000.0 to 999999.9.

The Priceless Asset

From the distinctive radiator grille to the matching walnut veneers, the Silver Wraith II is built almost entirely by hand.

In tribute to this enduring Rolls-Royce tradition, it is no coincidence that more than half of all the motor cars we have ever built remain very much on the road.

And, in return for the purchase price of $49,000,* it is little wonder that a Silver Wraith II speaks so warmly of the past and so surely of the future.

A collection of Rolls-Royce masterpieces is waiting at your nearest Authorized Rolls-Royce Dealership. For further information, call 800-325-6000 and give this ID number: 1000.

*Suggested U.S. Retail Price March 1, 1977.

The heart and soul of a masterpiece
ROLLS
RR
ROYCE

Economical Family Transportation Doesn't Have To Be Dull.

IT'S MORE FUN TO TAKE THE BUS.

Has the size of your family driven you into a car you can't afford? Does the car that fits your budget squeeze the fun out of your family? If so, you've missed the Bus. The 1978 Volkswagen Bus.

The '78 Bus costs less than most big station wagons. And to run, it's ahead by miles. The Bus' peppy, fuel-injected, two-liter engine is not only quiet, it's also very economical. It helps the Bus deliver an estimated 25 mpg on the highway, 17 in the city with standard transmission, according to the 1978 EPA tests. (Of course, actual mileage may vary depending on how and where you drive, optional equipment, such as automatic transmission, and the condition of your Bus.)

And nothing beats the Bus for family fun. It's easy to park, easy to handle, and it gives everyone in your family enough elbow room to relax in comfort. With space left over for your dog, your luggage, or just about anything else you want to carry. The Bus is 70% roomier inside than a full-sized domestic station wagon. And with the Bus' eight picture windows, everyone in the family gets the best seat in the house. And that's not all. The VW Bus is very versatile. The rear seat folds down to provide extra carrying space and that rear hatch and big sliding door lets you load everything from antiques to zithers.

So, when you want to uncramp your family's style, nothing compares to the Bus.

See your Volkswagen dealer today. And prove to yourself it's more fun to take the Bus. The 1978 Volkswagen Bus.

"That's IT"

Just as a great painting is more than canvas and paints, there are some things that go beyond the sum of their parts. The Porsche Targa is such an object.

It is a piece of machinery whose purpose far exceeds transporting you from one point to another. The Targa's goal is to afford the ultimate driving experience. In performance, in engineering, in comfort.

The Targa has come amazingly close to that goal; each year, with subtle improvements, a bit more.

First, consider its superbly thought-out features. It has a built-in roll bar, and a huge fixed rear window. To give the car the practicality of a hardtop coupe. And you the exhilarating experience of a roadster.

It has an aerodynamic shape, to protect you from wind blast. And a rear-engine design that has been steadily improved upon for 25 years.

All controls are meticulously engineered to be functional and logically accessible.

Yet it is the total effect of these innovations that impresses.

With the removable top stored in the trunk, cushioned in luxurious bucket seats, you ride in "Belle Epoque" comfort.

But the grandest feature of the Targa is the experience of driving it.

The handling is quick, correct, precise, because of Porsche's legendary engineering. Putting the driver and car in perfect collaboration. It is almost as if you just "think" where you want the car to go.

The Targa is available in all three 911 models: 911T, 911E, and 911S.

But be warned.

It is very difficult to be humble about owning any Porsche. And if it's a Targa, that's IT.

Porsche 911 Targa, 1973

Volkswagen Bus, 1978 ◂

The exciting new Sedan deVille and Fleetwood Sixty Special Brougham

Never has the introduction of a new Cadillac so dramatically established Cadillac's undeniable leadership in the world of fine motor cars.

All nine of the magnificent 1971 Cadillacs are totally new. They are completely new in looks—with crisper, more classic contours, greater glass area and doors designed to permit easier entry and exit.

They are new in luxury—with a completely redesigned instrument panel, new lower profile seats and a wide selection of rich new fabrics. And they are new in convenience, including a unique light monitoring system available on all models.

You will discover new performance, too. The superb Cadillac ride has never been smoother. The quietness of operation will impress even long-time Cadillac owners. And all Cadillac V-8 engines deliver their famed performance on the new no-lead, low-lead fuels.

See—and drive—the brilliant new 1971 Standard of the World, now at your authorized dealer's. Leadership has never been so elegantly presented.

The new Eldorado. . .the world's most elegant personal cars.

In the Eldorado Coupe and Convertible, Cadillac presents two completely new and completely distinctive automobiles. A new, longer wheelbase provides superb riding qualities and new, more impressive beauty.

Individual touches, such as the jewel-like stand-up crest and the exclusive coach windows on the Coupe, typify the Eldorado's many styling innovations.

The Convertible, now the only luxury convertible built in America, comes equipped with an ingenious new inward-folding Hideaway Top. It provides a more graceful top-down appearance and allows greater room for rear-seat passengers.

Both Eldorados share the same 8.2 litre V-8 (the world's largest production passenger car engine) in combination with the precise handling of front-wheel drive, variable-ratio power steering, power front disc brakes and Automatic Level Control.

Surely, these are the two most excitingly luxurious automobiles in the world of personal motoring . . . the Fleetwood Eldorados by Cadillac.

Cadillac for 1971 the New Look of Leadership

Cadillac Fleetwood, DeVille, and Eldorado, 1971

Length still mattered to the traditional buyer in 1970, and Cadillac was unabashed by its massive models.

Traditionsbewusste Käufer legten auch 1970 weiterhin Wert auf Länge und Cadillac ließ sich das nicht zweimal sagen.

En 1970, la taille importe encore à l'acheteur traditionnel et le constructeur ne lésine pas sur le gigantisme.

► Chrysler Cordoba, 1976

This is Cordoba. The small Chrysler. An automobile in which you will enjoy not only great comfort . . . but great confidence. It is confidence you can see, the confidence of knowing your automobile possesses a look of great dignity. It is confidence you can *feel*, in thickly cushioned contour-seats available in rich crushed velour or soft Corinthian leather. It is confidence you experience when you are in control of a truly road worthy automobile. This is the confidence you will find in a most surprisingly affordable small Chrysler. Cordoba.

We hate to dampen the spirits of other trucks. But scrappage records show Chevy pickups outlast others.

What makes us so tough? For one thing, we use two pieces of sheet metal in our cab. Double-wall it, for strength.

And we build our independent front suspension to expect the worst from a road. Without getting rattled.

Another thing. We just won't leave well enough alone. For instance, you can now order a powerful new additive for regular gas: a 400-cubic-inch V8.

It's not that we're out to make it tough for other trucks. We're out to make it easier for you.

Because putting you first, keeps us first.

You'll still be washing it when other '70's are washed up.

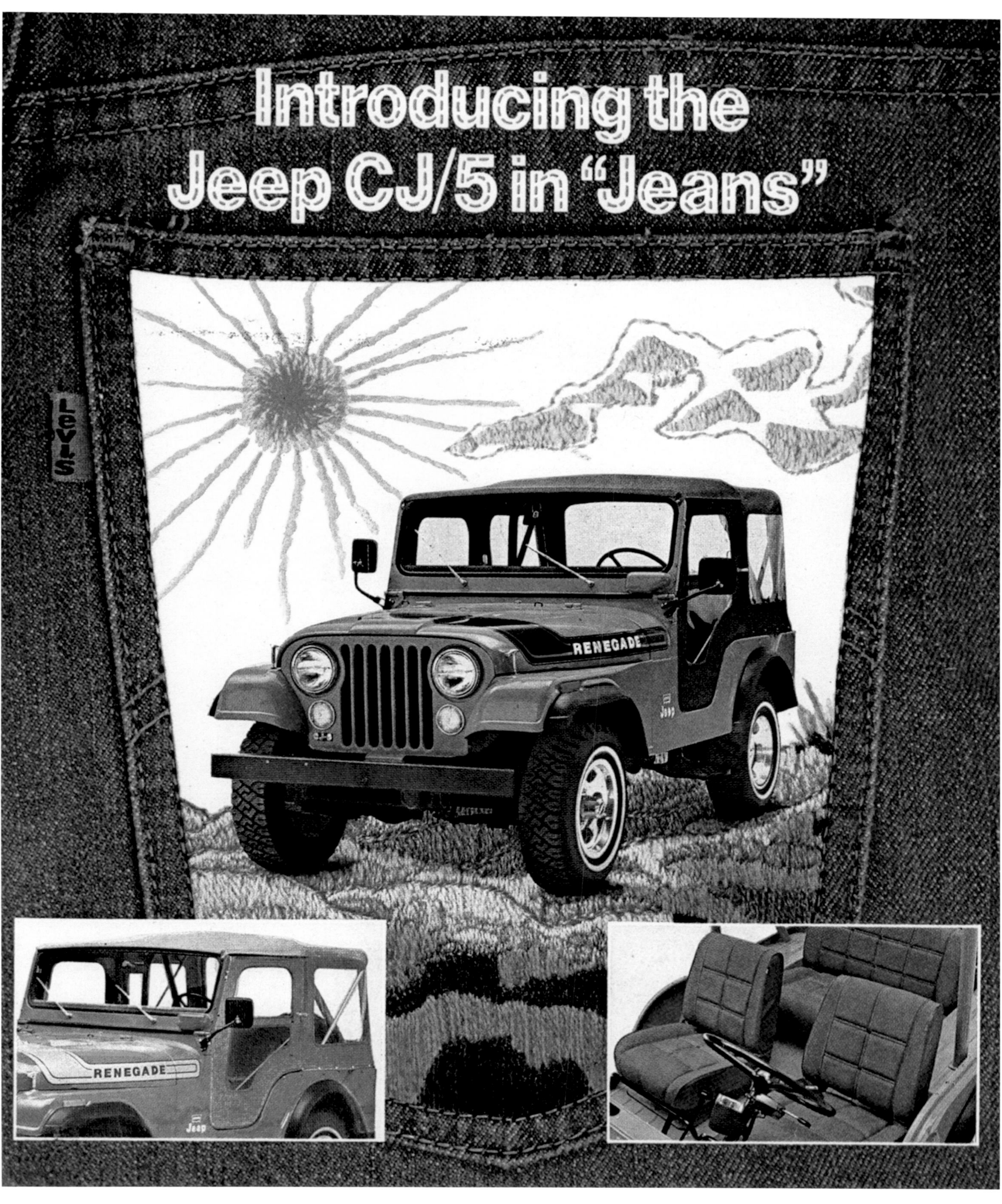

Jeep CJ/5, 1975

Chevrolet Pickup, 1970 ◂

▸▸ Chevrolet Monte Carlo, 1974

THE SLOW TIMES OF THE EARLY 1980S WERE SUCCEEDED BY A BOOM THAT REVELED IN CONSPICUOUS CONSUMPTION IN A WAY NOT SEEN SINCE THE GILDED AGE. "GREED IS GOOD," DECLARED GORDON GEKKO, MICHAEL DOUGLAS'S CHARACTER IN OLIVER STONE'S FILM *WALL STREET* (1987).

AUF DIE TRÄGHEIT DER FRÜHEN ACHTZIGER FOLGTE EIN WAHRER BOOM MIT DEMONSTRATIVEM KONSUM, WIE MAN ES SEIT DEM GOLDENEN ZEITALTER NICHT MEHR ERLEBT HATTE. „GIER IST GUT", ERKLÄRTE MICHAEL DOUGLAS ALS GORDON GEKKO IN OLIVER STONES FILM *WALL STREET* (1987).

LE RALENTISSEMENT DU DÉBUT DES ANNÉES 1980 CÈDE LA PLACE À L'EXPLOSION DE LA CONSOMMATION OSTENTATOIRE, DU JAMAIS VU DEPUIS LA CROISSANCE DE LA FIN DU XIXE SIÈCLE. « LE FRIC, C'EST CHIC », DÉCLARE GORDON GEKKO, PERSONNAGE INTERPRÉTÉ PAR MICHAEL DOUGLAS DANS LE FILM *WALL STREET* (1987), D'OLIVER STONE.

1980

GREED IS GOOD

GIER IST GUT

LE FRIC, C'EST CHIC

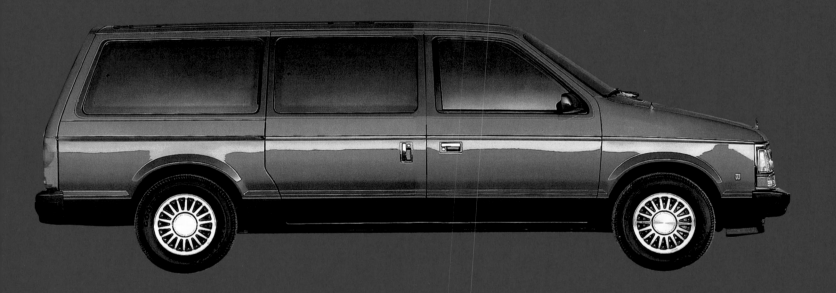

-1989

Driving takes on a new

The Scirocco was not built for this country. It was made to be driven in Germany.

And it is for this precise reason that you should be interested in it.

Consider the following: There is no speed limit on Germany's autobahns.

Think about that for a moment.

Think about the level of engineering required to make a sports car that can respond precisely under such driving conditions.

Now consider the fact that most other sports cars on the market today are created to perform in, shall we say, a less demanding world?

It is this difference of standards th makes the Scirocco superior.

Any test drive will prove it.

When you get into a Scirocco, the fir thing you notice is getting in. The seat set low to the ground.

Now, as you drive along, you'll notic the Scirocco's linear response.

ɔerspective in a Scirocco.

What that means is that the suspen-
on, braking, and steering systems com-
ıunicate with you directly. And they
ɘact predictably to your commands.
s you accelerate down straightaways
nd track through turns, you feel that
ɔu are an integral part of the car.
It's an exhilarating feeling.

To enhance this performance, VW engineers recently broke new ground with techniques as simple as cutting grooves down the roof. Better aerodynamics lessen drag and enable the car to move faster.

What's more, the Scirocco has maximal glass space, making it easier to see everything around you.

But that shouldn't come as a surprise. Like we said at the beginning, the Scirocco gives you a new viewpoint on driving. Seatbelts save lives.

Nothing else is a Volkswagen

Volkswagen Scirocco, 1983 ◄◄

Mercedes-Benz 380SE, 1983 ◄

Pontiac Fiero, 1983

THE U.S. GOVERNMENT LENT CHRYSLER MORE THAN ONE BILLION DOLLARS TO AVOID BANKRUPTCY AND LAYOFFS IN 1980. To persuade citizens this was a good investment, and to persuade customers to buy cars, Chrysler boss Lee Iacocca, trusted as the creator of the Ford Mustang, took to advertising in magazines and on the airwaves as the personal face of the company. Like Henry Ford and Walter Chrysler before him, Iacocca became the spokesman for the company he headed, pushing the bare-bones, basic Chrysler K-cars, such as the Dodge Aries, Plymouth Reliant, and Chrysler LeBaron.

One answer to the new constraints and austerity of the industry came with the "aero" look, pioneered by Ford, which combined a sense of visual excitement—smooth, flowing forms that made for dramatic advertising photos—with practical claims of economy. In the Ford Taurus, which drew from the European lines of the Ford Sierra and Audi 100, the spirit of the streamlined 1930s was reborn, but with a practical argument to consumers: reducing drag by streamlining increased fuel mileage.

The slow times of the early 1980s were succeeded by a boom that reveled in conspicuous consumption in a way not seen since the Gilded Age. "Greed is good," declared Gordon Gekko, Michael Douglas's character in Oliver Stone's film *Wall Street* (1987). Now, greed was directed at new models. Until the 1970s, luxury European cars had been a minority taste. Despite technical and safety advantages, Mercedes and BMW sold only a fraction of the number of cars registered by Cadillac and Lincoln. But the '80s saw that change; BMW, in particular, became a new status symbol.

Entirely new types of vehicles were now available to consumers: The minivan, developed by Chrysler in 1983 as the Dodge Caravan, Plymouth Voyager, and Chrysler Town and Country, succeeded the station wagon as America's favorite family car. General Motors' "dust buster"-style minivan and Ford's Aerostar never quite caught on, and the minivan eventually became burdened with a soccer-mom image that left many males unwilling to be seen in them.

Far more macho was the sport-utility vehicle, or SUV. Based on the Jeep or pickup truck with a shell added on, the SUV began with the old Jeepster, the Jeep Cherokee, and the International Harvester Scout. Ford's crude Bronco arrived in the 1970s, but its more refined Explorer helped lead the transition to SUVs. Introduced in 1990, the Explorer was the quintessential suburban SUV, combining luxury features with towing capacity, lots of interior space, and other practical elements. It rarely left the pavement, of course, but it carried kids and groceries.

1980

1980 Mercedes-Benz introduces airbags as Supplemental Restraint System (SRS)

Airbags als Bestandteil des Insassen-Rückhaltesystems von Mercedes-Benz eingeführt

Mercedes-Benz lance le coussin gonflable de sécurité, ou airbag

1980 *Magnum*, P.I. TV series debuts, starring Tom Selleck and a Ferarri 308 GTS

Start der Fernsehserie *Magnum* mit Tom Selleck und seinem Ferrari 308 GTS

Débuts de la série *Magnum*, avec Tom Selleck et sa Ferrari 308 GTS

1981 Giorgetto Giugiaro-designed DeLorean DMC-12 sports car unveiled

Vorstellung des von Giorgetto Giugiaro entworfenen Sportwagens DeLorean DMC-12

Lancement de la DeLorean DMC-12 dessinée par Giorgetto Giugiaro

1982 Honda becomes first Japanese carmaker to open plant in U.S.

Honda eröffnet als erster japanischer Autobauer ein Werk in den USA

Honda est le premier constructeur japonais à s'installer aux États-Unis

DIE US-REGIERUNG HATTE CHRYSLER 1980 MEHR ALS EINE MILLIARDE DOLLAR GELIEHEN, UM KONKURS UND ENTLASSUNGEN ABZUWENDEN. Mit dem Ziel, die Bürger davon zu überzeugen, dass dieses Geld gut angelegt sei und um sie zum Autokauf anzuregen, ging Chrysler-Boss Lee Iacocca, dem man als Schöpfer des Ford Mustang vertraute, dazu über, in Zeitschriften und Rundfunk persönlich für sein Unternehmen zu werben. Wie bereits Henry Ford und Walter Chrysler vor ihm, machte Iacocca sich zum persönlichen Sprecher des Unternehmens, dem er vorstand, und warb für die einfachen, eine gemeinsame Plattform besitzenden „K-Cars" wie den Dodge Aries, Plymouth Reliant und Chrysler LeBaron.

Ford reagierte auf den neuen Sparzwang mit dem „Aero-Look", einer Kombination aus optischer Attraktivität (die fließenden Formen ermöglichten dramatische Werbefotos) und handfester Sparsamkeit. Mit dem am europäischen Ford Sierra und Audi 100 orientierten Ford Taurus erlebte die Stromlinien-Idee der Dreißiger eine Renaissance, diesmal jedoch verbunden mit dem praktischen Argument einer größeren Reichweite dank geringerem Luftwiderstand.

Auf die Trägheit der frühen Achtziger folgte ein wahrer Boom mit demonstrativem Konsum, wie man es seit dem Goldenen Zeitalter nicht mehr erlebt hatte. „Gier ist gut", erklärte Michael Douglas als Gordon Gekko in Oliver Stones Film *Wall Street* (1987). Nun gierte man nach neuen Automodellen. Bis in die 1970er-Jahre hatten europäische Luxuskarossen nur eine Minderheit angesprochen. Trotz (sicherheits)technischer Vorteile erzielten Mercedes und BMW nur einen Bruchteil der Verkaufszahlen von Cadillac und Lincoln. Das sollte sich in den Achtzigern ändern, denn vor allem BMW stieg zum neuen Statussymbol auf.

Den Kunden standen nun auch ganz neue Autotypen zur Verfügung: 1983 von Chrysler als Dodge Caravan, Plymouth Voyager und Chrysler Town and Country eingeführt, trat der Minivan die Nachfolge des Kombis als beliebtestes US-Familienauto an. Der einem Handstaubsauger ähnelnde Minivan von GM und der Aerostar von Ford vermochten nie so recht Fuß zu fassen. Und auf dem Minivan lastete zunehmend ein „Fußball-Mutti-Image", weshalb viele Männer sich nur ungern in einem solchen Gefährt blicken ließen.

Viel männlicher war dagegen ein SUV. Basierend auf einem geschlossenen Jeep oder Pick-up nahm das Sport Utility Vehicle mit dem alten Jeepster, dem Jeep Cherokee und dem International Harvester Scout seinen Anfang. In den Siebzigern folgte der gröbere Ford Bronco, doch erst der gediegenere Explorer beschleunigte die Hinwendung zu den SUVs. Luxus mit Zugkraft, reichlich Platz und weiteren praktischen Merkmalen vereinend, war der 1990 eingeführte Explorer gleichsam die Quintessenz des suburbanen SUV. Selbstredend ließ er den Asphalt nur selten hinter sich, doch er beförderte die Kinder und Einkäufe.

1983

1983 Motorola DynaTAC 8000x first cellular mobile phone; initially sells for $3995

Erstes Mobiltelefon: Das Motorola DynaTAC 8000x kostet zunächst stattliche 3995 US-Dollar

Premier téléphone portable commercialisé par Motorola : DynaTAC 8000x (3 995 dollars)

1983 American Motors first to offer remote keyless entry systems

Funkfernbedienung erstmals von American Motors angeboten

American Motors est le premier à proposer le système d'accès à distance sans clé

1984 Chrysler introduces first minivans: Dodge Caravan and Plymouth Voyager

Chrysler präsentiert mit dem Dodge Caravan und Plymouth Voyager die ersten Minivans

Chrysler lance les premiers monospaces : le Dodge Caravan et le Plymouth Voyager

1986 Ford's new "aero" style Taurus resembles Audi 100 and European Ford Scorpio

Mit seinem „Aero-Look" ähnelt Fords neuer Taurus dem Audi 100 und dem europäischen Ford Scorpio

La nouvelle Ford Taurus au style « aérodynamique » rappelle l'Audi 100 et la Ford Scorpio

Ford
RADIAL
GOODYEAR
Get it together—Buckle up!

Renault 18i, 1981 ◄◄

Ford Bronco II, 1985 ◄

►► Jensen Car Audio, 1984

EN 1980, LE GOUVERNEMENT AMÉRICAIN PRÊTE À CHRYSLER PLUS D'UN MILLIARD DE DOLLARS POUR EMPÊCHER DÉPÔT DE BILAN ET LICENCIEMENTS. Afin de convaincre le citoyen de la valeur de cet investissement et de persuader le consommateur d'acheter ses voitures, Lee Iacocca, le patron de Chrysler auquel on doit la Ford Mustang, devient l'ambassadeur de la firme dans la presse et à la radio. Comme Henry Ford et Walter Chrysler avant lui, Iacocca devient le porte-parole de l'entreprise qu'il dirige et vante ses modèles les plus basiques : Dodge Aries, Plymouth Reliant et Chrysler LeBaron, autrement dit les modèles K.

En réponse aux nouvelles contraintes et à l'austérité qui s'imposent au secteur automobile, on voit surgir le look « aéro » lancé par Ford ; il allie esthétique – formes arrondies et fluides, parfaitement adaptées à la mise en scène dans les photos publicitaires – et fonctionnalité, comme l'exige l'économie. Avec la Ford Taurus, inspirée des lignes européennes de la Ford Sierra et de l'Audi 100, on retrouve l'esprit aérodynamique des années 1930, mâtiné d'arguments pratiques à l'adresse du consommateur : réduire les frottements en perfectionnant l'aérodynamisme améliore le taux de consommation de carburant.

Le ralentissement du début des années 1980 cède la place à l'explosion de la consommation ostentatoire, du jamais vu depuis la croissance de la fin du XIXe siècle. « Le fric, c'est chic », déclare Gordon Gekko, personnage interprété par Michael Douglas dans le film *Wall Street* (1987), d'Oliver Stone. Désormais, le chic, c'est l'Europe. Jusque dans les années 1970, les voitures de luxe européennes ne plaisaient qu'à une minorité d'Américains. Malgré leurs avantages sur les plans de la technique et de la sécurité, Mercedes et BMW ne vendaient qu'une fraction de véhicules par rapport à Cadillac et Lincoln. Dans les années 1980, la tendance s'inverse : BMW, en particulier, devient un nouvel emblème de statut social.

Des types de véhicules entièrement nouveaux s'offrent désormais au consommateur : le monospace, élaboré par Chrysler en 1983 pour les Dodge Caravan, Plymouth Voyager et Chrysler « Town and Country », remplace le break au rang de véhicule familial préféré de l'Amérique. Néanmoins, le monospace style « aspirateur » de General Motors et l'Aerostar de Ford ne marcheront jamais vraiment, car le monospace est rapidement associé à l'image de la femme au foyer qui fait le taxi pour ses enfants, de sorte que beaucoup d'hommes répugnent à se laisser voir au volant de ce type de voiture.

Le SUV convient beaucoup mieux au macho. Tenant à la fois de la Jeep ou du pick-up et de la voiture de luxe, ce 4x4 de ville est un hériter des modèles Jeepster, Jeep Cherokee et International Harvester Scout. Au rudimentaire Ford Bronco des années 1970 succède l'Explorer, une version plus raffinée qui contribue largement au développement des SUV. Lancé en 1990, l'Explorer représente la quintessence du 4x4 de ville ; il combine des caractéristiques de luxe avec une capacité de remorquage, un habitacle spacieux et d'autres éléments pratiques. Il quitte rarement le goudron, bien sûr, mais il permet de transporter enfants et courses.

1986

1986 Honda introduces first Japanese luxury brand, Acura

Honda lanciert mit Acura die erste japanische Nobelmarke

Honda lance la première marque de luxe japonaise : Acura

1986 Hyundai becomes first Korean car brand to sell in U.S.

Hyundai als erste koreanische Automarke auf dem US-Markt vertreten

Hyundai est la première marque coréenne à pénétrer sur le marché américain

1989 "Fahrvergnügen" (German for "driving pleasure") slogan adopted by Volkswagen

Volkswagen USA wirbt mit „Fahrvergnügen"

Volkswagen adopte le slogan « Fahrvergnügen » (« le plaisir de conduire »)

1989 Ford acquires Jaguar Cars Limited for $2.5 billion

Ford übernimmt Jaguar Cars Limited für 2,5 Mrd. US-Dollar

Ford rachète Jaguar Cars Limited pour 2,5 milliards de dollars

VOLUME
TUNER PSCAN
SEEK/SCAN
JENSEN
COMPUTER CONTROLLE
87.9
FM

TZ500
AM/FM
MEM
PLAY PROG
EJECT
REW
DOOR
FF
MAN
TUNE
1
2
3
4
5
6
TUNER ADVANCE
REPEAT
MTL TAPE
TUNER STANDBY
SCAN

THE LUXURY CAR FOR THOSE WHO REFUSE
TO RELAX THEIR STANDARDS.

Anyone who pays $40,000 for a luxury sedan should not be asked to do so in a spirit of forgiveness for its deficiencies.

The BMW 733i makes no such requests. And one of the world's most unforgiving production processes makes certain that none is ever needed.

That process mandates over 3 million operations for the assembly of the body alone. It controls chassis alignments to within 4/1,000ths of an inch. And it assesses the corrosion-resistance of structural metals by submerging them in salt water for at least ten days.

It also endows the BMW 733i with such technological innovations as an optional four-speed automatic transmission that doesn't force you to sacrifice the precision of a manual gearbox, but rather "gives the best of both worlds" (Autosport magazine).

But the 733i is freer of compromise than even that implies. Of its more than 4,000 parts, none ever suffers from inattention because it's judged 'minor.'

The electrically-powered leather bucket seats are orthopedically molded to the contours of the spine. And because they're infinitely adjustable, being uncomfortable is all but an anatomical impossibility.

Human anatomy even dictates the design of the buttons that operate the power windows and the two-position electric sunroof: They are precisely shaped to fit the natural curvature of the fingertip.

The 733i, in short, is an automobile in which nothing has been left to chance, in which luxury is the result of—rather than a substitute for—genuinely superior design and craftsmanship.

Providing something life commonly denies the perfectionist: Vindication, instead of disappointment.

THE ULTIMATE DRIVING MACHINE.

BMW 733i, 1984

▸ Volvo 740, 1987

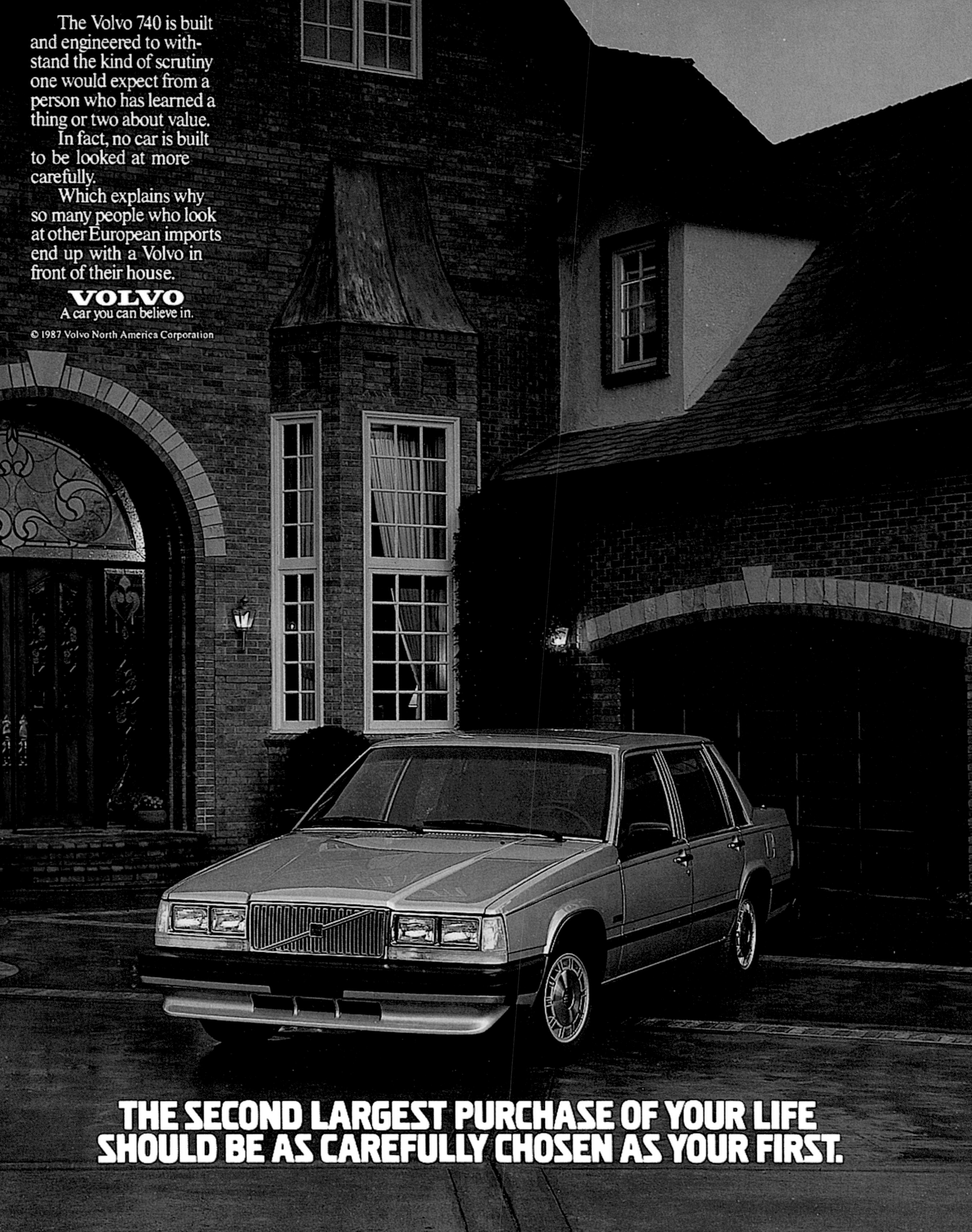
The Volvo 740 is built and engineered to withstand the kind of scrutiny one would expect from a person who has learned a thing or two about value.
In fact, no car is built to be looked at more carefully.
Which explains why so many people who look at other European imports end up with a Volvo in front of their house.
VOLVO
A car you can believe in.
© 1987 Volvo North America Corporation
THE SECOND LARGEST PURCHASE OF YOUR LIFE SHOULD BE AS CAREFULLY CHOSEN AS YOUR FIRST.

Consumer Orientation

No. 4 in a Series
of Technical Papers

4

Subject:
Body Longevity.
The Cathodic Rust
Protection of Zinc.

Porsche 924

Porsche+Audi
Nothing
Even Comes
Close

Paint alone is no protection against rust. Moisture—and other corrosive elements—can attack metal through pinholes on a painted surface. Unchecked, rust can expand, mar the finish, and weaken an ordinary steel body. And so, in addition to a 4-step paint process, the Porsche 924, like all Porsches, is protected by a hot dip galvanizing process.
All of the sheet steel in the 924 is hot dip galvanized in a zinc bath. This produces a zinc oxide that actually grows into any damaged portion of the paint skin—plugging pinholes and preventing further corrosion. In fact, with the introduction of the 1980 model year, Porsche warrants the entire lower body shell against rust perforation for 6 years.*

418

1. The Porsche 924's sheet steel is drawn through a 500°C liquid zinc bath.

2. The high temperature causes the zinc to diffuse into the steel, creating an iron-zinc fusion layer.

3. When the galvanized sheet is taken out of the bath, a pure zinc protective coating forms on the fusion layer.
If the zinc coating is damaged so that the steel is exposed, and if moisture contacts the damaged spot, the moisture acts as an electrolyte, producing a local galvanic element.

4. Between iron and zinc, there is a voltage potential of approximately 0.3 volts. Because zinc has a negative potential, it becomes the anode.

5. The result is an ion migration from zinc to iron, neutralizing the exposed steel surface. The zinc sacrifices itself to the steel and protects the damaged spot against iron rust. The process is called the cathodic rust protection of zinc.

*Porsche+Audi warrants that Porsche vehicles are free from rust perforation for the duration of 6 years. If rust perforation develops under normal use and service and the vehicle has been maintained in accordance with manufacturer's requirements, any Porsche+Audi authorized dealer will replace or repair the defective parts free of charge.

For your nearest Porsche+Audi Dealer, call toll-free: (800) 447-4700. In Illinois, (800) 322-4400.

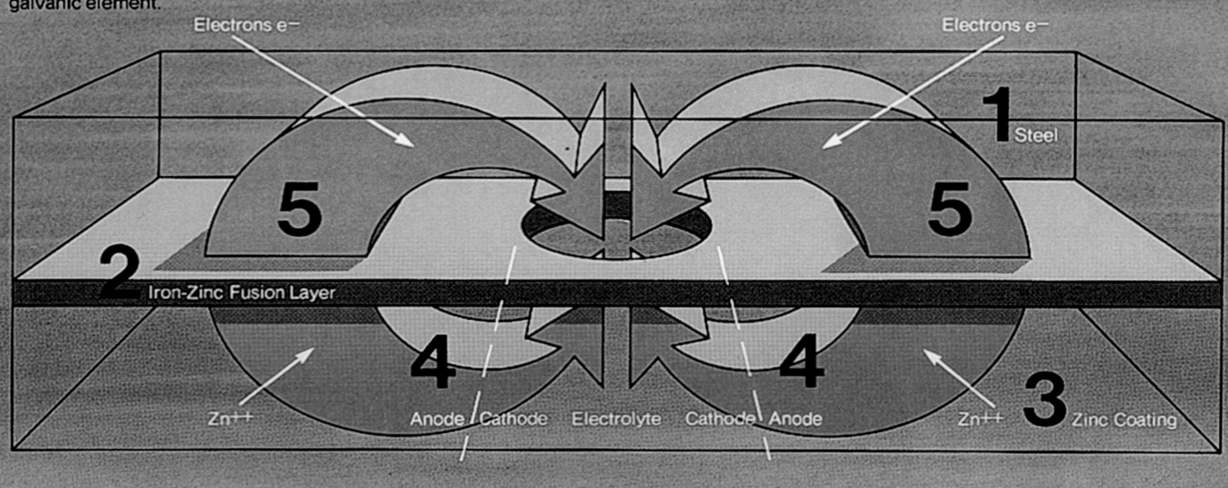

Porsche 924, 1980

► Chevrolet Corvette, 1985

CORVETTE

THIS AMERICAN WENT EYE TO EYE WITH EUROPE... AND EUROPE BLINKED.

Let's get it together...buckle up. GM

Exotic Europeans have traditionally dominated the high-performance sports car class. But in recent United States Auto Club performance trials, the exotic American was the overall winner. The 1985 Corvette. So please join Ferrari, Porsche, Lotus and Lamborghini in a hearty welcome to a new world-class champion. The 1985 Chevrolet Corvette.

USAC Competitive Rank

	Corvette	Lamborghini Countach	Porsche 944	Ferrari 308 GTSi	Lotus Esprit Turbo	Porsche 928S
Total Points	21	18	14	11	11	9
Acceleration 0-60 (sec.)	4 (6.00)	6 (5.33)	1 (7.95)	3 (6.43)	5 (5.95)	2 (6.66)
Braking 60-0 (ft.)	6 (129.2)	3 (135.7)	4 (135.2)	2 (143.1)	1 (144.7)	5 (135.1)
Slalom (sec.)	6 (6.13)	3 (6.38)	5 (6.33)	4 (6.36)	2 (6.40)	1 (6.62)
Lateral Acceleration (g's)	5 (.91)	6 (.92)	4 (.86)	2 (.83)	3 (.85)	1 (.82)
Price as Tested	$26,703	$103,700	$26,121	$60,370	$50,384	$49,495

Scoring based on an Olympic system in which first place is awarded 6 points for each event. USAC certified tests, January 1985. All cars listed were latest models available for sale in the U.S. at time of testing and were equipped with various high-performance options. Corvette's Manufacturer's Suggested Retail Base Price is $24,891 including dealer prep. Tax, license, destination charges and optional equipment additional.

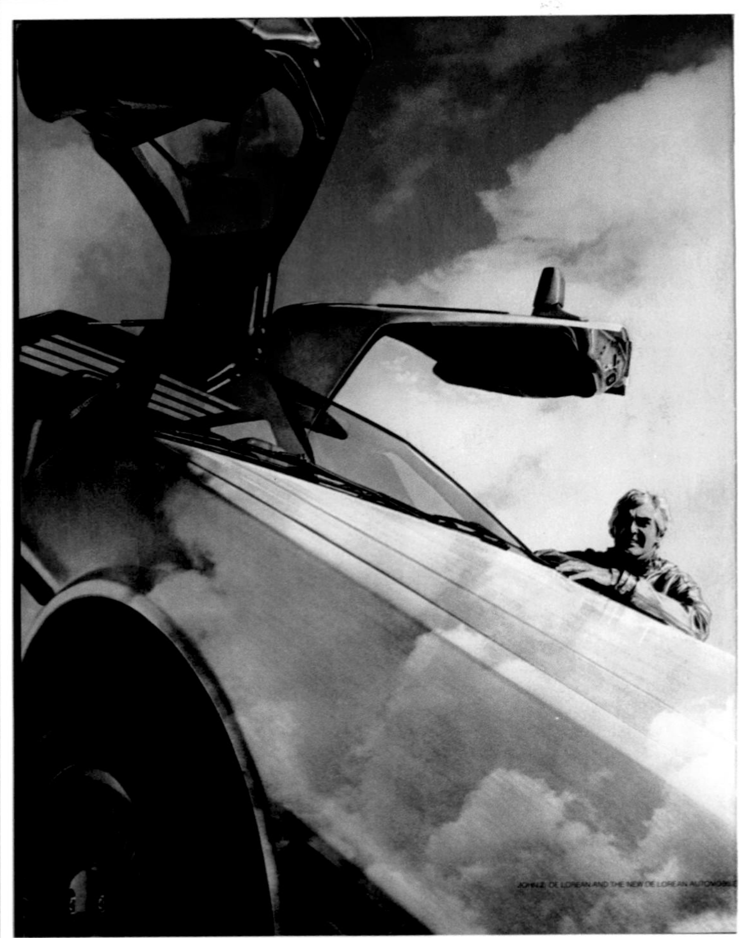

THE DE LOREAN. LIVE THE DREAM.

Your eyes skim the sleek, sensuous stainless steel body, and all your senses tell you, "I've got to have it!"

The counterbalanced gull-wing doors rise effortlessly, beckoning you inside.

The soft leather seat in the cockpit fits you like it was made for your body.

You turn the key. The light alloy V-6 comes to life instantly.

The De Lorean. Surely one of the most awaited automobiles in automotive history.

It all began with one man's vision of the perfect personal luxury car. Built for long life, it employs the latest space-age materials.

Of course, everyone stares as you drive by. Sure, they're a little envious. That's expected. After all, you're the one Living The Dream.

Start living it today at a dealer near you.

A dealer commitment as unique as the car itself. There are 345 De Lorean dealers located throughout the United States. Each one is a stockholder in the De Lorean Motor Company. This commitment results in a unique relationship which will provide De Lorean owners with a superb standard of service.

For the dealer nearest you, call toll free 800-447-4700, in Ill., 800-322-4400. DMC

DeLorean DMC-12, 1982

Famous for his 1964 Pontiac GTO muscle car, dreamed up while he was an executive at General Motors, John DeLorean tried his hand at entrepreneurship with his short-lived DeLorean Motor Company. He built cars for just two years (1981–1982), but his gull-winged, stainless-steel-bodied DMC-12 became legendary as the star of the *Back to the Future* movies.

Berühmt für sein Muscle-Car Pontiac GTO von 1964, den er als Geschäftsführer von General Motors ersonnen hatte, versuchte sich John DeLorean mit seiner DeLorean Motor Company als Unternehmer. Autos baute man nur zwei Jahre lang (1981–1982), doch der DMC-12, ein Flügeltürer mit Edelstahlkarosserie, wurde durch seinen Auftritt in der Filmtrilogie *Zurück in die Zukunft* zur Legende.

Célèbre pour sa Pontiac GTO 1964, une grosse cylindrée dont il rêvait déjà chez General Motors, John De Lorean tente brièvement sa chance aux commandes de l'éphémère firme qui porte son nom. Il ne construit des voitures que pendant deux ans (1981–1982) mais sa DMC-12 en acier inoxydable, avec portières papillon, est entrée dans la légende grâce aux films *Retour vers le futur*, dans lesquels elle tient la vedette.

► Ferrari 308 GTB, 1981

Only those who dare... truly live

For the name of the authorized Ferrari dealer nearest you, call these numbers toll-free:
(800)477-4700 or, in Illinois, (800)322-4400, in Alaska and Hawaii, (800)477-0890.

Ferrari

DATSUN OFFERS
BLACK GOLD
10TH ANNIVERSARY 280-ZX
Here is precious metal many will desire, but few will possess. It's the limited-edition Datsun 280-ZX – created to celebrate the first decade of the legendary Datsun Z-car.
Come. Stroke its rich leathers on the thick, cushioned bucket seats. Ignite its restless soul with a fuel-injected six-cylinder power source. Control its seething passion with all around disc brakes, independent four-wheel suspension and road-feeling power steering.
Whisk over a twist of scenic route with the T-bar roof open to the sky.
So rare each is numbered on an engraved plaque. So rich all are lavished with optimum luxury – from pre-flight computer read-out to 40-watt power-boosted, four-speaker stereo.
It's Black. It's Gold. And it is awesome.
Appraise one now at your Datsun dealer.
10
DATSUN
WE ARE DRIVEN
NISSAN

Toyota Corolla Tercel, 1981

Toyota Celica Supra, 1980

Datsun 280-ZX, 1980 ◂

Sometimes your toughest competition is yourself.

Motor Trend magazine recently named its 1984 Import Car of the Year. And for the first time ever, one manufacturer swept the top three places. Thank you, thank you, thank you.

Motor Trend
Import Car of the Year

HONDA

424

© 1984 American Honda Motor Co., Inc.

Honda Civic, Prelude, CRX, 1984

While Japanese makers reduced the number of colors and other options available, they upgraded their models more often than their American rivals.

Während die japanischen Hersteller nun weniger Farben und Optionen boten, betrieben sie eine intensivere Modellpflege als ihre amerikanischen Mitbewerber.

Les constructeurs japonais réduisent le nombre de coloris et d'options disponibles mais améliorent leurs modèles plus souvent que leurs concurrents américains.

► Dodge Colt, 1989

Colt joins the crème de la 最高.

The totally re-designed Colt GT Turbo. Recently named one of *Car and Driver* magazine's 10 best cars of the year.

"One of the 10 best cars of the year."
Car and Driver magazine

And it earned that distinction by delivering something Colts aren't known for. *A rush.*

With performance enhancements that include a turbocharged 16-valve, DOHC 1.6 liter powerplant, power rack and pinion steering, power 4-wheel disc brakes, taut sports suspension, performance radials, a super slippery new profile and more spunk than a lot of high-ticket turbo coupes.

3/36
Bumper To Bumper Warranty
See limited warranty at dealer, restrictions apply. Excludes normal maintenance, adjustments and wear items.

Its refinements didn't stop under the hood, either.

Inside you'll find the Colt GT has ample elbow room, comfortable sport buckets, a telescoping tilt steering wheel, an ergonomically advanced interior and impressive dash graphics and instrumentation.

They're available in limited numbers at Plymouth and Dodge dealers who can promise you one thing:

A test drive that's a real kick in the 後背部.

優秀 Colt

It's all the Japanese you need to know.

TURBO
Chrysler technology makes Made in America mean something again.
The 1986 Chrysler LeBarons are the most technologically advanced LeBarons ever. This is a series of cars that expresses Chrysler's commitment to be the best.
This year they're re-designed with gracefully sculpted new lines and meticulous detailing.
They're re-equipped with even more standard features than Buick Century.
A new, larger 2.5-liter engine is available and electronic fuel injection is standard. Or you may choose a turbocharged engine that gives you the power of a V-8 with the fuel efficiency of a four cylinder.
Whatever LeBaron you choose, you enjoy the confidence of front-wheel drive handling, and the comforts of Chrysler luxury.
And LeBaron's protection is outstanding. Your engine, drivetrain and even your turbo are backed by a 5-year or 50,000-mile Protection Plan, while outer body rust-through is covered for the same period.*
Test drive LeBaron at your Chrysler-Plymouth dealer, where purchase or lease may be arranged.
Chrysler
Division of Chrysler Corporation
THE COMPETITION IS GOOD. WE HAD TO BE BETTER.
*See limited warranty at dealer. Excludes leases. Restrictions apply.
Buckle up for safety.

Chrysler LeBaron, 1986

One of the K-cars that saved the company, this convertible LeBaron was pitched by actor Ricardo Montalbán, whose accented pronunciation of "Corinthian leather" became a tagline for comedians of the era.

Als eines der K-Cars, die das Unternehmen retteten, wurde das LeBaron-Cabrio von Schauspieler Ricardo Montalbán beworben. Seine Aussprache des „korinthischen Leders" wurde zur Zielscheibe der Komiker.

Cette décapotable, un des modèles K qui sauveront la firme, sera vantée dans la publicité par l'acteur Ricardo Montalbán, dont l'accent pour prononcer « cuir corinthien » inspirera les humoristes.

► Cadillac Seville, 1982

Seville by Cadillac

...a remarkable automotive investment any way you look at it.

Since its inception, more Americans have chosen to own Seville than any luxury import model.

They've come to appreciate Seville's engineering excellence—from four-wheel independent suspension to electronic level control. They've discovered the exceptional roominess and legroom of front-wheel drive. And Seville's superb ride. Plus an abundance of standard features that often cost extra on luxury imports (if they're offered at all).

With styling imitated but never equalled... Seville is an American standard for the world. Buy or lease, see your Cadillac dealer soon. Seville... remarkable any way you look at it, and...

Best of all...it's a *Cadillac*

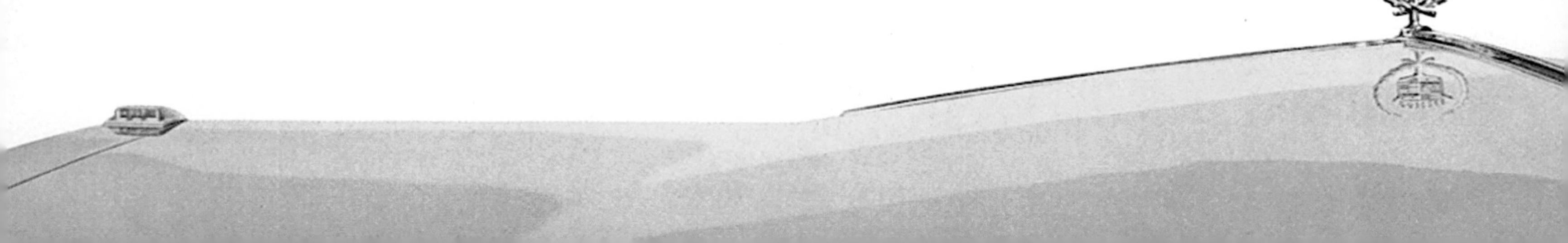

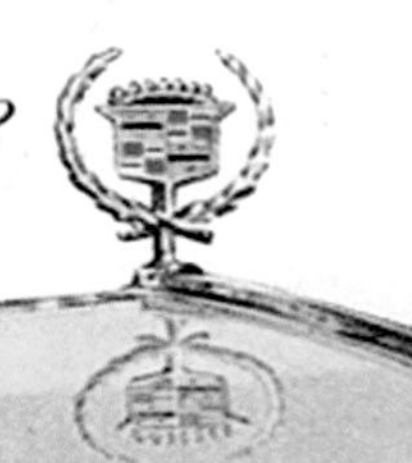

Still, The Standard.

Today, the Honda Accord 4-Door Sedan is bigger than when it was first introduced. Both inside and out. It is more aerodynamic. More powerful. More luxurious. And it has become the number one selling small car in America.*

Only one thing has not changed. It is still the standard by which every car in its class is judged.

HONDA
Accord 4-Door Sedan

 *Based on 1983 calendar year *Ward's Automotive Reports* and EPA Interior Volume Index for subcompacts.

TAURUS
One of the many examples of Ford's attention to detail is the cargo restraining net on the LX. It helps keep grocery bags from tipping over and loose packages from sliding around.
The optional electronic instrument panel is designed to be "user friendly." All instruments are easy to read and all controls are placed where your hands can easily find them.
THE NEW FORD TAURUS. ITS PERFORMANCE ISN'T LIMITED TO WHAT'S UNDER THE HOOD.
The secondary sun visor helps eliminate glare from the front and side simultaneously, so you don't have the inconvenience of constantly swinging the visor back and forth. It's not available on the L model.
Even the smallest details have been carefully thought out. For example, the shape of this light switch and its position on the instrument panel make the simple task of turning on the lights as easy as possible.
OFF
LIGHTS
The mark of a well-designed automobile is total performance.
In the case of Taurus, that means a powerful 3-liter, V-6 engine. Plus dozens of other features that not only respond to the needs of the driver, but to those of the passengers as well.
As a result, Taurus performs beautifully.
Right down to the smallest detail.
The best-built American cars.
At Ford, Quality is Job 1. A 1985 survey established that Ford makes the best-built American cars. This is based on an average number of problems reported by owners in a six-month period on 1981-1984 models designed and built in the U.S.
MPH
km/h
ODO
SEL
TRIP
RESET
SPEED
ALARM
FUEL
ECON
DTE
ECON
RESET
The trip computer is part of the optional electronic instrument cluster. It provides valuable travel information such as rate of fuel consumption and the distance you can travel until empty.
Have you driven a Ford...lately?
Ford
Buckle up–Together we can save lives.

429

Ford Taurus, 1986

The round, full shapes of the Taurus's aerodynamic family sedan and wagon evoked both European cars, such as the Audi 100, and a 1949 Ford.

Die Rundungen des aerodynamischen Taurus erinnerten sowohl an europäische Modelle wie den Audi 100 als auch an einen 1949er Ford.

Les formes rondes, pleines et aérodynamiques de la berline et du break Taurus évoquent les modèles européens comme l'Audi 100, mais aussi l'ancien modèle Ford de 1949.

Honda Accord, 1985 ◂

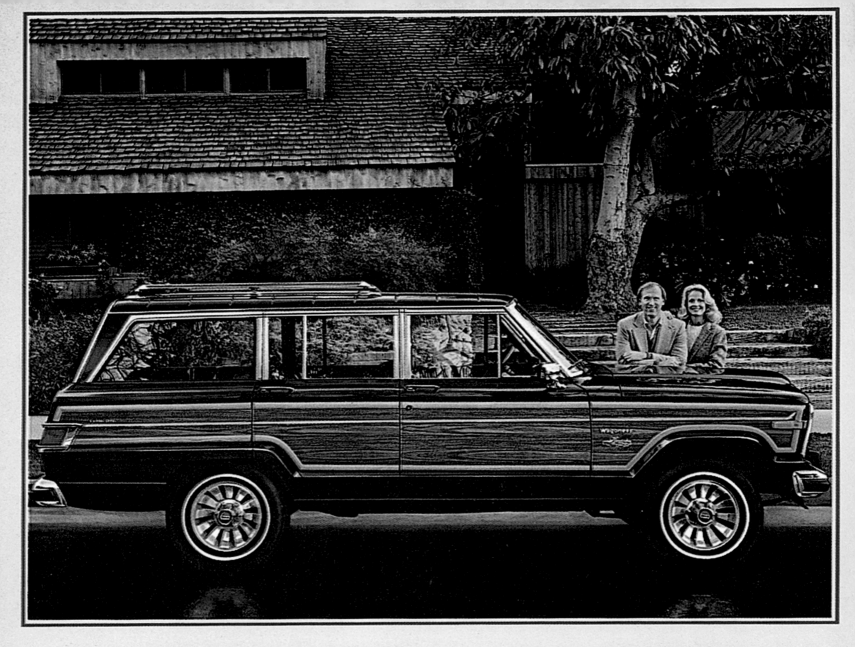

Anyone who'd call Wagoneer a station wagon has obviously never driven one.

Any similarity between the Jeep Wagoneer Limited and a conventional two-wheel drive wagon is purely coincidental.

Because no conventional full-size wagon gives you all the security, luxury and economy of Wagoneer.

For security, it's the Wagoneer's sure-footed four-wheel drive, performing deftly under all kinds of pressure...snow buried highways, icy roadways, torrential downpours. Or just digging in off-road to take you far from the maddening crowds.

For luxury, it's an interior filled with supple leathers, thick carpeting, and a wealth of comfortable appointments you would expect to find only in the plushest automobiles.

And for economy, it's better EPA estimated mileage than *any* full-size two-wheel drive wagon.*

Luxury, economy *and* the security of four-wheel drive. With all this, and surprisingly affordable prices, why would anyone drive anything else?

The Jeep Wagoneer Limited. We call it the Ultimate Wagon. You'll call it *beautiful*.

18 EST* EPA MPG 25 HWY EST

Jeep® Wagoneer Limited. The Ultimate Wagon.

AT AMERICAN MOTORS

*Use these figures for comparison. Your results may differ due to driving speed, weather conditions and trip length. Actual highway mileage lower.
Jeep Corporation, a subsidiary of American Motors Corporation.

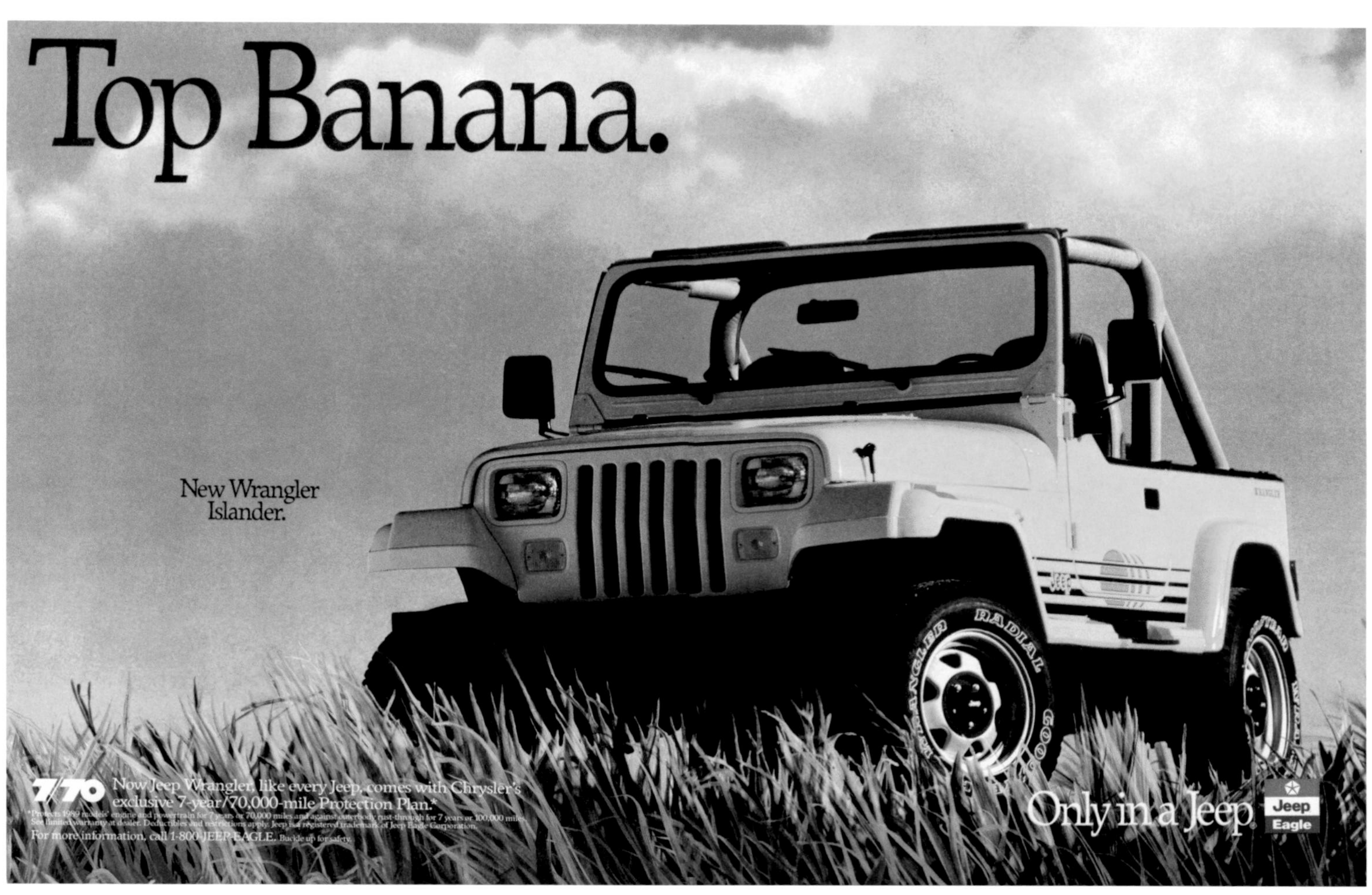

Top Banana.
New Wrangler Islander.
7/70 Now Jeep Wrangler, like every Jeep, comes with Chrysler's exclusive 7-year/70,000-mile Protection Plan.*
For more information, call 1-800-JEEP-EAGLE. Buckle up for safety.
Only in a Jeep
Jeep Eagle

Jeep Wagoneer, 1982 ◂

"Roughing it easy" increasingly became a theme of the automobile as rugged models were outfitted with leather seats, high-end audio systems, and other luxuries, so that they came to resemble elaborate camping trailers.

„Aber dennoch bequem" wurde zunehmend zum Thema des Jeep, als Ledersitze, hochwertige Audiosysteme und weitere Luxuskomponenten Einzug hielten.

La Jeep se décline sur le thème du « tout terrain tout confort » : les modèles ordinaires s'équipent de sièges en cuir et de systèmes audio performants, entre autres luxes.

Jeep Wrangler, 1989

▸▸ Nissan Pickup, 1988

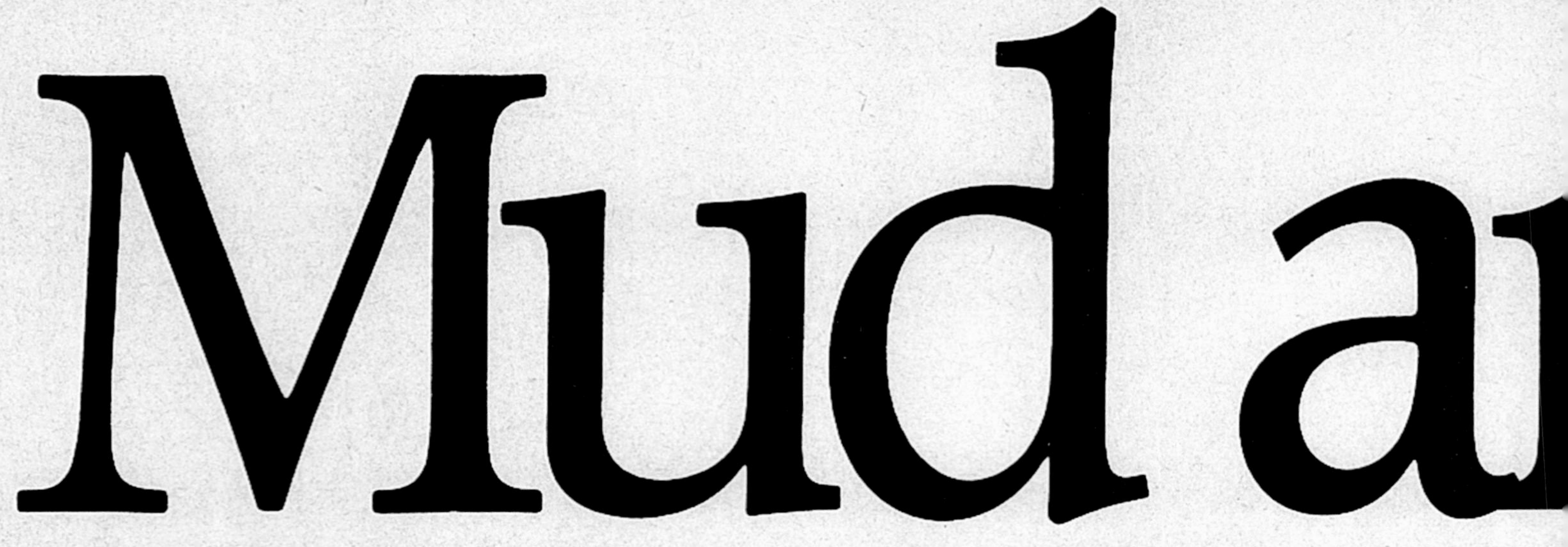

It takes a lot of both to build a great truck.

And, to know one.

Now if you don't like to go out every once in awhile and just plain get your truck dirty, you may not appreciate all the effort that goes into making a Nissan® Hardbody™ what it is.

But if you're interested in a really tough truck, you'll be glad to know that the Hardbody goes through a lot to make sure you can do the same.

For instance, Nissan tests its special anti-ru and corrosion protection in tons of gritty, grim and very salty mud. For what is the equivalent ten long and torturous years.

All just to make absolutely sure that you

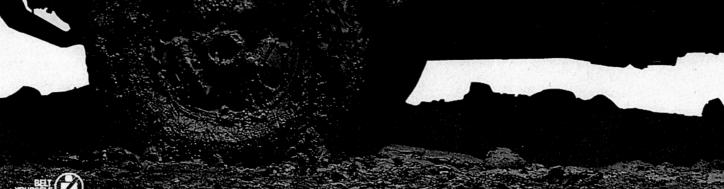

Nissan Hardbody SE King Cab® 4x4. Equipped with Sport and Power Packages, including standard fuel-injected V6 and automatic-locking front hubs.

BELT YOURSELF

Nissan Hardbody's body stays just that way.

And when it comes to guts, the Hardbody's got gobs of that, too. As in 145 hp. and 166 ft./lbs. of torque, from an optional 3.0-liter fuel-injected overhead cam V6. So you can haul, tow and go to your heart's content.

But, hey, don't just take our word for it. Go out in a Hardbody 4x4 and find yourself some mud. And then, punch it.

If you've got the guts.

NISSAN®

Built for the Human Race.™

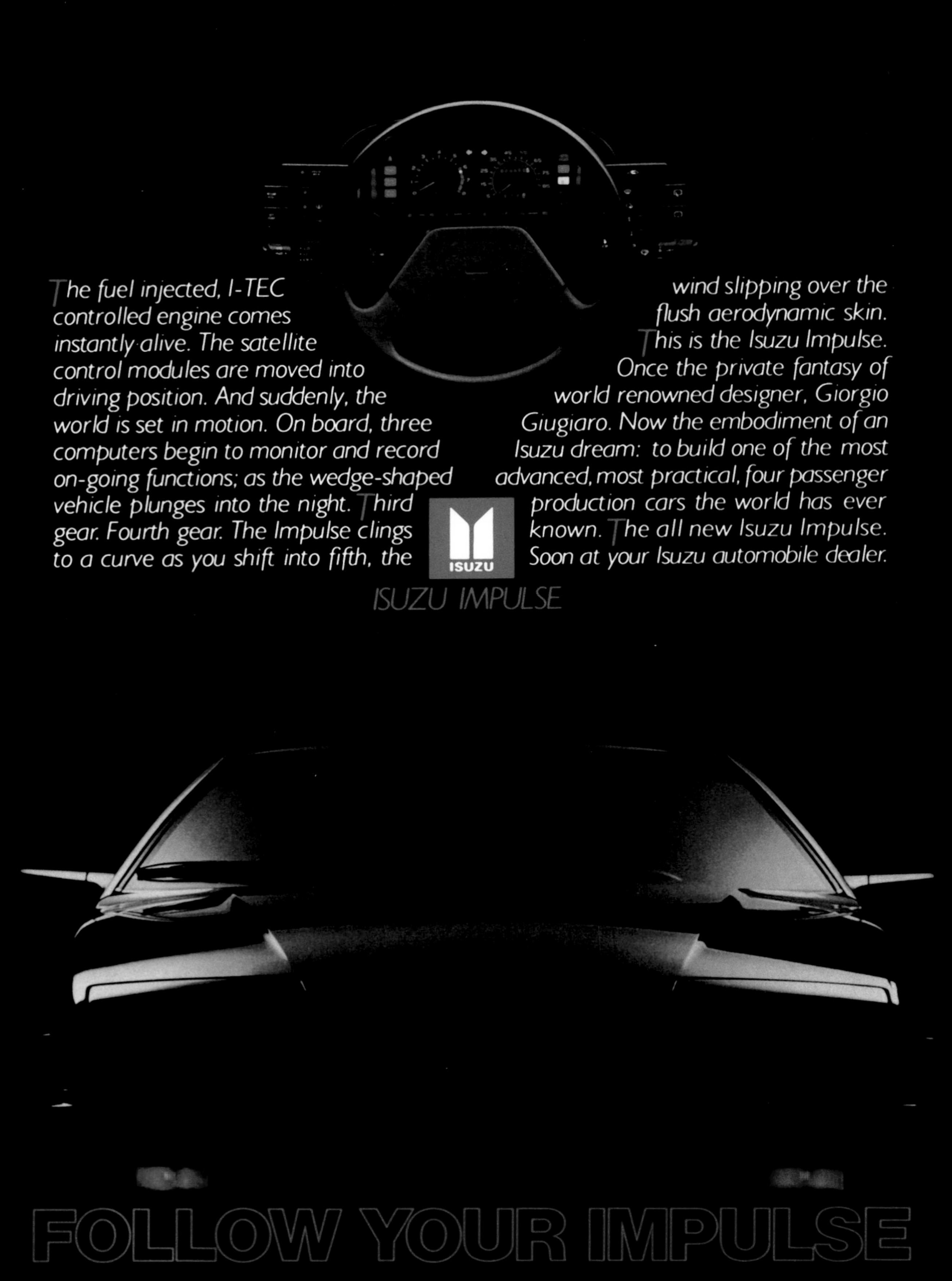

The fuel injected, I-TEC controlled engine comes instantly alive. The satellite control modules are moved into driving position. And suddenly, the world is set in motion. On board, three computers begin to monitor and record on-going functions; as the wedge-shaped vehicle plunges into the night. Third gear. Fourth gear. The Impulse clings to a curve as you shift into fifth, the wind slipping over the flush aerodynamic skin.
This is the Isuzu Impulse. Once the private fantasy of world renowned designer, Giorgio Giugiaro. Now the embodiment of an Isuzu dream: to build one of the most advanced, most practical, four passenger production cars the world has ever known. The all new Isuzu Impulse. Soon at your Isuzu automobile dealer.
ISUZU
ISUZU IMPULSE
FOLLOW YOUR IMPULSE

Isuzu Impulse, 1983

► Chevrolet Spectrum, 1988

The sequel with no equal.
Introducing the new Grand Caravan.
From the company that wrote the book on minivans comes another surefire success story. Introducing Dodge Grand Caravan.
Like Caravan, the new Grand Caravan has some unique advantages over imitators, Aerostar and Astro. Such as a shorter step up for easy ins and outs. A lower lift-over height for easy loading and unloading. A shorter height overall for easy maneuvering in and out of your garage. Front-wheel drive to move you easily through mud, snow and rain. And Dodge's outstanding 7/70 Protection Plan* for more peace of mind down the road.
More room than before.
Yet, Grand Caravan extends itself even further. It offers 170% more total knee room in the back seats, and 100% more cargo space than an original Caravan with 7-passenger seating.
And, with the seats out, Grand Caravan goes to even greater lengths to accommodate. Offering enough floor space for a full 4x8 sheet of plywood. And a generous 150 cubic feet of cargo room.
All new V-6 power.
Both Caravan and Grand Caravan give you a powerful new choice of engines. Dodge's proven 2.2 liter 4-cylinder, standard on Caravan. The spirited 2.5 liter 4-cylinder, standard on Grand Caravan. Or the newly available 3.0 liter V-6 power plant.
So now you have an unequaled choice.
Buy or lease the original Caravan. Or the new, longer wheelbase Grand Caravan. At your Dodge dealer.
Dodge
7/70
DIVISION OF CHRYSLER MOTORS
Setting new standards of performance.
Chrysler Motors: Best built, best backed American cars and trucks*
*Based on survey of owner problems with '86 cars & light trucks (combined) sold Oct-Nov '85 (5 mos. avg. usage) and a warranty comparison of competitively priced models for vehicles designed & built in No. America. See 7/70 powertrain & 7/100 outer body rust-through limited warranty at dealer. Restrictions apply.
BUCKLE UP FOR SAFETY.

Dodge Grand Caravan, 1987

Successor to the station wagon, the witty combination of *car* and *van* into Dodge's Caravan could not disguise the boxy, mundane quality of the vehicle. Despite the dream of owning a sports car, consumers with families had to admit that minivans were the vehicles that met most of their real, daily needs.

Als Nachfolger des Kombi konnte auch die geistreiche Kombination von „car" und „van" zum Dodge Caravan die kastenförmige Schlichtheit des Vehikels nicht verbergen. Auch wenn sie lieber einen Sportwagen gehabt hätten, mussten die Verbraucher mit Familie doch einräumen, dass ein Minivan das Gros ihrer realen, alltäglichen Bedürfnisse abdeckte.

Pour remplacer le break familial, Dodge propose un astucieux modèle entre « voiture » (*car*) et « camionnette » (*van*), dont la forme reste toutefois un peu trop carrée et banale. Malgré ses rêves de voitures de sport, le consommateur doit bien admettre que le monospace est le véhicule le mieux adapté à ses besoins quotidiens.

► GMC Safari, 1986

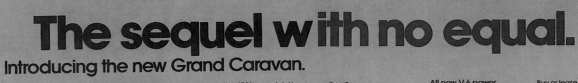

GM
RODEO DR.
GMC
BEVERLY HILLS NEW YORK
Safari is ideal for all sorts of demanding expeditions.
Any van is useful for the mundane, dreary, go-to-the-market episodes of life.
Certain kinds of more vibrant lifestyles, however, demand a certain kind of vehicular style. It's found at last in Safari, a van one can take anywhere.
With available seating, Safari has room for eight friends and/or family members. And the creature comforts they're accustomed to expecting from fine automobiles.
You demand the best from life. So don't just get a van. Demand a Safari. By GMC. From your nearest GMC Truck dealer. You'll find a listing in the Yellow Pages.
GMC
TRUCK
A truck you can live with
Let's get it together. . . buckle up.

438

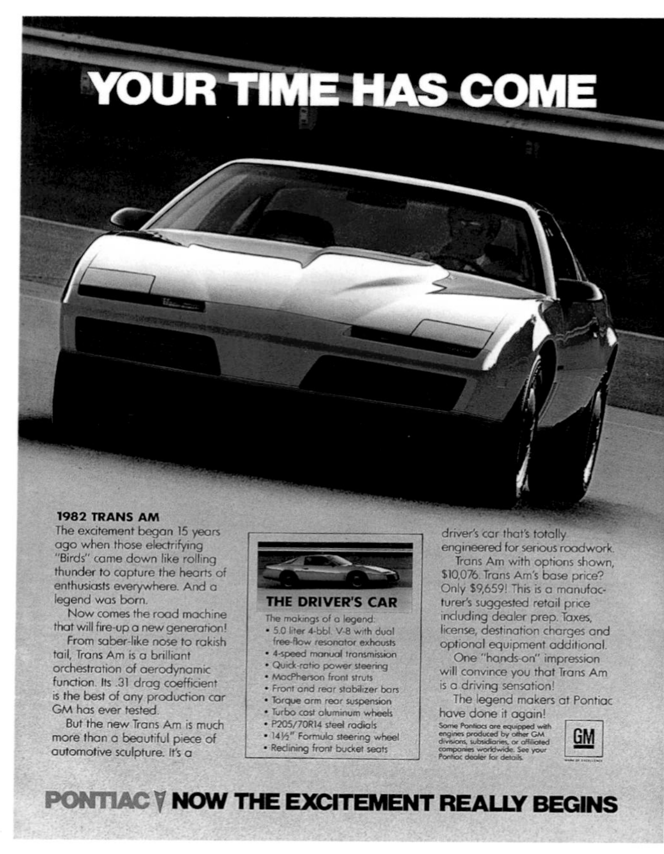

Dodge Charger 2.2
A lot of go without the guzzle.
0 to 50 in 6.6 seconds. 41 EST. HWY 26 EPA EST. MPG mpg.*

The Charger legend lives again in the new Charger 2.2. A sports car that we call a Driving Machine.

A Driving Machine that's a performance machine.

We took Chrysler's gutsy 2.2 liter OHC powerplant that cranks out 111 foot pounds of torque at 2800 RPM. Hooked it on a 3.13:1 final drive ratio and put it together with a slippery aerodynamic exterior that weighs-in under 2400 pounds. On the street, according to NHRA acceleration tests, that translates into 0 to 50 in only 6.6 seconds!

We've got a lot more than just muscle up our sleeve.

MODEL	EPA* EST.	HWY* EST.	ENGINE	DSPL/WT†	0-50††
'82 Charger 2.2	26	41	2.2-Liter 135 CID	.060	6.62
'81 Datsun 280ZX 2+2	21	32	2.8-Liter 168 CID	.056	7.30
'81 Mustang Cobra	23	34	2.3-Liter 140 CID	.053	9.04
'81 Porsche 924	20	35	2.0-Liter 121 CID	.046	7.77
'81 Pontiac Trans Am	16	22	4.9-Liter 301 CID	.087	7.32

With all that torque Charger 2.2 zips past the pump at an incredible 41 EST. HWY. 26 EPA EST. MPG.*

Only a handful of other machines can even compete with Charger 2.2. Those that do, for the most part, are conventional rear-wheel-drive. Years behind the technology that makes Charger 2.2 a driving machine.

A USAC certified sports car.

There's a good reason why USAC certified Charger 2.2 as a sports car. It gives you the handling you can expect from front-wheel-drive and rack-and-pinion steering. It sits firmly on the road with its Sports Suspension System and performance raised white letter tires. Notice that Charger 2.2 comes with a Rallye Instrument cluster that includes a tachometer and quartz clock. Notice the reclining bucket seats with lateral support, remote control dual sport mirrors and performance exhaust system. All standard equipment. And if you're into off-road racing, there's a Direct Connection dealer waiting to help you tool up your Charger 2.2.

A Driving Machine for less than the cost of a lot of cars. $7,242.**

Dodge Charger 2.2. The new standard by which all thoroughbred driving machines will be judged. Buy or lease one at your Dodge dealer. You'll have a hard time beating her on the road. At $7,242** you'll have an even harder time beating the price. The Charger legend lives again. Unchallenged.

Dodge
America's Driving Machines

*Use EPA EST MPG numbers for comparison. Actual mileage may vary depending on speed, trip length, and weather. Actual HWY mileage probably lower. CA mileage lower.
**Sticker price excluding taxes and destination charges. †Calculated by dividing cubic inch displacement by curb weight. ††Based on National Hot Rod Association acceleration tests.

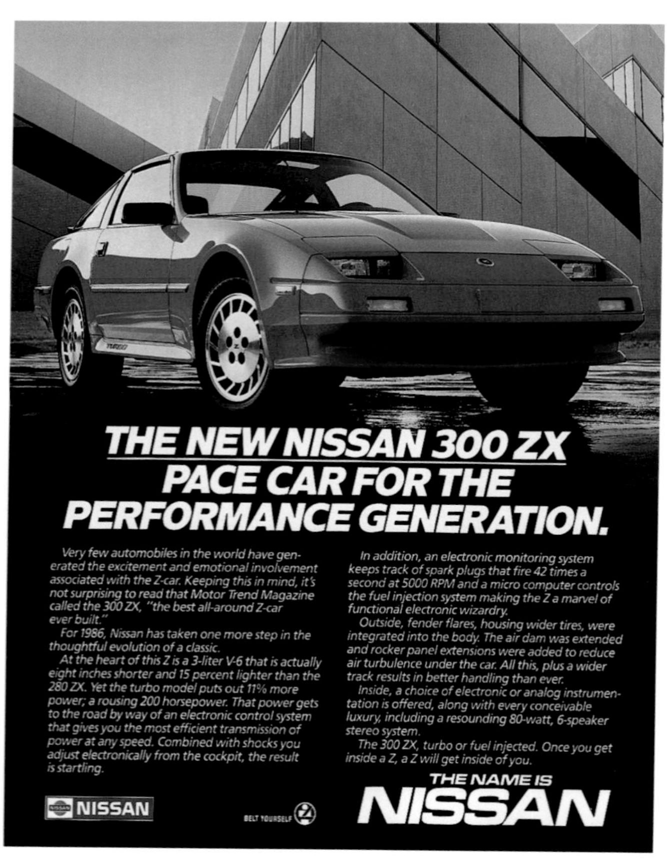

Chevrolet Camaro, 1983 — Pontiac Trans Am, 1982

Dodge Charger, 1981 — Nissan 300 ZX, 1985

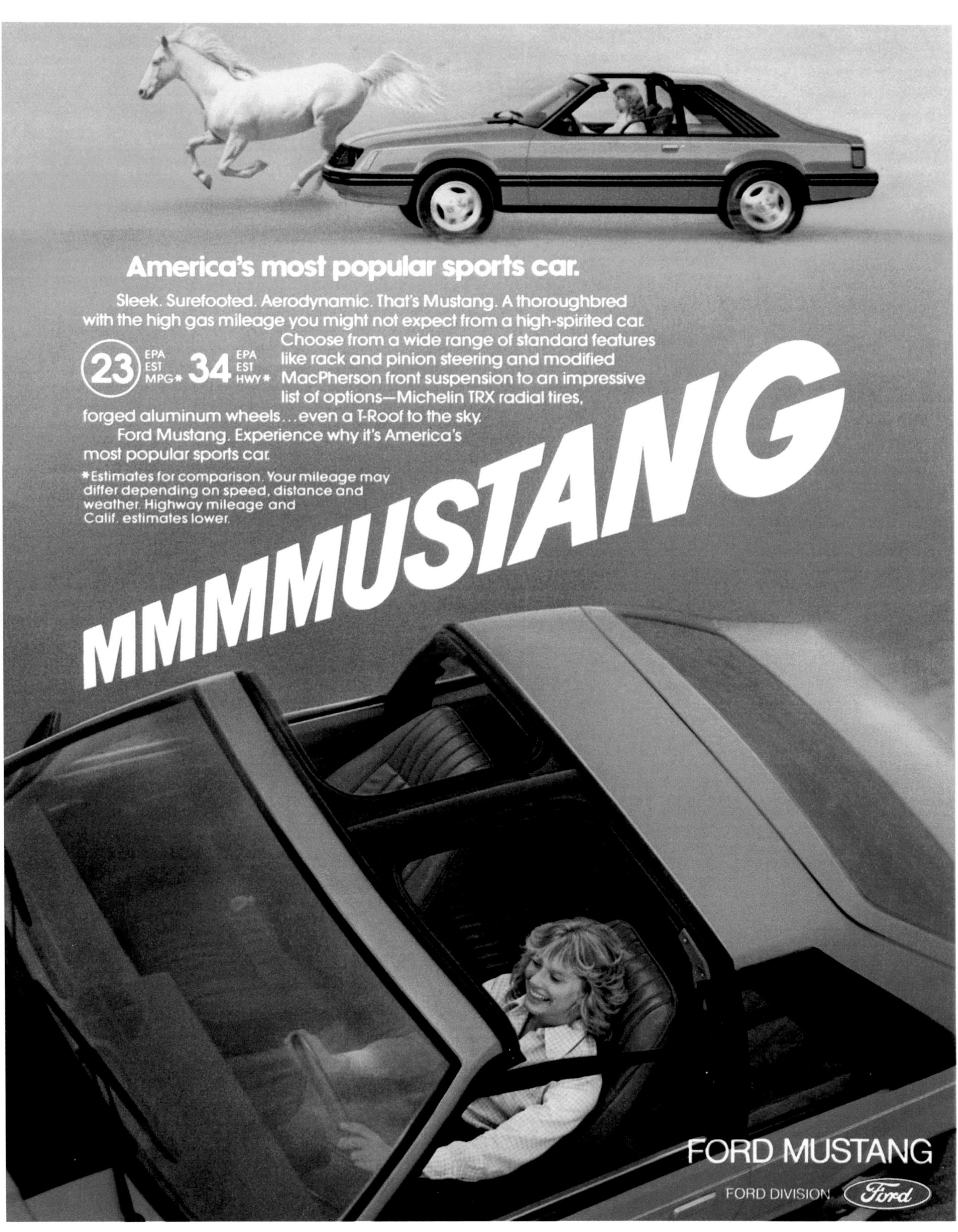

America's most popular sports car.
Sleek. Surefooted. Aerodynamic. That's Mustang. A thoroughbred with the high gas mileage you might not expect from a high-spirited car.
23 EPA EST MPG* 34 EPA EST HWY*
Choose from a wide range of standard features like rack and pinion steering and modified MacPherson front suspension to an impressive list of options—Michelin TRX radial tires, forged aluminum wheels . . . even a T-Roof to the sky.
Ford Mustang. Experience why it's America's most popular sports car.
*Estimates for comparison. Your mileage may differ depending on speed, distance and weather. Highway mileage and Calif. estimates lower.
MMMMUSTANG
FORD MUSTANG
FORD DIVISION
Ford

Ford Mustang, 1981

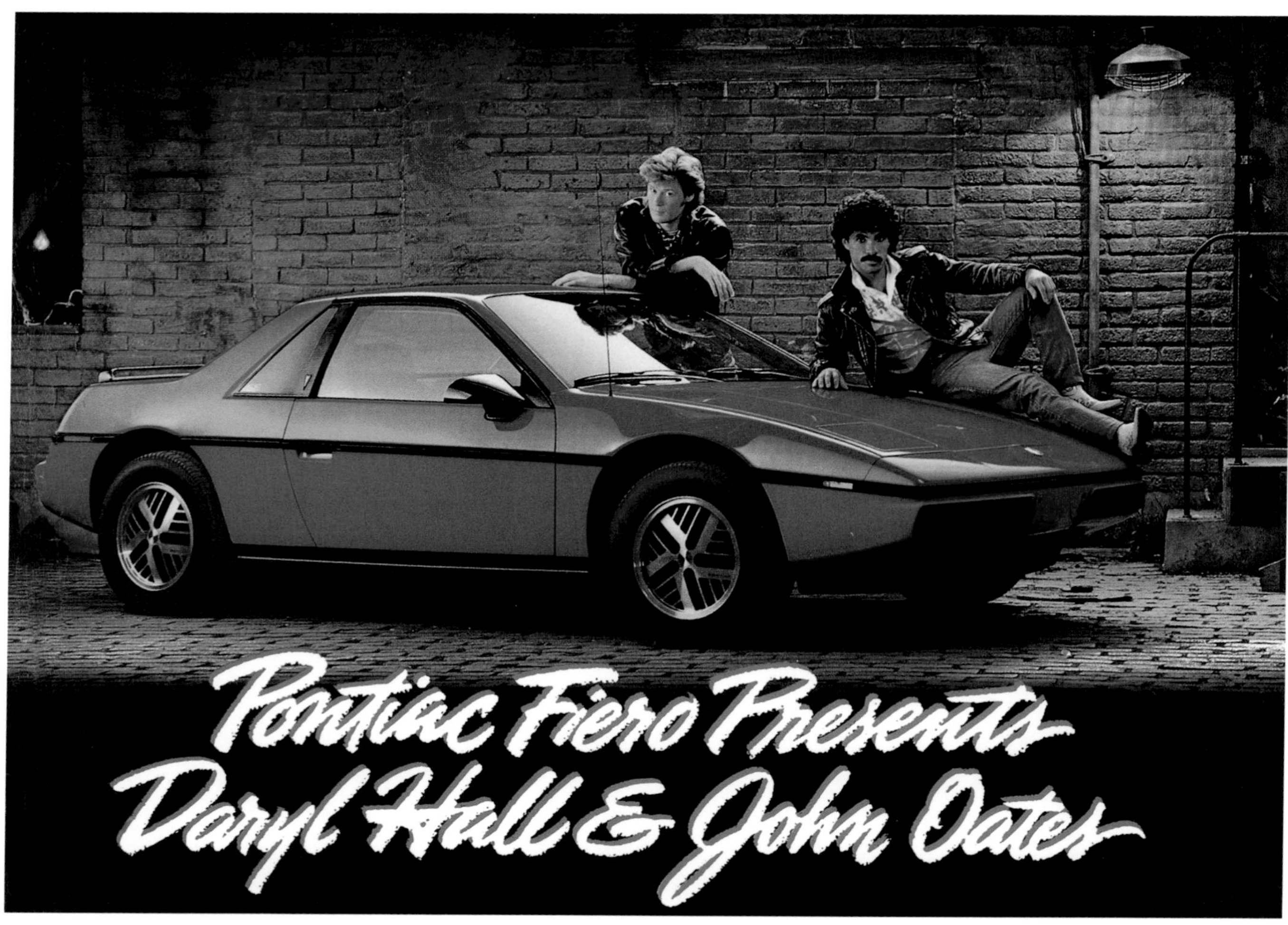

Pontiac Fiero, 1984

General Motors' efforts to tie its sporty cars to pop music no longer had the resonance in the 1980s, with Hall and Oates, that they'd had in the '50s and '60s when Elvis and the Beach Boys sang about their cars.

Der Versuch von General Motors, seine sportlichen Autos mit Popmusik zu verbinden, stieß in den Achtzigern mit dem Popduo Hall and Oates nicht mehr auf die Resonanz wie in den Fünfzigern und Sechzigern, als Elvis und die Beach Boys ihre Autos besungen hatten.

Les efforts de General Motors pour associer ses voitures de sport à la musique pop ne trouvent plus d'écho dans les années 1980, comme c'était le cas dans les années 1950 et 1960 avec Elvis ou les Beach Boys.

▸ Lotus Esprit, 1980

▸▸ Mercury Cougar, 1986

A Lotus is a rare sight.

Look at the Lotus Esprit.
The exotic car that holds the road like nothing else.

The roadholding secrets of the Esprit reach from Formula One to US 1.
The powerful four-cylinder 907 aluminum engine is placed amidships.
The gasoline supply is balanced ingeniously by connecting port and starboard tanks.
The low aerodynamic drag is enhanced by a wraparound spoiler.
The wide-track alloy wheels are widened further by hub-cap offsets.
The remarkable glass-fibre body is made even stronger by a steel-backbone chassis.
The gear box puts a fifth dimension at your fingertips.
And to dazzle the eye, the cockpit is finished by hand.
British inventor Colin Chapman and Italian designer Georgetto Giugiaro would have it no other way.
Just so you can escape in an exotic car today that no one can touch tomorrow.

For the name of the Lotus Authorized Dealership nearest you, call 800-325-6000 and use ID number 1000.
The two-passenger mid-engine Esprit S2. The Éclat 2 + 2. The four-passenger Elite 503.
One look will tell you: there is nothing else in sight.

Lotus

The rarest exotic cars.

1986 Mercury Cougar.
It moves the way it moves
because it looks the way it looks.
MERCURY. The shape you want to be in.

For more information, call 1-800 MERCFAX
LINCOLN-MERCURY DIVISION
Ford

AS THE 20TH CENTURY DREW TO A CLOSE, THE 1990s TOOK ON A RETROSPECTIVE, NOSTALGIC MOOD. SO-CALLED RETRO DESIGNS LIKE VOLKSWAGEN'S NEW BEETLE, FORD'S THUNDERBIRD, AND THE NEW MINI COOPER TOOK A POSTMODERNIST LOOK AT A VANISHED PAST, PART ELEGIAC, PART WRY.

DIE LETZTEN JAHRE DES AUSGEHENDEN 20. JAHRHUNDERTS STANDEN IM ZEICHEN EINER NOSTALGISCHEN RÜCKSCHAU. SO GENANNTE RETRODESIGNS WIE VWs NEW BEETLE, DER FORD THUNDERBIRD UND DER NEUE MINI WARFEN EINEN POSTMODERNEN, TEILS ELEGISCHEN, TEILS IRONISCHEN BLICK AUF EINE FERNE VERGANGENHEIT.

ALORS QUE LE XXE SIÈCLE TIRE À SA FIN, LES ANNÉES 1990 SE CARACTÉRISENT PAR UNE CERTAINE NOSTALGIE. LES MODÈLES SOI-DISANT RÉTRO, À L'INSTAR DE LA NOUVELLE COCCINELLE VOLKSWAGEN, DE LA FORD THUNDERBIRD ET DE LA NOUVELLE MINI COOPER, JETTENT UN REGARD POSTMODERNE, À LA FOIS ÉLÉGIAQUE ET IRONIQUE, SUR UN PASSÉ DISPARU.

1990-

THROUGH THE REARVIEW MIRROR

IM RÜCKSPIEGEL

COUP D'ŒIL DANS LE RÉTROVISEUR

-1999

Bentley Azure

185

Bentley Azure, 1996 ◄◄

Chevrolet Blazer, 1999 ◄

Ford Escort, 1997

AMERICANS HAD NEVER BEFORE BEEN SO AMBIVALENT ABOUT THE AUTOMOBILE AS THEY WERE IN THE 1990S. While some of them, mostly those in rural areas and the West, gloried in ads that showed ever larger SUVs — giant Suburbans, Escalades, Excursions — others, mostly in cities and the East, looked enviously at new compact European models. New York's Museum of Modern Art showed some of these in 1999: Ford's Ka (cute as a Beetle or a Twingo, but sold only in Europe), the then-new Toyota Prius, the prototype for BMW's new Mini Cooper, and others.

As the 20th century drew to a close, the 1990s took on a retrospective, nostalgic mood. So-called retro designs like Volkswagen's New Beetle, Ford's Thunderbird, and the new Mini Cooper took a postmodernist look at a vanished past, part elegiac, part wry. Jaguar looked to its own models of decades gone by as inspiration and templates for new designs, based on the classic D- and E-types. The designers of Chrysler's PT Cruiser made use of the input of a psychologist to tap into primal memories of cars past, in films and fiction: It was more abstract in its evocations of the past. It did not channel the soul of a single model, but seemed part delivery truck, part gangster getaway car, part Model A hot rod in its visual associations.

Recalling the gadget pitches of the 1950s, the decade's advertising increasingly emphasized interior features and electronic systems. Chrysler promoted comfortable leather "captain's chairs" in front and folding "Stow 'n Go" seats in back. Cup holders and map pockets multiplied in interiors. Seats and even steering wheels were heated. More models had navigation units for the driver to find her way, CD players, and video screens for watching movies in the car. With increased traffic and longer commuting times, the car was more and more becoming what the ads had long boasted: a rolling living room.

Another form of nostalgia was the sport-utility vehicle, which seemed to yearn for the size of big cars past and the wide-open, rough ride of the days before towns and highways. The SUV was as much symbol as real vehicle.

Arguably as old as the Jeepsters and Wagoneers made from military equipment in the late 1940s, the SUV kept alive the dream of the open road and the expanding frontier, even in a period of limits.

Ad firms often placed Ford Explorers, Jeep Cherokees, Chevrolet Suburbans, and GM's massive, military-grade vehicles called Hummers in Western and wilderness backdrops. The vehicles provided symbolic security in a dangerous world. Even if they spent more time in rush hour traffic than off-road, the toughness of these SUVs assured car owners they could go anywhere — as long as they had the gas. But by the end of the century, new kinds of cars — small hybrids, which were part electric, part gasoline-driven — signaled an alternate route to the new automotive millennium. Small was becoming beautiful again, in a new way.

1990

1990 Ford contributes to SUV craze with Explorer sports-utility vehicle

Ford bedient den Run auf SUVs mit dem Modell Explorer

Ford contribue à l'engouement pour les 4x4 avec l'Explorer

1990 First Saturn driven off assembly line; promoted as "a different kind of car company"

Erster Saturn läuft vom Band; „Saturn – eine andere Art von Unternehmen"

La première Saturn, produite par un « constructeur différent », sort des chaînes

1991 Three years after launch, Lexus becomes number one-selling luxury import in U.S.

Drei Jahre nach Markteinführung wird Lexus zur meistverkauften US-Importmarke der Oberklasse

Trois ans après son lancement, la Lexus devient numéro un des importations de luxe aux États-Unis

1992 AM General starts production of Humvee, marketed as Hummer for civilian use

AM General beginnt mit der Produktion des als Hummer für die zivile Nutzung beworbenen Humvee

AM General entame la production du Humvee, commercialisé sous le nom de Hummer dans le civil

IN DEN NEUNZIGERN STANDEN DIE AMERIKANER DEM AUTO SO ZWIESPÄLTIG GEGENÜBER WIE NOCH NIE. Manche, vor allem die Menschen auf dem Land und im Westen, konnten sich für immer größere SUVs begeistern, für riesige Suburbans, Escalades und Excursions. Andere wiederum, hauptsächlich Städter und die Bewohner der östlichen Bundesstaaten, warfen einen neidvollen Blick auf die neuen europäischen Kompaktwagen. Einige von ihnen präsentierte das Museum of Modern Art im Jahr 1999: so z.B. den Ford Ka (niedlich wie der Käfer oder Twingo, doch nur in Europa erhältlich), den neuartigen Toyota Prius oder den Prototyp des neuen Mini.

Die letzten Jahre des ausgehenden 20. Jahrhunderts standen im Zeichen einer nostalgischen Rückschau. So genannte Retro-Designs wie VWs New Beetle, der Ford Thunderbird und der neue Mini warfen einen postmodernen, teils elegischen, teils ironischen Blick auf eine ferne Vergangenheit. Jaguar ließ sich von eigenen Klassikern wie dem D- und dem E-Type inspirieren. Unterstützt von einem Psychologen, versuchten die Designer des Chrysler PT Cruiser das in Film und Fiktion verankerte Urbild vergangener Automodelle zum Leben zu erwecken. Der Cruiser nahm eher abstrakt Bezug auf die Vergangenheit, indem er nicht an ein spezielles Modell anknüpfte, sondern visuell zugleich einen Lieferwagen, ein Fluchtauto und einen Model A Hot Rod anklingen ließ.

An den Ausstattungs-Tamtam der Fünfziger erinnernd, rückte die Werbung Innenausstattung und elektronische Systeme zunehmend in den Mittelpunkt. Chrysler warb für komfortable „Captain's Chairs" aus Leder. Klappbare Rücksitze wie Chryslers „Stow 'n Go" ergänzten das Angebot. Plötzlich wimmelte es von Becherhaltern und Staufächern. Beheizbare Sitze und sogar Lenkräder wurden offeriert, und immer häufiger auch Navigationssysteme, CD-Player und Video-Bildschirme. Angesichts der erhöhten Verkehrsdichte und der längeren Fahrten zum Arbeitsplatz wurde das Auto mehr und mehr zu dem, was die Werbung schon seit langem behauptet hatte: ein fahrendes Wohnzimmer.

Eine andere Form der Nostalgie verkörperte das SUV, Ausdruck der Sehnsucht nach den großen Schlitten vergangener Tage und dem freien, wenngleich holperigen Fahrvergnügen jener Zeit, da Ballungsgebiete und Highways noch nicht existierten. Wohl so alt wie die Ende der Vierziger aus Militärrestbeständen gefertigten Jeepsters und Wagoneers, hielt das SUV den Traum von der freien Fahrt und dem vorrückenden Horizont auch in einer Zeit der Beschränkungen lebendig.

Die Werbung präsentierte den Ford Explorer, Jeep Cherokee, Chevrolet Suburban oder den gewaltigen, an ein Armeefahrzeug erinnernden Hummer oftmals in einer Art Wildwest-Szenerie – als Symbol der Sicherheit in einer Welt voller Gefahren. Auch wenn sie mehr Zeit im Stau verbrachten als im Gelände, waren die SUVs robust genug um ihren Besitzern die Gewissheit zu geben, jedes Ziel erreichen zu können – genug Benzin vorausgesetzt. Gegen Ende des Jahrhunderts signalisierte eine neue Art von Autos – kleine Hybridfahrzeuge, wahlweise per Elektro- oder Verbrennungsmotor angetrieben – einen alternativen Weg in das neue Jahrtausend. Klein wurde neuerlich schick, nun jedoch auf andere Weise.

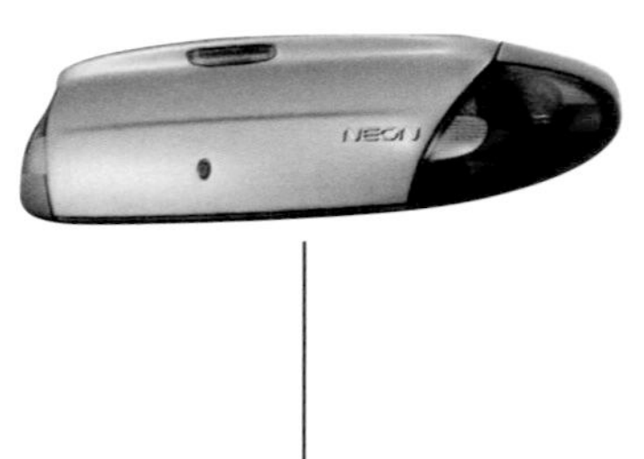

1994

1994 Center High-mounted Stop Lamp (CHMSL) required above the trunk area

Dritte Bremsleuchte oberhalb des Kofferraums in den USA nun auch für Vans vorgeschrieben.

Le feu stop arrière central devient obligatoire

1994 British SUV marque Land Rover acquired by BMW

Britische SUV-Marke Land Rover von BMW übernommen.

Land Rover, marque britannique de 4x4, est racheté par BMW

1995 James Bond drives first non-British car in *GoldenEye*

James Bond fährt in *GoldenEye* mit dem BMW Z3 das erste nicht-britische Auto.

Pour la première fois, dans *GoldenEye*, James Bond conduit une voiture non britannique

1996 GM releases electric EV1; then, three years, later "kills the electric car"

GM präsentiert das Elektroauto EV1; drei Jahre später wird das Projekt eingestellt.

GM lance l'EV1, un modèle électrique ; puis, trois ans plus tard, « tue la voiture électrique »

RANGE ROVER

A
B

Land Rover Range Rover, 1995 ◂◂

BMW 3 Series, 1999 ◂

Mercedes-Benz E-Class, 1995 ▸▸

JAMAIS LES AMÉRICAINS N'ONT EU UNE ATTITUDE AUSSI AMBIVALENTE VIS-À-VIS DE L'AUTOMOBILE QUE DANS LES ANNÉES 1990. Tandis que certains, dans les zones rurales et l'Ouest du pays pour l'essentiel, mordent à l'appât de publicités pour des SUV toujours plus imposants, d'autres, surtout en ville et à l'est, lorgnent avec envie vers les nouveaux petits modèles européens. Le musée d'Art moderne de New York en expose quelques-uns en 1999, parmi lesquels la Ford Ka (aussi mignonne que la Coccinelle ou la Twingo, uniquement vendues en Europe), la Toyota Prius et le prototype de la nouvelle Mini Cooper pour BMW.

Alors que le XXe siècle tire à sa fin, les années 1990 se caractérisent par une certaine nostalgie. Les modèles soi-disant rétro, à l'instar de la nouvelle Coccinelle Volkswagen, de la Ford Thunderbird et de la nouvelle Mini Cooper, jettent un regard postmoderne, à la fois élégiaque et ironique, sur un passé disparu. Jaguar s'inspire de sa propre gamme des décennies précédentes pour créer de nouveaux modèles, comme les classiques types D et E. Pour concevoir le PT Cruiser, Chrysler fait appel à un psychologue afin d'exploiter la mémoire collective des voitures du passé, nourrie par les films et les romans. Le résultat est un peu abstrait, car ces associations visuelles ne canalisent pas l'âme d'un modèle unique; elles donnent à voir un curieux mélange de camion de livraison, de voiture de gangster et de Ford modèle A.

S'inspirant des lancements de gadgets des années 1950, la publicité de cette décennie souligne de plus en plus les équipements intérieurs ainsi que l'électronique. Chrysler vante ses confortables « sièges capitaine » en cuir, à l'avant, et son système « Stow'n Go » de sièges escamotables, à l'arrière. Les porte-gobelets et les poches aumônières se multiplient dans l'habitacle. Les sièges et mêmes les volants deviennent chauffants. Le GPS aide le conducteur à trouver son chemin, les lecteurs de CD permettent d'écouter de la musique et les écrans vidéo de regarder des films pendant les trajets. Avec la circulation croissante et l'allongement du temps passé dans les allées et venues en voiture, l'automobile se conforme toujours plus à l'image qu'en donne la publicité depuis longtemps : celle d'un salon ambulant.

Autre témoignage de l'humeur nostalgique de l'époque : le SUV semble envier aux voitures du passé leurs généreuses dimensions ainsi que la possibilité de s'aventurer dans la nature, comme à l'époque d'avant les villes et les autoroutes. Le SUV symbolise le vrai véhicule. Soi-disant aussi vieux que les Jeeps Jeepster ou Wagoneer issues de l'équipement militaire de la fin des années 1940, le SUV entretient le rêve de la conduite hors des sentiers battus et des frontières sans cesse repoussées, même dans une période pleine de limitations.

Les publicitaires présentent souvent sur fond de vastes paysages sauvages les Explorer, Jeep Cherokee, Chevrolet Suburban et autres gigantesques Hummer – véhicules également issus de l'environnement militaire produit par GM. Ils offrent une sécurité symbolique dans un monde dangereux. Même si ces 4x4 de luxe passent plus de temps dans les embouteillages que sur les chemins de terre, leur allure robuste assure à leurs propriétaires qu'ils peuvent aller où ils veulent – tant que le réservoir est plein. La fin de ce siècle voit l'arrivée de nouveaux types de voitures – de petites hybrides, fonctionnant à l'électricité et à l'essence, indiquent une voie alternative pour l'automobile du nouveau millénaire. « Petit » redevient synonyme de « beau », mais d'une manière différente.

1997

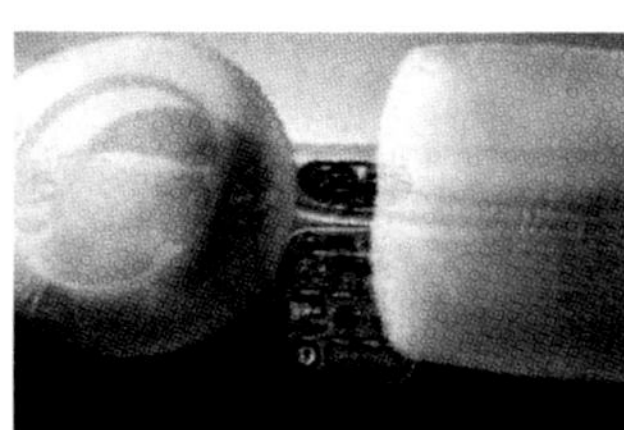

1997 American sales of Mazda Miata, introduced in 1989, surpass 400,000 units

Der 1989 in den USA eingeführte Mazda Miata übertrifft die Verkaufsmarke von 400 000 Einheiten

Les ventes américaines de la Mazda Miata, lancée en 1989, dépassent les 400 000 exemplaires

1997 DVD players available as optional accessory from many manufacturers

DVD-Player als Zubehör von zahlreichen Herstellern angeboten

Le lecteur DVD est proposé en option par de nombreux constructeurs

1998 Dual front "de-powered" airbags required on all new cars in U.S.

Front-Airbags der zweiten Generation für Fahrer und Beifahrer in den USA bei allen Neuwagen vorgeschrieben

Les doubles airbags deviennent obligatoires à l'avant sur toutes les nouvelles voitures aux États-Unis

1999 Daimler AG introduces Smart car in Europe; U.S. launch stalled until 2008

Daimler AG präsentiert den Smart in Europa; Smart Fortwo seit Februar 2008 an US-Kunden ausgeliefert

Daimler AG lance la Smart en Europe ; sa commercialisation aux États-Unis attendra 2008

Starts at $39,900*

Dynamic new styling, more standard equipment, a roomier interior, a sportier driving experience. To learn more about the makings of another milestone, visit your authorized Mercedes-Benz dealer or call 1-800-FOR-MERCEDES.

Bing Crosby
Yul Brynner
Marlene Dietrich
Gary Cooper
Errol Flynn
Clark Gable

Volkswagen New Beetle, 1999 ◂

The New Beetle, introduced in 1998, represented a retro, pop aesthetic, rendering idealized memories of the past in bright contemporary colors – like Swatch watches.

Der 1998 eingeführte New Beetle repräsentierte eine Retro- und Pop-Ästhetik, indem er idealisierte Erinnerungen mit bunten modernen Farben verband – ähnlich den Swatch-Uhren.

Lancée en 1998, la nouvelle Coccinelle incarne une esthétique pop rétro, qui fait revivre un passé idéalisé dans de vives couleurs contemporaines – qui ne sont pas sans évoquer les montres Swatch.

Lotus Esprit, 1995

Mercedes-Benz E-Class, 1995 ◂◂

By the go-go '80s, European luxury models – and, later, Japanese ones – moved ahead of Cadillac and Lincoln in the United States. The Mercedes-Benz E-Class represented a tradition of excellence traceable back to the beginnings of the automobile.

In den dynamischen Achzigern wurden Cadillac und Lincoln in den USA durch europäische (und später auch japanische) Luxusmodelle überholt. Die E-Klasse von Mercedes-Benz stand für eine Tradition hervorragender Leistung seit den Anfängen des Autos.

Dans les prospères années 1980, les Européennes de luxe – et plus tard leurs consœurs japonaises – jouissent d'un plus grand prestige que les Cadillac et les Lincoln aux États-Unis. La Mercedes Classe E incarne une tradition d'excellence qui remonte aux débuts de l'automobile.

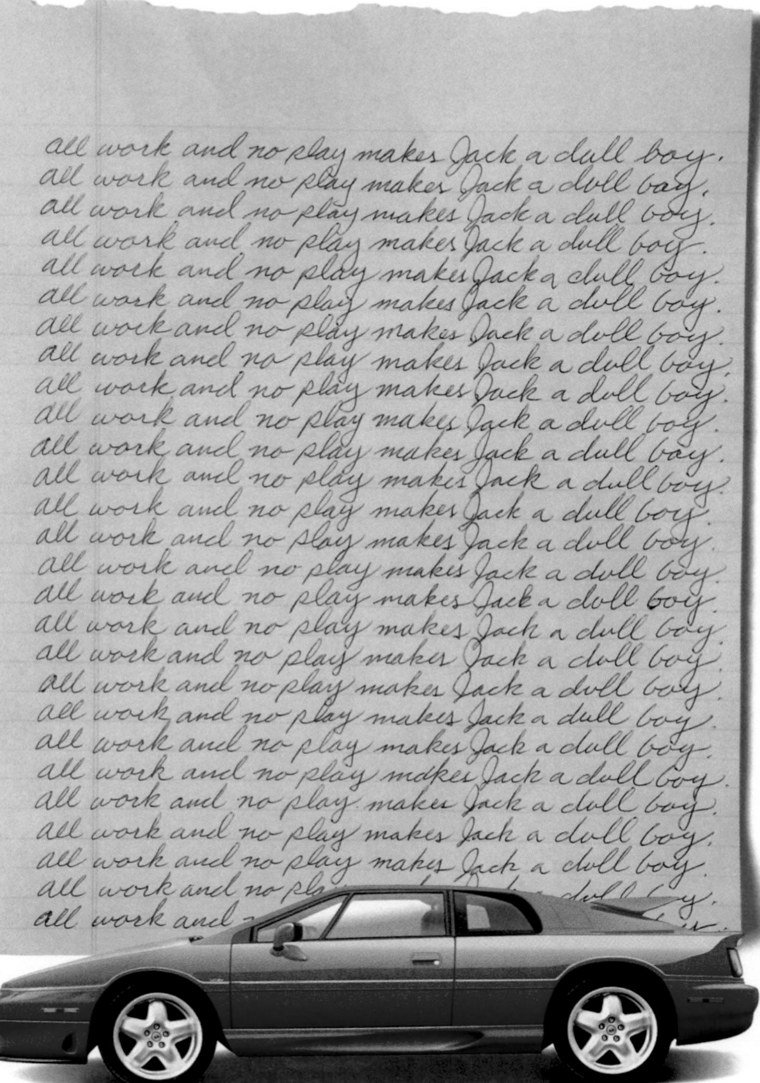

Just a reminder.

For the few that know the difference. ESPRIT S4

For the location of the Lotus retailer nearest you call: 1-800-24-LOTUS

Sales, there's always a future in sales.

You can make tons of money on a fishing boat in Alaska.

Be virtual, man.

Emu. It's the meat of the future.

Did you know you can get an MBA by mail?

It's not just me, me, me, anymore. You have a family to think about.

What happened to medical school?

Join the Navy. See the world.

It's the franchise opportunity of the '90s.

Lots of changes in direction. One car. Make it a good one. The Civic Sedan.

1-800-33-HONDA, ext. 381 and www.honda.com.

HONDA
Simplify.

► Honda Civic, 1996

As Japanese cars grew larger and more mainstream in the U.S. by the early 90s, the Honda Accord and Toyota's Camry and Corolla traded honors for best-selling car; though they were still outsold by Ford's F-Series pickup truck. The Japanese car makers' legendary reliability wouldn't outpace Americans' love of trucks until the middle of 2008, when Honda's fuel-efficient Civic finally bested them all.

Als die japanischen US-Importwagen Anfang der Neunziger größer wurden und sich dem Mainstream annäherten, wechselten sich der Honda Accord und Toyotas Camry und Corolla als meistverkaufte Pkws ab – wenngleich sie weiterhin vom Pickup der Ford F-Serie übertroffen wurden. Die legendäre Zuverlässigkeit der japanischen Autohersteller sollte sich erst Mitte 2008 gegen die Vorliebe der Amerikaner für Pickups durchsetzen, da nun der genügsame Honda Civic alle übertrumpfte.

Au début des années 1990, les Japonaises s'agrandissent et touchent un plus large public américain. La Honda Accord ainsi que la Camry et la Corolla de Toyota caracolent tour à tour en tête des meilleures ventes, derrière les séries F de Ford. La légendaire fiabilité des constructeurs japonais ne parviendra en effet à détrôner l'amour des Américains pour les pick-ups qu'à l'été 2008, avec le succès de la très peu gourmande Honda Civic.

Honda Civic, 1997

Now you'll be able to hear people in the backseat. Sorry.

The bigger, more powerful, and yes, quieter Civic Hatchback is a noteworthy achievement. A car that knows when to shut up, even when nobody else seems to be capable of that simple act.

To reach this peaceful place, teams of engineers, clad in white coats, armed with security badges, studied noise.

They used scientific instruments to take precise measurements. They took voluminous notes on clipboards. They brought prototypes to concerts by aging English metal bands (well, not quite).

The result, a very quiet car. Even the layout of the new cabin is designed to impart a sense of true harmony. In other words, it even looks quiet.

And let's not forget to discuss all the room inside. Your friends will be relaxed and comfortable. Which means you'll be driving those freeloaders all over town.

Here, the car is pictured with a spiffy set of accessory wheels that cost extra. We know, it's a conspiracy. Please call for more information at 1-800-33-HONDA, ext. 360. Or http://www.honda.com.

Many nice folks suggested we go the extra step and add ejector seats to deal with backseat drivers. We appreciate all the input. But the costs are prohibitive at the present time.

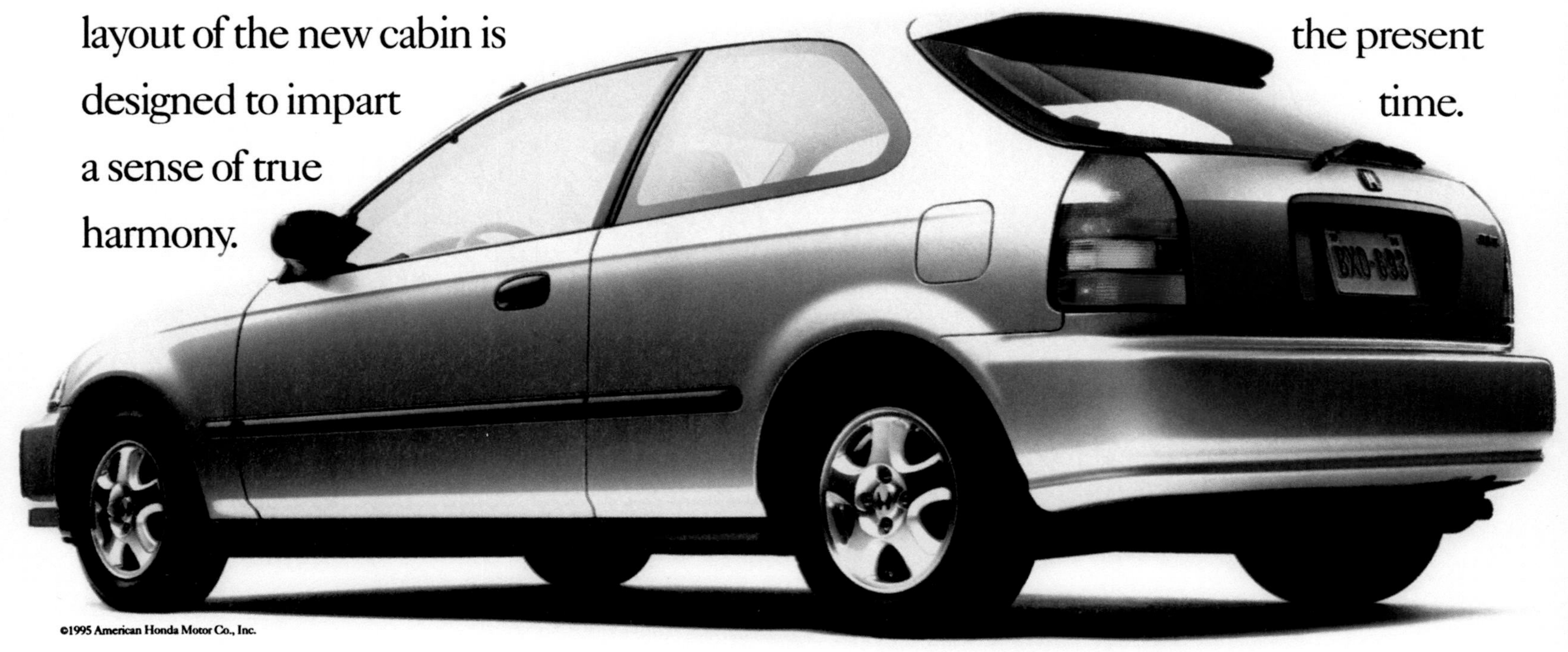

The new Civic Hatchback HONDA

IT ONLY SEEMS LIKE YESTERDAY.

Miata Special Edition They had names like Healey, MG, Triumph and Jag. They smelled of engine oil and leather. And a chosen few were the deep green of the English countryside. If these memories are familiar, this Miata is for you. Its coat of British Racing Green and tan interior evoke the best of the classic roadsters.

Settle into the cockpit and revel in the scent of leather. Other than the standard CD player and power accessories, you'd think little has changed since 1960. But as you bring the eager twin-cam engine to life and grab the wood shift knob, you find that everything's changed. Everything except the fun.

Take the inside line through a curve, and the rigid unibody works in concert with four-wheel double-wishbone suspension. Handling has come a long way in the last 30 years. So has reliability. The Miata may well be the most trouble-free sports car you'll ever own. Small wonder that with such virtues, *Road & Track* recently named it "One of the Ten Best Cars in the World."*

So come experience the old magic in a new way. See your Mazda Dealer and take the Miata Special Edition for a spin. There will only be a few. And a car like this only comes along every now and then.

36-MONTH/50,000-MILE WARRANTY

No-deductible, "bumper-to-bumper" protection. See your dealer for limited warranty details. For information on any new Mazda car or truck, call toll-free, 1-800-345-3799.

Mazda Miata, 1991 ◂

The Mazda Miata married an abstracted composite of the British sports car tradition – the Triumph and the Austin, and others – to Japanese economy and reliability.

Der Mazda Miata vereinte das Wesen der britischen Sportwagentradition (Triumph, Austin etc.) mit japanischer Wirtschaftlichkeit und Zuverlässigkeit.

La Mazda MX5, appelée Miata aux États-Unis, offre un modèle de sportive mêlant tradition britannique – inspirée des Triumph, Austin et autres – et économie et fiabilité japonaises.

Acura Legend, 1996

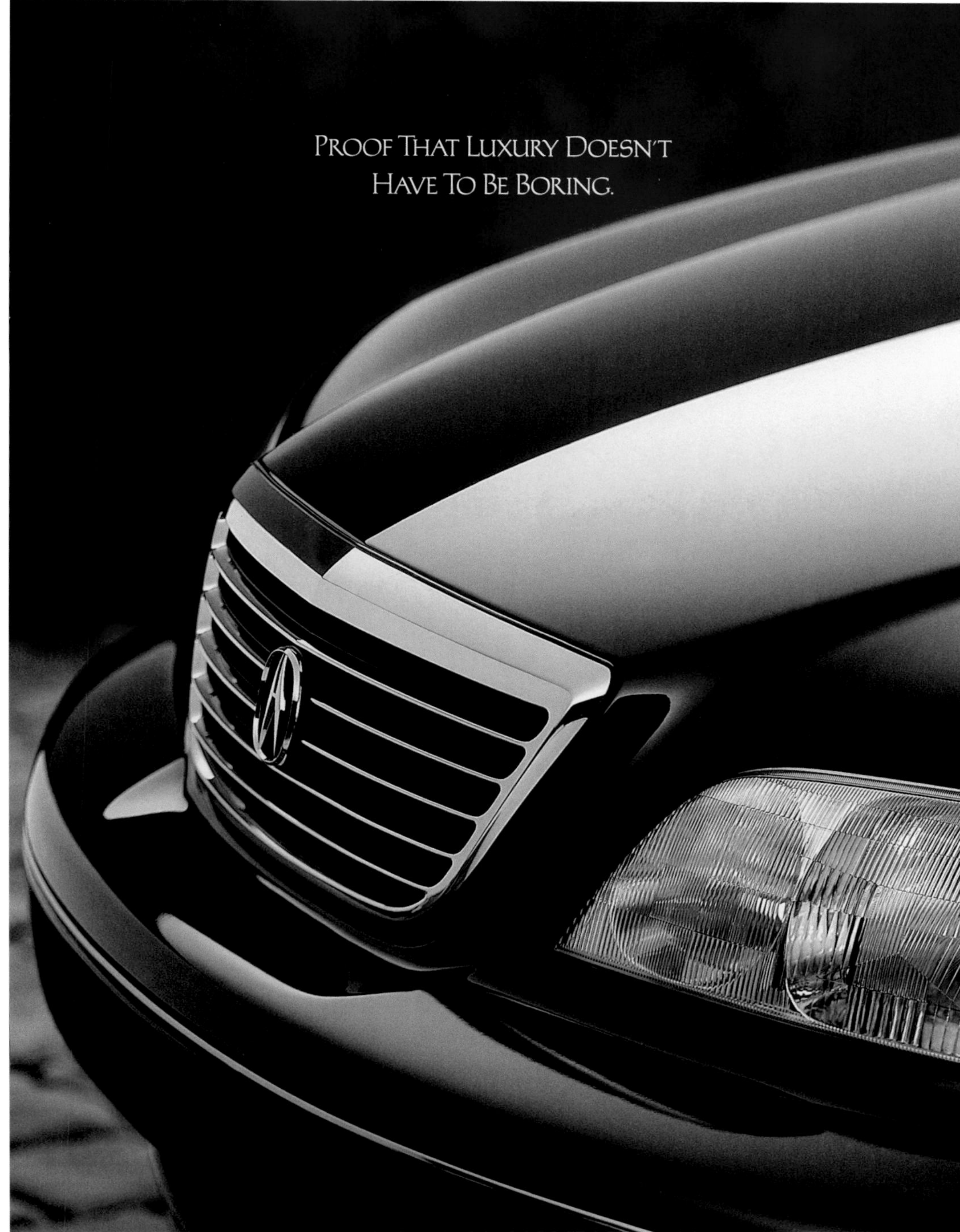

PROOF THAT LUXURY DOESN'T
HAVE TO BE BORING.

THE ABILITY TO SCALE AN 18-INCH VERTICAL WALL. THE ABILITY TO FORD TWO FEET OF WATER. THE ABILITY TO MAKE A SEMI THINK TWICE ABOUT CUTTING YOU OFF.

It's not a car. It's not a truck. It's not another 4X4. It's a Hummer. A vehicle not in a class, but a universe all its own. A Hummer is what it is. A wolf in wolf's clothing. A vehicle that looks the way it does because of what it was designed to do. With its 16 inches of ground clearance (twice that of any 4X4), steep approach and departure angles, stable 72-inch track width, and unique geared hub assembly, a Hummer can go places and do things that would be impossible for any other vehicle. A street-legal Hummer can climb a 60% grade. Traverse a 40% side-slope. Plow through three-foot snow drifts. And claw its way across even the deepest sand. With its unique Central Tire Inflation System, you can even inflate and deflate all four tires right from the driver's seat for better traction in varied terrain. Of course, a Hummer is also perfectly capable of behaving admirably within the confines of polite society. You'll find parallel parking, going though the bank drive-through, and zipping in and out of rush-hour traffic not only easy, but a blast. In fact, the only problem you're likely to run into in town is working your way through the crowds that invariably form wherever it's parked. For more information, call 1-800-732-5493.

► Ford Explorer, 1994

Ford's immensely popular Explorer was the best-executed version of the '90s SUV formula: road worthy, and tough enough to actually go off-road; a piece of sports equipment made into a style statement.

Fords überaus populärer Explorer war das gelungenste SUV der 1990er-Jahre – straßentauglich, einigermaßen geländegängig und zugleich Sportgerät und Statement in Sachen Stil.

Ce modèle connaît un immense succès car il offre la meilleure version du SUV des années 1990 : une bonne routière, parfaitement à la hauteur sur tous les terrains – un équipement sportif qui permet d'affirmer son style.

Hummer, 1995

Best-in-Class Passenger/Cargo Room Side Door Guard Beams Hidden Underbody Spare
4-Wheel ABS 4x4 Touch-Drive 6-Way Power Sport Buckets

Eddie Bauer Model. Some Features Shown May Be Optional.

FIND YOURSELF IN AN EXPLORER.

The world's just too big to be left unexplored.

SAAB
SCANIA
SAAB

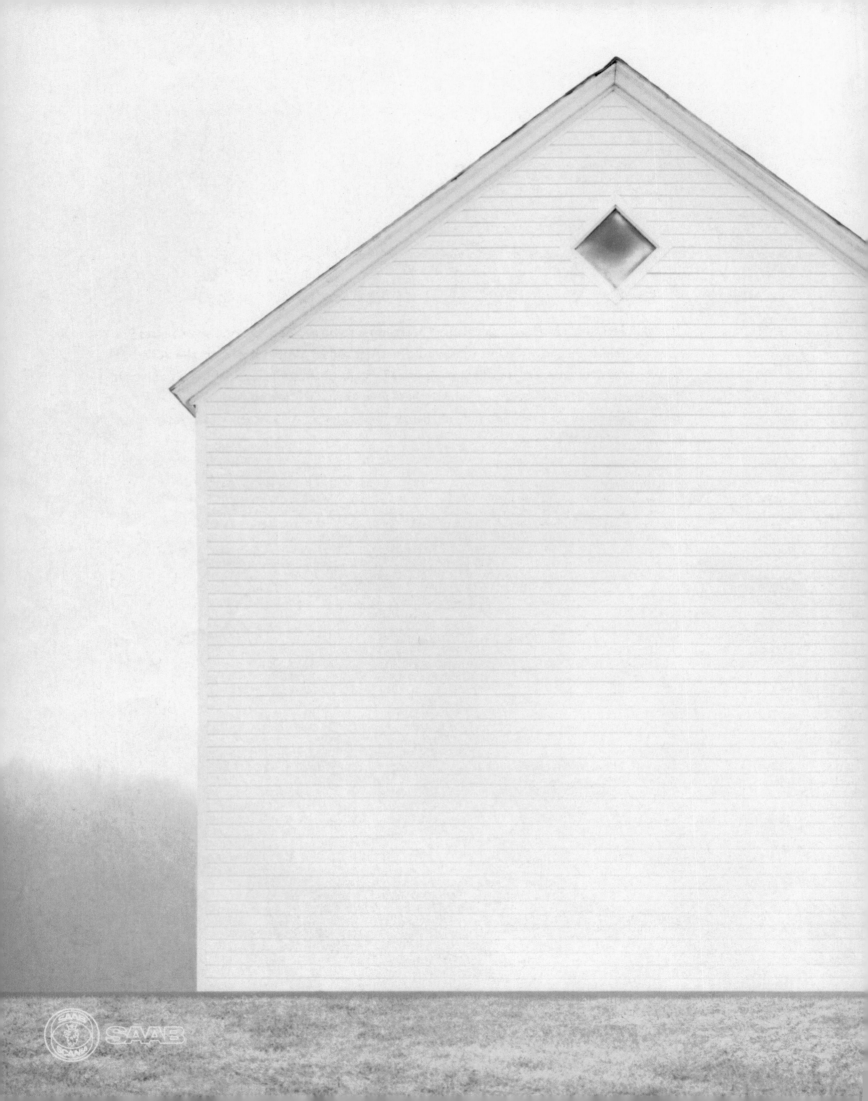

Beautiful dreamer, awake unto me,
Stereo and six speakers are waiting for thee.
Sounds of the rude world heard in the day,
Curtailed by a barrier, have all passed away.
A lot more to love.
The Next Neon
Dodge·Plymouth

Saab 9-3 Convertible, 1999 ◄◄

So globally interlinked had the automobile industry become that by the end of the 20th century the quirky, Swedish Saab became property of the giant General Motors.

Die Automobilindustrie war inzwischen derart stark global verflochten, dass der eigentümliche schwedische Saab Ende des 20. Jahrhunderts unter die Fittiche des Riesen General Motors gelangte.

À la fin du XXᵉ siècle, le secteur automobile s'est tellement mondialisé que le Suédois Saab devient la propriété du géant General Motors.

Dodge and Plymouth Neon, 1999

► Oldsmobile Silhouette, 1998

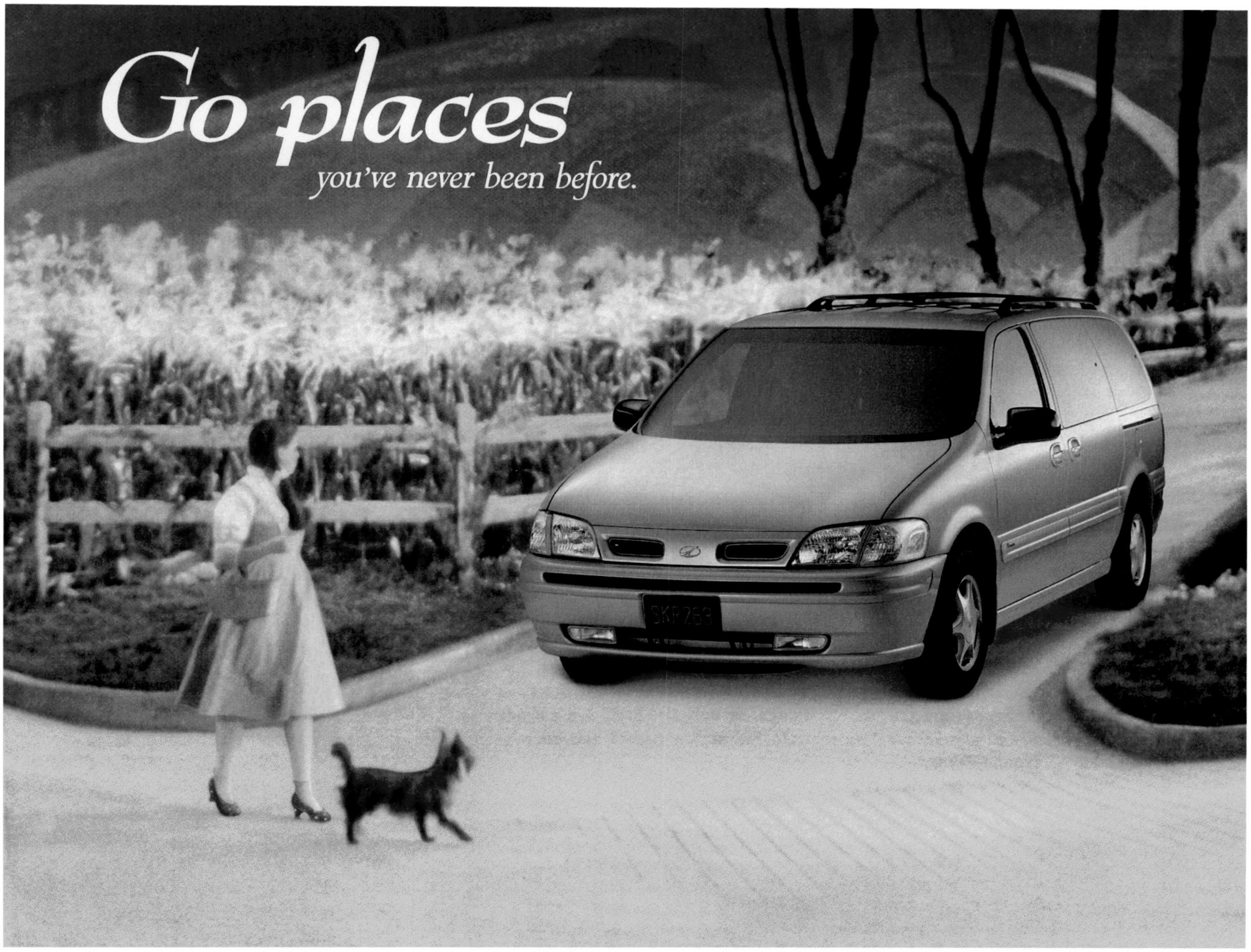

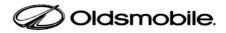

Imagine a Rollerblade® with fuel injection.

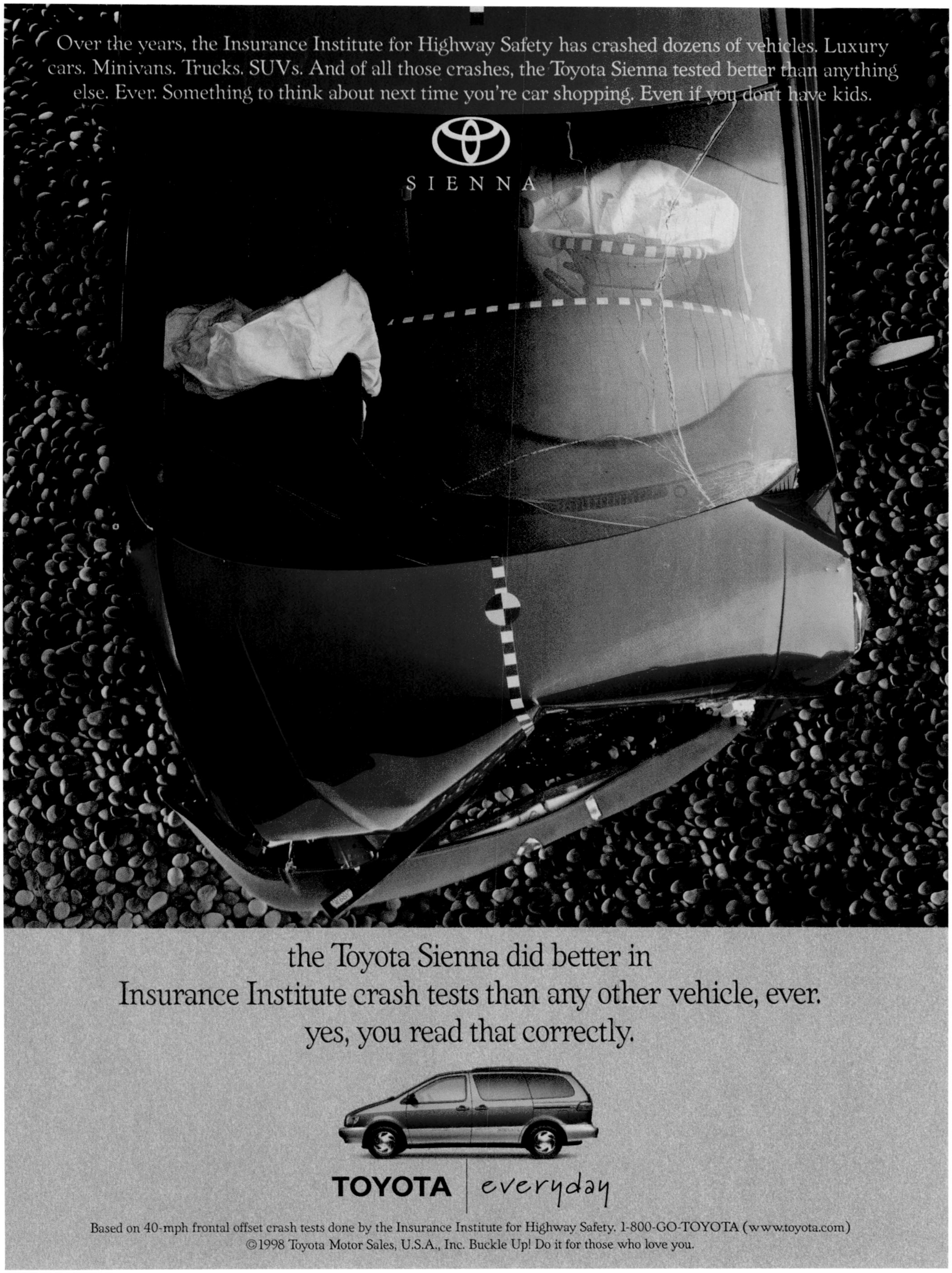

Over the years, the Insurance Institute for Highway Safety has crashed dozens of vehicles. Luxury cars. Minivans. Trucks. SUVs. And of all those crashes, the Toyota Sienna tested better than anything else. Ever. Something to think about next time you're car shopping. Even if you don't have kids.

SIENNA

the Toyota Sienna did better in
Insurance Institute crash tests than any other vehicle, ever.
yes, you read that correctly.

TOYOTA | everyday

Based on 40-mph frontal offset crash tests done by the Insurance Institute for Highway Safety. 1-800-GO-TOYOTA (www.toyota.com)
©1998 Toyota Motor Sales, U.S.A., Inc. Buckle Up! Do it for those who love you.

Toyota Sienna, 1998

Infiniti G20, 1992 ◂

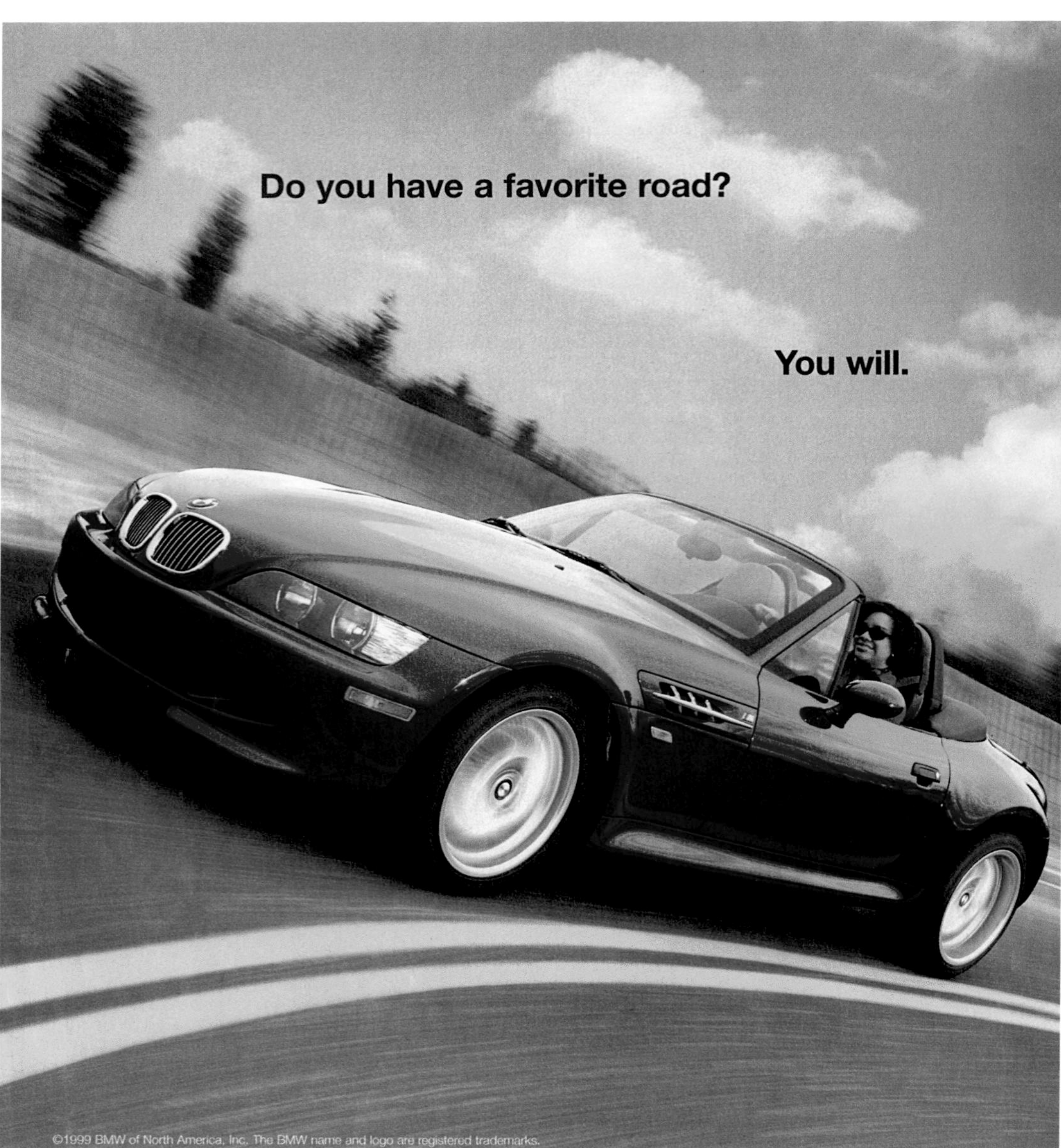

Do you have a favorite road?
You will.
©1999 BMW of North America, Inc. The BMW name and logo are registered trademarks.

In a BMW, the highway suddenly becomes more inviting. The curves more exhilarating. You'll realize there are so many roads to choose from... and there is one car waiting to help you make the most of them all.

The Ultimate Driving Machine®

BMW Z3, 1999

BMW, almost unknown in the United States as late as the 1970s, established itself in the '80s as "the ultimate driving machine" in ads from the Minneapolis-based advertising agency Fallon McElligott.

Noch in den 1970er-Jahren in den USA nahezu unbekannt, etablierte sich BMW in den Achtzigern in den Anzeigen der in Minneapolis ansässigen Werbeagentur Fallon McElligott als „die ultimative Fahrmaschine".

Encore pratiquement inconnue aux États-Unis à la fin des années 1970, « l'ultime machine à conduire » s'impose dans les années 1980 grâce aux publicités conçues par l'agence Fallon McElligott, dont le siège est à Minneapolis.

► Volkswagen Jetta, 1990

►► Pontiac Trans Am, 1998

ONCE YOU'VE EXPERIENCED FAHRVERGNÜGEN IN A JETTA, THE ROAD WILL NEVER BE LONG ENOUGH.

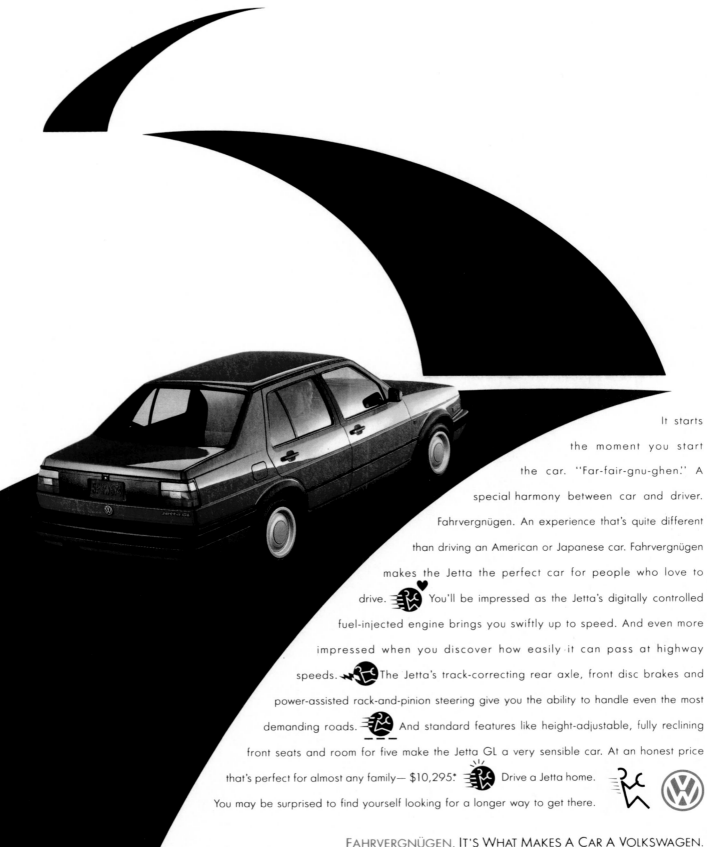

It starts the moment you start the car. "Far-fair-gnu-ghen." A special harmony between car and driver. Fahrvergnügen. An experience that's quite different than driving an American or Japanese car. Fahrvergnügen makes the Jetta the perfect car for people who love to drive. You'll be impressed as the Jetta's digitally controlled fuel-injected engine brings you swiftly up to speed. And even more impressed when you discover how easily it can pass at highway speeds. The Jetta's track-correcting rear axle, front disc brakes and power-assisted rack-and-pinion steering give you the ability to handle even the most demanding roads. And standard features like height-adjustable, fully reclining front seats and room for five make the Jetta GL a very sensible car. At an honest price that's perfect for almost any family— $10,295.* Drive a Jetta home. You may be surprised to find yourself looking for a longer way to get there.

FAHRVERGNÜGEN. IT'S WHAT MAKES A CAR A VOLKSWAGEN.

Seatbelts save lives. Don't drink and drive.

©1990 Volkswagen

*Base MSRP excludes taxes, license, transportation and dealer charges. For details, call 1-800-444-VWUS.

RED MEAT.

INDUCTION, 320 HORSEPOWER AND 6-SPEED TRANS.*

FIREBIRD TRANS AM THE MUSCLE CAR LIVES

INDEX

CHEVROLET
GOODRICH TIRES
STOP
Will Rogers Highway
BMW